NONPRINT MATERIALS ON COMMUNICATION

An Annotated Directory of Select Films,
Videotapes, Videocassettes, Simulations and Games

by

JUNE D. BUTEAU

The Scarecrow Press, Inc.

Metuchen, N.J.   1976

Library of Congress Cataloging in Publication Data

Buteau, June D
    Nonprint materials on communication.

    Includes index.
    1. Communication—Audio-visual aids—Catalogs.
I. Title.
P93.5.B8   016.0015   76-21857
ISBN 0-8108-0973-7

This book is dedicated to
Michelle, Brandon and Bernard
who share the real meaning
of communication

PREFACE

This volume is an attempt to provide, in one central source, a compilation of select nonprint materials classified primarily for communication needs. The proliferation of available related materials has become overwhelming. Locating, comparing and evaluating these materials in several media is now almost as time-consuming as digesting the information itself. The many favorable responses to requests for catalogues and related information--their sheer volume as well as the encouraging covering letters--suggest that there is no known equivalent single source available which duplicates the purpose or scope of this directory.

The nonprint materials listed include film (primarily 16mm and a few kinescopes), videotapes, videocassettes, and a selection of simulations and games. Communication industry specialists and educators suggest that there is a particular need for resource material to maximize the effective use of these media.

For our purpose, communication is interpreted as a reflection of the process, primarily oral--the exchanges of messages, meaning, information. The written criticism and evaluation, however, plus the research preparation related thereto, must of necessity be included.

Concentration, in addition, is on materials about communication. It is virtually impossible to divorce materials for analysis as communication from those about communication. A few primary source films, for example, chosen essentially as enrichment potential, supplement process concepts and may be examined for original rhetorical strategies.

Speech and hearing science materials, because of their technical specificity, are excluded. Unless related to some prime phase of our objectives, theatre and oral interpretation listings are also rejected. By definition, they encompass the entire gamut of English and American literature, and, in addition, are often incorporated in other current manuals.

Finally, evaluation of individual listings is not an objective of this directory. Individual needs determine effectiveness and use of these materials. No intentional effort, therefore, has been made to impose the author's personal standards or provide such an analysis. No attempt has been made to judge the character, worth or use of the materials by any subjective criteria--philosophic, political, artistic or technical.

ACKNOWLEDGMENTS

The completion of this directory is testimony to a collective recognition of its need. The author is grateful for the assistance of the many educators--in communication and educational media--throughout the country who contributed to its comprehensiveness. The generous university media centers donating directories are listed in Part IV, "Sources."

The author is also indebted to many special individuals: for helpful suggestions and for sharing their knowledge of film materials, Ms. Carol Valentine, Arizona State University and chairperson of the Speech Communication Association Learning Resources Committee, and Dr. John Jellicorse, Associate Editor of Bibliographic Annual for Speech Communication; for suggestions for the simulation (game) segment, Dr. Jean Grambs, University of Maryland, and Dr. Michael Weatherly, University of Dayton.

Special acknowledgment is given for encouragement and pertinent recommendations to Dr. Andrew Wolvin, Chairman, Speech Communication Division, and Dr. Kathleen Jamieson, both of the University of Maryland Speech and Drama Department, and Dr. Ross Hempstead, Director, Educational Media Center, University of Maryland.

J. D. B.

CONTENTS

"Knowledge is of two kinds. We know a subject ourselves or we know where we can find information about it."

--Samuel Johnson, Boswell's Life of Johnson, April, 1772.

INTRODUCTION

What could be more mutually motivating than a conceptual alliance of nonprint materials and communication--a merger of messages and media, communication and communications?

This directory attempts to synthesize select nonprint materials with a communication focus and organize them systematically. To centralize, to integrate diverse materials, to suggest a framework within which they may be utilized--there are our objectives. Within reasonable time limits, it is the intention, therefore, to be comprehensive, definitive and orderly.

Three fundamental factors suggest that there is a valid need for this type of directory: 1) The dynamic communication concept continues to change; 2) Current resource directories of nonprint materials are inadequate; and 3) An awareness of the scope of available materials is a positive, productive generating force in itself.

The communication concept is changing from a narrow, static and structured philosophy to a broader base, overlapping and interactive with other disciplines of the behavioral and social sciences. The stress is on the interrelationship of interpersonal, intrapersonal and socio-cultural systems of communication.

The "new" communication, in addition to theory and interaction, focuses on concepts of proxemics in small group settings, kinesics, linguistics, psychology, sociology, information sciences, media, and philosophic issues or movements. Boundaries also touch upon history, political science, literature, the arts and other areas. The diversity of the field is reflected by the many subspecialties, such as political, cross cultural and business/organizational communication.

As with many interdisciplinary areas today, there are also newer approaches and processes for learning. The transactional process/approach, for example, is currently introduced, where students learn fundamentals that apply to any area--intrapersonal, interpersonal, small group, public speaking and/or mass communication. Communication concepts also encompass techniques (the how), content (the what), and theory (the why). Research continues and curricula, methodology and texts have been and are being redesigned.

Parallelling the revolutionary changes in communication con-

1

cepts is the simultaneous growth and diversification of the available
resource materials and media, the hardware.

Inadequacies include both the lack of a central source for information about communication materials and contradictions in listed
classification concepts. All available central directories, catalogues
and sources were researched in preparing this volume. This survey
of existing resources, which included both published and unpublished
documentary studies, bibliographic sources, ERIC location directories
and equivalent anthology references, confirmed the inadequacy of
current resources.

Terminology in the mushrooming communication and educational media areas has never been truly standardized. There is a
multiplicity of unintegrated listings, and the inconsistency of definition creates major barriers. The older directory categories, in
particular, need redefinition and reclassification.

Media products have also proliferated. A host of new videocassette information systems has been developed or are in the
course of development. Also referred to as videodisc, videorecord
and cartridge television, they are manufactured in nineteen different
formats of various sizes and shapes. And "Involvement Learning"
has become the trade name for the growing simulation/game industry. The extensive range of varied topical divisions include: learning games (with rules in varied applications); actual case studies
(exercises); educational simulations (replicas); and life skills (decision-making).

Probably the primary justification for this directory is to
create awareness of the scope of existing materials, which in turn
should encourage their use. None of us can retain all the information produced by the many data banks (catalogues), nor perceive the
context within which the materials may be used. Given an overview,
one becomes conscious of supply--overlaps or duplication of materials, a paucity or surplus in particular categories. And, since it
concentrates solely on communication concepts, the directory should
save time for the reader.

As a collection of the vast volume of materials available for
potential use the directory functions dually--as a mirror of what
exists in the field, and as a molder of what can be. The innovator
may find here materials that open doors in both directions.

PROCEDURES

More than 1,400 sources--publishers, distributors, organiza-
tions--were asked to supply their current media catalogues and/or
other pertinent data. These sources ranged from vendors and manufacturers to university media centers, and included associations,
libraries, political, religious, philanthropic and educational institutions.

Materials solicited were considered, in particular, in terms of: timeliness; significance; popular appeal; authoritativeness; credibility; reputation of producer, distributor, artist, or publisher; format and/or price.

Those solicited initially were usually the original producers, vendors and sponsors of films, cassettes, videotapes, simulations and games. Communication societies also contributed suggestions, as did associations, organizations, legal and civil rights groups, institutions, societies, and others contacted about "missing" primary source materials. Although the goals, philosophies and organization of these sources may differ, for the needs of this directory they all possess one common denominator: they provided a service. Every accessible primary and secondary source responding and every obtainable guide listing known producers and distributors was examined. All contributing sources are listed, with addresses, in Part IV, "Sources."

The Classification

The classification divisions are a reflection of the "new" communication as previously described and represent organizational attempts at clarification within the directory. There is no magic formula for channeling communication into neat little structured packages of specialized subject content. The final composite overview represents a consensus of the above sources as related to the objectives of this directory.

Since all available materials from available reliable distributors could not be listed, a conscious attempt was made to select those items which could be described as relevant, recent, timely, provocative, authoritative, or rare. Also considered were potential effectiveness of primary source materials in teaching concepts that are difficult to teach by other means, and the development by universities of local productions for specific instructional needs.

The Categories

Because of the increasingly interdisciplinary nature of communication, some of the listings are appropriate in more than one category. It is impossible to limit categories and subcategories to rigid structural interpretations. Boundaries are purely arbitrary. If possible, categories are defined in terms of the anticipated outcome (behavioral objectives) and/or particular content emphasis. Films on "Feedback," for example, may be listed under the Process/ Theory category or under Business/Organizational, depending upon the thrust of the presentation, content, setting or application. For this reason, a cross-reference index is provided, in which the reader may find listings with multiple reference potential.

For convenience, categories are listed alphabetically (see

Table of Contents). The following categories may need further ex-
plication: Business/Organizational, Cross-Cultural, Dyadic, Educational Technology, Freedoms, Information Systems, Intrapersonal,
Learning Theory, Movements, Perception, Political, Process, Rhetorical Topics and Therapy.

Business/Organizational divides conveniently into communication categories: Management, Negotiation, Personnel Development, Sales, with some overlap between Personnel Development and
Management content. Cross-Cultural categories--Ethnic, International and Urban all relate; however, in general, Ethnic has a special race/religious group orientation, International refers to global
concerns, and Urban covers communication problems indigenous to
the cities. The Prejudice category interacts with the aforementioned
three. Ethnic, of course, also overlaps with Civil Rights.

The thrust of the Dyadic category is the informal one-to-one
concept, while the Family category orientation has the same in-
formality in a family problem-setting. And, the Interview, also
one-to-one communication, is in a separate category of its own,
although many listings are associated with business/organizational
applications.

Educational Technology includes the teaching facets of technical communication systems (television, satellites), while the essence of Information Systems, of course, is computer-related communication. Mass Media: Broadcasting is more concerned with the
process/art aspects of television, as well as with radio, than is
Educational Technology. Films on Civil Liberties--the Bill of Rights,
constitutional amendments, guarantees of speech, privacy, etc. --
are in the Freedoms category.

Intrapersonal, Learning Theory and Therapy all overlap; however, Intrapersonal contains primarily materials on communication
problems with self; Learning Theory focuses on behavioral and other learning communication methodologies; and Therapy, is "ventila-
tion" problem-oriented, subdivided into both Individual and Group.

Movements and Rhetorical Topics coincide but materials on
three major movements are so extensive and worthwhile that they
justify separate categories: Civil Rights Movement, Peace Movement,
Women's Movement. Materials in Civil Rights, of course, overlap
with Freedoms' category materials.

Listening relates to Process/Theory, yet is in a separate
category, as is Perception, also associated with Process/Theory,
as well as with Language. Parliamentary Procedure subdivides into
Campaigns and The System, and has, of necessity, some overlap in
these categories and also with the Freedoms category.

Rhetorical topics are concerned with topic choices: History/
Criticism, Philosophic, Religious, War. Among these, War, on occa-
sion, relates to its counterpart--Movements: Peace. Finally,

Interpersonal is not listed as a separate entity because of its broad, obtuse interpretation and application. Almost every category listed contains some materials which are, by definition, interpersonal.

The Entries

The model (see end of Introduction) exemplifies a typical entry for a film, with accompanying relevant statistical data. Videotape, videocassette, simulation/game abstracts vary slightly according to content information available and pertinence.

The content description represents a composite of all accessible source material available to the author. If data are missing, it is because they were not available. Videotape and videocassette descriptive material may appear sketchy in some listings. Both media suffer from a shortage of available supply distributors and understaffed service divisions with inadequate facilities to acknowledge information requests.

Titles are listed alphabetically, word-by-word, within each category and subcategory. Some titles are listed both as part of a series and individually, when particularly significant. At least one major distributor or availability source is listed. When known, production dates are included. Data concerning running time (playing time for simulations/games), size of film, whether black or white or color, tape size (for videotapes), are listed when available. Film materials available on videotape and/or videocassette are designated as vt (for videotape) and vc (for videocassette). Conversely, videotape and videocassette listings are designated F (for Film), if also available on film. Within the videotape and videocassette listings, in addition, the respective media available--videocassette or videotape--are indicated with the vt or vc directly after the title of the material. Simulation data also include the number of suggested players.

Listings are geared to junior college to university students, with many appropriate for the average adult. Although lower academic levels are not included in this directory, when appropriate and known, notations are incorporated for possible application of materials for the secondary level. Many of the more recent materials are not rated by publishers or producers according to audience level and some of those rated are suggested for "any age." Letters used are self-explanatory: c = college; s = secondary; a = adult. The directory replicates the practice of some university guides and capitalizes the "c" to "C" when material is particularly effective for university use.

Primary source materials--offerings which may be studied as communication--are intermixed and, for convenience, are "starred" ("*") in the categories: Mass Media: Film; Political; Rhetorical Topics: Philosophic, War; Movements: Women's Movement.

Data Not Included

Because of the lack of standardization in nonprint material catalogues, the following data are not included in the annotated listings:

1. Code numbers of organizations, producers, distributors. Distributors invariably list different numbers from catalogue to catalogue. In the interest of efficiency and clarity, therefore, these diverse and changing numbers are omitted.

2. Prices for rental and/or purchase. Several of the same films are listed for rental at one fee from a university media center, for another fee from an area public library and for a third from a vendor's distributing company. Many of these fees differ by a considerable amount. Prices also change periodically and such listings would not necessarily be valid indicators of current fees.

3. Rental and price agreements. Every catalogue and directory listed special individual rental and/or purchase plans.

4. Preview/auditioning arrangements. Contractual agreements differ among distributors and availability sources.

Reminders

Because of the disparate sizes and formats of videocassettes and videotape systems and materials, as well as the changing "standardization" rulings for format compatibility, the reader is urged to check current industry and government product decisions. The industry is also awaiting critical national and international copyright law revisions as they relate to videotape and videocassette material content. Prior to purchase, rental and/or use, therefore, it is suggested that recent interpretations be considered.

Finally, because of the unceasing demands for use of nonprint materials today, materials will frequently not be available when needed unless they are reserved or requested months in advance. The reader is also cautioned that listed materials may now be out of circulation or out of print.

Model Entry

(A) THE CASE HISTORY OF A RUMOR

(B) CBS   (C) CBS   (D) 1963   (E) Part I: 27 min.; Part II: 26 min.   (F) b/w   (G) s/C/a
(H) From CBS Reports Series
(I) New York Film Festival Award

(J) This social documentary relates the hate, hostility and threats to freedom created by political "extremism," ignorance, prejudice and suspicion. It details how an unfounded rumor regarding an anti-communist military maneuver in the south and a series of events lead to widespread media coverage.

(A) Title of Film
(B) Producer/Vendor/Sponsor
(C) Distributor/Releasing Agent
(D) Date Produced and/or Released
(E) Running Time
(F) Other Data (black and white or color; kinescope; silent; availability on videotapes and/or videocassettes)
(G) Audience Level
(H) Series Reference (and/or revision information)
(I) Awards
(J) Synopsis

PART I

FILMS

FILMS

ANIMAL

1. ANIMAL COMMUNICATION
    Time-Life 1971 30 min. color vt/vc s/c/a
    Based on the Life Nature Library: Life Around Us Series
        The premise of this film is that the study of animal com-
        munication will yield new insights into how man communi-
        cates. The study reviews a variety of signals used by a
        dozen different species from insects to primates.

2. ANIMAL COMMUNICATION
    American Association for the Advancement of Science Pennsyl-
    vania State University 1966 30 min. color c/a
        Dr. Martin Schein, Pennsylvania State University, discusses
        active and passive communication among animals. Also ana-
        lyzed are techniques of the study of communication systems
        and marine life communication as well as communication
        among invertebrates.

3. ANIMALS--HOW THEY COMMUNICATE
    Coronet 1968 11 min. color s/c/a
        This film illustrates the role of communication in animal
        life and survival. Wide examples are illustrated, ranging
        from courtship displays among birds to social life of prairie
        dogs. According to this documentary, "animals communi-
        cate fear, presence, interest, alarm and many other as-
        pects of behavior" by sound, sight and movement.

4. LANGUAGE WITHOUT WORDS
    Bailey Film Associates 9 min. b/w
        This film explores methods of communication among such
        animals as wolves, grouse, beavers, blackbirds and Sia-
        mese fighting fish. Viewers are then asked to observe and
        analyze complex systems of related human behavior.

5. MESSAGES
    Graphic Curriculum National Educational Association 1967
    24 min. color s/c/a
    From the Animal Secrets Series
    Awards: CINE; many others
        The viewer learns of signs and signals of animal communi-
        cation. Analyzed is the evolution of language, from ancient
        to contemporary times.

11

6. TALKING WITH DOLPHINS
    United States Navy   National Audiovisual Center   1970   15 min.
    color
        Filmed at the Naval Undersea Research and Development
        Center at Coconut Island, Oahu, Hawaii, this research
        documentary describes studies and experiments with under-
        water sound.   Scientists investigate the life of the dolphin,
        particularly his adaptability to a communication system with
        man.

7. TEACHING SIGN LANGUAGE TO THE CHIMPANZEE, WASHOE
    Pennsylvania State University   1973   48 min.   color   s/c/a
        A scientific experiment at the University of Nevada illus-
        trates how a young chimpanzee was taught, over a number
        of years, to communicate by means of Ameslan, the sign
        language of the North American deaf.   The film depicts the
        range of Washoe's vocabulary, the development of sentence-
        like sign sequences and spontaneous comments and questions
        initiated by Washoe.   Scientific commentary is interspersed
        with interviews with the subject.

8. UNEXPLAINED, THE   (PARTS I, II)
    Columbia Broadcasting System   1970   52 min.   color   s/c/a
    From the "21st Century" Series
        This film investigates the "last" unexplored frontiers of
        knowledge: communication with dolphins in their own lan-
        guage; life in outer space.   Experiments include some of
        the mysteries of the human brain, extra-sensory perception,
        the future of "cyborgs," creatures who are part man, part
        machine.

                              ARGUMENT

9. ARGUING A MOTION
    Pound   University of Utah   1970   11 min.   b/w   C
    From the Civil Advocate Series: #8
        This film illustrates protocol and the court rules to be fol-
        lowed while arguing a preliminary to dismiss the case.

10. ARGUMENTATIVE SITUATION, THE
    University of Iowa   1959   30 min.   b/w   c
        A profitable argument must be "problem-" rather than "per-
        sonality-centered."   Examples and analysis are presented
        of three types of argument concerning fact, policy and value.

11. CASE OF THE DISAPPEARING PRESUMPTION, THE
    University of California   1967   35 min.   b/w   c
    Award winner
        Based on the presumption provisions of the California Evi-
        dence Code, this film clarifies the confusing law of evidence.
        Shown are problems of the operations and use of presumptions

in three dramatized situations. Attorneys test their clients' problems in relation to presumptions, both conclusive and rebuttable.

12. COMMON FALLACIES
University of Iowa 1959 30 min. b/w s/c/a
As an introduction to the persuasive process in argumentation, the viewer learns fallacies of reasoning: overgeneralizing, vague appeals to crowds, use of statistics, attacking the person rather than the argument.

13. CONFERENCE IN CHAMBERS
Pound University of Utah 1970 11 min. b/w C/a
From the Civil Advocate Series
This film shows the chambers conference immediately prior to a trial, with the exclusion of prejudicial matters by both the plaintiff and the defendant attorneys.

14. CONFERENCE ON TRIAL TACTICS
Pound University of Utah 1970 11 min. b/w C/a
From the Civil Advocate Series: #11
The viewer sees the plaintiff attorney and his subordinates' conference which focuses on the central theme they seek to establish in a court trial.

15. CROSS-EXAMINATION I
Pound University of Utah 1970 11 min. b/w C/a
From the Civil Advocate Series: #21
This film details a cross-examination during which the credibility of a witness is attacked. Involved are such evasions as "refused" and "didn't recall."

16. CROSS-EXAMINATION II
Pound University of Utah 1970 11 min. b/w C/a
From the Civil Advocate Series: #22
The details of the cross-examination during a witness' testimony are challenged. The film evaluates the use of prior statements and lack of experience.

17. CROSS-EXAMINATION DEBATE: A DEMONSTRATION AND CRITIQUE
University of Iowa 1968 48 min. b/w s/c
The viewer sees an entire debate on the topic "That Congress Should Establish Uniform Regulations to Control Criminal Investigation Procedures." In addition, a critique is presented on strategy, the speaker's responsibility and rebuttal.

18. DEBATE: '68
Northwestern University 1968 35 min. b/w s/c/a
Thomas McLain, Northwestern University, criticizes the techniques of four debaters who stage a demonstration debate on the national topic for the year.

19. DEDUCTION, INDUCTION AND SEMANTICS
     University of Utah 1966 27 min. b/w c/a
     From the Introduction to Philosophy Series: #4
          This film summarizes principles used by philosophers to
          examine knowledge claims/arguments. It classifies them:
          semantics--the use of words; deductive logic; arguments
          and contraries; and inductive logic--facts and examples.
          The film concludes that philosophical reasoning is a method
          of careful analytical effort.

20. EVIDENCE: THE FOUNDATION OF REASONING
     University of Iowa 1959 30 min. b/w
          The information in this film is intended primarily for
          speech amplification based on supporting evidence.

21. GREAT DEBATE: LINCOLN VERSUS DOUGLAS, THE
     Encyclopaedia Britannica 1965 30 min. b/w and color
     vt/vc s/c/a
          Key segments of the debates and national issues relating
          to them are reenacted. Examined are moral and political
          issues involved, with viewers as "eyewitnesses." Princi-
          pals are: Hal Holbrook as Lincoln, Jack Bittner as Doug-
          las.

22. HONEST TRUTH, THE
     National Film Board of Canada 1953 5 min. b/w s/c
     From What Do You Think? Series: #3
          A short drama introduces the question of whether an honest
          judgment is preferable to a tactful evasion of criticism.
          Audiences are invited to resolve the discussion.

23. HOSTILE WITNESS, THE
     Pound University of Utah 1970 11 min. b/w C/a
     From the Civil Advocate Series: #6
          This film illustrates a trying but factual interview between
          the plaintiff's attorney and the attending doctor. It illus-
          trates the hostility and reluctance of a witness who has
          reservations regarding an appearance at the trial.

24. HOUSE DIVIDED: THE LINCOLN-DOUGLAS DEBATES
     Time-Life 1972 54 min. color vt/vc
          The highlights from the debates in Hannibal, Missouri are
          reenacted. Lincoln examines the war in Mexico and the
          slavery issues at home in the interchanges with Douglas.

25. HOW TO JUDGE FACTS
     Coronet 1948 11 min. b/w s/c
          Common causes in errors of thinking are explored. These
          include words with several connotations, false analogies,
          irrelevant facts, unreliable data.

26. LAWYERS, THE
     Time-Life 87 min. b/w vt/vc c/a

This study reviews the history of English Common Law,
upon which our own system of jurisprudence is based. The
documentary was filmed on location in England and Wales
with real lawyers, clients, law students, clerks.

27. LEARN TO ARGUE EFFECTIVELY
Coronet 1951 11 min. b/w s/c/a
This film stresses the necessity of being informed, of listening, of understanding, of finding a common basis of argument. To clarify the role of persuasive argument, it
demonstrates when arguments are purposeful, what subjects
are desirable and what is a basis for a "good" argument.
It contrasts the serious use of argumentation with the ir-
relevant, purposeless argument.

28. OBJECTIONS AND OFFERS OF PROOF
Pound University of Utah 1970 11 min. b/w C/a
From the Civil Advocates Series: #10
The viewer learns how an attorney should demonstrate an
offer of proof. The film illustrates how a court can be
forced to make a direct ruling upon an objection.

29. OPENING STATEMENT, THE
Pound University of Utah 1970 11 min. b/w C/a
From the Civil Advocates Series: #10
Preliminary scenes of a court trial are shown. The film
emphasizes the significance of the plaintiff attorney's open-
ing statement remarks.

30. PROBABILITY
National Broadcasting Company 1970 13 min. b/w
Based on the study of statistics, this animated film demonstrates the application of probability to a variety of situations.

31. PROBABILITY AND STATISTICS AND THE TEACHING OF
PROBABILITY AND STATISTICS SERIES
Indiana University 1963 b/w s/c/a
A semester's course includes subject matter for the stu-
dent and pertinent method programs for the instructor.
These 80 programs were originally presented as "Conti-
nental Classroom" on NBC-TV from February to May 1961.
Instructors are Dr. Frederick Mostelle, Harvard Univer-
sity, and Professor Paul C. Clifford, Montclair State College.

32. PROCESSES OF REASONING
University of Iowa 1959 28 min. b/w c
This film explores the basic types of reasoning used in
argument and the relationship of reasoning to evidence. Included are analyses of reasoning from general principles
and from particulars, a complete explanation of the difference between inductive and deductive reasoning and the
strengths and weaknesses of each. In addition, discussion

includes material concerning causal reasoning, reasoning
by analogy and from authority.

33. SCIENTIFIC METHOD, THE
     Encyclopaedia Britannica 1954 12 min. b/w vt/vc
        Steps of the scientific method are illustrated. The film
        explores the technique of problem-solving by scientists and
        discusses the value of scientific thinking in dealing with
        life's various problems.

34. SCIENTIFIC METHOD, THE
     University of Utah 1966 27 min. b/w C/a
     Introduction to Philosophy Series
        An eight-fold "evaluation" path used by specialists involves
        the problem, hypothesis, experimentation, theory and con-
        clusion for developing an idea.

35. SCIENTIFIC METHOD IN ACTION
     International Film Bureau 19 min. b/w and color
        This film presents examples of the scientific method in
        everyday life. It suggests techniques to use as "flexible
        checkpoints" for evaluation.

36. STATISTICS AT A GLANCE
     John Wiley 26 min. b/w
        An introduction to descriptive statistics is presented.
        First, statistics are explained in terms of daily activities
        and, finally, in the areas of specific concepts.

37. STORY OF A TRIAL
     Business Education Films 22 min. b/w s/c
        Two young men are accused of a misdemeanor offense.
        Following them from their arrest through their trial, the
        film stresses the importance of due process of law. The
        participating judge, lawyers and police use their own lan-
        guage.

38. UNCALCULATED RISK, THE
     Roundtable 26 min. color
     From the Communication Series
        Communications specialist Dr. William Haney demonstrates
        how to distinguish guesswork from fact and how to mini-
        mize the risk of uncritical inferences.

                        BUSINESS/ORGANIZATIONAL

                              Management

39. ANATOMY OF A PRESENTATION, THE (PARTS I, II)
     Roundtable 1967 Part I: 30 min.; Part II: 5 min. color
     and b/w

From the Communication Series
> These films demonstrate how to organize, prepare and de-
> liver business speeches for department and intracompany
> communication. More specifically, they examine tech-
> niques for technical management personnel to present oral
> reports, ideas and proposals effectively. Guidelines in-
> cluded are audience analysis, preparation, delivery.

40.   ARE YOU EARNING THE RIGHT TO MANAGE OTHERS?
Bureau of National Affairs 1974 27 min. b/w
> Bill Gove describes how a manager learns to be supportive:
> have confidence in subordinates, be a good listener, get
> subordinates "involved," make problem-solving a group
> event.

41.   ASSESSING MANAGEMENT POTENTIAL
Bureau of National Affairs   1972 27 min. color
> Saul Gellerman and five practicing behavioral scientists of-
> fer innovative solutions to problems involving managerial
> succession, promotion policy, practice, managerial selec-
> tion techniques, career counseling. Douglas Bray, Direc-
> tor of Personnel Research at American Telephone and Tele-
> graph, does the commentary.

42.   BREAKING THE DELEGATION BARRIER
Roundtable 1971 30 min. b/w and color
> This film analyzes why many managers fear the delegation
> of authority and responsibility. Discussed are topics re-
> lating to delegation methodology and the potential for in-
> creased efficiency and improved communication.

43.   CHALLENGE OF LEADERSHIP, THE
Bureau of National Affairs 1972 10 min. color
> In a setting completely removed from that of a normal
> workday, this film shows leadership in action. Designed
> to help supervisors identify and analyze the qualities which
> make a leader effective, the film reviews topics such as
> morale, productivity, assignment of work, leadership
> styles, persuasion, interpersonal communication.

44.   COMMUNICATING MANAGEMENT'S POINT OF VIEW
National Educational Television Bureau of National Affairs
1965 24 min. color and b/w C/a
From the Berlo Effective Communication Series
> Dr. David Berlo explains the role of the manager in chang-
> ing attitudes and behavior of his staff. Suggesting that
> managers can become more skillful with communication
> techniques, he makes specific recommendations. These in-
> clude: acknowledgment of the significance of perception of
> other's point of view and learning communication skills.
> Demonstrated are ingredients of persuasion, empathy and
> credibility.

45. COMMUNICATING WITH A GROUP
     Roundtable 1972 23 min. color
          Supervisors, managers and salesmen learn techniques of
          group communication. Simple established rules include:
          deciding why the group has assembled, what the purpose of
          the gathering is, what one intends to say, who the group
          members are, how the message(s) are to be delivered.
          Included is an analysis of problems such as nonparticipa-
          tion, heckling, maintaining interest.

46. COMMUNICATION IN INDUSTRY
     University of Ohio 6 min. b/w s/c/a
          A leading airline uses telephone conference lines to keep
          its top executives informed on current company business.
          Restricted to on-campus use.

47. COMMUNICATION OF PURPOSE, THE
     Roundtable. 40 min. b/w
          This film distinguishes between "what people work at and
          what they work for" to demonstrate that the manner in
          which managers communicate frequently determines their
          eventual success.

48. COMMUNICATION PROBLEMS
     American Medical Association 1967 3 min. color
     From the Supervisory Leader Series, Case Study: #5
          A case study demonstrates communication breakdown be-
          tween supervisors and subordinates. The case in question
          involves a superintendent who "misunderstands" an em-
          ployee's remarks.

49. COMMUNICATIONS
     McGraw-Hill 12 min. b/w c/a
          Effective communication in industry is explored, with the
          focus on methods of communication between management
          and employees.

50. COMMUNICATIONS CASEBOOK
     Strauss Perennial 1956 15 min. b/w c/a
          This film presents four cases dealing with one of manage-
          ment's needs: effective on-the-job communication. Illus-
          trated in a work situation in a factory are: two-way com-
          munication, audience reaction, significance of feelings and
          nonverbal communication. Case titles: The Tuned-Out
          Mind (Case I); The Wrong Wave-Length (Case II); The Chain
          Reaction (Case III); The Silent Yell (Case IV).

51. CONFLICT
     Roundtable Part I; 14 min.; Part II: 20 min. color
          This two-part film is designed to develop an awareness and
          understanding of the causes and consequences of interper-
          sonal conflict. Two managers, one in design, the other in
          production, can't reach agreement on the design specifica-

tions for a new product.   Conflict resolution is learned by
solving the problems in a "flexible" communicative manner.

52.   CRITICAL PATH IN USE
      Roundtable   28 min.   b/w
            Supervisors and managers are trained to oversee a pro-
            ject efficiently, to anticipate crisis situations and to moti-
            vate employees on all levels to use a "critical path" meth-
            od for efficiency.

53.   DIVIDED MAN, COMMITMENT OR COMPROMISE?, THE
      Didactic   color
            This film presents a complex dilemma of choice, useful
            for programs in management decision-making, leadership,
            supervisory skills and organizational development.

54.   DO NOT FOLD, STAPLE, SPINDLE OR MUTILATE (PARTS
      I, II)
      National Film Board of Canada   McGraw-Hill 1968   50 min.
      Award: International Labor Film Festival, Montreal
            This film questions the impact of social change on organi-
            zations and their respective leaders. It contrasts the re-
            lationship of union-management as it existed in the early
            part of the century and the relationship as it exists today.
            Explained are reasons for the effect of external forces on
            change and how technical advances affect both union leader
            and the man he represents.

55.   EFFECTIVE BRIEFING
      United States Air Force   National Audiovisual Center   1960
      24 min.   color
            The viewer is shown how to plan, organize, prepare, re-
            hearse and deliver staff and command briefings.   The film
            stresses accuracy, brevity, clarity in communications.

56.   EFFECTIVE DECISIONS
      Bureau of National Affairs   1968   25 min.   color
      From the Peter Drucker Series
            Mr. Peter Drucker describes how effective constructive
            discussion is used by executives to make certain that each
            decision is the best choice among many alternatives.

57.   EFFECTIVE EXECUTIVE THE, SERIES
      Bureau of National Affairs   1968   25 min. each   color vt/vc
      See individual film listings
            Peter Drucker, major management consultant, presents
            five films on executive organizational management: 1. Man-
            aging Time; 2. What Can I Contribute?; 3. Focus on To-
            morrow; 4. Effective Decisions; 5. Staffing for Strength.

58.   EFFECTIVE LEADERSHIP
      University of California   1968   32 min.   b/w

From the Management Development Series
   In this filmed lecture, Dr. Robert Tannenbaum defines and
   analyzes characteristics of effective leadership. He concludes that effective leadership requires a consistent attempt to perceive and understand people around us. He
   refers to his solution as "social sensitivity and action flex-
   ibility."

59. EFFECTIVE ORGANIZATION SERIES
     Bureau of National Affairs 1972 6 films vt/vc
     Revision of the Gellerman--Motivation and Productivity Series:
     See relevant individual title listings
        Dr. Saul Gellerman, business coordinator, represents the
        thinking of men associated with particular organizations
        where behavioral-science-based ideas have been applied
        intensively. Film titles include: 1. Assessing Manage-
        ment Potential; 2. Management by Participation Potential;
        3. Pay for Performance; 4. Making Human Resources
        Produce.

60. EXECUTIVE SPEAKING
     Bureau of National Affairs 1971 30 min. color
        Joe Powell leads you from the moment you are selected to
        the time you deliver your business speech. Instructions
        are given concerning the choice of occasion, location and
        advice relative to stage fright ("relax and enjoy").

61. FLOOR IS YOURS, THE
     Bureau of National Affairs 1972 26 min. color
        This is the story of Jim, young executive, who has to give
        his first presentation. As a neophyte manager, proper
        procedures suggested are: setting the objective, planning
        the presentation, preparing the materials.

62. FOCUS ON TOMORROW
     Bureau of National Affairs 1968 25 min. color
     From the Effective Executive Series
        Mr. Peter Drucker suggests that "yesterday's successes
        linger on beyond their productive life." He describes
        them as "investments in managerial ego," and recommends
        changes in thrust for decisions.

63. FOLLOW THE LEADER
     Strauss Didactic 11 min. color
        As a training tool, this film aids in developing leadership
        tools that are immediately useful. The problems, pitfalls
        and barriers facing the would-be leader or newly-appointed
        supervisor are analyzed in terms of his interpersonal com-
        munication.

64. FUNCTIONS OF MANAGEMENT, THE
     Roundtable 40 min. b/w
        Mr. William Oncken, management consultant, explains how

a manager can improve his leadership skills by developing
himself. He discusses the five functions of management--
organizing, planning, directing, coordinating, controlling.

65. GET 'EM UP, SCOUT
Bureau of National Affairs 1974 27 min. color
Dr. David Berlo points out that the manager who relies on
authority and traditional notions of how to "get the work
out" finds that he's still accountable but not in control.
Practical suggestions are included.

66. GRID ORGANIZATIONAL DEVELOPMENT
University of California 1970 35 min. color
Robert Blake and Jane Mouton, pioneers of the grid organizational development concept, discuss management developments of the past twenty years. Using the grid approach,
they present current thinking about the management of
people.

67. HOW FAR CAN I TRUST YOU?
Bureau of National Affairs 1974 30 min. color
Dr. David Berlo challenges some of the conventional
clichés about personal trust. He points out that "once information is released, it cannot be ignored."

68. HOW GOOD IS A GOOD GUY?
Roundtable 1971 21 min. b/w and color
Awards: Ohio, California
This film analyzes qualifications for effective leadership
and explores why some leaders fail to receive respect
from their subordinates.

69. I'D RATHER NOT SAY
Roundtable 30 min. color
From the Communication Series
This film examines the responsibilities managers and supervisors have to receive needed information to solve problems and make decisions. It suggests that "understanding
and trust" will help overcome communication defensive-
ness.

70. INSTRUCTIONS OR OBSTRUCTIONS
Bureau of National Affairs 1951 14 min. color
Seven steps for supervisors in presenting orders or instructions are offered: planning, preparation, presentation, verification, action, follow-up and appraisal.

71. MAKING OF A DECISION, THE
Roundtable 1968 32 min. b/w and color
This "open-end" film is about the decision-making process
and is designed to train managers to follow a specific logical program. Illustrated to improve decision-making are:
not jumping to conclusions, overcoming fear of making

mistakes, avoiding decisions and a tendency to have un-
realistic values. Stressed is the significance of insight
and perception in making a decision.

72.   MAN THE MANAGER
      Strauss   Perennial   19 min.   b/w and color
      Award Winner
           This animated film may be used independently or with the
           other related case history studies. It traces vital aspects
           of the management process to stimulate constructive think-
           ing towards solutions of specific problems.

73.   MAN THE MANAGER: CASE HISTORIES
      Strauss   Perennial   7 min.   b/w   c/a
           Illustrated in three two-minute case histories are stories
           that dramatize basic managerial principles and the conse-
           quences of ignoring these concepts. Titles include: Mak-
           ing Problems (Case I); Anticipating Problems (Case II);
           Solving Problems (Case III).

74.   MANAGEMENT BY OBJECTIVES SERIES
      Bureau of National Affairs   27 min. each   1972   color   vt/vc
      Film coordinator: John Humble, Management Consultant
           This structured six-part series stresses communication of
           "management by objectives" in a wide range of manage-
           ment training courses.

75.   MANAGEMENT BY PARTICIPATION
      Bureau of National Affairs   1974   30 min.   color
           Dr. Alfred J. Marrow, Board Chairman of Harwood Com-
           panies, describes how to apply behavioral science to busi-
           ness problems. Psychologists divided employees into
           three groups, each applying different methods of handling
           a new procedural change. Attitudes and communication
           problems are discussed.

76.   MANAGEMENT DEVELOPMENT SERIES
      University of California   1963   35 min. each   color
           Pertinent series discussions include: Effective Leadership;
           Grid Organizational Development; Human Considerations in
           Management; Managerial Grid; Organizational Development;
           Problem-Solving in Groups; Some Personal Learnings about
           Interpersonal Relationships; Ways of Dealing with Conflict
           in Organizations.

77.   MANAGEMENT, MOTIVATION AND THE NEW MINORITY
      WORKER
      Roundtable   1974   30 min.   b/w and color
           Role-playing and reverse role-playing dramatize the sensi-
           tive areas of culture gap and motivation and suggest help-
           ful training techniques and attitudes. The film is moder-
           ated by Dr. Allan Katcher.

78. MANAGER WANTED
     Roundtable   1964   28 min.   b/w and color
     Awards: CINE and California special awards
         This film explores the weakness of the selection process
         for supervisors.   Criteria for personnel choice are dis-
         cussed.   Questions asked include "Why do men of real abil-
         ity often fail to make the grade as managers?"

79. MANAGERIAL GRID
     University of California 1963   35 min.   b/w
     From the Management Development Series
         Robert Blake presents the managerial grid technique as a
         way of evaluating various approaches to management.   Val-
         ues from one to nine are assigned to the grid areas.   Five
         intersectional points at coordinates are discussed in terms
         of the degree of commitment, creativity and conflict that
         can be expected under such management.

80. MANAGING TIME
     Bureau of National Affairs 1968   27 min.   color
     From the Effective Executive Series
         Mr. Peter Drucker demonstrates why every executive needs
         to understand about the effective use of time, and how to
         maximize its use by specific planning.

81. MATTER OF METHOD, A
     Roundtable   16 min.   plus two four-min. case studies   color
         To demonstrate to supervisors who use planning and prob-
         lem-solving, this film documents a case study of the basic
         responsibilities involved in two-way communication of man-
         agement and the working group.   Suggestions for problem-
         solving include: analyze, plan, execute.

82. MODERN MANAGEMENT SERIES, THE
     Bureau of National Affairs   7 films; each 10 min.
     See individual listings
         This film series surveys areas of supervisory responsibil-
         ity as applied to the relationship with subordinates.   Titles
         are: 1.   Challenge of Leadership; 2. Trouble with Arch-
         ie; 3. Instructions or Obstructions; 4. A Good Beginning;
         5. A Case of Missing Magnets; 6. Listen, Please; 7.
         Winning Combination.

83. NATIONAL MANAGERIAL TEST, THE
     Roundtable   1 hour (two reels) b/w and color
         Managerial skills are covered in this film test to measure
         training needs and results.   The test may be administered
         at the inception of a training program to measure strengths
         and weaknesses of trainees, or at the conclusion of the
         program to measure results.

84. ONE-SIDED TRIANGLE, THE
     Bureau of National Affairs 1974   25 min.   color

Production department managers at Harrison Brothers learn
that their communication behavior at staff meetings is not
conducive to top-flight problem-solving and decision-making. Opportunities for teamwork are hindered by those
who don't participate or who are not candid, those who
monopolize discussions or try to manipulate others.

85. OVERCOMING RESISTANCE TO CHANGE
     Roundtable 30 min. b/w and color
     Awards: National Association of Manufacturers' Awards
        This film demonstrates to supervisors how resistance to
        change is caused by their people's varying perceptions of
        that change. Resistance may be cleared by resolving mis-
        perceptions, opening communication channels, developing
        participation, ventilating feelings.

86. PARKINSON'S LAW
     Mass Media Associates 1971 7 min. b/w
     Zagreb Film Production; Awards: Atlanta, Philadelphia
        Bureaucracy is satirized. The parts-makers have man-
        agers, who have managers, who, in turn, have managers.
        The man at the lathe is eventually "pushed" completely out
        of the picture frame, and hence, also out of the organiza-
        tion.

87. PROBLEM-SOLVING--SOME BASIC PRINCIPLES
     Roundtable 18 min. color
        This film spotlights principles that underlie sophisticated
        problem-solving techniques if a manager is to identify cor-
        rectly problems and to resolve them.

88. PROBLEM-SOLVING IN GROUPS
     University of California 1961 25 min. b/w
     From the Management Development Series
        The film outlines the function of management committees.
        It describes the best method of improving decision group
        problem-solving procedure.

89. QUESTION OF MAY, A
     Bureau of National Affairs 23 min. color
        A communication misunderstanding concerns an order to be
        delivered in May. Managers encounter basic communica-
        tion principles concerning the process, listening, percep-
        tion.

90. STAFFING FOR STRENGTH
     Bureau of National Affairs 1968 25 min. color
     From the Effective Executive Series
        Mr. Peter Drucker suggests that effective executives never
        ask questions about what subordinates cannot do. Instead
        they apply behavioral principles by using a reward system
        as a result of asking, "What can they do uncommonly
        well?"

91. STRENGTH OF LEADERS, THE
     Roundtable   40 min.   b/w
         Mr. William Oncken, management consultant, reviews four
         positions of strength from which managers exercise leader-
         ship--competence, position, personality and communication.
         He shows the dramatic effects of each of the positions of
         strength on motivation.

92. STYLES OF LEADERSHIP
     Roundtable   1962   26 min.   b/w and color
         This film demonstrates a common business problem re-
         garding a new contract.   The primary characteristic of
         each leadership style and its effects on subordinates is
         compared and contrasted.   Shown are how four different
         types of leaders "perform."   The styles of the autocratic,
         democratic, manipulative and consultative, and their ef-
         fects on subordinates, are explained.

93. SUPERVISORY CONFERENCES
     McGraw-Hill   1953   14 min.   b/w   c/a
     From the Personnel Management Series
         To explain the purpose of training programs, this film for
         managers offers a dramatization of related conferences.

94. TAKE THE CHAIR
     Roundtable   26 min.   b/w
         Five managers confer to learn how to plan and conduct ef-
         fective conferences.   Details and actions that make the dif-
         ference between a meeting's success and failure are drama-
         tized.

95. TEAM BUILDING
     Bureau of National Affairs   1972   30 min.   color
         Sheldon Davis, Director of Industrial Relations of the Sys-
         tems Group of TRW, Inc., identifies barriers to collabora-
         tion.   Plans are detailed concerning specific improvement
         actions involving inter-group sessions.

96. TIME TO THINK
     Roundtable   1974   20 min.   color
         This film urges self-analysis and self-management as keys
         to managerial effectiveness.   It suggests that insecure man-
         agers often fail because they never plan, never coordinate,
         never delegate.

97. TWO-PERSON COMMUNICATION, A SERIES
     Bureau of National Affairs   1974   b/w and color
         Dr. David Berlo contends that management communication
         is more than a useful tool.   It has "become a control sys-
         tem itself because organizational productivity and develop-
         ment are increasingly based on information relationships
         and less on traditional concepts of authority."

98.   WHAT CAN I CONTRIBUTE?
       Bureau of National Affairs 1968 25 min. color
            Mr. Peter Drucker stresses that promotions in the mana-
            gerial ranks should go to those who assume more re-
            sponsibility and not merely to those who have done jobs
            well. Information needs of colleagues to make team man-
            agement a reality are also discussed.

                              Negotiation

99.   ALL I NEED IS A CONFERENCE
       Strauss Perennial 1964 28 min. b/w c/a
       Versions in French, Spanish and Swedish
            This film suggests that conferences can save businesses
            time and money and can resolve problems "if people learn
            how to work together." A particular case is depicted,
            wherein a serious industrial problem is reconciled by a
            conference of all supervisors involved.

100.   BARGAINING COLLECTIVELY
       Teaching Film Custodians 1952 9 min. s/c/a
            A committee of workers meets with plant directors to set-
            tle a strike. Arguments are presented from both labor
            and management personnel for and against union recogni-
            tion. The film concludes with the board chairman calling
            for a vote on the issue.

101.   BEGINNINGS OF CONFLICT
       University of Indiana 29 min. b/w
       From the Mediation: Catalyst to Collective Bargaining Series
            Dramatized is an upcoming labor-management contract dis-
            pute in a fictitious metals company. Some of the issues
            to be worked over in bargaining sessions are out-
            lined.

102.   CASE OF INSUBORDINATION, A
       Roundtable 1972 20 min. b/w and color
            One incident is presented as perceived by four people:
            an employee, a supervisor, a witness and an arbitrator.
            The series of short case studies and comments teaches
            disciplinary and grievance procedures regardless of indus-
            try or union status. It can also be used as a series of
            case studies in perception, communications or
            conflict.

103.   CHANGE: HANDLE WITH CARE
       Fortune Magazine Crowell, Collier and Macmillan 1971 25
       min. b/w s/c/a
            This film reviews the verbal and visual confrontation be-
            tween major executives of a large corporation and educa-
            tors and students. Questioned are the issues of individu-
            alism, justice, free enterprise.

104.   CONFERENCE
       Ohio State University   13 min.   b/w   1961
          Conference among instructor, supervisor and principal
          promotes reconciliation of specific problems.

105.   DEMOCRACY: THE ROLE OF DISSENT
       Coronet   1970   13 min.   color   s/c/a
          A group of tenants is faced with the question of appropri-
          ate channels for the redress of grievances.   They dem-
          onstrate and consider a rent strike in protest against liv-
          ing conditions in their apartment building.

106.   DISPUTE
       Time-Life   1974   Two parts: 50 min. each   vt/vc   b/w
       From BBC-TV
          These two on-the-spot films were produced while disputes
          were actually taking place, with separate filming units
          following each side.   What employers and union men say
          to each other and behind each others' backs, how the
          workers behave, how management resolves the problems
          --all are explored.

107.   ENGINEERING OF AN AGREEMENT, THE
       Roundtable   21 min.   b/w and color   c/a
       Awards: Belgium, Seattle, Educational Film Library Assoc.
          To teach managers and supervisors communication meth-
          ods, this film explains basic techniques for directive and
          non-directive persuasion.   The film analyzes the agree-
          ment process and presents effective ways of overcoming
          barriers to agreement.   It is designed for use both in
          management and sales training.

108.   FOLLOW-THROUGH
       University of Indiana   29 min.   b/w   s/c/a
          Mediators have specific functions in settling contract dis-
          putes: advisement, motivation, listening.   A group of
          company employees asks union leaders for reaction on
          anticipated problems.

109.   GRIEVANCE, THE
       National Film Board of Canada   McGraw-Hill   1954   30 min.
       b/w
       From the Labor in Canada Series
          Through several stages of negotiation between union and
          management, this film examines the orderly processing
          of a grievance.

110.   GRIEVANCE HEARING
       McGraw-Hill   1953   15 min.   b/w   C/a
          To illustrate how hearings are conducted, this film re-
          views what their purpose is, the function of compromise
          and how disputes can be settled.   A case study of a
          grievance is explored.

111.   HARD BARGAINING
        University of Indiana   29 min.   b/w   s/c/a
        From the Mediation: Catalyst to Collective Bargaining Series
            The mediator's role is defined as he resolves personal
            attacks between labor and management, gets each side to
            outline its views, earns respect from each side and meets
            independently with each side in the dispute.

112.   LET THE BUYER PREPARE
        National Audiovisual Center   1969   35 min.   color
            Procurement by negotiation is the theme of this film deal-
            ing principally with six major steps in the negotiation
            process. Four basic negotiations objectives are identi-
            fied and some important do's and don'ts relating to nego-
            tiation are recommended.

113.   NO COOPERATION
        Eastern Pennsylvania Psychiatric Institute   1970   7 min.
        color   c/a
            The absence of communication and consideration leave a
            supervisor, his supervisor and fellow workers dissatis-
            fied with their work and each other. The results are
            frustration and hostility and the demand for some type of
            reconciliation.

114.   WAYS OF DEALING WITH CONFLICT IN ORGANIZATIONS
        University of California at Los Angeles   1962   27 min.   b/w
        From the Management Development Series
            Professor of Behavioral Science, Herbert Sheppard, Case
            Institute of Technology, reviews three optional methods
            of resolving conflicts in bargaining and problem-solving.
            Each method specifies procedures, tools and objectives.

115.   YOU ARE THERE AT THE BARGAINING TABLE
        American Medical Association   Encyclopaedia Britannica
        1955   50 min.   b/w   vt/vc   s/c/a
            This film presents negotiations between the Rogers Cor-
            poration and the AFL International Brotherhood of Paper
            Makers. It details the background to wage discussions,
            pointing out the specific bargaining techniques.

                            Personnel Development

116.   BOB KNOWLTON STORY, THE
        Roundtable   28 min.   b/w and color
            Based on the real life case written by Dr. Alex Bavelas,
            this film shows how psychological barriers can interrupt
            communication and job performance. A production-ori-
            ented boss puts a brilliant individualist under the super-
            vision of a highly effective but team-oriented supervisor.
            The importance of managers and subordinates keeping the
            channels of communication mutually open is demonstrated.

117. BUILDING A CLIMATE FOR INDIVIDUAL GROWTH
Bureau of National Affairs   25 min.   color
> Six stages of psychological growth are explained, with or-
> ganizational policies and practices applied for personnel
> at each stage.

118. BUSINESS, BEHAVIORISM AND THE BOTTOM LINE
CRM Films 1971 20 min. color
> Dr. B. F. Skinner discusses the behavioral modification
> of workers which, in turn, is interpreted and applied by
> Edward Fenney, Emery Air Freight. In contrast with the
> standard management development film, this film intro-
> duces the viewer to techniques of behavioral change and
> how they affect strategies.

119. CHANGING ATTITUDES THROUGH COMMUNICATION
National Educational Television Bureau of National Affairs
1965 24 min. b/w and color s/c/a
From the Berlo Effective Communication Series
> Dr. David Berlo, Michigan State University, illustrates
> that rejection, distortion and avoidance are major ways
> of resisting change which a manager must anticipate and
> correct. He points out the necessity for using persua-
> sion when introducing policies which require changes in
> an organizational system.

120. COMMUNICATING WITH THE PUBLIC
Encyclopaedia Britannica 1971 12 min.   color vt/vc
s/c/a
> A series of filmed interviews with office workers illus-
> trate vignettes of business situations to stress specific
> qualities necessary to resolve communication difficulties
> when dealing with the public.

121. COMMUNICATION
Oregon State University 30 min.   b/w kinescope c/a
From the Business Supervision Series: #2
> The importance of communication within the business sys-
> tem is stressed.   Obstacles to effective communication
> include: 1.   need for feedback; 2. importance of the
> culture in shaping things we perceive; and 3. the role of
> experience and background.

122. COMMUNICATIONS
McGraw-Hill 1963 12 min.   c/a
From the Personnel Management Series
> The viewers learn how gossip and rumor may affect peo-
> ple in an organizational setting.   Discussed are communi-
> cation methods recommended to supplant rumors with
> facts, not only in sales and production operations but also
> in matters concerning the whole plant and its personnel.

123.   CONFRONTATION, SEARCH AND COPING
       Bureau of National Affairs   1969   25 min.   color
       From the Organizational Renewal Series
           This film approaches the problem of conflict in an organi-
           zation. It reviews how to achieve "leveling" and "open-
           ness" in relations between people and groups. It ex-
           plains that mere confrontation is insufficient, that prob-
           lems must be resolved so that experience gleaned will en-
           able everyone to cope with future challenges.

124.   CORRECT TELEPHONE COURTESY
       Business Education Films   22 min.   b/w   s/c/a
           The viewer learns how one answers a business phone to
           reflect a positive image of both self and company.

125.   DON'T TELL ME WHAT'S GOOD FOR ME
       Bureau of National Affairs   1974   30 min.   color
           Dr. David Berlo delves into the increasing importance of
           individual and organizational development. He gives the
           basis for effective counseling, practical "how-to-do" steps
           in development. "As rule changes become central to or-
           ganizational stability, the manager becomes less of a
           coach and more of a referee."

126.   EFFECTIVE COMMUNICATION SERIES
       Bureau of National Affairs   1965   24 min. each
       See individual film listings.
           This film series surveys communication problems on ev-
           ery organizational level. Dr. David Berlo comments on:
           1. Avoiding Communication Breakdowns; 2.   Meanings
           Are in People; 3. Communication Feedback; 4. Chang-
           ing Attitudes through Communication; 5. Communicating
           Management's Point of View.

127.   ENGLISH ON THE JOB: LISTENING AND SPEAKING SKILLS
       Coronet   1972   14 min.   color   s/c/a
           The importance of listening and speaking skills are illus-
           trated: in getting and holding a job, in obtaining possible
           promotion.

128.   ENGLISH ON THE JOB: WRITING SKILLS
       Coronet   1972   14 min.   color   s/c/a
           Almost everyone uses on-the-job writing skills, from
           completing forms to writing memos and reports. The ex-
           periences of workers illustrate how writing that is clear,
           complete and accurate adds to total communication.

129.   FAREWELL TO BIRDIE McKEEVER
       Stuart Reynolds Production   University of California   1959
       25 min.   b/w   s/c/a
           This is a story of a receptionist, her employers and a
           provocative situation involving employer-employee rela-
           tionships. The whole gamut of understanding and misun-

derstanding among office personnel is reviewed.

130. FIRST IMPRESSIONS
United States Navy   National Audiovisual Center   1942   21
min.   b/w
The film emphasizes the importance of first impressions
on the job and demonstrates step-by-step a technique of
introducing a new employee to other office personnel.

131. GELLERMAN MOTIVATION AND PRODUCTIVITY SERIES
Bureau of National Affairs   1967-68   color
Moderator: Dr. Saul Gellerman, behavioral consultant
See pertinent individual titles for listings
This series of films is concerned with job motivation, potential and personnel improvements. Titles are:
1. Strategy for Productive Behavior (20 min.);
2. Motivation through Job Enrichment (28 min.);
3. The Self-Motivated Achiever (25 min.);
4. Understanding Motivation (28 min.);
5. Theory X and Theory Y, Part I: Description (25 min.);
6. Theory X and Theory Y, Part II: Application (25 min.);
7. Human Nature and Organizational Realities (28 min.);
8. Human Assets (28 min.)

132. GETTING AHEAD: THE ROAD TO SELF DEVELOPMENT
Roundtable   28 min.   b/w and color
This is an informational and motivational documentary to
encourage self-evaluation, goal-setting, continuing education, on-the-job learning and activities essential to self-
development at all levels.   Interviews with a number of
successful people describe techniques, education, preparation needed for success in their positions.

133. GOOD BEGINNING, A
Bureau of National Affairs   1974   10 min.   color
The viewer sees a demonstration of the "right" way to introduce a new employee to his department, job and job
training.

134. HOW ORGANIZATIONAL RENEWAL WORKS
Bureau of National Affairs   1969   25 min.   color
The film analyzes and demonstrates who should take leadership and how he should go about getting support of management.   The role of "resource" people or "internal con-
sultants" is also discussed.

135. HUMAN NATURE AND ORGANIZATIONAL REALITIES
Bureau of National Affairs   1967   28 min.   color
From the Gellerman Motivation and Productivity Series
Dr. Chris Argyris, Professor and Chairman of Administrative Sciences, Yale University, discusses experiments
in redesigning routine jobs to motivate individuals at the
lower organizational levels.   Examined is the human tend-

ency to fear change and responsibility. Improvements for executive action are suggested with methods of T-group training encouraged.

136.   I JUST WORK HERE
       Roundtable   17 min.   b/w and color
       Awards: Columbus, Ohio
           Dramatized are the damaging effects of negative, self-centered attitudes. Self-defensiveness, indifference, arrogance, hostility, insincerity and irritation hamper interpersonal relationships in the office. Mutual respect opens avenues of communication.

137.   I UNDERSTAND, YOU UNDERSTAND
       Crowell Collier Macmillan   1975   32 min.   color.
           Management consultant Joe Batten explains the principles and techniques of transactional analysis (TA), employing dramatized scenes from everyday business life. He shows how TA can change attitudes, increase motivation and productivity and bridge gaps in communication.

138.   IF AN ELEPHANT ANSWERS
       Bell Telephone Co.   26 min.   color   s/c/a
           This film shows how business customers can receive full benefits from their communication facilities.

139.   IMAGINATION AT WORK
       Roundtable   21 min.   b/w and color
       Awards: San Francisco, California
           This film illustrates how anyone can do more creative thinking and develop an atmosphere where creative abilities are encouraged. Four factors pertinent to creative ability are discussed: sensitivity, fluency, flexibility and originality. The major barriers to creative thinking are also reviewed.

140.   IN THE COMPANY OF MEN
       Greaves   1969   52 min.   b/w
       Award-winner
           Designed for in-plant training, this film explores the breakdown and reconstruction of communication between "unemployables" and personnel managers. It explores sensitivity sessions and role-playing as productive techniques.

141.   INDUSTRIAL MODEL
       University of Ohio   2 min.   b/w   s/c/a
           The training of hostesses at the United Airlines Educational Center in Chicago is the setting for this application of the communications model to skills training. Message content is largely fixed; objectives are clear, varied and direct; feedback is tolerated but not essential.

142. INNER MAN STEPS OUT
      General Electric   32 min.   b/w   c/a
          The film discusses working with people to obtain the best
          relationships and maximum productivity. It compares
          the "harsh" military boss to the understanding, consid-
          erate type.

143. INTRODUCTION TO WORK SAMPLING
      Northeastern University 1956 19 min. b/w and color
          To determine various solutions to problems affecting of-
          fice personnel, this film demonstrates techniques of ran-
          dom sampling as they relate to substantiation of evidence
          for businessmen.

144. JOB ENRICHMENT IN ACTION
      Bureau of National Affairs 1974 25 min. color
          Some of the most common problems and pitfalls in the
          way of successful job enrichment are explored. Accord-
          ing to the theory, it is the actual job content which al-
          lows for motivation or accounts for the lack of it.

145. JUDGING PEOPLE
      Roundtable 23 min. b/w
          This film explains some of the costly errors a manager
          can make in judging others. Specific techniques to judge
          ability, personality, intelligence, character and potential
          are explained.

146. KITA, OR WHAT HAVE YOU DONE FOR ME, LATELY?
      Bureau of National Affairs 1974 27 min. color
          A presentation with humorous touches explains all about
          KITA ("kick in the pants") or the simplest way to moti-
          vate people to work. The film states that it "depends on
          how people are used job-wise, not on how well they are
          treated."

147. LET'S GET ENGAGED ...
      Bureau of National Affairs 1975 28 min. color
          Dr. David Berlo deals with the fact that all communica-
          tion relationships are voluntary, even the supervisor-
          subordinate relationship. As work becomes more infor-
          mational and less physical, either party can disengage--
          often without getting caught. "Information relationships
          have to be maintained as a cost of doing business."

148. MAKING HUMAN RESOURCES PRODUCTIVE
      Bureau of National Affairs 1974 30 min. color
          Dr. M. Scott Myers, Organization Development Consult-
          ant for Texas Instrument Company and an expert in ap-
          plying job enrichment concepts, stresses that the aim of
          job enrichment is not merely to provide satisfaction, but
          also to make the organization more effective. Two dra-
          matic cases are presented: a supervisor ignores the

ideas of an employee; feedback and performance is
thwarted. In the final analysis, it is the employee's
feedback meshed with managerial expertise that promotes
organizational efficiency.

149.   MAN OR WOMAN FOR THE JOB, THE
       University of California   14 min.   color
            The film points out the importance of effective employee
            recruitment and selection procedures. Brief vignettes re-
            flect various sources of employees.

150.   MANNER OF SPEAKING
       Bell Telephone Co.   28 min.   color   s/c/a
            This film illustrates satisfactory telephone conversation
            for business people. It demonstrates how "badly handled"
            telephone calls can result in the customer suspending re-
            lations, how efficient use builds profits, creates "good
            will."

151.   MEETING THE PUBLIC
       Encyclopaedia Britannica   1952   12 min.   vt/vc   b/w
            This film describes techniques for workers in meeting
            and working with persons outside the company, face-to-
            face and over the telephone.

152.   MORE THAN WORDS
       Strauss   Perennial   1959   14 min.   color   s/c/a
            This film outlines basic methods of acceptable communi-
            cation applicable to activities where the fundamental role
            is dealing with people. Through a combination of anima-
            tion and live sequences, the film explores communication
            by management supervision, sales, public and community
            relations.

153.   MORE THAN WORDS
       Strauss   Perennial   1969   14 min.   color   c/a
            A revision of the above film, this version stresses the
            need for acceptance and understanding between two per-
            sons.

154.   ORGANIZATIONAL DEVELOPMENT
       University of California   1968   30 min.   color
            Behavioral science techniques are applied to organization-
            al development. The film suggests methods to produce
            lasting cultural changes.

155.   ORGANIZATIONAL RENEWAL SERIES
       Bureau of National Affairs   1972   approximately 25 min.
       each   color
       With Gordon Lippitt
       See individual title listings
            To define and illustrate research on organization develop-
            ment, this series includes: 1. Growth Stages of an Or-

ganization; 2. Confrontation, Search and Coping; 3. Individual and Teamwork; 4. Coping with Change; 5. How Organizational Renewal Works.

156. ORGANIZING FOR POWER: THE SAUL ALINSKY APPROACH --SERIES
National Film Board of Canada 1971 b/w
These five films explain organizational communities in terms of participatory democracy. Titles are: People and Power (17 min.); Deciding to Organize (35 min.); Building an Organization (38 min.); Through Conflict to Negotiation (43 min.).

157. PATTERN FOR INSTRUCTION
Roundtable 21 min. b/w and color
This film relates the basic steps in job instruction training to the principles of learning. It is designed for use with new supervisors.

158. PERSON TO PERSON COMMUNICATION
Roundtable 1956 14 min. b/w and color s/c/a
A valued employee asks his boss for a week off. The boss is so preoccupied with his thoughts that he doesn't hear why the man wants the time off. The film proves itself a valuable aid in "improving the ability to communicate with others in the office."

159. PERSONAL PROBLEM, THE
McGraw-Hill 1959 7 min. b/w C/a
From the Plant Supervisor's Problems Series
This film suggests that a supervisor who avoids discussing an employee's personal problems with him can precipitate production fall-off by the worker. Suggestions are made as to what and how much assistance with a personal problem a supervisor should offer.

160. PERSONALITY CONFLICT
McGraw-Hill 1959 7 min. b/w C/a
From the Plant Supervisor's Problems Series
What happens when two conflicting types of personalities must work together is exemplified in this film. It discusses the necessity for adjustments, compromise and communication in the interests of harmony and efficiency.

161. REWARDS OF REWARDING, THE
Roundtable 24 min. color
Part I of the Thanks A'Plenty Boss Series
This film deals with behavior modification--the favorable changing of people's behavior. It details how approval can affect job performance, job tenure, employee turnover and costs. Principles used include those of Skinner, Maslow and Blake.

162. SELF-MOTIVATED ACHIEVER
      Bureau of National Affairs 28 min. color s/c/a
          Dr. David McClelland discusses his research on the
          achievement motive: identifying problems with a high
          need for achievement, how to deal with them when they
          are discovered in an organization. Case problems drama-
          tized include several motivation and productivity prob-
          lems.

163. SOCIOTECHNICAL SYSTEMS
      University of California 1974 33 min. b/w
          G. K. Javaram, noted organizational consultant, presents
          a lecture summarizing the history of organizational theory
          and explaining the concept of open and sociotechnical sys-
          tems. He suggests that the proponents of sensitivity
          training generally overemphasize social factors in organi-
          zational life.

164. SOMETHING TO WORK FOR
      Roundtable 30 min. b/w and color
      Awards: CINE
          This film stresses the importance of setting high stan-
          dards, communicating clearly and giving encouragement
          and support to subordinates.

165. STATUS AND ROLE
      University of Utah 1963 29 min. b/w
      From the Human Relations Series: #16
          This film discusses the general potential structure of so-
          ciety and the variable features entailed in its formation.
          Specifically, it evaluates the relationship between job
          workers and their standing in the community.

166. TALKBACK: A STUDY IN COMMUNICATION
      Roundtable Association Films 18 min. b/w
          Highlights of fundamental communication aspects in any
          organization and in our working lives are discussed. The
          film stresses the need for open dialogue, clear direc-
          tions and constructive feedback to help eliminate any mis-
          understanding.

167. TELEPHONE AT WORK, THE
      Roundtable 15 min. color
          The film shows how the telephone can be used as a valu-
          able aid to business communication, rather than merely
          an instrument of frustration. It makes the point that a
          polite, efficient telephone call is not just a message, but
          a part of the company's total image.

168. THAT'S NOT MY JOB
      Roundtable 26 min. b/w and color
          When employees fail to cooperate, productivity and morale

suffer. This film attacks the problem on two levels. It
encourages employees to recognize the relationship of
their work to that of others; it helps supervisors develop
their ability to deal with uncooperative employees. It is
useful as a training and attitude-formation film.

169. TROUBLE WITH WORDS, THE
Association Films Crowell, Collier, Macmillan 1968 15
min. color c/a
Award: Most honored labor film of 1968
Explored are solutions to communication problems in
worker-job situations, with recommended solutions for
those problems.

170. TRY TO TELL IT LIKE IT IS
Bureau of National Affairs 1975 30 min. color
Problems of appraisal, giving instructions and evaluations
to help people understand what you want--are all discussed. The focus is on the practical requirements of
effective communication, the importance of "talking sense
rather than nonsense."

171. UNDERSTANDING MOTIVATION
Bureau of National Affairs 1967 28 min. c/a
From the Gellerman Motivation and Productivity Series
Dr. Saul Gellerman, Executive Research Consultant at International Business Machines Corporation, explains the
scope of behavioral science as it applies to the field of
management. Suggestions are made to initiate activity by
behavioral techniques.

172. VOICE OF YOUR BUSINESS
Business Education Films 12.5 min. color
This film portrays an animated cartoon showing the value
of good telephone habits for business users. It points out
that "answering quickly, taking messages properly, trans-
ferring a call, leaves the strong impression that you're
really on the ball."

173. WELCOME ABOARD
Roundtable 21 min. color
Awards: CINE; Columbus, Ohio
For first-line supervisors, this film stimulates viewers
to assess their own roles and responsibilities in helping
new people to become oriented quickly and productively.

174. WILL TO WORK, THE
Roundtable. 22 min. plus two 4-min. case studies color
To explain the factors that motivate working people, this
film presents the confrontation of a low-producing supervisor with the Devil. The supervisor is forced to live
again through his supervisory misdeeds.

175.   YOU CAN SURPASS YOURSELF
        Ramic Productions 1975 color
        A motivational film that deals with successful meetings,
        the subject of teachability. The "Four Levels of Teachabil-
        ity" are explained and the use of the concept is explored.

176.   YOUR JOB: YOU AND YOUR BOSS
        Business Education Films Coronet 16 min. b/w
        The relationship between employee and boss is explored
        from both points of view. Interviews with supervisors
        and employees at their jobs answer many of the questions
        faced by young people regarding dependability, familiarity
        and authority.

177.   YOU'RE COMING ALONG FINE
        Roundtable 23 min. b/w and color
        This film explains how to make appraisals vital and use-
        ful tools. Its purpose is to illustrate the importance of
        establishing mutually shared objectives and giving honest
        feedback for progress toward their realization.

                                   Sales

178.   ARE YOU EARNING THE RIGHT TO ASK THEM TO BUY?
        Bureau of National Affairs 1971 28 min. color
        Bill Gove explains effective selling techniques by first an-
        alyzing the problems of the salesman who has particular
        difficulties in consummating final sales.

179.   AVOIDING COMMUNICATION BREAKDOWN
        Bureau of National Affairs 1963 24 min. color and b/w
        From the Berlo Effective Communication Series
        In this dramatization of how a key account is lost, Dr.
        David Berlo analyzes warning signals to defective com-
        munication. He points out that communication breakdown
        costs money, affects employee morale and results in lost
        sales.

180.   BEN FRANKLIN SELLS TODAY
        Jam Handy Business Education Films 23 min. b/w s/c/a
        Ben Franklin comes to modern life in this illustration of
        common mistakes in selling. We learn of the application
        of his methods: for getting the other person to talk; for
        keeping out of arguments; for putting across your opinions;
        for saving time while selling.

181.   CAREERS IN SALES: THE JOY OF SELLING
        Bureau of National Affairs 26 min. color
        Every industry, business and community employs some
        sales personnel. The film explores some directions of a
        sales career for those motivated.

182. CLOSE THAT SALE
      Roundtable 11 min. color
          This motivational sales film explains techniques for
          "closing the sale": the direct, the trial, the assumptive,
          the inducement and the summary.

183. CONFRONTING CONFLICT
      Bureau of National Affairs 1974 30 min. color
          The advertising group with Sheldon Davis, trainer-con-
          sultant, holds a team-building session. Filmed extempo-
          raneously, it provides insight into team building practice
          and advertising techniques for selling.

184. CUSTOMER-ORIENTED SELLING
      Roundtable 1973 30 min. color
          Two young men at a sales seminar compete for the at-
          tention of a celebrity. Customer-oriented selling tech-
          niques are applied to achieve effective results.

185. DIALOGUE WITH A YOUNG MAN
      General Motors 14 min. color s/c/a
          A young man is challenged to consider the possibilities
          offered in the profession of selling. He gives his gen-
          eration's point of view.

186. EFFECTIVE SELLING THROUGH PSYCHOLOGY
      Roundtable 30 min. color
          Salesmen are helped in learning communication skills and
          in "closing" more sales. Techniques presented include
          those of motivation, coaching and counseling.

187. FOCUS ON SALES
      Roundtable 15 min. color
      From the Communication Series
          This film stimulates self-appraisal and improvement in
          the basics of selling. Contrasts are made between suc-
          cessful selling techniques and an effective athletic contest.

188. HABIT OF WINNING, THE
      Bureau of National Affairs 1974 30 min. color
          This motivational film relates the philosophy of the late
          Vince Lombardi and associates. Jerry Kramer narrates
          as an inspiration for a positive attitude change.

189. HARRY WOODS IS AT THE DOOR
      Communications Group West 13 min. color vt/vc s/c/a
          This film follows Harry Woods through a typical day of
          selling. He is a specialist in "selling people the things
          they would not ordinarily purchase." Throughout the
          film, he explains exactly what psychology and techniques
          he uses.

190.   HIDDEN SIDE OF SELLING, THE
       Roundtable 1961 34 min. b/w and color
       Awards: Columbus, Ohio Restricted to educational institu-
       tion use only
            Designed to show new and experienced salesmen how to
            "close" more sales, this film presents practical methods
            every salesman can use to improve his abilities. Ex-
            plained are: how to find common areas of interest, how
            to get a customer to answer his own objections.

191.   I'LL BUY THAT
       Roundtable 30 min. color
            Meredith MacRae stars in this humorous application of
            sales techniques to "date-getting." Suggestions include:
            do pre-call research, planning; discover and concentrate
            on the customer's needs; develop an effective opening;
            emphasize customer's benefits; be sensitive to the opti-
            mum closing time.

192.   LISTEN, PLEASE
       Bureau of National Affairs 1974 10 min. color
            This film demonstrates that failure to really listen is of-
            ten the key to a lost sale. Viewers are shown that they
            often think they're better listeners than they actually are.

193.   LITTLE WHITE CRIMES: A QUESTION OF ETHICS
       National Film Board of Canada 1969 28 min. b/w
            This film suggests various behavior patterns and situa-
            tions of ethical conflict that exist in the business world.
            A young advertising executive, intent on building his im-
            age to match his aggressive ambitions, has difficulty in
            relating to the needs of his peers.

194.   MOST IMPORTANT THING IN THE WORLD
       Pioneer Screw and Nut Company San Francisco State 1970
       7 min. color s/c/a
            A prize-winning marketing/sales film depicts the various
            operations and activities of a manufacturing company.
            It illustrates the use of filmic self-parody to establish a
            favorable attitude in the mind of the viewer.

195.   PRESENTING THE OFFER
       National Institute of Real Estate Brokers 1969 20 min. color
            Market analysis forms in persuasion are explained.
            Techniques are dramatized that are effective in "closing"
            the sale.

196.   SALES GRID, THE (Parts I and II)
       Bureau of National Affairs 1975 30 min. each color
            In Film I, Blake and Mouton present their ideas to four
            salesmen who question them on various aspects of the
            selling relationship. Film II covers the principal seller
            styles.

197. SALESMAN ISN'T DEAD, HE'S DIFFERENT, THE
      Fortune Crowell, Collier, Macmillan 21 min. b/w s/c/a
      This film shows what today's successful salesman does
      and how he does it, the responsibility involved and the
      benefits he derives. The change in salesmen, from
      stereotyped characterizations of the past to the modern
      representative of his company, is portrayed.

198. SELLING TODAY
      Jam Handy 1960 22 min. b/w s/c/a
      Rules are described which may be applied to modern sell-
      ing, from Benjamin Franklin formulations to those of cur-
      rent hucksters. Suggestions include: determine the
      buyer's real wants, avoid absolute statements, preface
      rebuttals with "yes, but," don't contradict, don't waste
      time, and use persuasive techniques.

199. SHARPER FOCUS, A
      Strauss 1974 10 min. color c/a
      Through the film we see how words affect a customer's
      emotions, how actions affect his point of view, how si-
      lence can be a powerful tool in allowing the customer to
      participate.

200. WHAT EVERY MANAGER NEEDS TO KNOW ABOUT MAR-
      KETING (Parts I, II)
      Bureau of National Affairs 1972 30 min. each color
      Part I: The Merritt Case; Part II: What Businesses
      Are You Really In? Part One contrasts marketing with
      selling. Part Two provides analysis of marketing by
      Theodore Levitt, Harvard School of Business.

201. WHO KILLED THE SALE?
      Roundtable 21 min. color
      Awards: Columbus, Ohio, British Industrial Film Award
      This film is a case study showing how a company fails to
      win a large sale. Its purpose is to develop teamwork in
      a sales organization and make all personnel cognizant of
      the sales effort.

202. WINNING COMBINATION, THE
      Bureau of National Affairs 1974 10 min. color
      Emphasized are the principles of good salesmanship and
      how they are applied in everyday supervision.

203. YOU AND YOUR CUSTOMERS
      Bureau of National Affairs 14 min. color
      Since the customer is "always right," this film presents
      sales situations and techniques to satisfy him.

204. YOU PACK YOUR OWN CHUTE
      Ramic Productions 1972 30 min. color
      Dr. Eden Ryl, management motivation consultant, demon-

strates that personal responsibility is the keystone of
sales success.   The film is designed to motivate achievement in sales and training programs.

CROSS CULTURAL

Ethnic

205. AMERICAN INDIAN INFLUENCE ON THE UNITED STATES,
THE
Dana   1971   20 min.   color
Barry Sullivan, narrator
      This film depicts how United States life today has been in-
      fluenced sociologically, philosophically and culturally by
      the American Indian.   The aim of the film is to help
      "break the communication barrier" through multi-cultural
      understanding.   The stress is on the contribution of mi-
      norities to the building of this country.

206. BLACK AFRICAN HERITAGE: A SERIES
Learning Corporation of America   1971   50 min. each   color
vt
      Produced and directed by Eliot Elisofon, this series fo-
      cuses on environmental studies, national development and
      prejudice.   Titles are: 1. The Congo;   2. The Bend of
      the Niger;   3. The Slave Coast;   4. Africa's Gift;   5.
      Combination.

207. BLACK AND WHITE TOGETHER
National Educational Television   Indiana University   58 min.
b/w   s/c/a
      Interracial understanding between students in Atlantic City,
      New Jersey, was promoted by conducting two six-week
      sessions of living and learning together at a local hotel.
      Dissension occurs when a staff member challenges the
      premise of the experiment.

208. BLACK FRONTIER, THE: A SERIES
University of Nebraska (KUON-TV)   color   four 59 min. programs.
      The Ford Foundation financed this series which focuses on
      several distinguished blacks who settled in the Great
      Plains areas.   Host-narrator is William Marshall.   Titles
      are: 1. New Americans; 2. Cowherders; 3. Buffalo
      Soldiers; 4. Exodusters.

209. BLACK HAS ALWAYS BEEN BEAUTIFUL
Indiana University   1971   17 min.   b/w
      Black photographer James Van DerZee documents the black
      experience in Harlem for more than sixty years.

210.   BLACK HISTORY: LOST, STOLEN OR STRAYED (PARTS I, II)
        Bailey Film Associates 1968 I: 26 min. II: 27 min.
        color s/C/a
        Award winner
            Bill Cosby narrates black achievements unrecorded in
            American history. The film explores the history of atti-
            tudes (black and white) and their effect on the black Amer-
            ican.

211.   BLACK MUSIC IN AMERICA
        Learning Corporation of America 1972 color 29 min.
            Musical performances interspersed with woodcuts show
            the history of the black man in America. The musical
            contribution is traced by performances of Louis Arm-
            strong, Mahalia Jackson, others.

212.   BLACK MUSLIMS SPEAK FROM AMERICA
        BBC-TV Time-Life   33 min. b/w s/c/a vt/vc
            Malcolm Muggeridge reviews comments from the Black
            Muslims, including their hopes and their influence on in-
            tegration in America. In an interview with seven young
            Black Muslims, he learns that they believe in the "de-
            struction" of America.

213.   BLACK VIEWS ON RACE: ADAM CLAYTON POWELL
        Time-Life 1970 4 min. color vt/vc s/c/a
        From Black Views on Race Series
            "We're not anti-white ... we're pro-black. Black is the
            way you think. There are a lot of people who can think
            black and still be white," according to the late Mr. Pow-
            ell.

214.   BLACK VIEWS ON RACE: BOBBY SEALE
        Time-Life 1970 4 min. color s/c/a vt/vc
        From the Black Views on Race Series
            Bobby Seale expounds his beliefs: "... if you're going to
            shout about differences ... you must have the proper
            tools and the proper tool is the gun.... We want free
            medicine, free health clinics in black communities."

215.   BLACK VIEWS ON RACE: CARL STOKES
        Time-Life 1970 4 min. color s/c/a vt/vc
        From Black Views on Race Series
            "Never put yourself in the position that you do the very
            thing that we have been fighting," advises Carl Stokes to
            political candidates.

216.   BLACK VIEWS ON RACE: DICK GREGORY
        Time-Life 1970 4 min. color s/c/a vt/vc
        From Black Views on Race Series
            Dick Gregory, philosophizing, states "As dirty as Amer-
            ica is, she's still Momma. I will die for her but I will
            never kill for her...."

217.   BLACK VIEWS ON RACE: MALCOLM X
       Time-Life 1970 4 min. color vt/vc s/c/a
       From Black Views on Race Series
           Malcolm X suggests: "Whenever a black man attains a
           high level, he forgets that his people still live in severe
           conditions."

218.   BLACK VIEWS ON RACE: MARTIN LUTHER KING
       Time-Life 1970 4 min. color vt/vc s/c/a
       From Black Views on Race Series
           "I don't believe in riots so my slogan is 'build, baby,
           build' ... 'organize, baby, organize' ... 'learn, baby,
           learn' so you can earn, earn," stated the late Mr. King.

219.   BLACK VIEWS ON RACE: MUHAMMAD ALI
       Time-Life 1970 4 min. color vt/vc s/c/a
           According to Muhammad Ali, "the suffering forced upon
           us by white America justifies our demand for a complete
           separation in a state or territory of our own."

220.   BLACK VIEWS ON RACE: SERIES
       Time-Life 1970 4 min. each color vt/vc s/c/a
           Twenty prominent blacks speak out about racial problems.
           Individual segments include speeches, interviews, dia-
           logue: 1. Ralph Abernathy; 2. Harry Belafonte; 3. Jul-
           ian Bond; 4. Edward Brooke; 5. H. Rap Brown; 6.
           James Brown; 7. Jim Brown; 8. Stokely Carmichael;
           9. Shirley Chisholm; 10. Muhammad Ali; 11. Dick
           Gregory; 12. Coretta King; 13. Martin Luther King;
           14. Sidney Poitier; 15. Adam Clayton Powell; 16.
           Jackie Robinson; 17. Bayard Rustin; 18. Bobby Seale;
           19. Carl Stokes; 20. Malcolm X. Some individual titles
           are listed.

221.   BLACK WORLD
       CBS News 1968 53 min. color s/c/a
       From the Of Black America Series
           Mike Wallace moderates a round-robin conversation on
           the black man's position in the world today. Panelists in-
           clude Representative John Conyers, Jr., Washington,
           D.C.; Honorable Thomas Mboya, Kenya; Floyd McKissick,
           CORE; and Dr. Alex Kwapong, Vice Chancellor, Univer-
           sity of Ghana.

222.   BLUES
       Bailey Film Associates 18 min. color s/c/a
           This is a film about the awakening racial awareness in
           a secondary school. The goal is to "delineate the di-
           lemma confronting the gifted young black in a society
           structured by white men's rules."

223.   BODY AND SOUL (PARTS I, II)
       Bailey Film Associates 1968 Pt. I: 24 min; Pt. II:

28 min. color s/c/a
> Part I examines the black American's contribution to
> sports.   Harry Reasoner and others interview and report.
> Part II focuses on Ray Charles and his description of the
> development of the language of black music and the econ-
> omics of black depravity.   Featured are noted musicians/
> vocalists from the black music fields.

224. CELEBRATIONS
United States Information Agency   National Audiovisual Center
1966   19 min.   color
> Ethnic celebrations retained from the "old country" by
> Americans are shown.   The diverse national origins in-
> clude: the Feast of San Gennaro, Blessing of the Ani-
> mals, Chinese New Year, Zuni Indian dances, the Mexi-
> can Pinata festival and an Italian-American wedding.

225. COLOR US BLACK
National Education Television   Indiana University   1968   60
min.   b/w   c/a
> Black students from Howard University, Washington,
> D. C. , explain their concepts of black identity.   Shown is
> the four-day takeover of the administration building by
> students.

226. CONFRONTATION: DIALOGUE IN BLACK AND WHITE
National Educational Television   Indiana University   1968
35 min.   b/w
> One hundred citizens from Chicago confront each other in
> the studios of WTTW to discuss racial tensions.   The de-
> bate is preceded by a film of the Chicago west side, pro-
> duced and directed by a black militant.

227. END OF THE TRAIL: THE AMERICAN PLAINS INDIAN
McGraw-Hill   53 min.   b/w
> The film explores the folklore of the American Plains In-
> dians, specifically examining the history of the American
> Indian in the post-Civil War era.

228. EXILES, THE
McGraw-Hill   72 min.   b/w
> American Indians are shown "caught" between two cul-
> tures: those of the reservations they have left and the
> chosen new environment.

229. FORTY-SEVEN CENTS
University of California   1973   25 min.   b/w
Emmy Award
> This is a documentary of how officials of the Bureau of
> Indian Affairs, the Indian Claims Commission, and an In-
> dian lawyer obtained a land settlement that "many" Indi-
> ans did not want.   Officials explain the government's po-
> sition.

230. HARLEM RENAISSANCE: THE BLACK POETS
     Carousel 1972 20 min. color s/c/a
          This film examines the historical as well as the literary
          significance of the "black experience" from childhood to
          old age.

231. HEART OF APARTHEID, THE
     Time-Life 39 min. b/w vt/vc s/c/a
          In South Africa, the black man's views are "usually" rep-
          resented by white spokesmen or political refugees. In
          this film, he is given the opportunity to speak frankly
          about the separation policy in South Africa.

232. HERITAGE IN BLACK
     Encyclopaedia Britannica 27 min. color vt/vc s/c/a
          A panorama of two hundred years shows the first strug-
          gles of black people as well as today's experiences. Il-
          lustrated are contributions in sciences, industry, educa-
          tion, music, sports, labor movement and entertainment.

233. HUELGAL
     McGraw-Hill 50 min. color
          This is the filmed story of a job-walkout by Mexican and
          Filipino-American grape pickers in 1965. It examines
          their struggle to raise the standards of living, recording
          the genesis of a union and its effects on the lives of its
          members.

234. I AM JOAQUIN
     San Francisco State 1969 color s/c/a
          Based on a poem by R. C. Gonzales, this film explores
          the Mexican-American's struggles with ruling white cul-
          tures.

235. IF THERE WERE NO BLACKS WE'D HAVE TO INVENT THEM
     American Documentary Films 1968 58 min. b/w
          John Speight's English play focuses on social issues of
          racism. An assortment of character/symbols act out a
          Brechtian comedy of prejudice, militarism and class con-
          flict.

236. INDIAN DIALOGUE
     National Film Board of Canada 1972 18 min. b/w
          Canadian Indians discuss many problems that cause con-
          cern, particularly the threat to their own culture by a
          predominantly white society. Many "younger generation"
          Indians are involved in the dialogue.

237. INDIAN FOR A CHANGE
     U.S. Department of Labor   National Audiovisual Center   1970
     28 min. color

Old stereotypes are corrected with the presentation of candid, insightful portraits of five young Indian men and women.

238. INDIAN LAND
Crowell, Collier, Macmillan 21 min. color s/a
In candid vignettes, American Indians discuss their veneration for the Earth--their concept of land as being free for use by everyone.

239. INDIAN MAINSTREAM
University of California 1975 25 min. color
This film examines a movement to develop an economic base for the native Americans of Northern California. The film shows the construction of ancient Hupa and Hurok villages and a "walking university of Indian heritage."

240. INDIAN SPEAKS, THE
McGraw-Hill National Film Board of Canada 41 min. color
This film is about Canadian Indians who are concerned with the preservation of what is left of their culture and the restoring of what is gone.

241. INDIAN TO INDIAN
U.S. Department of Labor National Audiovisual Center 1970 26 min. color
Indians who are part of the work force explain their lives and work. They describe how, though part of the work force, they retain their tribal heritages.

242. INDIANS AND CHIEFS
University of California 1972 40 min. b/w
This narrationless documentary shows problems of American Indians trying to maintain their Indian identity while they learn to master the White Man's world on his terms. It focuses on one summer's events, the Los Angeles Indian Center, and Indian-run urban meeting place that provides help for thousands of emigrating Indians.

243. INJUN TALK
Standard Oil Ideal 32 min. b/w
More than 150 Indians in colorful regalia appear in this film, photographed in Glacier National Park to demonstrate the "graphic beauty and symbolism" of the Indian sign language.

244. LEE SUZUKI--HOME IN HAWAII
Learning Corporation of America 1974 19 min. color
This simple episode in the life of a fourteen-year-old Hawaiian boy provides a view of the island people whose multi-ethnic society makes them unique among our fifty states.

245. LIKE ME, LIKE YOU
     Mass Media Associates 1972 22 min. b/w
         A party provides the occasion for a white and a black
         couple to become acquainted. It comes to grips with
         some of the basic emotional reactions to racial issues.

246. MEXICAN-AMERICAN, THE: HERITAGE AND DESTINY
     Handel 29 min. b/w s/c/a
         Roberto, a young Chicano, feels that he has little control
         over his destiny. The narrator, Ricardo Montalban,
         "leads" him back through the pages of Mexican history.
         The film emphasizes the necessity for bridging "communi-
         cation gaps" between the two countries.

247. MEXICAN-AMERICAN--THE INVISIBLE MINORITY
     National Educational Television Indiana University 1969
     28 min. s/c/a
         This film explains the identity-struggle of the five million
         Mexican-Americans who are "our fastest-growing ethnic
         minority." It stresses the need for understanding that the
         Mexican-American has unique aspirations which include
         retaining a cultural identity.

248. MEXICAN-AMERICAN CULTURE: ITS HERITAGE
     Communication Group West 1970 18 min. color s/c
         The impact of Mexican history and culture on the United
         States is recalled in this survey designed to remind the
         viewer of the closeness of the two countries in ways other
         than purely their geographical locations. Ricardo Montal-
         ban narrates.

249. MEXICAN OR AMERICAN
     McGraw-Hill 17 min. color s/a
         Through the eyes of an educated Mexican-American family
         man, the film provides insight into the problems of the
         Spanish-speaking minority of America.

250. NATION OF IMMIGRANTS
     Xerox Time-Life 60 min. b/w vt/vc
         Underscoring that our nation's history is the history of
         our immigrants, the film traces the successive waves of
         ethnic groups that migrated to the United States, beginning
         with the English aboard the Mayflower. Narrated by Rich-
         ard Basehart.

251. NAVAJO
     Crowell, Collier, Macmillan 1971 16 min. color s/c
         The land of the Navajos is visited, where the remnants of
         a matriarchal society remain. Tribes discuss their out-
         door lives and the changes that most disturb them.

252. NAVAJO (PARTS I, II)
     National Educational Television 29 min. b/w

The film visits a Navajo reservation to discover the values held by the community. Part II presents a visit to Windrock, Arizona to interview members of the Navajo Tribes Council to discuss tribal organizational patterns.

253. NAVAJO: THE LAST RED INDIANS
Time-Life 35 min. color vt/vc s/c/a
This film is about the Navajo's fight for existence of life against the inroads of the white man's culture. It contains many exclusive and uncensored scenes of rituals and ceremonies.

254. NAVAJO LIFE
National Educational Television 9 min. b/w and color
The film visits Navajo Indians living in the Canyon de Chelly in Arizona. The viewer learns how the Indians farm, build their homes, communicate.

255. NAVAJOS AND ANNIE WAUNEKA
CBS News Crowell, Collier, Macmillan 25 min. b/w
This documentary is about a 54-year-old Navajo woman who has devoted her life to helping her people in the field of public health.

256. NEGRO AMERICAN
Bailey Film Associates 15 min. color animation
The brief history of Negroes in the United States illustrates how they were involuntarily uprooted from homes in Africa and sold into slavery. Background material is offered to trigger discussions on the subjects of freedoms, prejudice, bigotry.

257. NO MAN IS AN ISLAND
Columbia Broadcasting System Associated Instructional Materials 39 min.
From the CBS Look Up and Live Series
The story of two army men, one white, one black, and the prejudices they encounter when they attempt to maintain their friendship in civilian life.

258. NORTH AMERICAN INDIAN, THE (PARTS I, II, III)
Contemporary Films 1972 Pt. I: 18 min.; Pt. II: 25 min.; Pt. III: 24 min. color
Narrated by Marlon Brando
These three segments relate the plight of the American Indians, from the opening of the West to the present. Titles include "Treaties Made, Treaties Broken," "How the West Was Won ... and Honor Lost," and "Lament of the Reservation."

259. NOTHING BUT A MAN
Roemer-Young Brandon 92 min. b/w
This drama about the personal struggle of a Southern

Negro and his wife in a "hostile society" tells the story of a young railway worker who gives up a good job to marry the preacher's daughter. The problems of earning a livelihood, living in peace and dignity, and refusing to "play the expected Negro role" are all examined.

260. NOW IS THE TIME
Carousel Associated Instructional Films 36 min. b/w
Ruby Dee and Ossie Davis narrate this documentary of the history, strength and militancy of the black American. The script is drawn from the poetry of Langston Hughes and the writing of James Baldwin, plus others.

261. OUR COUNTRY, TOO
National Educational Television Indiana University 1965 30 min. b/w s/c/a
This film explores the inner world of the American Negro --his values, attitudes and impressions of life. Interviews are in various settings: an African rite in Harlem, a debutante ball, the office of a Negro newspaper and a Negro-owned radio station.

262. PORTRAIT IN BLACK AND WHITE, A
CBS News Bailey Film Associates 1968 54 min. b/w c/a
CBS News prepared a 45-minute questionnaire and interviewed 1,500 people to learn black attitudes toward the white community and the reverse. The results of these interviews are examined. General conclusions show attitudes and feelings to be both "subtle and complex."

263. PRIDE AND THE SHAME, THE
Time-Life 1974 30 min. b/w vt/vc s/c/a
This study focuses on the Sioux Indians of the Black Hills of North Dakota as examples of the half-million American Indians across the country who still live on reservations.

264. RACE RELATIONS
University of California 1971 22 min. color
This film probes recent history, examining possible directions for blacks in the United States. Current economics as well as existent discrimination are examined.

265. RENDEZVOUS WITH FREEDOM
Crowell, Collier, Macmillan 56 min. color s/c/a
This film traces the history of the Jews in America, from the arrival of the earliest Jewish settlers in New Amsterdam in 1654 through the present. Commentary is spoken by Herbert Kaplow. Narration, readings and songs are by Zero Mostel, Sam Jaffe, Marian Seldes, George Segal.

266. SOME OF MY BEST FRIENDS ARE WHITE
Time-Life 1975 30 min. b/w vt/vc s/c/a

This is a provocative face-to-face social study of a middle-class black's attitudes, values and approach to the achievement of racial equality.

267.   STORM OF STRANGERS, A
       ACI Films, Inc.   1970   27 min.   b/w and color
       Award Winner
           Narrator Herschel Bernardi reminisces about Jewish immigration to New York's Lower East Side around 1910. The comedies and tragedies are remembered and compared with the obstacles of the black and Puerto Rican families today.   Educators claim this film is "already on its way to becoming a film classic."

268.   STRANGERS IN THEIR OWN LAND: THE BLACKS
       American Broadcasting Company   12 min.   color
           The film's message is: "to be young, gifted and black--that's where it's at."   The creativity of black youth today is shown in urban black ghettos, with dance, fashion, literature, art.

269.   STRANGERS IN THEIR OWN LAND: CHICANOS
       American Broadcasting Company   16 min.   color
           Questions are discussed that are pertinent to the future of the Mexican-Americans in the United States.

270.   STRANGERS IN THEIR OWN LAND: THE PUERTO RICANS
       American Broadcasting Company   16 min.   color
           Typical problems of a Puerto Rican family in Brooklyn are examined.   Economic, education, social conditions are discussed with the Puerto Rican Family Institute directors.

271.   TALKING HANDS
       University of Oklahoma   1954   20 min.   b/w   s/c/a
           The film presents a basic introduction to the universal sign language of the American Indian.   A storyteller recounts the battle of the Washita in Hand Talk.

272.   TELLING IT LIKE IT IS AND HOW IT OUGHT TO BE
       Crowell, Collier, Macmillan   30 min.   b/w   c/a
           Frank Robinson of the Baltimore Orioles and Joe Garagiola of National Broadcasting Company discuss the problems related to being black in a white-dominated society.

273.   THEY BEAT THE ODDS
       University of California   1965   22 min.   color
           This film shows a series of highly successful minority people who have completed their education and worked diligently despite the odds against them.

274.   TO BE BLACK
       American Broadcasting Company   McGraw-Hill   54 min.   b/w

Resentments and frustrations of black Americans are revealed in a personalized dialogue of contemporary concerns.

275. TREASURE, THE
      Bailey Film Associates   13 min.   color   s/c/a
      This contemporary study explores the conflicting values of
      two Indian brothers, impatient with their father's tradi-
      tional ways.

276. WAYS OF OUR FATHERS, THE
      University of California   1974   33 min.   color
      Members of several Northern California Indian tribes de-
      pict unique elements of a way of life as it flourished be-
      for the imposition of a foreign culture.   Several Native
      American teachers discuss historical methods of Indian
      education.

277. WHAT ABOUT TOMORROW?
      National Dental Association   Modern Talking Picture Service
      (Free Loan Film)   28 min.   color
      Caught up in the pressures of racial consciousness, a
      black youth searches for identity and a life goal.

278. WHAT IS THE FUTURE OF THE BLACK AMERICA?--A SE-
      RIES
      Holt   26 min.   b/w   s/C
      Dr. Vincent Harding, moderator; participants: James Fore-
      man, Reverend Albert Cleague and John Hendrik Clarke.
      Individual program listings are: 1. Our Spiritual and Cul-
      tural Future; 2. Our Political Future; 3. Our Future
      with the Third World.

279. WHERE IS JIM CROW?   A CONVERSATION WITH LENA
      HORNE
      University of California   1967   30 min.   b/w
      Miss Horne discusses herself as a symbol of the Negro
      "pinup" image, the representative Negro woman of "this
      year's black," and tells how she had to conquer this im-
      pression for her own sake.

280. WHERE IS JIM CROW?   A CONVERSATION WITH NANCY
      WILSON
      University of California   1967   30 min.   b/w
      Singer Nancy Wilson discusses the Negro in show busi-
      ness, African heritage, discrimination and civil rights ac-
      tivities.

281. WHERE IS JIM CROW?   A CONVERSATION WITH ...:   A
      SERIES
      University of California   1967   30 min. each   b/w and color
      Black personalities discuss personal experiences with
      discrimination and the necessity for attitude changes.

Individual titles include: "A Conversation with Godfrey Cambridge"; "A Conversation with Lena Horne"; "A Conversation with Nancy Wilson"; "A Conversation with Stokely Carmichael."

282. WRITERS, BRUCE JAY FRIEDMAN AND BLACK HUMOR
National Educational Television Indiana University 1966 30 min. b/w c/a
Black humor is defined as "humor that probes characteristics that distinguish this genre and its historical perspectives." Panelists include George Mandel, Leslie Fiedler and R. V. Cassill.

283. YO SOY CHICANO
Indiana University 1972 50 min. color
Depicted is the Chicano experience--from its roots in pre-Columbian history to the present--using actors to recreate key events and portray important individuals in Chicano history. In addition, there are interviews with contemporary Chicano leaders.

284. YOU ARE ON INDIAN LAND
Contemporary Films 1974 37 min. b/w
This is a cinéma-vérité presentation of a confrontation between the Cornwall, Ontario, police and a group of Mohawk Indians. The thrust of the message is the need for understanding of the needs of all people for self-expression.

International

285. ALL KINDS OF PEOPLE
Mass Media Associates 1966 13 min. color s/a
Viewers are asked to consider the many different people living in the world and the ways in which they may live together peacefully.

286. ALLO! HELLO! ALLO!
McGraw-Hill Contemporary Films 1963 9 min. color
Co-production of: UNESCO and Bucharest Studio
Awards: New York Film Festival, Oberhausen Festival
Ion Poepsco Gopo's "littleman" stars in an animated history of communications, emphasizing the significance of worldwide communication and the rapidly developing technology.

287. AS OTHERS SEE US
Crowell, Collier, Macmillan 26 min. b/w s/c/a
From a CBS Twentieth Century program
With a new look at the "American image," the viewer learns what people in other nations think of the American people. Street-corner interviews in eight foreign cities tell the story.

288. BANNER, THE
     McGraw-Hill 1965 7 min. color s/c/a
     Award winner
         This animated fantasy from Poland makes a comment on
         conformity, organization and the individual in society.
         A group of identical men are lined up with identical flags.
         A missing comrade finally arrives, without his flag, but
         with all kinds of "irrelevancies." Anarchy occurs which
         almost disrupts the official event.

289. BEYOND ALL BARRIERS
     Pacific Telephone Company (Free Loan Film) Associated
     Sterling 18 min. b/w s/c
         To demonstrate how modern science is breaking down bar-
         riers of distance and time, this film travels around the
         world to present contrasts in cultures.

290. BORN CHINESE
     Time-Life 1974 57 min. b/w s/c/a
         Since one person in every four on the face of the earth
         is Chinese, this film attempts to visit a typical Chinese
         family. The camera follows them closely, studying their
         daily routine and the motives behind their behavior.

291. BOUNDARY LINES
     McGraw-Hill 1947 11 min. color s/c/a
         This film pleads for the elimination of arbitrary boundary
         lines which divide peoples and nations from each other in
         terms of color, origin, wealth and religion. Animated
         paintings and abstract symbols are used to demonstrate
         differences in cultures.

292. BROTHERHOOD OF MAN
     United Auto Workers McGraw-Hill 1946 11 min. color
     s/c/a
         This animated film cartoon emphasizes man's interrela-
         tionship in the world, stressing that dissimilarities be-
         tween people are based on superficial environmental in-
         fluences and are not "fundamental." There is conflict
         between desire to be friendly and fears and suspicions.

293. CHALLENGE AND THE PROMISE, THE
     UNESCO McGraw-Hill 1963 18 min. b/w s/c/a
         The viewer learns of UNESCO's role, from origin to the
         present fight against illiteracy and promotion of knowl-
         edge and understanding. The film highlights the challenge
         posed by the developing countries and UNESCO's contri-
         bution in a world of "rising expectations and exploding
         knowledge."

294. DESPITE MAN'S DIFFERENCES
     McGraw-Hill 1970 20 min. color s/c/a
         According to this film, man must learn that he shares

membership in a single human species and to accept the
differences that exist among separate members of the
species.   Pride is discussed in terms of attitudes and
prejudice toward others.   It is suggested that attitudes
are learned and, therefore, can also be unlearned.

295.   DIALOGUE FOR A DECADE
       Encyclopaedia Britannica 1962   49 min.   b/w vt/vc
             Political and economic leaders are interviewed about com-
             munication between labor union and industry, between dif-
             ferent nations, in changing societies.

296.   EXCHANGE OF WORDS
       Crowell, Collier, Macmillan Associated Instructional Films
       28 min.   b/w s/c/a
             Some of the bridges and barriers to international under-
             standing are revealed in this documentary of an actual
             encounter between American and Polish students.   Filmed
             in Poland at an advanced English Language Summer Work-
             shop, the film provides "insights for dialogue and discus-
             sion."

297.   EXPANDING WORLD RELATIONSHIPS
       National Audiovisual Center   1946 11 min. color s/c
             This film traces the development of economic and social
             interdependence from Jefferson's time to the forties.
             Stressed are the complexities of a modern industrial so-
             ciety which have increased the interdependence of men
             and nations.   It suggests that dialogue must exist, for
             isolation no longer is an "effective method" of settling
             differences peacefully.

298.   FABLE FOR FRIENDSHIP
       UNESCO McGraw-Hill 1958 11 min.   b/w and color
             This animated film portrays the aims and ideals of
             UNESCO.   It deals with self-imposed "walls" that sepa-
             rate nations and people from each other: ignorance and
             self-interest.   After these walls have been destroyed, we
             can begin to exchange knowledge through communication
             and shared experiences.

299.   FENCE, THE
       Bailey Film Associates 1969 7 min.   color no narration
             With animation, this film illustrates the wisdom and rele-
             vance of the Golden Rule.   It portrays a man who throws
             trash over his fence into a neighbor's yard, encouraging
             retaliation.   This leads to the destruction of his house.
             Later, he tosses a flower over the fence into the same
             yard.   The moral of the film is, "difference in strate-
             gies leads to considerable difference in results."

300.   GENTLE WINDS OF CHANGE
       Crowell, Collier, Macmillan 33 min.   color

The pace and effects of the westernization occurring
throughout Africa are examined, with a focus on the influences from the "outside." This film suggests a less dramatic characterization of the changes occurring in Africa.

301. INTERPRETER, THE
      McGraw-Hill 1951 25 min. b/w
      From the United Nations International Zone Series
          This film illustrates the diplomatic interpreter as the in-
          dispensable middleman of diplomacy in our age of "con-
          ferences."

302. JOURNEY OF FABIO PACCHIONI, THE
      McGraw-Hill 1967 28 min. color
      From the United Nations Film International Zone Series
          Fabio considers that for public communication, the drama
          "should reflect community goals and aspirations as a pow-
          erful resource." He takes his Italian traveling theatre
          troop through the Ecuadorian countryside to "entertain."
          Climax of the film is the education of the players them-
          selves--adjustment of their own attitudes as their message
          reaches the villagers.

303. NORSTAD OF NATO: WAR OR PEACE?
      Brandon 52 min. b/w
      From the "Twentieth Century" Series
          This is a filmed interview with the man who spent twelve
          years helping build up Europe's military and economic de-
          fense through the North Atlantic Treaty Organization.

304. PICTURE IN YOUR MIND
      International Film Foundation 1949 color s/c/a
          Philip Stapp's animation presents the earliest roots of
          cross-cultural barriers and prejudice and the reasons why
          any group, tribe or nation thinks its way of life is superi-
          or to the other man's mode of living. A plea is made to
          every individual "to re-examine his own thinking."

305. POP BUELL: HOOSIER AT THE FRONT
      Crowell, Collier, Macmillan 26 min. b/w s/a
      A "Twentieth Century" Series
          This profile of a retired Indiana farmer who helps Lao-
          tians help themselves in guerri'la-occupied territory is
          testimony to the oneness of man, no matter "what cultur-
          al or language barriers individual men hurdle."

306. PRODUCTION 5118
      Modern Learning Aids Modern Talking Picture Service 1955
      32 min. color s/c/a
          Communication significance is explored on every level of
          a human relationship: personal, civil, national and inter-
          national.

307. RACE RELATIONS
      University of Utah   1963   29 min.   b/w   c/a
      From the Human Relations Series: #14
            This film elaborates upon the qualities and characteris-
            tics involved in defining a "race" of people.   It discusses
            features that make one race different from another.

308. SAN FRANCISCO 1945
      Department of Defense   National Audiovisual Center   1945
      17 min.   35 mm
            A study of the conference at which the United Nations was
            founded, this film illustrates differences and interprets
            meanings and reconciliations of the nations involved.

309. SOCIAL PROCESSES: VALUES AND INSTITUTIONS
      Encyclopaedia Britannica   1952   30 min.   b/w   vt/vc   s/C/a
      From the American Democracy Series
            Harold Lasswell, political scientist, conducts a seminar
            on the patterns and concepts of behavior common to all
            cultures.   He develops the thesis of "the social process"
            from the statement "man seeks values through institu-
            tions using resources" and explains a terminology result-
            ing from this statement.

310. SUMMIT
      Stan Vanderbeek   Film-Maker's Cooperative   1963   12 min.
      b/w and color
            This film symbolizes world leaders at the "crossroads."
            A plastic universe is constructed where familiar objects
            lose their usual relationships.   When another shuffle oc-
            curs, then we "must become adjusted to the new picture."

311. TOO YOUNG TO HATE
      Crowell, Collier, Macmillan   26 min.   b/w   s/a
      From the Twentieth Century Series
            The subject is an innovative experiment in international
            understanding, the Children's International Summer Vil-
            lages, Inc.   A camp-like experience for children from
            many lands, the experiment is analyzed in terms of how
            the children come together to work, play, learn.

312. UNANSWERED QUESTION, THE
      Crowell, Collier, Macmillan   Brandon   1966   5 min.   b/w
      s/c/a
      Awards: Many film festivals
            Amram Nowak Associates asked people on the street,
            "What is Brotherhood?" for an interview television spot
            on "Brotherhood" prepared for the National Conference
            of Christians and Jews.   The film was put together from
            the "outtakes" of these street interviews.   The producers
            feel that this is a more truthful film than the later tele-
            vision announcements.

313. UNITED NATIONS: THE INTERPRETERS
      National Education Television 28 min. b/w s/a
         The importance of the interpreters during proceedings of
         the United Nations is shown to two students from the
         U. N. International School. Several fine points of inter-
         pretation are discussed.

314. UNITED NATIONS: V.I.P. TOUR
      National Educational Television 29 min. b/w s/a
         In addition to the examination of the lobby area, an exten-
         sive U. N. tour includes the work of each council as each
         chamber is visited.

315. UNITED NATIONS CONFERENCE IN SAN FRANCISCO
      Thorne 4 min. b/w any age
         The first session of the United Nations is opened with an
         address by George Bidault. Later scenes show the Earl
         of Halifax calling for a vote, the voting and the signing
         of the Charter by various delegates. President Truman
         addresses the assembly.

316. U. N. IN A REVOLUTIONARY WORLD
      Indiana University 29 min. b/w s/c/a
         The role of the United Nations in maintaining world peace
         is discussed: the revolutionary approach to the peace
         problem through organized, international cooperation,
         mediation.

317. U. S. IN A REVOLUTIONARY WORLD
      National Educational Television 29 min. b/w
         This film reviews U. S. participation in the League of Na-
         tions, neutrality acts of the thirties, foreign aid, the
         Korean conflict.

318. WARSAW GHETTO
      Time-Life 1974 51 min. b/w vt/vc s/c/a
         Heinrich Himmler's album, documenting the life and death
         of the Jewish people, consisted of photographs and films
         taken from the German Army, the S. S. and the Gestapo.
         BBC has synthesized this material and recreated the
         period.

319. WHO SPEAKS FOR MAN?
      Indiana University 1970 56 min. b/w
         This film evaluates the original goals of the U. N. , con-
         tending that it has remained primarily a central debating
         society for the world's superpowers. Interviews are in-
         cluded.

320. WORLD AT UNITED NATIONS PLAZA, THE
      State Department Oregon State University 1968 38 min.

b/ w
> Arthur Goldberg discusses life at the U. N. and, more
> specifically, presents glimpses of diplomacy, debates,
> conferences.

321. WORLD WITHOUT END
Crowell, Collier, Macmillan   45 min.   b/w   s/a
> This story of the work of UNESCO and three other U. N.
> agencies was filmed in Mexico and Thailand.

Prejudice

322. AN AMERICAN GIRL (THE PROBLEMS OF PREJUDICE)
Brandon   1958   28 min.   b/w   s/a
Award: Columbus, Ohio Film Festival, Vancouver, other
Film Festivals
> Focusing on the problem of anti-Semitism, the film re-
> lates a true incident of an American girl who defends her
> rights at a meeting.   Norma Davis, who is not Jewish,
> wears a bracelet that has Jewish symbols on it.   She is
> accused of trying to "pass" and told to "stick to her own
> kind. "   She exposes her experience with anti-Semitism
> and explores the problem by reading her diary at a
> school meeting.

323. BEYOND BLACK AND WHITE
Motivational Media   1975   28 min.   color   s/c/a
> This film deals with the reasons why so-called educated
> people continue to perpetuate clichés about minorities
> which have no factual validity.   These acts of racism,
> sexism and prejudice too often have no other motive than
> one of profit or fear.   Narrated by Eddie Albert.

324. BILL COSBY ON PREJUDICE
Pyramid   1972   26 min.   color   s/c/a
> Bill Cosby expresses just about every prejudice ever
> thought or spoken by a bigot.   The film was made to cata
> lyze thought and lead to an honest examination of atti-
> tudes.

325. BLACK AND WHITE UPTIGHT
Bailey Film Associates   1970   35 min.   color   s/c/a
> Myths are examined that perpetuate prejudice.   Explained
> are the subtle ways in which hate is learned.   Historical
> inequities in education and opportunity accentuate dif-
> ferences between social and racial economics.

326. CAN WE IMMUNIZE AGAINST PREJUDICE?
Center for Mass Communication   1954   7 min.   b/ w
s/ c/ a

Award Winner: Boston Film Council, Cleveland Film Council
An animated film narrated by Eddie Albert, the story
concerns how three sets of parents try to raise their
children free from prejudice.

327. CHANGING IMAGES: CONFRONTING CAREER STEREOTYPES
University of California 1975 17 min. b/w
This film examines the influence of sex role stereotypes
in the career expectations of school children. It illustrates that children are aware of evidence contradicting
most stereotypes.

328. COMMON FALLACIES ABOUT GROUP DIFFERENCES
McGraw-Hill 1957 15 min. b/w c/a
This film analyzes seven common notions about prejudice,
races, heredity and group differences in the light of known
scientific evidence.

329. CONFORMITY (PARTS I, II)
Carousel 1962 Part I: 23 min.; Part II: 26 min. b/w
s/c/a
Conformist attitudes in American life and their inherent
dangers are analyzed. Discussed are advocates of censorship, bigots, "group think" educators. Depicted is the
trend toward homogenization and dehumanization as a paral-
lel to communism and a classless society. Examples are
illustrated from contemporary society.

330. DID I DO GOOD?
Teleketics 1972 30-second spot announcement color
This spot announcement contends that "name calling" is
a sign of a prejudiced mind. It points out that prejudice
is learned and can, therefore, be unlearned if there is
enough love.

331. EVERYBODY'S PREJUDICED
National Film Board of Canada 23 min. b/w
Compared are "minor" prejudices of most people and the
"major" prejudice of the bigot, who is labeled as "di-
vorced from all reason."

332. EYE OF THE STORM
ABC Media 1971 29 min. color
Award Winner
This documentary records Mrs. Elliott's innovative attempts to introduce students to prejudice in her sixth
grade all-white rural class. The color of the eyes was
the criterion of superiority. Each child spent one day as
the oppressor and one day as the oppressed. The academic performance of each group related to whether or
not they were "top dogs."

333. FRIENDLY GAME, THE
      Mass Media Associates   1968   10 min.   b/w
      CINE Gold Eagle Winner
          This interpretation of racist and capitalistic psychology
          concerns a chess game between two men. Whitey con-
          siders it the function of a chess club to help "novices"
          along, invites Blackie to play his friendly game. Trapped
          by his own pride, Whitey soon finds himself "beaten at
          his own game." The concept is developed in terms of
          the alienation of "opposites" by subtle but real prejudice
          toward each other.

334. FUTURE IS NOW, THE
      Associated Instructional Films   24 min.   b/w
          Problems of prejudice towards minority groups are dis-
          cussed. Topics, including areas of employment and edu-
          cation, are documented with interviews with both Jewish
          and black university students.

335. HARMONY
      Wombat Productions   1974   8 min.   color   s/c/a
          Stereotype roles with their inherent bias are examined.
          A bully husband executive becomes a meek, passive part-
          ner at home.

336. HIGH WALL
      Northeastern University   32 min.   b/w
          This film dramatizes a case study of prejudice as a con-
          sequence of economic frustration. It stresses that hatred
          is passed from parent to child, from gang member to
          gang member, from instructor to student.

337. INTOLERANCE
      Wayne State University   120 min.   color   silent   s/c/a
          This D. W. Griffith movie classic contains four separate
          stories, each illustrating how intolerance and hatred
          throughout the ages have battled love and charity.

338. KU KLUX KLAN: THE INVISIBLE EMPIRE
      CBS News American Documentary Films   1965   45 min.   b/w
          The Klan is studied as it operates in the South today.
          Rituals are illustrated, as are interviews with their "vic-
          tims."

339. OH DEM WATERMELONS
      Mass Media Associates   1965   12 min.   color
          A satirical comedy tells the adventures and misadventures
          of fifteen watermelons, symbolizing racial stereotypes.
          A commentary on the white man's concepts of black cul-
          ture, the satire was originally portrayed by the San Fran-
          cisco Mime Troupe's production.

340.   PEOPLE: ROOTS OF PREJUDICE
        National Educational Television Indiana University 30 min.
        b/w
            Memory operation is demonstrated to explain the main-
            tenance of prejudice. People "tend to recall concepts
            which favor their own beliefs."

341.   POINT, THE
        Audio/Brandon 1972 75 min. color
            Aimed at the elimination of prejudice and ignorance, this
            satire instructs that "it is not at all necessary to con-
            form to be contented." In an unusual kingdom where all
            have pointed heads, only one boy, named Oblio, has a
            round one. Along with his dog, he is banned from his
            kingdom because he does not conform "to the pointed
            heads."

342.   PREJUDICE
        University of Utah 1963 29 min. b/w
        From the Human Relations Series
            Theories to determine the presence of prejudice are dis-
            cussed. Meaning, nature, functions are explained.

343.   PREJUDICE FILM
        Mass Media Associates 1973 28 min. color
        Award Winner
            With a series of vignettes, this film examines the history
            of contemporary forms of racial, ethnic and religious
            prejudice in our society. David Hartman narrates.

344.   SOCIAL ACTION: PART III
        CBS News Associated Instructional Films 28 min. b/w
            Attitudes on race relations from both the minority and the
            majority viewpoints stimulate discussions on prejudice and
            how it may be overcome.

345.   WHAT ABOUT PREJUDICE
        Centron McGraw-Hill 1959 12 min. b/w and color s/c
        From Discussion Problems in Group Living Series
            Examined is the damage done to a classmate by his peers
            because of prejudice directed against parental origin.

346.   WHERE IS PREJUDICE?
        National Educational Television Indiana University 1968 60
        min. b/w s/c/a
            Twelve university middle-class students with diverse ra-
            cial and religious backgrounds live together for a week.
            For some, the encounter results in apprehension and con-
            cern about deep-seated prejudices.

347.   YOU AND YOUR ATTITUDES
        Association Films 1950 10 min. b/w
            A family is analyzed in terms of its attitudes toward

several situations--the new family who moved into the
neighborhood, foreign groups and prejudices that inhibit
intelligent attitudes.

Urban

348.   ASK ME, DON'T TELL ME
American Friends Service Committee 1960 22 min. b/w
The viewer learns of a successful project in San Francisco where juvenile gangs are given an opportunity to
interact with people in the community who are there to
provide assistance.   Much of the film concerns the dialogue between the gang members and the community people.

349.   BARBARA LINDEN
National Educational Television Indiana University 30 min.
color
Barbara Linden, artistic director of the Theatre Workshop, Boston, designed a children's theatre to involve
children with their environment and society.   The emphasis is on self-expression, free association and communication with the audience.

350.   BESIEGED MAJORITY, THE (PARTS I, II)
National Broadcasting Television 1970 Part I: 30 min.;
Part II: 30 min. color s/C/a
The film deals with the urban issues of crime in the
streets from the victim's point of view.   It surveys
criminal courts, points of law enforcement and the need
for solutions to social causes of crime.

351.   BLACK COP
National Educational Television 15 min. b/w
The relationship of the black policeman to other blacks is
explored by interviewing those on both sides in New York
City and Los Angeles.

352.   CONFLICTS IN AMERICAN VALUES: URBAN + RURAL VIEW-
POINTS
Bailey Film Associates 18 min. b/w s/c/a
This documentary film helps identify different ways in
which urban and rural Americans see life.   Increased
urban living in the last century has changed the pace,
needs and aspirations of large numbers of people.

353.   DETACHED AMERICANS
Carousel 1964 33 min. b/w
Narrated by Harry Reasoner
Widespread problems of apathy are examined.   Shown are
examples of "apartness" in our society, including New
Yorkers who stood by and watched the murder of a neigh-

bor, Chicagoans who ignored a policeman's call for help.
The breakdown in family relationships has contributed to
the phenomenon.

354.   FELICIA
University of California   1966   13 min.   b/w
Filmed in Watts, California, this is an assessment of one
girl's situation as part of a minority group coupled with
the frustrations of living in an urban environment.

355.   FROM THE INSIDE OUT
Metro Goldwyn Mayer   1967   24 min.   b/w
Made in a neighborhood house, directed by black teenagers, the participants tell their story in this film: to
resolve awareness in the white community there must be
dialogue with ghetto teenagers.

356.   GETTING THE FACTS
Encyclopaedia Britannica   1954   11 min.   b/w   vt/vc
s/c/a
Discussed are the agencies existing in the average urban
area which disseminate facts: newspapers, broadcasting
facilities, libraries, other channels of information.

357.   GROUP STUDIES AND SOCIAL PSYCHIATRY
Psychiatry Department, Harvard   National Institute of Health
1967   20 min.   b/w   c/a
Dr. Erich Lindemann stresses the importance of the study
of social systems, institutional and structure, in terms of
the concept of role.   He recommends a large variety of
group studies which have contributed to the development
of community communication.

358.   GWENDOLYN BROOKS
University of California   1967   30 min.   b/w
A view of the city of Chicago from the poetry and philos-
ophy of Gwendolyn Brooks, the prize-winning black poet.

359.   HITCH
International Film Bureau   90 min.   color
This feature-length film explores ghetto life in Harlem.
Based on experiences of the Northside Center for Child
Development, Inc., suggestions are realistic attempts to
make things better for those who live there.

360.   HOW COMMUNICATIONS HELP IN THE COMMUNITY
Cahill   1968   11 min.   color   any age
This film portrays the vital role of community communications.   Documentary sequences relate the story of a
lost dog and communication attempts with police head-
quarters, radio/television stations, others.   It illustrates
the success of total urban community action.

361. I WISH I KNEW HOW IT WOULD FEEL TO BE FREE
Yale   McGraw-Hill   1968   20 min.   b/w
Ghetto area black people are interviewed in New Haven,
Connecticut.   Their ambitions are described as well as
their frustrations, fears, struggles and advocacy.

362. IMAGE CHANGERS, THE
New York University   19 min.   b/w
The viewer explores a relationship between the police,
young people and members of the community at large.

363. JUNGLE, THE
Churchill   21 min.   b/w   s/c/a
Gang life in the ghettos is explained by the 12th and Ox-
ford Street Gang of Philadelphia, now the 12th and Oxford
Street Film Makers Corporation.

364. KATSUMI HIRANO: CONVERSATION BETWEEN A NAIL AND
A STOCKING
Film-makers Cooperative   1958   25 min.   b/w
With the assistance of Nippon University students, this
surrealist short story deals with the "terror that results
from a breakdown in communication in modern society."
The film "expresses confusion resulting from conflicting
of reality and hallucination in the life of modern Japan."

365. NO HIDING PLACE and WHO DO YOU KILL?
Talent Associates/Paramount   American Documentary Films
1964   51 min.   b/w
Two dramas from "East Side, West Side" present indict-
ments of conditions in black ghettos and problems of moving to middleclass neighborhoods.

366. NOT ALL COPS, NOT ALL KIDS
Northeastern University   30 min.   b/w
In the area of communication, this film deals with problems faced by both police and youth in urban areas.   It
presents dialogue that takes place between police and
teenagers, with fears and resentments from both sides
ventilated.

367. OPERATION BOOTSTRAP
Encyclopaedia Britannica   58 min.   b/w   vt/vc   s/c/a
Watts is examined in terms of the methods used by the
demonstrators of the area.   The film reflects the language of the streets, unedited and often profane.

368. PHYLLIS AND TERRY
University of California   1965   36 min.   b/w
This is improvised filming of two teenage black girls who
have grown up in the slums of New York's Lower East
Side and who face the prospect of adult life in the ghetto.

369.   STOREFRONT
       National Audiovisual Center   1969   40 min.   b/w   vt/vc
              This film documents the training and role of a non-pro-
              fessional aide in a neighborhood storefront center.
              Filmed in south Bronx, New York, it shows the anger
              and frustrations of ghetto life.

370.   STREET CORNER RESEARCH
       Center for Mass Communication   1969   30 min.   b/w
       Filmed by Dr. Edward A. Mason, Harvard University
              The viewer sees a recorded interview between a psychol-
              ogist and two teenage boys he approaches in Harvard
              Square.   The initial contact and dialogue that follows are
              examined.

371.   THAT'S ME
       Contemporary Films   15 min.   b/w
              A social worker attempts to "redeem" a young Puerto
              Rican in Central Park.   Examined are life in an urban
              area as well as personal fulfillment priorities.

372.   WELFARE REVOLT
       University of California   1968   60 min.   b/w
              This film documents how women on welfare in some
              northern ghettos have tried organizing local unions to
              change what they consider to be intolerable conditions.
              Grievances are described and leaders of the movement
              discuss group pressures and means of forcing change.

                              DELIVERY

373.   BODILY ACTION
       University of Iowa   1959   30 min.   b/w   C
              The visual aspect of effective speaking is analyzed.   The
              emphasis is on the relationship of action to ideas ex-
              pressed, with such action "animated, with appropriate
              gestures and without distracting mannerisms."

374.   COMMUNICATING CORRECTLY
       McGraw-Hill   1969   13 min.   color   s/c
       From the Oral Communication Series
              Diverse examples of correct and incorrect communication
              are illustrated: audience awareness, liveliness, natural
              gestures.   Presented are a variety of relevant situations.

375.   COMMUNICATION BY VOICE AND ACTION
       Centron   1969   14 min.   color   s/c/a
       From the Art of Communication Series
       Award: Finalist, American Film Festival
              "Let go of my hands," an Italian once wrote, "I want to
              talk!"   That line from the film typifies its basic mes-

sage: that man is a social animal who wants to understand
and wants to be understood. The film details suggestions
for use of one's "natural" resources (voice, gesture, expressions, posture, inflections) to interpret thought and feeling.

376. DEVELOPING READING MATURITY: INTERPRETATIVE
MEANING
Coronet 1972 11 min. color and b/w
Specific steps are outlined for assistance with the explanation of the process of the fundamentals of literature interpretation. These include the necessity to: understand
the literal meaning of words, phrases and sentences; explore other meanings; evaluate one's own interpretation.

377. GETTING YOURSELF ACROSS
McGraw-Hill 1958 21 min. b/w s/c/a
From the Communication Series
This film demonstrates to novice speakers the function of
the speaker's personality in getting ideas to the audience.
Explained, in addition, are functional values, ways to
study movement and gestures in speaking, and the effect
"speaking practice" has on the personality development of
the speech student.

378. IMPROVE YOUR PRONUNCIATION
Coronet 1949 11 min. b/w s/c/a
A program for pronunciation improvement is presented.
Specifically offered are four basic rules for improving
speech troublespots: pronounce every syllable, pronounce
each sound correctly, use "acceptable" pronunciation and
use "natural" pronunciation.

379. LET'S TRY CHORAL READING
Centron (YAF) 11 min. s/a b/w
Simple rules and values of choral reading are presented.

380. MICROPHONE SPEAKING
Centron 1969 15 min. color s/c/a
From the Art of Communication Series
This film explores the correct use of microphones, public address systems and radio. As suggested, a microphone can be either a help or a hindrance, contingent on
the use by the speaker. Microphone techniques for "normal" situations are demonstrated.

381. PUBLIC SPEAKING: MOVEMENT AND GESTURE
Coronet 1955 11 min. b/w and color s/c/a
Collaborator Karl Robinson, Northwestern University,
demonstrates standard applicable and effective procedures
for public speakers. He recommends specific techniques
to develop ease, spontaneity of movement.

382.   SPEECH: PLATFORM POSTURE AND APPEARANCE
        McGraw-Hill Centron (YAF) 1949 11 min. b/w s/c/a
            The viewer learns of the importance of what the audience
            sees as well as what it hears. Discussed are good pos-
            ture, "proper" appearance.

383.   SPEECH: STAGE FRIGHT AND WHAT TO DO ABOUT IT
        McGraw-Hill Centron (YAF) 1949 11 min. b/w s/c/a
        From the Speech Series
            Analyzed are the causes of stage fright and what an inex-
            perienced public speaker can do to overcome it both in
            preparation and during the delivery of the speech.

384.   SPEECH: STAGE FRIGHT--WHAT YOU CAN DO ABOUT IT
        Centron 1969 11 min. color s/c/a
        From the Art of Communication Series
            This revising of the above film examines the physiologi-
            cal and psychological causes of stage fright, pointing out
            methods to overcome it. A parachute jump and the
            "equal" fright of making a speech are compared.

385.   SPEECH: THE FUNCTION OF GESTURES
        McGraw-Hill Centron (YAF) 1950 10 min. b/w s/c/a
        From the Speech Series
            The film illustrates the function of gestures in public
            speaking, pointing out that a speech can frequently be
            made more effective by using the "correct" gestures at
            the correct time.

386.   SPEECH: USING YOUR VOICE
        Centron (YAF) McGraw-Hill 1950 11 min. b/w s/c/a
        From the Speech Series
            This film illustrates how to use your voice effectively in
            everyday life situations. It is concerned primarily with
            the problem of common speech faults in both formal and
            informal speaking situations. Suggesting that "most
            speech faults are due purely to carelessness," the film
            demonstrates and explains how to correct such faults.

387.   SPEECH SKILLS: USING YOUR VOICE EFFECTIVELY
        Coronet 1969 14 min. color s/a
            In a television setting, pictures are projected onto a
            screen to exemplify the effective use of the voice. Prob-
            lems that are the result of a speaker's volume, voice
            quality and articulation are examined.

388.   SPEECH TECHNIQUES
        United States Army National Audiovisual Center 1956 11
        min. b/w
            Discussing the importance of effective speech techniques
            in military instructions, this film illustrates usable meth-
            ods. Suggestions include: eye contact, effective diction,
            proper gestures, speech pacing for understanding.

389.   USING VISUALS IN YOUR SPEECH
       Centron (YAF) McGraw-Hill 1959 14 min.   b/w   s/c/a
       From the Speech Series
            This film explores the various kinds of visual methods
            and devices for use in clarifying or increasing interest
            of a speech. Techniques are demonstrated.

390.   VOICE IN COMMUNICATION
       University of Iowa 1959 25 min. b/w C
            Analysis is made of the voice in oral communication in
            terms of pitch, intensity, duration, quality. The discus-
            sion includes the relationship of the voice to meaning,
            with methods suggested for increasing the vocal efforts.

391.   VOICE PRODUCTION: THE VIBRATING LARYNX
       Fleetwood Boston University 1969 42 min. b/w s/a
            The film tells of the way the human body produces sound.
            Shown are actual photos of the larynx in action.

392.   YOUR VOICE
       Encyclopaedia Britannica 1949 b/w vt/vc
            With animation, this film emphasizes the role of proper
            exercise in improving the voice. The drawings and live
            photographs exemplify four phases of voice production:
            respiration, phonation, resonance and articulation.

393.   YOUR VOICE IS SHOWING
       Association-Sterling Free Loan Film 12.5 min. color
            With humor, the "proper" handling of personal and busi-
            ness calls is illustrated. Pointers are made on how to
            "receive" from a productive telephone conversation. Spe-
            cific examples are given of the use and misuse of the
            telephone.

394.   YOUR VOICE IS YOU
       Southwest Bell Telephone Company 14 min. color s/c/a
            Five telephone operators demonstrate basic voice quali-
            ties: vitality, naturalness, expression, intelligibility,
            pleasantness. A narrator examines requirements and
            daily speech habits necessary to "cultivate" each voice
            quality.

                                  DYADIC

395.   BUILDING BRIDGES
       University of Nebraska 1972 b/w
            Dr. Robert E. Palmer, Professor, University of Nebras-
            ka, lectures on the "necessity for learning how to relate
            communication to other human beings ... to build a
            'bridge'."

396. CONVERSATION
McGraw-Hill 1953 11 min. b/w s/c/a
From the Speech Series
    Contrasts of conversational habits of a variety of partici-
pants are exemplified in social situations, on the job.
Recommendations for "useful" conversations are made.

397. DIALOGUE
Teleketics 1971 30-second spot announcement color s/a
    The theme of this brief announcement is that "communica-
tion is a sign of love." The object of the message is
that the daily routine should be shared to be meaningful.

398. DUET
Bailey Film Associates 1971 9 min. color no narration
    This animated puppet film comments on technology and the
breakdown in human values and communication. Two men
live in neighboring houses, enjoying each other's company,
sharing mutual pastimes. One brings home a phonograph,
forgets his plans with his friend. Hurt, the other obtains
his own phonograph and a rivalry begins. Friendship ends
as each man permits machines to replace shared social
activities. As the film ends, each man is watching television alone. Communication breakdown is now complete.

399. ENCOUNTER
Teleketics 8 min. each color 6 spot announcements
    Each spot announcement is a mini-drama of dyadic com-
munication, ranging from marital apathy to a child's view
of love. Titles include: 1. Listen Lady; 2. Can't I
Talk to You, Dad?; 3. Rat Race; 4. Say "Yes" to Love;
5. The Kiss; 6. Sleepy World. The premise of each
film is "communication infused with understanding concern
becomes communion."

400 ENCOUNTER, THE
Perennial National Institute of Mental Health 1971 10 min.
b/w s/c
From the University of Lund, Sweden
    This is a comedy about a shy young man attempting to ac-
quaint himself with a shy young woman in a bookstore.
Many amusing sequences follow with resulting fantasies
about the potential "encounter" and dialogue. The film is
a "springboard for discussion about communication in relationships."

401. EXCHANGES
Appleton-Century 1972 10 min. b/w
    This film relates an encounter between two train passen-
gers--a black man and a white girl. Fantasy interspersed
with reality provokes analysis of prejudice and related social issues. The film is "recommended for discussion in
interaction classes."

402. FUNNY THING HAPPENED ON THE WAY, A
      Associated Instructional Films   27 min.   any age
            A contemporary allegory of honesty and communication,
            this film portrays a couple whose lives are confused and
            unhappy.   They are "detoured" on the road of life, locked
            up with a computer/lie detector, and required to "help
            each other."   Eventually, they drop their pretense, admit
            their dissatisfaction with their lives and begin to com-
            municate.

403. INTRODUCTIONS
      Centron   1948   11 min.   b/w   s/c/a
      From Guidance and Human Relations Series
            The film explains how to confront situations requiring the
            introductions of family, friends and/or strangers.   Pre-
            sented are standard introductions in school, home, busi-
            ness, and at official and social gatherings, depicting a
            variety of greetings and conversations.

404. I'VE GOT THIS PROBLEM
      Crowell, Collier, Macmillan   1966   8 min.   b/w
      Awards: Cork International Film Festival
            This satire on non-communication shows a boy and a girl
            attempting to converse about life without ever really un-
            derstanding each other.

405. LET THE RAIN SETTLE IT
      Teleketics   1972   13 min.   color   s/a
      Awards: CINE
            Unforeseen circumstances throw two boys, one white, one
            black, together for twenty-four hours.   In that time they
            establish a fragile truce and eventually discover the be-
            ginnings of a friendship.

406. NEIGHBORS
      International Film Bureau   1954   9 min.   color   s/c/a
            This is a simple parable about two people who, after liv-
            ing side by side with mutual friendliness and respect,
            come to blows over the possession of a flower that one
            day grows on the line where their properties meet.

407. REASON WHY, THE
      Bailey Film Associates   1971   14 min.   color   c/a
            Starring Eli Wallach and Robert Ryan, this film shows
            two friends who express strong personal feelings relative
            to things they have destroyed in their lifetime.   It deals
            with their feelings concerning war, violence and their in-
            ability to communicate feelings in a positive fashion.

408. SOME PERSONAL LEARNINGS ABOUT INTERPERSONAL
      RELATIONS
      University of California   1967   33 min.   b/w
      From the Management Development Series

Dr. Carl Rogers discusses the business of relating to another, suggesting rewards of open and genuine communication, empathy and nonjudgmental listening. Described
is the satisfaction of quality communication with another
person.

409.   WAYS TO BETTER COMMUNICATION
       Coronet 1950 11 min. b/w s/c
       To interest a class in developing conversational skills,
       specific techniques are suggested: listening and being in-
       clusive. In addition, the film explains why these skills
       are recommended.

                      EDUCATIONAL TECHNOLOGY

410.   AND WONDERS NEVER CEASE
       National Education Association 1963 28 min. b/w c/a
       This film presents a survey of educational audiovisual ma-
       terials, including computers operated in large city sys-
       tems.

411.   AUDIOVISUAL AIDS TO LEARNING
       United States Information Agency National Audiovisual Center
       1951 11 min. b/w s/C/a
       Centralized audiovisual department services are discussed.
       Techniques for effective use are furnished for both edu-
       cational and civilian information programs.

412.   AUDIOVISUAL MATERIALS IN TEACHING
       Coronet 1956 14 min. color C/a
       This film explains how audiovisual materials can challenge
       attention and interest in a classroom. The viewer sees
       actual class situations at an audiovisual center.

413.   AUDIOVISUAL SUPERVISION
       International Film Bureau 1959 19 min. color c/a
       From the Audiovisual Training Series
       Methods and responsibilities of the supervisor of a typi-
       cal audiovisual department are outlined. Duties include:
       training teachers to use available materials, supervising
       students' participation in the department, working with
       curriculum planning groups.

414.   CETO TELEVISION FILMS
       Centre for Educational Television (London)
       24 presentations: 2 in b/w; 2 in color vc s/c/a
       These films about television production training offer wide
       and varied application on many subjects and at diverse
       levels.

415. CHOOSING A CLASSROOM FILM
McGraw-Hill 1963 18 min. color c/a
From the Audiovisual Series
Factors are explored which govern the selection for class
use of applicable films. Included are an analysis of
types of film, techniques, goals in terms of behavioral
changes in students. To help overcome barriers to learning, examples are shown of various types of appropriate
films.

416. CLASS OF '01: COLLEGE OF TOMORROW
CBS News McGraw-Hill 1972 25 min. color
This film presents a glimpse of what the university of the
future may be. Explored are advanced methods of teacher
training and new educational technologies. There will be
new multimedia methods such as "computerized control
centers" and closed circuit television plus the "bottling
in film" of great professors.

417. COLLEGE TEACHING WITH TELEVISION: AN INTER-INSTI-
TUTIONAL APPROACH
United States Office of Education Du Art 28 min. b/w
c/a
Through the cooperative use of broadcasting and closed
circuit television, the film explains how groups of colleges
in Texas, Florida and Oregon share courses and teaching
personalities.

418. COMMUNICATION CONFERENCE
Ohio State University U.S. Office of Education 1966
31 min. b/w C/a
The discussion film centers on the use of media in education. It explains how communication differs from other
social interactions and points up the social implications
of a wide-spread communication network. Additional topics include messages, nature and educational implications
of packaged instructional systems, teacher's role in class,
selection and arrangement of instructional systems and
materials. The film features James Finn, George Gerb-
ner, Edgar Dale, Franklin Knower, Charles Hoben and
Kenneth Norberg.

419. COMMUNICATIONS EXPLOSION, THE
CBS McGraw-Hill 1967 27 min. color s/c
From the Twentieth Century Series
This film traces the development of messages from the
beginning of man through the sixties, stressing that media
technology alone cannot produce understanding.

420. COMPLEAT AUDIOVISUALIST, THE
Trafco 1967 7 min. color s/c/a
This film presents a lighthearted look at some of the
problems of communicators who attempt to use projector

resources. Illustrated are various steps involved in the
correct utilization of films.

421. DEVELOPMENT OF COMMUNICATIONS
Encyclopaedia Britannica   11 min.   b/w vt/vc s/a
Modern methods of communication are traced, including
the inception of the telegraph, wireless, radio, others.

422. EDUCATIONAL TECHNOLOGY
National Audiovisual Center   12 min.   color
This film is a presentation of how teaching machines,
auditory aids, recording devices and visuals are used in
educational programs for the development of speech with
the hearing-impaired.

423. FILM AND YOU, THE: USING THE CLASSROOM FILM
Bailey Film Associates   1961   14 min.   color   C/a
The motion picture plays a unique instructional role in
the classroom. This film explains how an instructor prepares the class for the film showing and how to devise
relevant follow-up activities.

424. FILM RESEARCH AND LEARNING
International Film Bureau   1956   14 min.   b/w   C/a
From the Audiovisual Training Series
The viewer sees how a teaching film may improve the
learning process and retention. The selected film is incorporated in a reading readiness program. Stressed is
the necessity for appropriate preparation in order to maximize the learning situation.

425. FOCUS ON A CENTURY OF COMMUNICATION
Glatfelter Co.   27 min.   color
This film is presented in terms of the different ways in
which people communicated through history. The emphasis is on the contemporary associations with technologi-
cal message output.

426. FOURTH NETWORK, THE
Film Product Service of Virginia   Great Plains Instructional
Television   20 min.   color   vc
This film explores current uses of educational television
for both educators and laymen. With many of the advantages of commercial television, educational television can
be used as a cultural enrichment for the community. An
entire production sequence of a television lesson is presented.

427. HOW TO TEACH WITH FILMS
Cathedral   22 min.   b/w   c/a
With a tested method of using films, television-film dem-
onstrations of complete lesson plans are shown.

428.   INSTRUCTIONAL FILMS--THE NEW WAY TO GREATER ED-
       UCATION
       Coronet   1948   16 min.   b/w
              A lecturer discusses the place of educational films in the
              curriculum.   Covered in the analysis are topics of proper
              selection, integration and administration of film, and the
              problem of accessibility of general and specialized titles.

429.   INSTRUCTOR-DIRECTED TELEVISION INSTRUCTION
       Department of Health, Education and Welfare   National Audio-
       visual Center   1968   25 min.   b/w   c/a
              This is a film wherein faculty members demonstrate a
              "television facility which frees the instructor from some
              of the restrictions inherent in traditional television pre-
              sentations."   The equipment enables the instructor to con-
              trol by push-buttons the use of the medium to best serve
              his purposes.

430.   ITV IS WHAT YOU MAKE IT
       KQED   1966   30 min.   b/w   C
              Demonstrating the role of the teacher in making television
              teaching effective, this film specifies what to prepare for
              both the lesson and the class.   It examines what activities
              can be carried on, from follow-up work to reinforcement
              learning.

431.   LEARNING WITH TODAY'S MEDIA
       Encyclopaedia Britannica   1974   35 min.   color   vt/vc   c/a
              This documentary defines and describes the role of the
              modern media center at the high school and college level.
              Four case studies reveal ways in which media centers may
              be equipped to serve classroom needs.   Each offers an in-
              terpretation of the role and significance of the center.

432.   LET'S TALK ABOUT FILMS
       National Film Board of Canada   1953   18 min.   b/w   s/C/a
              This film shows a workshop meeting where group leaders
              discuss what happened when a leader, using film, elicited
              no audience response.   This experience is then compared
              with that of another leader who, using the same film, ob-
              tains a positive response.

433.   MAKING FILMS THAT TEACH
       Encyclopaedia Britannica   1954   19 min.   b/w   vt/vc
              Explained are the research associated with teaching film,
              script preparation, the role of the collaborator, types and
              techniques of production.

434.   NEW DIMENSIONS THROUGH TEACHING FILMS
       Coronet   28 min.   color   c/a
              For an in-service teachers' institute program on effective
              film usage, this film examines specific examples from
              Coronet films.   The Audiovisual Film Director says "the

film is an educational tool that is one of the most power-
ful ever devised.   It's been tried, tested and is effective."

435.   NEW YORK UNIVERSITY TELEVISION WORKSHOP
       United World Films   10 min.   b/w   s/C/a
            This film presents an overview of the various phases of
            television as they affect viewers today.   Showing a tele-
            vision workshop where students are learning techniques in-
            volved, it illustrates the way television works, the writing,
            direction and production of a program.

436.   OVERHEAD TELEVISION DEMONSTRATION
       University of California   30 min.   b/w
            Rudy Bretz, former chairman of Educational Television at
            UCLA, presents a new visual system he devised.   He ex-
            plains how a variety of instructional material can be pre-
            sented via the system to both large and small groups with-
            out special preparation.

437.   PROBING MIND, THE
       United States Office of Education   National Audiovisual Center
       1961   29 min.   b/w
            The uses of new educational media are illustrated: films,
            television, recordings and teaching machines.

438.   PROGRAMMED LEARNING
       Bureau of National Affairs   1975   31 min.   color
            The film deals with the philosophy, practicalities and some
            of the hardware.   Terminal tests relate precisely to ob-
            jectives.   There are many practical examples of the mix
            of principles and practice.

439.   RESOURCES FOR LEARNING
       McGraw-Hill   30 min.   b/w   C
            The viewer receives a perspective of available educational
            media for educators.   Also presented is an analysis of
            the changes taking place in patterns for learning and
            teaching with media.

440.   STAGING FOR TELEVISION
       Michigan State University   1965   30 min.   color
            Deals with various types of television programs: the in-
            terview, discussion, demonstration and the lecture.   The
            fundamental production elements involved in each type are
            discussed.   Also reviewed is the need for preliminary
            planning and the cogent relationship between the stage set
            and the rest of the program.

441.   STUDIO TEACHER, THE (PARTS I AND II)
       KNME-TV (Albuquerque)   University of Nebraska   1967
       Part I: 20 min.;   Part II: 27 min.   b/w   C/a
       The host: Dr. Hazen Schumacher, Associate Director of

Television, University of Michigan
For the studio teacher, the film introduces problems encountered when instructing from a television studio. Discussed are microphones, lighting, personnel, the instructor. The film explains the use of the chalkboard, models, other visual aids, as well as the limitations and production problems of the studio.

442. TEACHER AND TECHNOLOGY, THE
Ohio State University for U.S. Office of Education 1966 49 min. b/w c/a
From the Communication Theory and New Educational Media Series
The film traces the beginnings and history of the impact of technology on education. It illustrates some of the ways technology is being used to meet needs for individual instruction.

443. TEACHER-DIRECTED TELEVISION INSTRUCTION
United States Office of Education National Audiovisual Center 1968 28 min. b/w
How a television facility can free the instructor from some restrictions inherent in traditional television presentations.

444. TEACHER TELETIPS
Chicago Area School Television Great Plains Instructional Television 20 min. color vc
Skills are presented to enable teachers to "transport" students beyond the four walls of the conventional classroom. Fundamental information includes: proper physical arrangements of the room to maximize viewing for each student, how to choose from all the materials available, how to fully utilize the telecourse after it has been selected.

445. TEACHING MACHINES AND PROGRAMMED LEARNING
National Audiovisual Center 1969 29 min. b/w vc
B. F. Skinner explains the theory of programmed learning and the variety of teaching machines. Robert Glaser discusses the implications of such machines and materials for education.

446. TELEVISION: A POTENT MEDIUM
Great Plains Instructional Television 1964 29 min. b/w
The viewer learns how television can provide a number of instructional experiences. Discussed are the advantages of the medium: magnifying objects, spanning time and distance and presenting specialists.

447. TELEVISION: EFFECTIVE INSTRUCTION
Great Plains Instructional Television 1964 29 min. b/w
This film reviews research which has proved the effec-

tiveness of television for instruction of both teachers and
students in attitude change.

448.   TELEVISION: FOLLOW-UP THE LESSON
       Great Plains Instructional Television 1964 29 min. b/w
            Actual techniques used from a follow-up telecast are ex-
            amined.

449.   TELEVISION: IMPLICATIONS FOR INSTRUCTION
       Great Plains Instructional Television 1964 29 min. b/w
            The film describes the impact that television is having
            on educational programs at all levels.

450.   TELEVISION: INTER-INSTITUTIONAL USES
       National Audiovisual Center 1969 28 min. b/w vc
            This documentary explains patterns of inter-institutional
            and inter-regional college teaching by television in se-
            lected areas of the United States. Included are the edu-
            cational advantages for both staff and students who use
            cooperative television in college teaching.

451.   TELEVISION: THE PROFESSIONAL TEAM
       Great Plains Instructional Television 1964 29 min. b/w
            The viewer learns the procedure for planning an instruc-
            tional series, the people who make up the total team and
            the roles of the various crew members.

452.   TELEVISION: USING THE LESSON
       Great Plains Instructional Television 1964 29 min. b/w
            The role of the instructor during the telecast is dis-
            cussed. Suggestions concern note-taking, listening and
            viewing skills, assuming optimum learning situations and
            dealing with unavoidable interruptions.

453.   TELEVISION AT PENNSYLVANIA STATE
       Pennsylvania State University National Audiovisual Center
       26 min. C
            Closed circuit television teaching is demonstrated. Also
            examined is the management of these television facilities.
            Future realities of television facilities are explored.

454.   TELEVISION IN THE CLASSROOM
       KNME-TV (Albuquerque) 28 min. kinescope or vt b/w
            This film is directed primarily to teachers to explain the
            unique function of instructional television. As an intro-
            ductory course for a classroom series, the emphasis is
            on preparation, presentation and follow-up of a television
            lesson.

455.   TELEVISION TECHNIQUES FOR TEACHERS
       San Diego Area Instructional Television 1968 24 min.
       Great Plains Instructional Television color vc c/a
            An in-service utilization film gives practical answers for

instructors who must communicate in the classroom via instructional technology. Filming was accomplished in actual classroom demonstrations.

456. UNIQUE CONTRIBUTION, THE
Encyclopaedia Britannica 1959 30 min. color vt/vc C/a
This film considers elements in motion pictures that do the "unique" job in teaching. Cinematic devices are examined as to whether or not they contribute to learning. Examples of educational films are presented. Narrated by Maurice B. Mitchell, Chancellor, University of Denver.

457. VISUAL AIDS
Modern Learning Aids 1966 27 min. color
Produced for the British Navy, this film treats the value of visual aids humorously. It reviews general advantages of illustrative materials, making suggestions concerning use of film, models, projectors and a variety of other devices.

458. VISUALIZING YOUR SUBJECT
Michigan State University 30 min. b/w s/c/a
Johns Hopkins Science Review's producer shows how to use ingredients of showmanship to achieve an instructive television program.

459. WHY COMMUNICATION SATELLITES?
Bailey Film Associates 12 min. b/w s/a
Animation and live-action photography explain the need for satellites in long distance radio and television instructional communication.

FAMILY

460. ALL THE KIDS LIKE THAT
Learning Corporation of America 1972 50 min. color
Award: Dupont (Columbia University)
More than another drug story, this film aims at the "causes" of drug withdrawal. Filmed over a period of six months, it is a portrait of a fifteen-year-old and his family. The central problem of the family interaction is the lack of communication.

461. BETWEEN MAN AND WOMAN
Psychological Films, Inc. 1972 33 min. color
This film interview with Dr. Everett L. Shostrom and Mr. Howard Miller of ABC-TV, Chicago, depicts the various marital roles people play.

462.   BUT WHAT IF THE DREAM COMES TRUE?
        CBS News   Carousel   University of California   1971
        Award winner
            This revealing portrait of the goals and problems of an
            upper-class family examines the different pressures on
            each member of the family.   The unit--the Sam Green-
            walts--have children ages twelve and fourteen (daughters)
            and ten (a son).   It suggests that there can be "trouble
            in paradise."

463.   CHANGING
        University of California   31 min.   color
            Focusing on parent-child relationships, this film shows
            problems of a young family attempting to create alterna-
            tive life-styles that stress openness, spontaneity.

464.   DAVID AND HAZEL: A STORY IN COMMUNICATION
        National Film Board of Canada   McGraw-Hill   Perennial
        1964   28 min.   b/w   c/a
        From the Family Relations Series: #1
            Communication significance among members of a family
            is dramatized.   More specifically, the film is a study of
            what happens when a husband isolates his job from his
            family.

465.   FAMILY
        National Educational Television   1972   29 min.   b/w
            The change taking place in the structure of the American
            family is discussed.   Dr. Margaret Mead and Dr. Bert-
            ram Beck question the effect of cultural pressures on
            family life and distinctions between men and women.

466.   FAMILY, THE
        University of California   20 min.   b/w
            This film captures elements of family interaction that
            shows its impact on human growth and development.

467.   FAMILY: LIFESTYLES OF THE FUTURE
        Document Associates   University of California   1972   23 min.
        color
            Margaret Mead discusses stresses on the contemporary,
            isolated nuclear family and the growth of alternative,
            communal living groups.

468.   FAMILY ENCOUNTER
        Teleketics   1971   7 one-minute spot announcements   color
            These "public service announcements" depict various inci-
            dents regarding family communication.   Titles are: 1.
            Listen, Lady; 2. The Kiss; 3. War Games;   4. Like
            Father, Like Son;   5. Rat Race;   6. Can I Talk to You,
            Dad?; 7. Say "Yes" to Love.

469. FAMILY LIFE DISCUSSION GROUP
University of Wisconsin 1961 19 min. b/w s/c/a
Group discussion values are discussed, with indications
of the responsibilities of the discussion leaders. Suggestions include: participating parents should bring out common problems and conflicts within the family. Shown is
an actual discussion intended to communicate to parents
the kind of discussion group they might encourage.

470. FATHER/DAUGHTER
Teleketics 1974 10 min. color s/c/a
A documentary film relates the story of a California doctor who discovered his eighteen-year-old daughter using
drugs and the subsequent complex communication-related
problems.

471. FATHERS AND SONS
CBS News Carousel 1969 29 min. b/w
Two sons and their fathers speak frankly of their differences. Theo Jacob, young black student, works with minority children and his values are contrasted with those
of his parents. Francis Shor, SDS activist, refuses induction and faces a prison sentence. His father, a former army officer, doesn't understand.

472. FOUR FAMILIES
McGraw-Hill 60 min. b/w
Margaret Mead compares family life in four countries:
Canada, India, Japan and France. She discusses the up-
bringing of children as the contribution to each distinc-
tive national character.

473. GETTING ALONG WITH PARENTS
Encyclopaedia Britannica 1954 15 min. b/w vt/vc
This film explores the conflict between six teenagers and
their respective parents. In a situation designed to provoke discussion, it stresses that each generation must
perceive the generation difference in thinking and feeling
and be willing to compromise.

474. GETTING TOGETHER
Encyclopaedia Britannica 18 min. b/w vt/vc
Some of the problems of close family relationships are
dramatized in three "cinema verité" portraits of people
trying to deal with others close to them.

475. GUIDANCE FOR THE SEVENTIES: KIDS, PARENTS, PRES-
SURES
Bailey Film Associates 1971 color s/c/a
In a seminar, teenagers identify some of the everyday
pressures and tensions that confront them. Learning attitude control, they are encouraged to use positive channels as outlets to relieve pressures.

476.   HANDLING MARITAL CONFLICTS
        McGraw-Hill   Perennial   National Institute of Mental Health
        1965   12 min.   color   s/c/a
        From the Marriage and Family Living Series
                Five comparative points are made concerning the ele-
                ments of constructive and destructive conflict in marriage.
                This film portrays the development of an argument.   The
                Adams' conflict develops into a constructive one and the
                Kanes' into a destructive situation.

477.   HAVE I TOLD YOU LATELY THAT I LOVE YOU?
        Mass Media Associates   1958   16 min.   b/w   s/c/a
                One whole day in the life of a modern, suburban, afflu-
                ent family is followed: the lives of mother at home,
                father commuting, boy in school are all alluded to in a
                process of dehumanization through ritualized routine.

478.   HILLCREST FAMILY, THE--STUDIES IN HUMAN COMMUNI-
        CATION
        Pennsylvania State University   1968   4 films, varied lengths
                Separate interviews of the family by four psychiatrists
                reveal communication barriers.

479.   HOW CLOSE CAN YOU GET?
        Teleketics   1972   10 min.   color
                "No matter how close you get to another person, you are
                still alone."   This belief leads into an intense discussion
                of what people expect from marriage.

480.   I JUST DON'T DIG HIM
        Connecticut Department of Mental Health   International Film
        Bureau   1970   11 min.   color   s/c/a
                A communication problem between a father and son is
                dramatized--showing both points of view.   After each has
                had a chance to communicate with someone in the other's
                peer group, they become more objective and perception
                changes.   The film suggests that both sides' criticisms
                are parallel--hypocrisy, failure to follow through, lying
                --and concludes that misunderstandings can be overcome.

481.   LIKE FATHER, LIKE SON
        Teleketics   60-second spot announcement   color
                When a father lies about his son's age to get a reduced
                price on a theatre ticket, he becomes oblivious of the pow-
                er of his example to his children.

482.   LISTEN, LADY
        Teleketics   1972   60-second spot announcement   color
                A situation is illustrated wherein the wife appears to be
                listening, becomes bored, falls asleep.

483.   LISTEN, MAN
        Teleketics   1972   60-second spot announcement   color

The pressure of work and worry over bills cause a man
to ignore the problems of his wife. His lack of understanding of her world destroys communication.

484. LONELINESS AND LOVING
Learning Corporation of America 1972 17 min. color
A segment from the film "Five Easy Pieces," starring Jack
Nicholson
A young man is unable to communicate with his sister and
older brother, even through the music which they have
all loved.

485. MARRIAGE
Perennial 17 min. color s/c/a
This animated film is filled with concepts and ideas about
the subject of marriage, from the wedding to the golden
anniversary. It offers much latitude for the discussion
of communication barriers and breakdowns.

486. MARRIAGE PROBLEMS
University of California 1963 30 min. b/w
This dramatic vignette shows two sisters, one recently
married, the other about to have her second child. Each
shares problems with the other.

487. MOTHERS AND DAUGHTERS
American Documentary Films University of California 1969
27 min. b/w
This film focuses on two families in which daughters are
at odds with their mothers. In the first, the mother, a
devout Catholic, is outraged when her daughter marries
a young Jew; but after the daughter has a baby, the two
renew the relationship. In the second family, a 19-year-
old college student rejects her mother's values as too
conventional.

488. OLIVIA
Teleketics 1972 13 min. color
This documentary film is based on an unrehearsed dis-
cussion-role-playing group of young people. Olivia role-
plays a confrontation with her mother in which conflicts
based on cultural and ethnic customs, independence, prejudice are touched upon.

489. PEOPLE NEXT DOOR, THE
Bailey Film Associates 1969 79 min. b/w s/c/a
CBS Playhouse
Awards: Emmy
Some of the consequences of misunderstanding, lack of
communication and distrust associated with the "generation gap" are examined in this drama. Two families
face an ordeal involving a daughter, her brother and the
boy next door, involving stereotypes, evaluative listening
and bias.

490. PULL THE HOUSE DOWN
      WCU-TV Carousel 1969 38 min. color
            Harry Reasoner and his son, Stuart, discuss the "genera-
            tion gap" between the establishment and rebellious youth.
            Issues examined are the Vietnam War, sexual freedom,
            racism and campus revolt.

491. SOCIAL ENCOUNTER
      Teleketics 1971 8 min. color
            Seven one-minute spot announcements portray various in-
            cidents regarding family communication (some inter-
            changes are positive, some negative).

492. THREE GRANDMOTHERS
      University of California 1963 28 min. b/w
            The viewer gets a glimpse into the lives of three grand-
            mothers--a Nigerian (Muslim), a Canadian (Protestant),
            and a Brazilian (Catholic). The film shows that despite
            a great difference in the patterns of family life, the
            grandmothers have similar functions: to protect the young,
            guide the newlyweds and enjoy the freedom to help.

493. TROUBLE IN THE FAMILY
      National Educational Television 1965 90 min. b/w s/c/a
      From America's Crises Series: #10
            The emotional problems of a family from New England are
            analyzed with "family therapy." There are scenes from
            nine of the thirteen actual therapy sessions. Dr. Nathan
            Ackerman discusses group techniques of family therapy
            with Harold Mayer.

494. WAIT UNTIL YOUR FATHER GETS HOME
      Teleketics 1974 11 min. color s/c/a
            This film is taken from a six-day session in which a
            group of young people honestly and openly express their
            feelings, beliefs, hang-ups and problems.

495. WEEKEND
      Teleketics 1971 15 min. color s/c/a
            A rainstorm confines a vacationing couple to a hotel room
            and precipitates a discussion of their mutual dissatisfac-
            tion. Initially a game resulting from boredom, it evolves
            into an exploration of their marriage which reveals disap-
            pointment and fear. Barriers include communication
            blocks and the "inability to perceive them."

496. WORKOUT
      Teleketics 1971 15 min. color s/c/a
            This film explores the relationship between a father and
            son who understand the same values in totally different
            ways. Their major barrier to understanding is the ab-
            sence of communication.

FREEDOMS

497. AMERICAN REVOLUTION (PART I, II)
Learning Corporation of America 1972   each 24 min.   color
From the American Heritage Series
Awards: Columbus, Ohio; Media and Methods
    Part I, "The Cause of Liberty," is based on the actual
    interchange of correspondence between Henry Laurens,
    president of the First Continental Congress, and his son,
    John.   Part II, "The Impossible War," reviews John's
    patriotic return home, as a major in the army, while his
    father is elected president of the Congress.

498. BILL OF RIGHTS IN ACTION, THE: FREEDOM OF SPEECH
Bailey Film Associates 1969   21 min.   b/w or color
From the Bill of Rights in Action Series
    An in-depth study of the importance and complexity of is-
    sues involved in free speech.   This film follows the case
    of an unpopular speaker convicted of disturbing the peace.
    Lawyers argue constitutional issues to a court of ap-
    peals.   Viewers are asked to judge the ultimate verdict.

499. BILL OF RIGHTS IN ACTION, THE: FREEDOM OF THE
PRESS
Bailey Film Associates 1974   20 min.   color   s/c/a
    This film is structured around the issues of a reporter's
    loyalty to protect his sources.   The ultimate answer is
    left to the viewer.

500. BILL OF RIGHTS IN ACTION: THE PRIVILEGE AGAINST
SELF-INCRIMINATION
Bailey Film Associates 1974   23 min.   color   s/c/a
    The Fifth Amendment privilege against self-incrimination
    is examined.   Argued by lawyers, interpretations include
    those that protect those guilty of thought and speech
    crimes as well as those who are actually guilty of crimi-
    nal activity.

501. BILL OF RIGHTS IN ACTION: THE RIGHT TO PRIVACY
Bailey Film Associates 1970   23 min.   color
From the Bill of Rights in Action Series
    Attorneys argue whether the constitutional right to privacy
    of the accused was violated by surveillance.

502. BILL OF RIGHTS IN ACTION, THE: SERIES
Bailey Film Associates 1969-70   color
See individual title listings
    Cases involving constitutional issues are dramatized for
    analysis.   Titles include: Due Process of Law; Equal
    Opportunity; Freedom of Religion; Freedom of Speech;
    Right to Privacy; Story of a Trial; De Facto Segregation.

503.   BILL OF RIGHTS IN ACTION, THE: STORY OF A TRIAL
       Bailey Film Associates 1966 22 min. b/w and color
            This film introduces the procedures which protect the
            rights of citizens as guaranteed in the constitution.
            Stressed is due process of law, with an analysis of law
            courts and law enforcement agencies. The story follows
            two men from their accusation for a misdemeanor
            through their arrest and the trial.

504.   BILL OF RIGHTS IN THE UNITED STATES, THE
       Encyclopaedia Britannica 1956 19 min. vt/vc b/w
            What precipitated the adoption of the Bill of Rights is ex-
            amined: the struggle for official recognition of personal
            liberty and human rights in seventeenth century England
            and the American colonies.

505.   CARL SANDBURG
       National Broadcasting Company 1958 28 min. b/w
       From the Wisdom Series
            Carl Sandburg speaks of his lifelong dedication to the writ-
            ings and philosophy of Lincoln. Folk songs plus guitar
            accompaniment act as backdrop for his eloquence.

506.   CENSORSHIP: A QUESTION OF JUDGMENT
       International Film Bureau 1964 5 min. color s/C/a
       From the Citizenship: Whose Responsibility Series
            An argument develops between a student newspaper edi-
            tor and the sponsor over the publication of "sensational"
            news. The controversy is presented to foster audience
            discussion.

507.   CHAOS OR COMMUNICATION
       Doubleday 1969 b/w and color 15 min.
            This film explores the factors of alienation in our society
            and how they are related to the images reflected by the
            mass media. Questions concern the two-way communica-
            tion process and the status of the government in relation
            to various forms of dissent.

508.   CONSTITUTION, THE: THE COMPROMISE THAT MADE A
       NATION
       Learning Corporation of America 27 min. color s/c/a
            This dramatic reenactment focuses on the central argu-
            ment of the Constitutional Convention: the large state/
            small state controversy. It reveals the divergent views
            which had to be resolved by the men who first met to
            write the Constitution.

509.   CONSTITUTION AND CENSORSHIP
       National Educational Television Indiana University 1958
       30 min. b/w
       From the Constitution in Action Series
            Two court cases involving censorship on religious grounds

and by government agencies are presented. The film
traces the legal proceedings and precedents involved in
the banning of the film "The Miracle" and the case of
Cantwell et al. versus Connecticut. The conclusion of
the film examines opposing views of censorship.

510. CONSTITUTION AND FAIR PROCEDURE
Indiana University 29 min. b/w
The Leyra versus Denno case is presented. The right
to jury trial, right to be represented by counsel, protection against unreasonable counsel and protection against
unreasonable seizure are all dealt with in a broad framework of constitutional and civil liberties.

511. CROWD CONTROL
Free Circle Perennial 1970 11 min. s/c/a
An actual confrontation between demonstrators and police
provides an example for discussion of effective management of potentially violent situations. To insure the
First Amendment and limit violence becomes a mutual
challenge.

512. DARK CORNER OF JUSTICE
National Broadcasting Company 1970 19 min. color
Awards: Emmy, festival awards
This film tells the story of people awaiting trial in over-
crowded prisons with "hostility and bias" existing.

513. DEFINING DEMOCRACY
Encyclopaedia Britannica 1954 18 min. b/w vt/vc s/c
Dr. H. Lasswell, Yale University, compares a democratic community with those that favor despotic conditions,
in terms of freedom of ideas and expression.

514. DISSENTERS SERIES, THE
Indiana University 30 min. each b/w s/c/a
A series of six filmed interviews focus on dissenting edi-
tors and publishers of political opinion magazines: Dan-
iel Watts, Gilbert Harrison, Irving Howe, Dr. Billy
James Hargis, William F. Buckley, Joe Michael Cobb.

515. FIRST FREEDOM, THE
Time-Life 1974 90 min. color s/c/a
This dramatic reenactment is based on a full, authenti-
cated transcript of a trial of Andrei Sinyavsky and Yuli
Daniel, two Russian writers. It stars Arthur Hill as
well as Lee Montagne and Peter Vaughan.

516. FREE PRESS VERSUS TRIAL BY JURY: THE SHEPPARD
CASE
Encyclopaedia Britannica 1969 27 min. color vt/vc
s/c/a
Reviewed is the collision course of the rights of the

press and the rights of the accused to a fair trial in the
Sheppard case of 1954. In protecting the rights of Dr.
Sam Sheppard, the Supreme Court extended the rights of
fair trial to all persons accused of a serious crime.   Illustrated are readings from court decisions reversing the
original verdict, providing a "balance" between rights of
accused and press protection.

517. FREEDOM OF COMMUNICATIONS
National Educational Television Indiana University 18 min.
b/w
      Investigating the freedoms of the press, this film re-
      views the history, treats the problems facing publishers
      and the handling of news.

518. FREEDOM OF EXPRESSION
Oregon Bar Association (KGW-TV) 29 min.   kinescope
      The right of the individual to freedom of expression and
      to hear others express themselves is demonstrated in
      terms of the methods the government uses to protect
      these freedoms.

519. FREEDOM OF THE PRESS
United States Information Agency Duart National Audiovisual Center 1949 17 min.   b/w s/c/a
      A historical review of freedom of the press in America
      is presented, from Zenger's weekly journal to publica-
      tion of today's newspaper.

520. FREEDOM OF THE PRESS
United World Films 17 min.   b/w
      This film stresses the importance of presenting facts ac-
      curately and completely.   Reviewed are the responsibili-
      ties of the media.

521. FREEDOM TO SPEAK: PEOPLE OF NEW YORK VERSUS
IRVING FEINER
Encyclopaedia Britannica 1967 23 min.   b/w or color
vt/vc s/c
      This discussion film presents a case study of Feiner
      versus New York, 1951, an investigation of the basic
      freedom of expression. Specifically, the case is of a
      university student convicted of "disorderly conduct."   An
      analysis of the majority and dissenting opinions of the
      justices follows.

522. FRUSTRATED CAMPUS
National Educational Television Indiana University 1968
47 min.   b/w
      Several university students, faculty and administrators
      debate some of the issues confronting higher education.
      Infringement of others' rights is a major topic.

523. GREAT RIGHTS, THE
      Brandon 1963 14 min. color s/c/a
           Animated cartoons present an imaginative view to illus-
           trate what might happen if the Bill of Rights disappeared.

524. INGENIOUS REPORTER, THE
      Encyclopaedia Britannica 1974 26 min. color vt/vc
      s/c/a
           Obstruction of justice is the theme of this film. An
           American reporter, working for a Paris newspaper, de-
           vises a way to improve his paper's circulation.

525. INSIDERS, THE
      National Broadcasting Company 1970 22 min. color s/c/a
      Award: American Bar Association
           A film documentary by convicts at Missouri State Peni-
           tentiary exemplifies the weaknesses of the rehabilitation
           system.

526. JUSTICE AND THE POOR
      University of Indiana 1967 60 min. b/w
           The inequities of the judicial system as they affect the
           poor are reported. Cited are "bias in police bookings,
           the bail system, political relations with ghetto communi-
           ties." This film concludes with a report on the status of
           recommendations to improve these inequities.

527. JUSTICE BLACK AND THE BILL OF RIGHTS
      CBS News Bailey Film Associates 32 min. color
           In this interview with CBS News correspondents Eric
           Sevareid and Martin Agronsky, Associate Justice Hugo
           M. Black of the Supreme Court discusses the possible
           conflict between constitutional law and morality: the free-
           dom of speech and police powers versus the rights of the
           accused.

528. JUSTICE DELAYED, JUSTICE DENIED
      CBS News 1971 40 min. color s/c/a
      From the Justice in America Series
           The problem of court congestion is assessed, with a dis-
           cussion of what exists and what might be done about it.
           Illustrated are "plea bargaining," "closed door" deals.
           Narrator is Eric Sevareid.

529. JUSTICE DOUGLAS
      Carousel 1972 52 min. color
           Supreme Court Justice William C. Douglas is shown in
           an interview with CBS News reporter Eric Sevareid.
           They discuss government surveillance of dissidents, in-
           trusion into private citizens' lives, erosion of the Bill of
           Rights, the unconstitutionality of the Vietnam War and the
           court's decision that newsmen can be forced to reveal
           confidential sources of information in some cases.

530.   JUSTICE UNDER THE LAW: THE GIDEON CASE
       Encyclopaedia Britannica 1966 23 min. b/w and color
       vt/vc
       From Our Living Bill of Rights Series
           The Gideon case is reenacted as an examination of a
           principle of justice. The question asked is: Is an ac-
           cused person who cannot afford a lawyer entitled to
           counsel? Viewers see the first trial, the argument be-
           fore the Supreme Court and the attorney who arranges
           the acquittal at the second trial. The focus concerns the
           "overworked, apathetic" defense attorneys.

531.   MIGHTIER THAN THE SWORD: ZENGER AND THE FREE-
       DOM OF THE PRESS
       Teaching Film Custodians 1953 20 min. b/w s/c/a
       From the Cavalcade of America Series
           The film reports the arrest of the colonial publisher-edi-
           tor John Peter Zenger for printing attacks upon the ad-
           ministration of William Cosby, royal governor of New
           York in 1734. Alexander Hamilton defends Zenger, ad-
           vocating the principle that "truth is not libel," and urges
           that juries uphold Zenger's right to resist tyranny by
           speaking and printing the truth.

532.   ONE MAN'S OPINION
       National Film Board of Canada 1963 6 min. b/w
           This film analyzes the question of the individual's right
           to hold out against the opinion of the majority.

533.   OUR DECLARATION OF INDEPENDENCE
       Academic 22 min. b/w s/c/a
           The signing of the document and the years of struggle and
           strife before the signing are dramatized.

534.   OUR HERITAGE OF FREEDOM--A SERIES
       Audio/Brandon 12 films to celebrate the Bicentennial 1974
       color s/c/a
           Declaration of Independence (18 min.); Bill of Rights (17
           min.); Sons of Liberty (21 min.); Romance of Louisiana
           (19 min.); Give Me Liberty (17 min.); Song of a Nation
           (19 min.); Man Without a Country (22 min.); Lincoln in
           the White House (21 min.); Old Hickory (17 min.); Mon-
           roe Doctrine (16 min.); Under Southern Stars (20 min.);
           Teddy the Rough Rider (19 min.).

535.   OUR LIVING BILL OF RIGHTS--A SERIES
       Encyclopaedia Britannica b/w vt/vc
       Collaborator: Dr. Isadore Starr, Queens College, authority
       on the Bill of Rights and constitutional law
           These films are designed to help viewers relate to ab-
           stract concepts of justice, liberty, equality. Teaching
           methodology used is the case method. Students confront
           conflicting values and interests in liberty versus law;

rule versus rights; liberty versus license; right versus responsibility; freedom versus security.

536. PEACEFUL ASSEMBLY AND FREE SPEECH
McGraw-Hill 1955 21 min. b/w
From the See It Now Series
A group of citizens desirous of forming a chapter of the American Civil Liberties Union are refused a meeting place on the grounds that their meeting is of a controversial nature. Finally, when they are given a hall, the American Legion protests the arrangement. Edward R. Murrow presents both meetings as a political debate, with assertions and rebuttals from each side.

537. PRISON
National Educational Television Indiana University
American Documentary Films 1971 59 min. b/w
The film visits inside the Bucks County prison, Pennsylvania, to tell the story of the inmates in their own language. Built in 1884, the prison now holds men who talk of contemporary problems: racism, education in crime, dehumanization, lack of communication and homosexuality.

538. RIGHT OF DISSENT
Walt Disney Films 1972 20 min. color
In 1798, Representative Matt Lyon goes to prison for his outspoken remarks about President John Adams and starts a national controversy.

539. RIGHT OF PRIVACY
Associated Instructional Materials 59 min. b/w
This documentary reveals a report on government and business activities threatening individual privacy today. The possible elimination of all privacy should the proposed National Data Center be established is considered.

540. RIGHT TO LEGAL COUNSEL
Bailey Film Associates 14 min. color s/c/a
Gideon versus Wainright is a dramatic telling of the 1963 Supreme Court decision that ruled that indigent defendants must be offered the assignment of counsel.

541. SCHEMPP CASE, THE: BIBLE READING IN THE PUBLIC SCHOOLS
Encyclopaedia Britannica 35 min. b/w and color vt/vc s/c
An analysis is made of Bible reading and the reciting of the Lord's Prayer over a loudspeaker in a public school in terms of possible violation of the First Amendment. Reviewed are the issues, the background and the ultimate Supreme Court decision.

542.   SIT DOWN, SHUT UP OR GET OUT
       National Broadcasting Company 1971 58 min.   color
            This is an adaptation of an original allegorical play about a
            boy who chooses to be different, raising money questions
            about the threat to individual freedom involved in the
            suppression of dissent.

543.   SIX HOURS TO DEADLINE: A FREE AND RESPONSIBLE
       PRESS
       Teaching Film Custodians 1962 20 min.   b/w
            This film dramatizes the responsibilities as well as the
            freedom of journalism in this country. It provides a
            background for the analysis of publication ethics.

544.   SPEECH AND PROTEST
       Churchill 1967 22 min.   color
       From the Bill of Rights Series
            Questions are raised concerning the first amendment and
            the constitution. Rights of free expression are drama-
            tized.

545.   TOWARD THE EXPRESSION OF THE IDEA OF FREEDOM
       University of California 1971 53 min.   b/w c/a
            This documentary shows how it felt to instruct and to at-
            tend class during an experimental political science course
            at Berkeley during the 1966-67 academic year.

546.   UNDERSTANDING THE LAW: EQUAL JUSTICE FOR ALL
       Encyclopaedia Britannica 12 min.   b/w vt/vc s/c
            Dr. Robert Carr, Oberlin University, explains the rights
            of the individual to be protected by and from the law.

547.   UNITED STATES SUPREME COURT: GUARDIAN OF THE
       CONSTITUTION
       Encyclopaedia Britannica 24 min.   color vt/vc
            History and landmark cases of the Supreme Court are de-
            tailed in this second edition of the film.

548.   VOICES INSIDE
       University of California 1969 23 min.   color
            The voices are those of the men and women inside U.S.
            prisons, expressing their feelings and frustrations.

                            GROUP DISCUSSION

549.   ANATOMY OF A GROUP
       National Educational Television Indiana University 1963
       30 min.   b/w s/c/a
       From the Dynamics of Leadership Series
            This film explores the structure of group goals, standards
            and procedures during meetings. The quality of communi-

cation involved is analyzed, including characteristics patterns and differences relating to member interaction in
the group.

550. BLOWING HOT AND COLD
Bureau of National Affairs 1974 23 min. color vc
Rivalry between business groups is examined. With the
aid of a consultant, groups are encouraged to explore the
basis for their differences and to shift from a "win-
lose" to a "win-win" orientation.

551. CHALLENGE OF LEADERSHIP, THE
Bureau of National Affairs 1960 15 min. color c/a
Leadership is explained in terms of its effectiveness in
times of a crisis. Common personalities of leaders are
reviewed. Recommendations are made for the conference leader to explore group analysis and attitudes toward the leader.

552. COOPERATION AND CONFLICT
University of Utah 1963 29 min. b/w
From the Human Relations Series: #10
This film explores diverse forms of relationships exist-
ing between groups and individuals.

553. DIAGNOSING GROUP OPERATIONS
National Educational Television Indiana University 1963
30 min. b/w s/c/a
From the Dynamics of Leadership Series
This film treats the attitudes of both participant and observer in the group. It points out signs of conflict, withdrawal, factionalism and group indecision.

554. DISCUSSION--ITS BASIS AND FORMS
University of Iowa 1959 30 min. b/w C
Principles for class discussion are outlined. A mock
discussion of college cheating demonstrates a segment of
the discussion.

555. DISCUSSION IN DEMOCRACY
Coronet 1948 10 min. b/w s/c/a
Students learn of the relationship of organization to discussion in society. They also develop a three-fold program for leader and participants in any discussion:
preparation, planning, personalities.

556. DISCUSSION TECHNIQUE
Department of Defense National Audiovisual Center 1951
29 min. b/w s/c/a
Methods of discussion techniques are outlined. Included
are suggestions for discussion specifically for enlisted
military personnel. The use of the forum, panel, sym-
posium, debate, conference and informal groups are presented.

557.   DYNAMICS OF LEADERSHIP--A SERIES
       National Educational Television   Indiana University   1963
       30 min. each   b/w   s/c/a
       Commentary by Malcolm Knowles, Boston University
              See individual title listings:
              1. Anatomy of a Group
              2. Diagnosing Group Operation
              3. Individual Motivation and Behavior
              4. Roadblocks to Communication
              5. Sharing the Leadership

558.   GROUP DISCUSSION
       Centron   McGraw-Hill   1954, revised 1965   12 min.   b/w
       From the Speech Series
              Incidents dramatized include industrial events, the PTA
              meeting and techniques pertinent to all groups.   The dis-
              cussion leader's basic responsibilities are explained.

559.   GROUP MORALE
       University of Utah   1963   29 min.   b/w   C/a
       From the Human Relations Series: #28
              Team spirit is discussed in terms of group morale.   An
              evaluation is made of the reasons for strong team spirit.

560.   GROUP MOTIVES
       University of Utah   1963   29 min.   b/w   C/a
       From the Human Relations Series
              This film analyzes specific group needs and suggests
              ways for activity behavior to fulfill these diverse needs.

561.   GROUP PROBLEM-SOLVING
       McGraw-Hill   1969   13 min.   color   s/c
              Advantages of intelligent discussions versus irrational
              protest for problem-solving.   The subject for analysis
              is grading systems.   The specific procedures for effec-
              tive discussion are presented with stress on the levels of
              stages of development.

562.   GROUPS
       Oregon State University   29 min.   kinescope   c/a
       From the Business of Supervision Series: #9
              This film's message is that group formations have spe-
              cialized needs as contrasted with the needs of mere
              "collections" of individuals.

563.   GROUPTHINK
       CRM   1974   33 min.   color   s/c/a
              There are eight symptoms of "groupthink" illustrated:
              invulnerability, shared stereotypes of the enemy, ration-
              alization, the illusion of morality, self-censorship, the
              illusion of unanimity, direct pressure on the deviant
              member and mind guarding--a device to prevent the
              group from dissenting opinions.   Commentary by Dr. Irv-
              ing Janis.

564.   HEY, HOW ABOUT RIGHT NOW?
       Modern Talking Picture Service   Free Loan Film   28 min.
       color
              Told in contemporary fashion, the "generation gap" is
              bridged by both sides in this film portrayal of the rela-
              tionship between adults and young people.

565.   HOW TO CONDUCT A DISCUSSION
       Encyclopaedia Britannica   1953   22 min.   b/w   vt/vc
       s/c/a
              This film dramatizes eleven fundamental principles to in-
              sure effective and satisfying group discussions.   Depicted
              are a wide range of group and discussion topics and tech-
              niques for leaders.

566.   HOW TO ORGANIZE A DISCUSSION GROUP
       Encyclopaedia Britannica   1952   22 min.   b/w   vt/vc   s/c/a
              Diverse discussion group procedures involving group or-
              ganization are investigated.

567.   INDIVIDUAL MOTIVATION AND BEHAVIOR
       National Educational Television   1963   b/w   s/c/a
       From the Dynamics of Leadership Series
              The basis for group action is explored: anxiety, argu-
              mentativeness and domination.

568.   LARGE GROUP INSTRUCTION
       Stanford University   1968   28 min.   color
              Dr. John Allen analyzes the effective use of large
              groups.   He stresses the techniques, types of presenta-
              tion, modes and communication methods.

569.   LEADERSHIP IS
       Cornell University   1970   33 min.   b/w   vt
              The three segments of this program explore the signifi-
              cance of leadership in group situations.   Discussed are:
              leading at the right time and at the right place, knowing
              the subject area, and getting along with people.

570.   LEARNING FROM CLASS DISCUSSION
       Coronet   1950   10 min.   b/w   s/c
       From Basic Study Skills Series
              The fundamental values of basic discussion are reviewed.
              The film emphasizes that organized discussion presup-
              poses clarity of ideas and an interchange of information.
              Recommendations are made for effective discussion tech-
              niques.

571.   LET'S DISCUSS IT
       National Film Board of Canada   1956   39 min.   b/w   s/C/a
              With an active discussion group participating, this film
              dramatizes the principles of group discussion methods.
              It describes steps in group organization and rules for
              following a discussion.

572.   MEETING IN PROGRESS
        Roundtable   43 min.   b/w and color
           This film presents conference leadership teaching prin-
           ciples through group participation.   Trainees are asked
           to decide, at twelve critical levels in a typical problem-
           solving conference, which group relations or task func-
           tion they would use if chosen leader.

573.   MEETING IN SESSION
        Columbia University Teachers College   1953   20 min.   b/w
        c/a
           This film illustrates how small groups can learn to work
           together more effectively.   It explains cooperative group
           awareness of each other's feelings, working toward solu-
           tions of common problems.   It examines "concentrating
           sessions"--individuals intent on resolving their own prob-
           lems.

574.   ORGANIZING DISCUSSION GROUPS
        Encyclopaedia Britannica   1953   21 min.   b/w   vt/vc   s/c/a
           Specific steps are indicated to promote and form the or-
           ganization of an informal adult discussion group in vari-
           ous situations.   Methods used are applicable to both in-
           formal and formal groups.

575.   OUR INVISIBLE COMMITTEES
        National Training Laboratory   1951   25 min.   b/w   s/c/a
           The film explores the important obstacle to group-thought
           and decision-making: the conflict of social pressures
           which operate within individuals.

576.   ROOM FOR DISCUSSION
        Encyclopaedia Britannica   1952   24 min.   b/w   vt/vc   s/c/a
           In both its personal and professional approach, this film
           explores the nature and function of discussion.   It stress-
           es the need for all citizens living in a democracy to un-
           derstand the privilege and responsibility for informed
           community discussion.

577.   SCHOOL BOARD MEETING TONIGHT
        University of Colorado   1957   30 min.   b/w   c/a
           This University of Colorado Department of Broadcasting
           film was produced for the Colorado Association of School
           Boards.   It shows the incorrect and correct procedures
           for conducting a school board meeting.

578.   SHARING THE LEADERSHIP
        National Educational Television   1963   30 min.   b/w   s/c/a
        From the Dynamics of Leadership Series
           This film explains how group members begin to share the
           responsibility for success of the group.   It explores three
           categories of individual action and their relation to group
           leadership: self-serving functions, task functions and
           group-serving functions.

579. SMALL GROUP INSTRUCTION
Stanford 1966 25 min. color c/a
Dwight Allen analyzes some variables in the establishment of interaction: human and material resources
available; issues of leadership; discipline and preparation of leaders and participation.

580. SOCIAL ANIMAL, THE
National Educational Television Indiana University 1963
29 min. b/w s/C/a
From the Focus on Behavior Series
The film highlights some of the current research in experimental psychology, particularly the ways in which
man is influenced and changed by his society. Dr. Stanley Schacter of Columbia University demonstrates the
effects of pressure on the individual to conform to the
group mores. Leon Festinger of Stanford University
shows the consequences of stating publicly ideas contrary
to one's own beliefs.

581. SPEECH: CONDUCTING A MEETING
Centron (YAF) McGraw-Hill 1952 12 min. b/w s/c/a
As a typical meeting is held, the narrator indicates mistakes made by the participants and emphasizes significant points. The use of parliamentary procedure to get
work done is stressed.

582. TEACHING BY GUIDED DISCUSSION
United States Air Force National Audiovisual Center 21 min.
b/w
An Air Force University academic course seminar in
psychology is presented to demonstrate applicable techniques of teaching by the "guided discussion method."

583. TEACHING PUBLIC ISSUES: DISCUSSION TECHNIQUES
Xerox 1968 25 min. b/w C/a
Case studies in a classroom situation exemplify the
Socratic dialogue in different settings.

INFORMATION SYSTEMS

584. ACCESS
University of California 1975 20 min. color
Applications of the basic concepts and uses of computerized information access systems. Three types of data
bases are detailed. Simple animation describes basic
searching techniques.

585. BETTER WORLD, A
International Business Machines 1967 8 min. color
The computer's influence is described in the areas of
education, research, business and law enforcement.

586.   COMMUNICATIONS: THE WIRED WORLD
       University of California 1971 22 min. color
       From the Towards the Year 2000 Series
           Future communications and information storage and re-
           trieval systems are examined. Shown are: new techno-
           logical developments in telephones, cable television, satel-
           lite communications, laser systems, and computers
           whose information will be accessible to households by
           telephone and television. Includes interviews by Mar-
           shall McLuhan, Irving Kahn and communications scien-
           tists and engineers.

587.   COMPUTER AND THE MIND OF MAN SERIES, THE
       National Educational Television 1962 30 min. each b/w
           The series includes: 1. Logic by Machine; 2. Universe
           of Numbers; 3. Universal Machine; 4. Control Revolu-
           tion; 5. Managers and Models; 6. Engine at the Door.

588.   COMPUTER GLOSSARY, A
       Encyclopaedia Britannica 10 min. color vt/vc s/c/a
           The film emphasizes the challenge of computer program-
           ming that emerges from its precisely defined procedures
           which demand a technical jargon. The viewer pursues
           a computer data path.

589.   COMPUTER MODELS
       University of Ohio 14 min. b/w s/c/a
           Two computer-based teaching-learning systems (Socrates
           and Plato) at the University of Illinois are seen in opera-
           tion. Models of the total communication system/process
           are explained.

590.   COMPUTER REVOLUTION (PARTS I, II)
       Modern Talking Picture Service Free Loan Film b/w
           The film explores how man will meet the challenge of
           the computer and its implications.

591.   COMPUTER SKETCHPAD
       National Educational Television 29 min. b/w s/c/a
           A new computer-programming system developed at M.I.T.
           is discussed. It permits a man to communicate with a
           computer by drawing sketches on an oscilloscope. Dis-
           cussed are practical applications of the system in indus-
           try and research.

592.   COMPUTER STORY, THE
       North American Rockwell Corporation Business Education
       Films 1968 24 min. color
           The history of Autonetics, one of the foremost producers
           of computers for military applications through 1969.

593.   COMPUTER TUTOR, THE
       Corporate Communications Business Education Films 20
       min. color

A large-scale optical character-recognition system and some of its current applications are examined.

594. COMPUTERS AND HUMAN BEHAVIOR
National Educational Television Indiana University 1963
29 min. b/w s/c/a
From the Focus on Behavior Series
  Some of the research conducted at Carnegie Tech. with electronic digital computers is explored. Explained are demonstrations in perception of motion and depth.

595. COMPUTERS AT WORK
Business Education Films 12 min. color s/c/a
  The computer is viewed under actual working conditions; helping to produce toys; improving instruction techniques in schools. On-location filming offers realism necessary in emphasizing computer studies and relating those studies to work.

596. CONTROL REVOLUTION
National Educational Television 1962 30 min. b/w
From The Computer and the Mind of Man Series
  The film focuses on how the development of the computer has made possible the automatic control of routine tasks and decision-making related to the recording, storing and processing of data in government, industry and general business.

597. ELECTRONIC COMPUTERS IMPROVE MANAGEMENT CONTROL
University of California 1957 15 min. color
  This documentary demonstrates how electronic data processing machines improve management control situations, because of four computer characteristics: high speed combined with accuracy, phenomenal memory, ability to communicate efficiently, and ability to carry out a long series of operations without human intervention.

598. ENGINE AT THE DOOR
KQED National Educational Television 1962 30 min. b/w
s/c/a
From The Computer and the Mind of Man Series
  The question asked is, "Will Machines Ever Run Man?"
  The pros and cons of man's responsibility for the wise and beneficial use of computer technology are analyzed.

599. INFORMATION EXPLOSION, THE
Ohio State University, for the U.S. Office of Education
1968 34 min. b/w C/a
From the Communication Theory and New Educational Media Series
  The revolution in human communication is reviewed, with the thrust on information, verbal and pictorial,

that is stored, duplicated, transmitted, transferred, dis-
tributed, received. Of primary concern is how this
"flood" of information may be intelligently processed and
what effects it will have on the lives of the next generation.

600. INFORMATION MACHINE, THE
Encyclopaedia Britannica 1958 10 min. color vt/vc
This film places the computer in historical perspective,
showing it to be the culmination of the abstractions and
measuring tools that man has been developing since primitive times. Produced by film-makers Charles and Ray
Eames for the IBM exhibit at the Brussels World Fair.

601. INTERNATIONAL SCIENCE REPORT
State University of New York 25 min. b/w
A report including a computer programmer's description
of digital computers, new areas for computer use and the
use of computers in medicine in Germany.

602. IS KNOWLEDGE POWER?
Special Libraries Association 28 min. b/w
Hubert Humphrey discusses the problems of information
storage and retrieval in a society that is generating information on an unprecedented scale.

603. LOGIC BY MACHINE
National Educational Television 1962 30 min. b/w s/c/a
This film discusses the computer revolution, the relationship between man and machine and of the symbolic world
of mathematics to the real world of events.

604. MAN AMPLIFIERS
University of California 30 min. color kinescope
A television discussion focuses on ".cybernetic anthropo-
morphous machines," which are not self-regulating but
require interaction with man.

605. MAN AND COMPUTER: A PERSPECTIVE
Business Education Films 20 min. color s/c/a
The film shows some of the basic elements in data processing, such as input, output, storage and control. It
explains in detail how they work and what function they
perform.

606. MANAGEMENT AND THE COMPUTER
Republic Steel Corporation 1966 29 min. b/w vt
This film presents a functional introduction to computers
and illustrates the value of the computer in managerial
work.

607. MANAGERS AND MODELS
National Educational Television 1962 29 min. b/w

The design and simulation capacities of the modern digital computer are explored. Scenes are included from testing centers.

608. PAPER BLIZZARD (PARTS I, II, III)
Battelle Memorial Institute 1970 45 min. color
This documentary introduces the array of information sources within the Federal Government and identifies the use of these resources.

609. SPEAK TO ME IN FORTRAN
Northern Virginia ETV 1972 19 min. color
From the Know What I Mean Series: #6
Mr. Victor Kryston examines a wide array of computer applications: the Goddard Space Center, an instructional program in public schools, the computer study of chromosomes. Discussion includes the challenge of the "logic" of the new machines.

610. "THINKING" MACHINES
Educational Testing Service 1960 19 min. color
To explain the role of machines for gathering data, this film demonstrates the potential for storage of information bits. Also shown are how a computer chess game is played and an electronic device consisting of a mechanical mouse seeking an artificial cheese in a maze.

611. ULTIMATE MACHINE, THE
Time-Life 1974 30 min. color vt/vc s/a
The development and use of the computer is examined in this film. It studies an automated oil refinery, shows a child learning from a classroom computer, and shows scientists building a man-like robot. It raises questions about computers and human rights and the beginnings of study of mathematical symbolism.

612. UNIVERSAL MACHINE
National Educational Television 1965 30 min. b/w s/c/a
From The Computer and the Mind of Man Series
The capability of the computer to do whatever man is capable of instructing it to do is discussed. Limitations concern man's ability to feed it with data and instructions.

613. UNIVERSE OF NUMBERS
National Educational Television 1965 30 min. b/w s/c/a
From The Computer and the Mind of Man Series
The history of computer development is reviewed, from the first mechanical calculator to the first completely electronic calculator built in the mid-nineteen forties.

614. VIEW FROM THE PEOPLE WALL
Encyclopaedia Britannica 14 min. color vt/vc s/c/a

Computers solve problems by employing abstract models.
The film demonstrates physical, mathematical and spa-
tial models, traces steps in the problem-solving process
and illustrates the computer's role in solving complex
problems.

615.   WHAT EVERY MANAGER NEEDS TO KNOW ABOUT INFOR-
        MATION SYSTEMS (PTS. I, II)
        Bureau of National Affairs   1972   25 min. each   color
            Part I, "The Merritt Case," concerns computer prob-
            lems on a managerial level.   Part II, "The Computer and
            You," defines the information system and explains the dif-
            ferences between information and data.   Featured is
            Isaac L. Auerbach, President of Auerbach Associations,
            Inc., Philadelphia.

616.   WHAT IS A COMPUTER?
        Encyclopaedia Britannica   19 min.   color   vt/vc   s/a
            This film dispels some of the mysteries about how a com-
            puter operates.   A brief introduction to the binary system
            of numeration leads to a description of how numbers are
            punched into cards, converted into pulses, stored mag-
            netically in the computer memory.

617.   YOU AND THE COMPUTER
        Didactic   Strauss   9 min.   color
            Using live action plus animation, this film explains what
            the computer does in clear, everyday terminology.   Terms
            are defined, applied, demonstrated.

                              THE INTERVIEW

618.   AID TO FAMILIES WITH DEPENDENT CHILDREN: INTAKE
        INTERVIEW
        University of Southern California   1965   18 min. each   b/w
        From the Studies in Interviewing Series
            Four training films are designed to stimulate questions
            and discussion on the subject of interviewing.   They ex-
            plain how the interviewer's skills, values and attitudes
            affect the interview and determine its success.   Two in-
            terview situations are contrasted which involve the same
            case situation, client, worker, time and place.

619.   APPLYING FOR A JOB
        Encyclopaedia Britannica   1971   13 min.   color   vt/vc
        From the Careers in the Office Series
            After a series of discouraging interviews, a young woman
            learns specific guidelines to avoid future mistakes.   Her
            next interview results in a successful job offer.

620. APPRAISAL INTERVIEW, THE
      Bureau of National Affairs 1974 27 min. b/w
      From Great Britain
          This three-part dramatic film explores the concept of ob-
          jective appraisal of job performance based on previously
          agreed targets and the essential role of the appraisal in-
          terview.

621. COUNSEL INTERVIEW, THE
      Roundtable 15 min. color
          Using the new training technique of psychodrama, this
          film probes the thoughts and emotions of a manager and
          a subordinate as they explore the reasons for the latter's
          poor performance. In the interview a number of impor-
          tant factors surface, from poor interpersonal relation-
          ships to miscommunications.

622. DISCIPLINE INTERVIEW, THE
      Roundtable 16 min. b/w
          An illustration focuses on a badly handled interview, with
          distractions, poor preparation, personality conflicts. As-
          sessments are made to reconcile the conflicts.

623. EMPLOYMENT INTERVIEW
      McGraw-Hill 11 min. b/w s/c/a
          Stressed is the significance of an employment interview in
          terms of getting the "right" man for the job. Techniques
          offered involve friendly discussion, testing, rating scales.

624. FINDING THE RIGHT JOB
      Coronet 11 min. b/w s/c/a
          This film stresses the essentials of locating the right
          job: developing leads, letters of application and the im-
          portance of interviews and interview techniques.

625. GETTING A JOB
      Encyclopaedia Britannica 13 min. b/w vt/vc s/c/a
          Preliminary preparation for job-seeking, application let-
          ters and effective interviews are all examined.

626. GROUP WORKER, THE
      University of Michigan National Institutes of Health 1967
      30 min. b/w
          Showing interactions of persons in interview situations,
          questions are asked in four sample interviews: 1. In pris-
          on camp; 2. In a mental hospital; 3. In a classroom;
          4. In a session with a married couple.

627. HOW'S IT GOING?
      Didactic Strauss 11 min. color c/a
          Four filmed cases deal with the more difficult and sensi-
          tive situations in the evaluation of job performance.
          Case I: "More than Paperwork," examines ways to cre-

ate a favorable "climate" for the interview. Case II:
"Give and Take," focuses on the two-way communication
essential in reaching mutual agreement. Case III:
"Means to an End," defines the need for a plan of action;
Case IV: "The Way Ahead," stresses the importance of
conducting the interview so that both parties will gain.

628. IMPROVING INTERVIEWING
      Pennsylvania State University 1963 33 min. b/w
           Excerpts from hundreds of real interviews with "real
           life" situations are presented. A viewer's guide is avail-
           able.

629. INITIAL INTERVIEW
      University of Wisconsin 17 min. b/w
           The initial interview between a case worker and an appli-
           cant for a public welfare job is reenacted. The film en-
           courages the viewer to evaluate techniques used by one
           interviewer: putting a person at ease, asking questions,
           seeking information, controlling the interview.

630. INTERPERSONAL PERCEPTION SERIES
      University of Utah 1964 6 films: 10 min. each color C
           Each film of this six-part series is part of an interview
           with a person in the Salt Lake City area. In the same
           interview, each person is given a group of unrelated
           questions concerning religion, current events and famous
           people.

631. INTERVIEWING
      Oregon State University 29 min. kinescope c/a
      From the Business of Supervision Series
           This film investigates skills required to strengthen the
           supervisor-subordinate communication channels.

632. INTERVIEWING A CHILD
      University of Michigan 20 min. kinescope c/a
           This film explores the method of gaining relevant infor-
           mation when communicating with children. It contrasts
           ineffective, direct and authoritarian forms of inquiry with
           the indirect approach to establish rapport with and com-
           munication with the child.

633. JOB INTERVIEW--THREE YOUNG MEN
      Churchill Business Education Films 1968 17 min. color
      s/c/a
           Actual job interviews are photographed with hidden cam-
           eras. Three young applicants are interviewed for trainee
           positions. The viewers are asked to evaluate the appli-
           cants as an employer might. The film is suggested to
           provoke discussion about "attitudes, goals, preparation
           for interviews, values, jobs."

634.   JOB INTERVIEW--THREE YOUNG WOMEN
       Churchill Business Education Films 1968 17 min. color
       s/c/a
              Three types of young women are interviewed for a job.
              The discussion is centered on mistakes they make during
              the interview.

635.   PROGRAMMED INTERVIEW INSTRUCTION--A SERIES
       University of Southern California School of Medicine 1970
       12 interviews: 15-20 min. each b/w
       From the Programmed Instruction in Medical Interviewing Se-
       ries
              Twelve medical interviews demonstrate technique ranging
              from facilitation of time to "conducting an emotional cli-
              mate" for the interviewee.

636.   STUDIES IN INTERVIEWING (PARTS I, II, III, IV)
       University of Southern California 68 min. b/w s/c/a
              Four different versions of two interview situations are
              shown: how the interviewer's skills and attitudes affect
              the interviewee and determine the success of the inter-
              view. The film is designed for use in training social
              workers but is useful in other fields requiring effective
              interviewing.

637.   THAT JOB INTERVIEW
       National Audiovisual Center 1971 17 min. color
              Stressed are useful techniques for veterans to use in job
              interviews with prospective employers. The film illus-
              trates the possible application of military training to civil-
              ian job.

638.   UNCALCULATED RISK, THE
       Roundtable 26 min. color
              To help interviewers distinguish inference from observa-
              tions and make better personnel decisions, Dr. William
              Haney shows a young manager how to coach, interview
              and counsel an employee.

639.   WHAT'S THE MATTER WITH ALICE?
       Newsfilms University of California 1972 30 min. color
              The first segment, "Anatomy of Change," is a series of
              management, supervisory and employee interviews high-
              lighting examples of upward mobility. The case study,
              "What's the Matter With Alice?" provides an example of
              one supervisor's response to the needs of an employee.

640.   YOUR JOB: APPLYING FOR IT
       Coronet 14 min. b/w and color s/c/a
       Collaborator: D. H. Kruger, Professor of Industrial Relations,
       Michigan State University
              The viewer sees interviews with workers of varying ages
              and education to learn techniques for job application.

Encouraged is a planned procedure, including following-
up leads, selling oneself and interview preparation.

INTRAPERSONAL

641. ALTER EGO
      Macmillan 9 min. color
           Two images of one animated figure represent man's
           super-ego and his id. In the concluding sequence, the
           hedonistic figure, at odds with the conformist part of him-
           self, saves his counterpart from self-destruction.

642. AND ANYBODY ELSE WHO'S LISTENING
      Probe Associates 1971 23 min. color
           On February 14, 1970, Craig Gardner, Salt Lake City
           nineteen-year-old honor student, drove six hours into the
           Wyoming Desert and shot himself. A few hours before,
           alone in his apartment, he revealed his inner thoughts
           about his life to his tape recorder. The tape is the
           film's main soundtrack and reveals his feelings about the
           inability to cope and communicate.

643. AWARENESS
      Associated Instructional Films 1970 22 min. color s/c
           "Recommended for sensitivity groups," this film explores
           the expression of reverence for the universal truth of the
           ideals of Buddhism. Social consciousness and spiritual
           renewal are examined in terms of the awareness of one's
           self and the "fusion of one's being with all living things."

644. BIOFEEDBACK: LISTENING TO YOUR HEAD
      University of California 1973 22 min. color
           The film explores current investigations into the nature,
           effects and uses of biofeedback. Experiments are demon-
           strated to convince that a patient can control his own
           awareness.

645. CAGE, THE
      Crowell, Collier, Macmillan 1967 26 min. color
           This film, written, produced and directed by prisoners
           at San Quentin prison, California, was produced for its
           therapeutic value.

646. CAGES
      McGraw-Hill 8 min. b/w s/c/a
      Award Winner
           This animated film from Poland suggests that all human
           beings are prisoners of themselves and of their own ideas,
           dreams, place in the world.

647. CAROL AND DR. FISCHER
      Grove Press   Evergreen   45 min.   b/w
            A basic study of the process of self-awareness, this film
            shows the ways in which a skillful and sensitive adult can
            help a child to express and understand herself.   The
            child and the therapist discuss sibling rivalry, disguised
            aggression, problems of communication

648. FACING REALITY
      McGraw-Hill   1954   12 min.   b/w   s/c/a
            The film shows common ways in which people escape
            from reality--daydreaming, identification, suppression
            and malingering.   Illustrated are methods which help
            change negative attitudes.

649. FRANKL AND THE SEARCH FOR MEANING
      Psychological Films   30 min.   color
            Dr. Viktor Frankl describes man's search for meaning
            as a form of "height" psychotherapy, as opposed to the
            Freudian theory, described as "depth" psychology.   In
            man's continuous growth upward toward self-actualiza-
            tion, he discovers meaning is a form of personalized
            valuing.

650. GET HIGH ON LIFE
      Dana   10 min.   color
            Using a mix of story and music, this film explores the
            wonders of each day from dawn to dusk.   The philosophy
            stresses the need for a positive approach to one's self.

651. GOLD IS THE WAY I FEEL
      Learning Corporation of America   9 min.   color
            This film has applications for stimulating self-expression
            and is aimed at students in search of identity and aware-
            ness.

652. GUIDANCE FOR THE 70'S: PUTTING YOURSELF TOGETHER
      Bailey Film Associates   17 min.   b/w   s/c/a
            This film deals with the relationship between our own in-
            ner self-image and the external pressures from the peo-
            ple in our environment.   Techniques for coping with the
            pressure are examined.

653. GUIDANCE FOR THE 70'S: SELF-ESTEEM
      Bailey Film Associates   18 min.   color   s/c/a
            The focus is on the significance of building good feelings
            about ourselves.   Self-esteem is a quality basic for an
            effective human being.

654. HASSLES AND HANGUPS
      Learning Corporation of America   29 min.   color   s/c/a
            Without moralizing, this film points up the need for self-
            esteem and a positive relationship to reality to complete

an in-depth look at ourselves.   Narrator is Michael Douglas.

655.   I WHO AM, WHO AM I?
       Learning Corporation of America   15 min.   color
       From "The Swimmer," starring Burt Lancaster
              Ned Merrill, without family, job or material possessions,
              starts out on an allegorical journey in search of himself,
              meeting people who forcefully thrust him into a realiza-
              tion of his present condition.

656.   INTERVIEW WITH PROFESSOR ERIK ERIKSON (PARTS I, II)
       Macmillan   50 min.   each   b/w
              Part I examines the eight stages of psychosocial develop-
              ment, particularly the significant "identity crisis." Part
              II reviews ego states, therapy, cross-cultural research.

657.   JOY OF COMMUNICATION, THE
       Dana   1974   18 min.   color
              Communication between self and all people is explored.
              The joy of communication with nature is also portrayed.
              The message is "rejuvenation of the mind," motivate,
              assess one's values.

658.   MASLOW AND SELF-ACTUALIZATION (PARTS I, II)
       CRM Films   1971   each segment: 30 min.   color   c
       From the Psychology Today Films
              Dr. A. Maslow, founder of the concept of self-actualiza-
              tion, explains his theories.   Film I discusses: a sense
              of humor, social interest, honesty, awareness; film II
              examines freedom, including creativeness and attitude
              change.

659.   MEASURE OF UNDERSTANDING, A
       Roundtable   29 min.   b/w and color
       From the Communication Series
              This film explains that interpersonal communication is on
              at least two levels--the informational and the behavioral.
              When these two levels fail to communicate the same mean-
              ing, then understanding is stifled.   Suggestions are made
              of ways to eliminate double meanings and to determine
              the primary causes of incongruent communication.

660.   NO MAN IS AN ISLAND
       Dana   11 min.   color
       Award winner
              John Donne's poem is interpreted through film and music
              to emphasize positive behavioral objectives behind the
              words of the poem.

661.   ROLLO MAY AND HUMAN ENCOUNTER (PARTS I, II)
       Psychological Films   30 min.   each   color
              Film I concerns "Self-Self Encounter and Self-Other En-
              counter," with an analysis of self as both subject and

object. Film II deals with the subject of "Manipulation and Human Encounter," equating man's search for self with man's preoccupation with sex and death.

662. SHYNESS
National Film Board of Canada McGraw-Hill 23 min. b/w
This film examines shyness, its causes and how we deal with the problem through greater understanding. Three children are studied, as is the lonely existence of a shy adult.

663. SIXTEEN IN WEBSTER GROVES
Carousel 1966 47 min. color
Rebellion, dissatisfaction are exemplified in this exploration of attitudes of teenagers in an affluent suburban community. Examined are the superficial symbols of abundance.

664. SOCIAL ACCEPTABILITY
McGraw-Hill 1958 20 min. b/w s/C/a
The film examines the relationship of adjustment and happiness to social acceptability as the basis for acceptance in a group.

665. TARGET FIVE
Crowell, Collier, Macmillan 1967 48 min. color
Virginia Satir, family therapist, demonstrates four manipulative response forms. The film's conclusion illustrates that the "essential qualities of an actual relationship are: listening, understanding and mutual meaning."

666. TO SEE OR NOT TO SEE
Learning Corporation of America 1969 15 min. color
This animated Czech film takes a close look at our inner thoughts and fears. Suggestions for "coping" are presented.

667. WEBSTER GROVES REVISITED
Carousel 1969 53 min. b/w
This is a follow-up to the examination of values in Webster Groves.

668. WHAT IS NORMAL?
Indiana University 1965 30 min. b/w
Discussed are various "normal" reactions to stress. Exemplified is the story of one young man who loses his job.

669. WHAT TO DO ABOUT UPSET FEELINGS?
Coronet 1964 b/w & color 11 min.
This film discusses four ways of overcoming upset feelings, stressing the need for talking to someone about feelings and taking "positive action."

LANGUAGE

670. "A"
      Contemporary McGraw-Hill 1964 10 min. b/w
      Directed by Jan Lenica, this animated film is based on
      one of Ionesco's favorite preoccupations: the power of
      language. The letters symbolize invasion of privacy, op-
      pression or "one's own problem."

671. ABC'S
      University of Southern California 27 min. b/w
      Dr. Frank Baxter lectures on the class theories of the
      origin of our alphabet and what today's scholars believe
      to have been the probable origins.

672. ALONG THE NILE
      University of Southern California University of Hawaii
      27 min. b/w
      From the Written Word Series
      The fourth of this film series examines the variety of
      Egyptian writing and the significance of the Egyptian
      alphabet.

673. ALPHABET, THE
      National Educational Television 1957 30 min. b/w c/a
      From the Language and Linguistics Series
      Analyzing the English writing system, this film traces the
      origin, development and spread of the alphabet. Included
      are demonstrations of diverse writing systems and the
      significance of hieroglyphics in the development of written
      language.

674. ALPHABET, THE--MARK OF MAN
      Berne McGraw-Hill 1967 20 min. color
      This film analyzes how the Semitic alphabet was im-
      proved by the Greeks, later refined by the Romans.

675. ALPHABET CONSPIRACY, THE (PARTS I, II)
      Bell Telephone 1959 60 min. color s/c
      With animated cartoons, Dr. Frank Baxter teaches the
      fundamentals of linguistics. Viewers see the exact usage
      of language in the communication process.

676. AMERICAN SPOKEN HERE
      Teaching Film Custodians 1940 10 min. b/w
      From the Passing Parade Series
      A dramatic history of several slang expressions illus-
      trates their origin and how they came to be included in
      the American idiom.

677. BERFUNKLE
      Portofilms   Perennial 1964   color   s/c/a
      Award winning
           Berfunkle introduces problems involved in verbal commun-
           ication--in our use of words as symbols of things and
           concepts.   A poor soul tries to discover the precise
           meaning of the word "berfunkle," only to learn that "ber-
           funkle" means different things to different people.

678. BETTER CHOICE OF WORDS, A
      Coronet 1952 11 min. b/w s/c
           This film stresses the significance of an extensive vo-
           cabulary, the relationship of a mental picture and what
           one says and the ability to select the most applicable
           words.

679. BUILD YOUR VOCABULARY
      Coronet 10 min. b/w s/c
           Suggestions are made concerning the maintenance of a
           personal vocabulary notebook, and the observation of
           others' use of appropriate words.

680. CHANGE IN LANGUAGE
      National Educational Television Indiana University   1967
      30 min. b/w s/c/a
      From the English Fact and Fancy Series
           James Bostain considers the continuing changes in lan-
           guage.   Of primary concern are the ongoing efforts to
           standardize English and the reasons for the language
           changes.

681. COMMUNICATION: STORY OF ITS DEVELOPMENT
      University of Hawaii 11 min. b/w s/c/a
           Milestones in the history of transmission of spoken and
           written language are presented.   Shown are live action
           scenes and views of many original inventions, including
           the telegraph and first wireless radio broadcast facility.

682. CONCRETE POETRY
      Pyramid   University of California 1968 12 min. b/w
           An innovative film describes a worldwide experimental
           poetry movement--concrete poetry--which is meant to be
           "seen rather than read aloud."   Attempts are made to
           create meaning and elicit response from the arrangement,
           juxtaposition and fragmentation of words and phrases on
           specific pages and screens as well as from spoken words
           or phrases.

683. CORRECTNESS IN LANGUAGE
      National Educational Television Indiana University 1967
      30 min. b/w c/a
      From the English Fact and Fancy Series
           James Bostain amplifies the necessity of making choices

among competing phonetic, lexical, syntactic conventions.
He explores the adoption or the ignoring of refinements
in language, pointing out that the speaker and/or writer
is judged by choices he makes.

684. DEBT TO THE PAST: LANGUAGE AND COMMUNICATION
      Moody Institute of Science 1962 17 min. color s/c
          This film develops the viewpoint that man derives consid-
      erable power of accomplishment from his language. Three
      recognized stages in the growth of a written language are
      reviewed: the pictograph stage, the ideographic stage and
      the phonetic stage. The film traces the contributions of
      the Egyptians, Phoenicians, Greeks and Romans to mod-
      ern language based on the alphabet.

685. DEFINITION OF LANGUAGE, A
      National Educational Television Indiana University 1957
      30 min. b/w C/a
      From the Language and Linguistics Series
          Dr. Henry Smith reviews and continues the definition of
      language. Detailed is the relationship between language
      and culture.

686. DIALECTS
      National Educational Television Indiana University 1957
      30 min. b/w C/a
      From the Language and Linguistics Series
          Dr. Henry Smith explains and demonstrates dialect dif-
      ferences in standard English. He illustrates how English
      variations are divided into geographical areas. Guests
      from five different geographical areas in the United States
      demonstrate pronunciation differences.

687. DO YOU KNOW HOW TO MAKE A STATEMENT OF FACT?
      National Educational Television Indiana University 1956
      30 min. b/w s/c/a
      From the Talking Sense Series
          The late Dr. Irving Lee analyzes the difference between
      statements of fact and statements of inference. He ex-
      plains that when a person is unaware that there is a dif-
      ference, he may behave as if inference were fact, lead-
      ing to arrogant behavior, a failure to assess situations
      realistically, and friction in human relations.

688. EFFECTIVE CRITICISM
      Coronet 1951 10 min. b/w and color s/c/a
      From the Language in Action Series
          Primarily concerned with the skills and types of criticism,
      this film presents the similarities and differences between
      evaluative and instructive criticism.

689. ENGLISH AND LATIN
      National Educational Television Indiana University

1967 b/w c/a
From the English Fact and Fancy Series
James Bostain examines some of the byproducts that people expect to gain from the study of Latin. He concludes
that the irrelevance of Latin to English "has yet to be
fully appreciated."

690. ENGLISH FACT AND FANCY SERIES, THE
National Educational Television Indiana University 1967
b/w vt c/a
Fifteen films with James C. Bostain, scientific linguist.
This series is designed to improve teaching through the
treatment of the English language as a social and behavioral phenomenon. Individual listings include: Scientists and Advocates; Language as Behavior; Structure and
Content; Talking and Writing, Parts I and II; Correctness
in Language; What Are the English Language?; English
and Latin; The Search for a "Universal Grammar";
Change in Language; Problem of Meaning; A Communications Model.

691. ENGLISH LANGUAGE, THE: HOW IT CHANGES
Coronet 11 min. b/w and color s/c
Collaborator: Dr. Thomas H. Wetmore, Chairman, Department of English, Ball State College
This film shows how changes keep the language alive and
flexible, making it a useful tool for communication. By
addition of words, by changes in spelling, meaning, pronunciation of words, and by updating the rules of grammar, the English language continues to change.

692. ENGLISH LANGUAGE, THE: PATTERNS OF USE
Coronet 1970 11 min. b/w and color s/c
This film demonstrates how speech styles and acceptability vary within each culture group and in different situations.

693. ENGLISH LANGUAGE, THE: STORY OF ITS DEVELOPMENT
Coronet 1952 11 min. b/w and color s/c
The viewer learns of the visual history of the English
language, from the time of Celtic, Roman, Nordic and
Saxon tribes through the infusion of French and Latin
and its emergence as a printed language which is still
growing and changing. Changes in the language are related to the printing press, as well as to the developments wrought by the Church monks, William the Con-
queror, Chaucer and Shakespeare.

694. GRAMMAR (PARTS I, II)
National Educational Television Indiana University 1957
30 min. b/w
From the Language and Linguistics Series
Dr. Henry Lee Smith analyzes the structure, patterning

and classification of words.   More specifics about grammar and the criteria for classification are discussed.

695.   GROWTH OF A LANGUAGE--AMERICAN ENGLISH
        United States Information Agency   National Audiovisual Center
        1960   29 min.   b/w
            The development of American English is reported against
            a background of factors involved in language change and
            growth.   The film illustrates varieties of English spoken
            in many countries.

696.   HIDING BEHIND THE DICTIONARY
        National Educational Television   Indiana University   1956
        30 min.   b/w
        From the Language in Action Series
            Dr. S. I. Hayakawa illustrates the preparation of diction-
            aries, explaining that the dictionary writer is a historian,
            not a "lawgiver."   Word meanings are "inferred from
            both physical and verbal contexts."   He suggests that it
            is possible that no word has exactly the same meaning on
            successive occasions of use.

697.   HISTORY OF THE ENGLISH LANGUAGE, THE
        National Educational Television   Indiana University   1957
        30 min.   b/w   s/c/a
        From the Language and Linguistics Series
            Dr. H. S. Smith investigates the history, development and
            growth of the English language.   He explores dialects of
            England about 600 A.D., explaining the change in vocabu-
            laries and mingling cultures.   He surveys other world's
            languages and comments on the possibilities of a world
            language.

698.   HISTORY OF THE INDO-EUROPEAN LANGUAGE FAMILY
        National Educational Television   Indiana University   1957
        30 min.   b/w   s/c/a
        From the Language and Linguistics Series
            Dr. Henry L. Smith surveys the history of the Indo-Euro-
            pean language family and how the various languages are
            related.

699.   HOW DO WE KNOW WHAT WE KNOW
        National Educational Television   Indiana University   1956
        30 min.   b/w
        From the Language in Action Series
            Using Korzybski's "structure differential" diagram, Dr.
            S. I. Hayakawa develops the idea that what we know of the
            objective world is a product of our nervous systems.
            Hence, an abstraction from sensory data is used to trace
            the successive levels of abstraction from the event and the
            object through the first or descriptive verbal level to high
            level verbal abstractions.

700. HOW TO SAY WHAT WE MEAN
      National Educational Television Indiana University 1956
      30 min. b/w C/a
      From the Language in Action Series
           Dr. S. I. Hayakawa explains that the "primary factor in
           communication is translation." Translation involves find-
           ing experiences to match other experiences, not merely
           finding words or symbols to match each other. What
           you mean must also mean something to the listener. "It
           is never enough to simply say what you mean."

701. HUMANITIES, THE: WHAT THEY ARE AND WHAT THEY DO
      Encyclopaedia Britannica 1959 25 min. b/w vt/vc
           Clifton Fadiman introduces the visual arts, music, litera-
           ture. The stress is on the potentialities of enjoyment in
           terms of understanding their symbolic language.

702. INTERVIEW
      Pintoff Brandon Learning Corporation of America 1960
      5 min. color C/a
           Using contemporary jargon, this animated film presents
           a satirical interview between a "square" announcer and a
           "hip" musician. The announcer becomes confused by the
           musician's terminology and the latter discouraged by the
           announcer's ignorance.

703. IS THERE COMMUNICATION WHEN YOU SPEAK?
      McGraw-Hill 1958 17 min. b/w s/c/a
      From the General Speech Series
           Using a University of Iowa speech class as a basis for
           example, the film shows the process of communicating
           ideas to an audience. The stress is on language and use
           and physical obstruction to effective transmission of com-
           munication. Also demonstrated are uses of visual aids,
           speaker's voice, articulation, language, movements. Audi-
           ence response is analyzed as well as the processing of
           an idea from one to another.

704. JUST WHAT IS GENERAL SEMANTICS
      National Educational Television Indiana University 1956
      30 min. b/w s/c/a
      From the Talking Sense Series
           The late Dr. Irving Lee, Northwestern University, defines
           semantics as formulated by Alfred Korzybski, indicating
           concern with factors in communication that lead to misun-
           derstanding, conflict and tension. He suggests that to avoid
           unrealistic reactions to a communication, we must distin-
           guish evaluations which make sense from those which do not.

705. KEYS TO THE MYSTERIES
      University of Southern California 27 min. b/w
      From the Written Word Series

Dr. Frank Baxter reveals the dramatic story of the decipherment of cuneiform and hieroglyphics.

706. KNOW WHAT I MEAN--A SERIES
Northern Virginia Educational Television (WNVT)
Sponsored by the International Society for General Semantics
1972 color
Instructor: Victor Kryston; See individual titles
  Six films study the nature of language, verbal and nonverbal meanings. Illustrated are differences in perception, culture, race, past experiences and uses of language which affect the thinking, beliefs, attitudes and ability to relate to each other. Titles are:
  1. Maps, Models and Metaphors
  2. To Be a Man (see "Process")
  3. Mind the Gap
  4. Louder than Words (see "Nonverbal")
  5. Change (see "Mass Media: Broadcasting")
  6. Speak to Me in Fortran (see "Information Systems")

707. LANGUAGE: THE SOCIAL ARBITER SERIES
San Francisco State College 1965 Each: 22-28 min.
See individual title listings
  Stuart Finley, in association with the Center for Applied Linguistics, presents films to assist with language problems of students who do not speak standard English.
  Titles are: 1. The Nature of Language; 2. Language Problems in the Schools; 3. Linguistics and Education; 4. Regional Variations; 5. Social Variations; 6. English Teaching Tomorrow; 7. Language and Integration.

708. LANGUAGE AND BEHAVIOR
National Educational Television (WETA) Indiana University
1967 30 min. b/w
From the English Fact and Fancy Series
  Mr. James Bostain examines the role of convention in language, outlining areas to which rationalized appeals are made to defend linguistic preferences.

709. LANGUAGE AND COMMUNICATION
Moody Institute of Science 1963 16 min. color s/c
From the Debt to the Past Series
  This film presents an analysis of the spoken and written heritage of the English language and its essential role in the communication of ideas. It stresses the significance of developing communication skills. It traces three states through which language has developed: pictographic, ideographic and phonetic.

710. LANGUAGE AND INTEGRATION
San Francisco State College 1965 29 min. color c/a
From Language: the Social Arbiter Series
  A biracial panel of specialists, including Dr. William

Stewart, Center for Applied Linguistics, discuss how language complicates and occasionally disturbs the process of integration. This film analyzes the quality and depth of research into both the linguistic and social nature of urban black dialects and the contributions to more effective techniques of teaching English.

711. LANGUAGE AND LINGUISTICS: AN INTRODUCTION
National Educational Television Indiana University 1957
30 min. b/w C/a
From the Language and Linguistics Series
Dr. Henry Lee Smith discusses language significance, focusing on common misconceptions concerning language. He details what language really is, explaining how the words we use and the way we use them affect how we think and perceive the world. Finally, Dr. Smith explores the relationship between language, paralanguage and kinesics.

712. LANGUAGE AND LINGUISTICS SERIES
National Educational Television Indiana University 1957
Features: Dr. Henry Lee Smith, Jr., Professor of Linguistics and English, University of Buffalo
The series presents an introduction to linguistics, covering the nature of language, its structure and development. It considers language as a basis for all human interaction. See individual program titles: 1. Language and Linguistics (An Introduction); 2. Language and Writing; 3. A Definition of Language; 4. The Linguistic Approach to Language Learning; 5. Sounds of Language; 6. Dialects; 7. Grammar I; 8. Grammar II; 9. History of the Indo-European Language Family; 10. History of the English Language; 11. The Alphabet; 12. Linguistics, Science and the Teaching of Reading; 13. Language and Meaning.

713. LANGUAGE AND MEANING
National Educational Television Indiana University 1957
30 min. b/w C/a
From the Language and Linguistics Series
Dr. H. L. Smith defines meaning purely from the linguistic point of view. Explaining the part structure plays in determining meaning from language, he continues an analysis of the relationship of paralanguage and kinesics to language and meaning. In conclusion, he explains how linguistic science can be applied to the analysis of the psychiatric interview.

714. LANGUAGE AND WRITING
National Educational Television Indiana University 1957
30 min. b/w C/a
From the Language and Linguistics Series
Dr. H. L. Smith commences with a definition of language,

analyzing the logic of language. He then examines misconceptions about language and writing, explaining that language "symbolizes experience and writing symbolizes language." Using vowels, intonation, distribution patterns, he shows the relationship between the written and the spoken language.

715. LANGUAGE BY GESTURE
University of Michigan 1965 30 min. b/w C kinescope
This film teaches the viewer how to learn a language quickly by a knowledge of structural linguistics. Dr. Kenneth Pike, University of Michigan, demonstrates how to identify parts of speech of a new language to determine some of its grammar.

716. LANGUAGE GAP
University of Michigan TV Center 29 min. s/c/a
Techniques are presented to work with children who have less-educated backgrounds. Developing language skills are explained, correlating spoken English and written English.

717. LANGUAGE PROBLEMS IN THE SCHOOLS
Center for Applied Linguistics 26 min. color
Some of the problems faced by communication teachers are explained in terms of the spoken and written standard English taught in the public schools.

718. LINES OF COMMUNICATION
United Nations Film McGraw-Hill 1963 b/w any age
Narrator: Alistair Cooke
From the International Zone Series
The viewer examines the spectacular progress of communications. The film traces the story of early language--message exchanges from ancient civilizations to contemporary satellites.

719. LINGUISTIC APPROACH TO LANGUAGE LEARNING
National Educational Television Indiana University 1957
30 min. b/w c/a
From the Language and Linguistics Series
Dr. Henry Lee Smith points out the difference between literary and spoken language. He examines the meaning of "correctness" and the significance of "rules" in grammar. Analyzing four types of stress used in speaking (primary, secondary, tertiary and weak), he discusses the effect of these factors upon the learning of a foreign language.

720. LINGUISTIC APPROACH TO THE TEACHING OF READING
National Educational Television Indiana University 1957
30 min. b/w c/a
From the Language and Linguistics Series

Dr. Henry Lee Smith discusses the use of the linguistic
approach as a primary means of improving reading ability.

721. LINGUISTICS AND EDUCATION
San Francisco State 1965 23 min. color
From Language: The Social Arbiter Series
   Laymen and some educators present certain views about
   language which limit their effectiveness in teaching chil-
   dren standard English.

722. MAKING LANGUAGE APPROPRIATE AND EFFECTIVE
University of Iowa 1959 30 min. b/w
   This film states that communication is more effective with
   the use of language that has greater clarity, simplicity,
   economy and variety. The purpose of communication is
   to adapt "to the level of language."

723. MAPS AND TERRITORIES
National Educational Television Indiana University 1956
30 min. b/w
From the Language in Action Series
   Dr. S. I. Hayakawa points out statements that have some
   objective and verifiable meaning. Calling them "maps,"
   he suggests they, in fact, give us directions to "territories" of human experience. The problem, however, is
   that "maps" can be manipulated independently of "territories" represented. "It is further possible to make
   verbal maps representing no actual territories."

724. MAPS, MODELS AND METAPHORES
Northern Virginia Educational Television (WNVT) 1972
16 min. color
From Know What I Mean Series: #1
   Instructor Victor Kryston unfolds the concept basic to this
   series: language is a shorthand for shared experiences
   of any culture. It "provides users maps, metaphors and
   models" for living. However, inasmuch as language is a
   "map" and not the territory, it merely represents a model, not the experience.

725. MODERN TECHNIQUES IN LANGUAGE TEACHING
Teaching Film Custodians 32 min. b/w c/a
   This film presents a demonstration of classes of three
   age groups, with grammatical organization and lexicon of
   a language emphasized.

726. NATURE OF LANGUAGE AND HOW IT IS LEARNED, THE
Teaching Film Custodians 1961 30 min. b/w s/C/a
   This film explores the nature of language and how it is
   learned. Examples of the "living language" are drawn
   from reservoirs of world languages. Illustrations reveal
   how differently languages function in respective sound systems, grammatical organization and lexical developments.

Speech language is contrasted with written language.

727.   ON THE DIFFERENCE BETWEEN WORDS AND THINGS
       National Educational Television   Indiana University   1956
       30 min.   b/w
       From the Talking Sense Series
             The late Dr. Irving Lee explains the results of forgetting
             that words only point to things.   He stresses that it is
             easy to distort descriptions of reality and that exaggera-
             tion tendencies frequently ignore the current status of a
             person or thing.   He suggests use of the dimension of
             time and greater attention to reality while talking.

728.   ORGANIZATION OF LANGUAGE, THE
       Teaching Film Custodians   1961   31 min.   b/w   C
             This film demonstrates that language is learned by oral
             experience and that patterns of organization differ from
             language to language.   Language organization is based es-
             sentially on customs and conventions characteristic of
             each language.

729.   PICTOGRAPHS
       University of Southern California   10 min.   color
             Highlighted is the development of man's early efforts at
             written communication through picture writing and idea
             signs.

730.   PRINCIPLES AND METHODS OF TEACHING A SECOND LAN-
       GUAGE, THE
       Teaching Film Custodians   1961   b/w
       Each unit has three reels
       See individual title listings
             Sponsored by the Center of Applied Linguistics of the
             Modern Language Association, this series consists of five
             major subjects.   The films explain and demonstrate prin-
             ciples of modern language teaching and show how these
             principles of modern languages are applied to teaching
             procedures.   Presenting illustrations from many lan-
             guages, these films are multilingual in approach and use.
             The titles are: 1. The Nature of Language and How It
             Is Learned;   2. Sounds of Language;   3. Organization of
             Language;   4. Words and Their Meanings;   5. Modern
             Techniques in Language Teaching.

731.   PROBLEM OF MEANING, THE
       National Educational Television   Indiana University   1967
       30 min.   b/w   c/a
       From the English Fact and Fancy Series
             Mr. James Bostain analyzes the obstacles caused by a
             human nervous system filled with associations which serve
             as obstacles between talking and things to be discussed.
             Efficient operation in a language depends on becoming
             aware of the language's area of specificity.

732.   READING PROCESS: LANGUAGE CONCEPTS
        University of California 1969 16 min. color c/a
            This film illustrates teaching methods required for learn-
            ing fundamental language concepts: words that refer to
            objects, feelings and other qualities.

733.   REGIONAL VARIATIONS
        San Francisco State 1965 28 min. color
            The major regional dialects in the United States are dis-
            cussed by Frederic Cassidy, University of Wisconsin, and
            A. Hood Roberts, Center for Applied Linguistics.

734.   SAY WHAT YOU MEAN
        McGraw-Hill 1958 20 min. b/w
        From the Communications Series (General Speech)
            This film explains language as man's main communication
            instrument. It illustrates how to choose language that
            states an idea clearly, is appropriate and colorful.

735.   SCIENTISTS AND ADVOCATES
        National Educational Television (WETA) Indiana University
        1967 30 min. b/w c/a
        From the English Fact and Fancy Series
            Mr. James Bostain states that students of human affairs
            are defined as "either scientists or advocates." Con-
            trasts are made of different kinds of statements produced
            by each. He distinguishes between descriptive grammar
            (what people do) and prescriptive grammar (what people
            ought to do).

736.   SEARCH FOR A "UNIVERSAL GRAMMAR," THE
        National Educational Television (WETA) Indiana University
        1967 30 min. b/w c/a
        From the English Fact and Fancy Series
            Mr. James Bostain, linguist, explains that grammar is a
            "handmaiden to logic." He suggests that grammar--
            which is conventional--and logic are fundamentally incom-
            patible. He explores the continued search for a univer-
            sal language.

737.   SEMANTICS OF THE POPULAR SONG, THE
        National Educational Television Indiana University 1956
        30 min. b/w s/c/a
            Dr. S. I. Hayakawa examines the unrealistic dream life
            described in popular music and contrasts it with the
            "real" world of the blues, citing implications of each.
            Clancy Hays sings and plays the banjo for background and
            demonstrations.

738.   SIGN AND SYMBOL
        University of Southern California University of Hawaii
        27 min. b/w
            Dr. Frank Baxter shows how very elaborate messages
            were conveyed earlier by simple signs.

739. SOCIAL VARIATIONS
      San Francisco State College 1965 29 min. color c
      From Language: The Social Arbiter Series
            Dr. Charles A. Ferguson discusses ways that social vari-
            ations among people are revealed in their speech patterns.
            Speech diversity is discussed with representatives from
            creoles of the Caribbean to "hipsters."

740. SOUND OF A WORD
      University of Utah 1967 25 min. color c
            In a world where effective communication is essential,
            this film focuses on problems faced by people with speech
            defects. It dramatizes examples of the deleterious ef-
            fects parents can have on their child while they are
            teaching him to communicate.

741. SOUNDS OF LANGUAGE, THE
      National Educational Television Teaching Film Custodians
      1957 30 min. b/w C
      From the Language and Linguistics Series
            Dr. Henry L. Smith discusses a methodology of linguis-
            tic analysis and the classification of significant language
            sounds. He explores phonemics, phonetics and the sci-
            ence of speech sounds. He illustrates and demonstrates
            the organization of speech.

742. STORY OF COMMUNICATIONS, THE
      Encyclopaedia Britannica Educational 1947 15 min. color
      b/w vt/vc s/c/a
      From Our Land and People Series
            Produced in the late nineteen forties, this film corre-
            lates the transmission of thought and word with the condi-
            tions of the space age at that time. The focus is on the
            early stages of communication: writing and printing.

743. STRANGE CASE OF THE ENGLISH LANGUAGE (PART I)
      Bailey Film Associates CBS News 1968 48 min.
      b/w & color s/C/a
            This film examines idiosyncrasies of the English lan-
            guage as it is spoken and written today. Interviews with
            various language experts are featured as well as com-
            ments by CBS' Harry Reasoner about John F. Kennedy,
            Everett Dirksen, Billy Graham, many others. The se-
            quences help illustrate stylistic quirks and the overuse of
            pet phrases.

744. STRANGE CASE OF THE ENGLISH LANGUAGE (PART II)
      Bailey Film Associates CBS News 1968 23 min.
      b/w & color s/C/a
            Part II treats singular difficulties and advantages of Eng-
            lish as compared with other languages. A perspective
            gives the viewer the significance or lack of significance
            of certain grammatical "rules." The origin of words

and current fad phrases are also discussed.

745. STRUCTURE AND CONTENT
      National Educational Television (WETA) Indiana University
      1967 30 min. b/w c
      From the English Fact and Fancy Series
            Mr. James Bostain outlines two primary classes of
            grammatical entities: the dictionary unit and sign units.
            Demonstrating that sign units are not logical, but rather
            conventional, he investigates how sign changes structure
            and meaning.

746. SYMBOLS OF EXPRESSION
      Pennsylvania State University 1952 16 min. b/w silent
            Individual drawings--"doodlings"--are explained as "key
            symbols" of personality, more than mere signatures or
            written productions.

747. TALKING AND WRITING (PARTS I AND II)
      National Educational Television (WETA) Indiana University
      1967 30 min. each b/w c
      From the English Fact and Fancy Series
            Part I: Mr. James Bostain lectures on talking and writ-
            ing, examining various systems of expression used. He
            outlines talking and writing as parallel systems with a
            complex and partial relationship. Part II: The continua-
            tion considers the reform of our writing system to fit a
            multiplicity of speech systems. It examines ways in
            which speech and writing differ.

748. TALKING OURSELVES INTO TROUBLE
      National Educational Television (KQED) Indiana University
      1956 30 min. b/w c/a
      From the Language in Action Series
            Dr. S. I. Hayakawa introduces the subject of general
            semantics, laying groundwork for the remainder of this
            series. He suggests the inherent dangers in the use of
            the language tool and explains a cause of communication
            breakdown: the one-value and two-value processes.

749. TALKING SENSE SERIES
      National Educational Television Indiana University 1955
      Each: 30 min. b/w s/c/a
      See individual title listings
            The late Dr. Irving Lee, San Francisco State, lectures
            on the following subjects:
            1. Do You Know How to Make a Statement of Fact?
            2. Just What Is General Semantics?
            3. The Man Who Knows It All
            4. On the Difference Between Words and Things
            5. What Is a Good Observer?
            6. Why Do People Misunderstand Each Other?

750.   TO BE A MAN
       Northern Virginia Educational Television (WNVT) 1972
       18 min. color
       From Know What I Mean Series: #2
           Instructor Victor Kryston shows how language and our
           earliest experiences shape attitudes and how these atti-
           tudes differ with different cultures. Viewers are encour-
           aged to test their own assumptions.

751.   WAR ON GOBBLEDYGOOK
       OFM Productions 35 min. color
           Professor Edward Fischer, Notre Dame, brings the cam-
           era into his communication classroom for an analysis of
           the prevalence of "gobbledygook"--or "strangled communi-
           cation in the modern world." Illustrations are shown
           from government documents, management reports and in-
           surance policies.

752.   WE USE WORD POWER
       Churchill 1962 9 min. color s/c
           A satirical approach shows how words change the impact
           of the visual image. Parts of the film are done in four
           different narration styles: travelogue, industrial film,
           educational films and the original.

753.   WHAT ARE THE ENGLISH LANGUAGES?
       National Educational Television (WETA) Indiana University
       1967 30 min. b/w c
       From the English Fact and Fancy Series
           Dr. James Bostain examines the teaching of the diver-
           sity of linguistic form. He suggests that English is com-
           prised of a variety of dialects and fantasizes about possi-
           ble ways English might be spoken and/or written.

754.   WHAT HOLDS PEOPLE TOGETHER?
       National Educational Television (KQED) Indiana University
       1956 30 min. b/w C/a
       From the Language in Action Series
           Dr. S. I. Hayakawa proposes that man's main means of
           survival is communication. He discusses evolution of
           human societies through stages of organization--each stage
           based on the need to communicate.

755.   WHAT IS LANGUAGE?
       National Educational Television Indiana University 1956
       30 min. b/w C/a
       From the Language in Action Series
           Dr. S. I. Hayakawa explains that language is a series of
           self-contained systems, with symbols having different
           meanings within different systems.

756.   WHERE IS THE MEANING?
       National Educational Television Indiana University 1956

30 min. b/w c
From the Language in Action Series
   Dr. S. I. Hayakawa states that, in reality, meaning is
   in the nervous systems of both listener and speaker.
   He lists four fundamental conditions of meaningfulness:
   words which are physically verifiable by observation,
   words within the rules of language, within a particular
   society, and within its institutions.

757. WHY DO PEOPLE MISUNDERSTAND EACH OTHER?
      National Educational Television Indiana University 1955
      30 min. b/w c
      From the Talking Sense Series
         The late Dr. Irving Lee analyzes the effort of both lis-
         tener and speaker to give meaning to words. He investi-
         gates ignorance, inflection and voice control, the trans-
         mission of ideas, problems related to general semantics
         as well as inferences. Repeated is his contention that
         "words in themselves contain no meaning."

758. WORD GAME, THE
      Teleketics 1971 60-second spot announcement color
         This is a visual attempt to translate in a word game the
         word "God" into a "meaningful idea." When used at a
         cocktail party, the word "God" elicits no standard re-
         sponse.

759. WORDS AND THEIR MEANINGS
      Teaching Film Custodians 1962 32 min. b/w s/c/a
      From the Principles and Methods of Teaching a Second Lan-
      guage Series
         This film discusses how the meaning of words changes
         with usage. It explains the deficiencies of word-for-
         word translation. A French class demonstration is
         shown, explaining how words are taught in meaningful
         contexts and how the ranges of meanings are appropri-
         ately developed.

760. WORDS THAT DON'T INFORM
      National Educational Television (KQED) Indiana University
      1956 30 min. b/w c
      From the Language in Action Series
         Dr. S. I. Hayakawa discusses use of pre-symbolic lan-
         guage, stating that only a small portion of our life's ut-
         terances are purely informative. This film is a fuller
         rendition of a well-known Hayakawa essay, "Snarl Words
         and Purr Words."

761. WRITTEN WORD, THE--A SERIES
      University of Southern California Each: 27 min.
         Fifteen films with Dr. Frank Baxter of the University of
         Southern California cover the history of the development
         of language and words and the processes of forming and

printing the written word. Pertinent series films include:
1. Sign and Symbol; 3. Keys to the Mysteries; 4. Along
the Nile; 5. ABC's. [2. not pertinent. See individual listings.]

LEARNING THEORY

762. ASPECTS OF BEHAVIOR
      CRM Films Time-Life 1971 31 min. color vt/vc s/c/a
      From the Psychology Today Series
          An overview of various fields of contemporary psychology
          emphasizes four approaches: social, physiological, ab-
          normal and cultural. Through interviews with noted psy-
          chologists and by witnessing their experiments, the viewer
          is introduced to significant aspects of these four ap-
          proaches. Ethical issues are considered as are elements
          of prejudice and attitude change. Participating psycholo-
          gists are: John Darley, Bibb Latane (Social Psychology);
          J. Anthony Deutsch (Physiology); Silvano Arletti, Arnold
          Friedhoff, Jr., J. Silverman and the late Abraham Mas-
          low (Cultural Psychology).

763. B. F. SKINNER AND BEHAVIOR CHANGE
      University of California 1975 42 min. color
          B. F. Skinner is shown in a variety of situations--work-
          ing in the laboratory, addressing students, talking with
          colleagues, reviewing important contributions.

764. B. F. SKINNER FILM SERIES, THE
      Learning Corporation of America Each film: 20 min.
      color s/c/a
      See individual title listings
          This three-film series consists of "A Conversation with
          B. F. Skinner," "Token Economy: Behaviorism Applied,"
          and "Business, Behaviorism and the Bottom Line."

765. BEHAVIOR MODIFICATION IN THE CLASSROOM
      University of California 1970 24 min. color c/a
          Teachers, psychologists and educational specialists learn
          methods of operant conditioning and modeling procedures
          for classroom application. Contrasts are made of be-
          havior before and after the introduction of behavior modi-
          fication techniques.

766. BEHAVIOR THEORY IN PRACTICE (PARTS I, II, III, IV)
      Appleton-Century-Crofts 1965 Each segment: 18 min.
      b/w and color C/a
          Psychologist B. F. Skinner analyzes methods psycholo-
          gists use to explore behavior science. He examines con-
          ditioning behavior, reinforcement, avoidance, motivation,
          sequences.

767.   BEHAVIORISM (BEYOND, BEYOND)
       CRM Films   1972   20 min.   color   c/a
       From the Psychology Today Series
            This film illustrates the study of the origins of behavior
            analysis.   An interview with Dr. B. F. Skinner concerns
            the meaning and implications of his summary work on
            behavior modification.

768.   BEHAVIORISM (TOKEN ECONOMY)
       CRM Films   1972   20 min.   color   c/a
       From the Psychology Today Series
            Dr. B. F. Skinner's educational theory applications are
            examined in this film.   Behavioral modification tech-
            niques are studied at a specific mental health facility.
            The film commences with Dr. Skinner's classical ex-
            amples and concludes with behavioral therapy at the Ill-
            nois Department of Mental Health facility.

769.   BRAIN AND BEHAVIOR
       National Educational Television   Indiana University   1963
       30 min.   b/w   s/c
       From the Focus on Behavior Series
            Dr. Donald B. Lindsey, UCLA, has done extensive re-
            search on the complex mechanisms of the brain which
            underlie human and animal behavior.   Historical develop-
            ment of brain concepts is traced.

770.   CASE METHOD OF INSTRUCTION (PARTS I, II, III)
       United States Army   National Audiovisual Center   1959
       Segments: from 19 min. to 23 min. each b/w
            Principles, application and value of method, role of the
            instructor and case issues are discussed.   Role-playing
            techniques are examined.   Discussion process maximizes
            theories.

771.   CAUSALITY
       New York University   1971   23 min.   b/w
            This film focuses on early cognitive development, particu-
            larly the growth of abilities to comprehend cause and ef-
            fect relationships.

772.   COGNITION
       Harper   1972   30 min.   color   c/a
            Jerome Kagan and H. Gardner of Harvard University ex-
            plain how thought processes--cognition--improve with age.
            The development of perception, memory, evaluation and
            reasoning change.   The film examines these changes,
            most particularly Piaget's description of the major stages
            of intelligence (sensory motor, pre-operational, concrete-
            operational, formal).

773. CONDITIONED REFLEXES
      Crowell, Collier, Macmillan 19 min. b/w
          This film reviews the most famous experiments of Ivan
          Pavlov. It explains behavior as a compound of instinct
          and conditioning and is illustrated with some of physiol-
          ogist Pavlov's experiments with reflexes.

774. CONFLICT
      McGraw-Hill 1956 18 min. b/w s/c/a
      From the Psychology Series
          Four basic types of conflict are dramatized from an an-
          alysis of student situations. The same types of conflict
          are also induced in rats in laboratory-controlled environ-
          ments.

775. CONTROLLING BEHAVIOR THROUGH REINFORCEMENT
      McGraw-Hill 1956 16 min. b/w C/a
      From the Psychology Series
          Psychologist Dr. B. F. Skinner demonstrates how a vary-
          ing reinforcement schedule affects the behavior of pigeons.
          The outcome of tests of similar experiments made in
          classrooms is compared. Explaining that this schedule
          produces "persistent" behavior, he affirms that it is dif-
          ficult to extinguish.

776. CONVERSATION WITH B. F. SKINNER, A
      CRM Films 1972 20 min. color vt/vc s/c/a
      From the B. F. Skinner Film Series
          Dr. B. F. Skinner discusses the meaning and implica-
          tions of his work, Beyond Freedom and Dignity. He an-
          swers some of his most persistent critics, detailing
          some of his concepts for the origin of behaviorism.

777. DEVELOPMENT
      CRM Films 1972 32 min. color vt/vc s/c/a
      From the Psychology Today Series
          This film examines the stages of growth, introducing con-
          cepts of human psychological development. It also ex-
          amines the investigation of the phenomena--their milieus,
          methods, findings. Focus is on a child's cognitive de-
          velopment, as well as on the acquisition of particular
          speech.

778. DISCUSSION WITH DR. CARL G. JUNG
      Brandon Ideal 32 min. b/w
          In this film, Dr. Jung explores his relationship with
          Freud and his differences with Freudian theory, his views
          of the conscious, his introversion-extroversion theories,
          his concept of archetypes and reactions to his contempo-
          raries.

779. DISCUSSION WITH DR. GARDNER MURPHY (PARTS I, II)
      Brandon Ideal Each segment: 50 min. b/w

Dr. Murphy presents his views on motivation, learning, perception, ego autonomy and self-determination in Part I. Part II examines extrasensory perception and uniqueness of personality.

780. DISCUSSION WITH DR. GORDON ALLPORT (PARTS I, II)
Brandon Ideal Each segment: 50 min. b/w
Dr. Allport reviews his relationship with Sigmund Freud and his own basic contributions to human analysis, including trait-theory and the functional autonomy of motives.

781. DISCUSSION WITH DR. HENRY MURRAY (PARTS I, II)
Brandon Ideal Each segment: 50 min. b/w
Dr. Murray shares his impressions of Drs. Freud and Jung and discusses the thematic aperception test, personology, molar versus molecular personality.

782. DIALOGUES: DR. J. B. RHINE DISCUSSES ESP (PARTS I, II)
Crowell, Collier, Macmillan 1969 Each segment: 45 min. color c
In Part I, Dr. Rhine discusses definitions of clairvoyance, PSI, telepathy. Part II analyzes current research in the field, whether there is a psychic personality and some of Dr. Rhine's most significant contributions in this area.

783. DIALOGUES: DR. JEAN PIAGET (PARTS I, II)
Crowell, Collier, Macmillan 1970 Each segment: 40 min. color c
In Part I, Dr. Piaget and his associate, Dr. Barbel Inhelder, are interviewed about the important stages of cognitive development that characterize Piaget's contribution to the study of child development. Part II examines Piaget's contact with Freud and reactions to criticims or misuses of Piaget's theories.

784. EDUCATIONAL GAMING
University of California 1970 59 min. b/w kinescope
A television discussion with two educational gaming experts examines the ramifications of such games for learning and the change this portends in teacher-student relationships.

785. ESP: THE HUMAN "X" FACTOR
Indiana University 1966 30 min. b/w
Dr. J. B. Rhine is interviewed at the Duke University Parapsychology Laboratory, where he discusses forty years of research on ESP. Experiments reviewed include: clairvoyance, psychokinesis, precognition, psychic abilities.

130

Communications

786. FILM DIALOGUE WITH ARTHUR MILLER (PARTS I, II)
Association Films 1967 Each segment: 50 min.
Arthur Miller discusses the concept of motivation and the
relationship of his life to his work, the impact on the
audience and attitudes toward psychological theories and
methods.

787. FREDERICK PERLS AND GESTALT PSYCHOLOGY
Psychology Films 2 films: Pt. I: 39 min.; Pt. II: 36
min. b/w c/a
These films focus on behavioral psychology: 1. Cliché
Behavior, Role Playing and Manipulation; 2. Demonstra-
tion of Actual Techniques of Gestalt Psychology.

788. FREUD: THE HIDDEN NATURE OF MAN
Learning Corporation of America 1969 29 min. color
Award: Canadian Film Festival
This film reveals Freud's "radical" concept of the human
personality--with the confused ego torn between the id and
the superego.

789. HUMAN BRAIN, THE
Encyclopaedia Britannica 1954 11 min. b/w vt/vc s/c
The brain development of several animals and men is in-
vestigated, with analysis of perception, integration responses in critical situations.

790. HUMANISTIC REVOLUTION, THE: PIONEERS IN PERSPEC-
TIVE
CRM Films 1971 32 min. b/w c
From the Psychology Today Series
The "new" revolutionists in psychology are featured:
Carl Rogers, Gardner Murphy, Rollo May, Paul Tillich,
Fred Perls, Viktor Frankl, Alan Watts, and the future
of self-actualization and humanistic psychology.

791. INTERVIEW WITH DR. B. F. SKINNER (PART I)
National Science Foundation Crowell, Collier, Macmillan
1966 50 min. b/w c
From the Psychology of Personality Series
Part I explores Dr. Skinner's evaluation of the Freudian
theory, views on motivation, operant conditioning, sched-
ules of reinforcement, punishment and teaching machines.

792. INTERVIEW WITH DR. B. F. SKINNER (PART II)
National Science Foundation Crowell, Collier, Macmillan
1966 50 min. b/w c
From the Psychology of Personality Series
Part II reviews the problems of creating a society based
on positive rather than negative control. Evaluating the
American educational system, he discusses the applica-
tion of operant conditioning to society-at-large.

793. INTERVIEW WITH DR. ERNEST R. HILGARD (PARTS I, II)
      Macmillan 27 min. each b/w
           Part I examines a brief history of Dr. Hilgard's work on
           learning theory. Part II reviews his involvement with
           hypnosis and the misconceptions associated with it.

794. INTERVIEW WITH DR. HANS EYSENCK
      Macmillan 32 min. color
           Dr. Eysenck, professor of psychology at the Institute of
           Psychiatry, London, discusses class criticisms of Freud-
           ian theory and psychoanalysis, explains behavior therapy
           and discusses its widespread use in treatment.

795. INTERVIEW WITH DR. NEVITT SANFORD (PARTS I, II)
      Macmillan   Pt. I: 31 min. Pt. II: 26 min. b/w
           In Part I, Dr. Sanford discusses the history of research
           on learning, the authoritarian personality and psychoanaly-
           sis. Part II examines the interdisciplinary attack on sig-
           nificant social problems.

796. JUNG SPEAKS OF FREUD
      Pennsylvania State University 1957 29 min. b/w
           Dr. Carl Jung tells of the origin of his type of psycho-
           therapy, the influence of Freud and the relationship to
           current learning theory.

797. KOESTLER ON CREATIVITY
      Time-Life 1971 40 min. color vt/vc s/c/a
           Writer Arthur Koestler discusses his theories concerning
           the processes underlying creativity and how creativity af-
           fects learning and our daily thoughts.

798. LEARNING
      CRM Films 1972 31 min. color vt/vc s/c/a
      Award: CINE Golden Eagle Award
           "The most comprehensive film available on learning," this
           film includes illustrations of theories from Dr. B. F.
           Skinner to Lewis Lipsitt and David McClelland. The focus
           is on laboratory demonstrations of the ways in which hu-
           mans and animals react to various stimuli.

799. LEARNING ABOUT LEARNING
      National Educational Television Indiana University 1963
      29 min. b/w s/C/a
      From the Focus on Behavior Series
           Different strategies are explored in terms of the develop-
           ment of theoretical concepts about man's ability to learn.
           The film details the work of Dr. Howard Kendler of New
           York University, Dr. Tracy Kendler of Barnard College,
           Dr. Kenneth Spence of Iowa State University, Dr. Harry
           Harlow of the University of Wisconsin, and Dr. B. F.
           Skinner of Harvard.

800. LEARNING AND BEHAVIOR: THE TEACHING MACHINE
      CBS Carousel National Institute of Health 1959 26 min.
      b/w C/a
      From the Conquest Series
            Drs. B. F. Skinner and R. J. Hernstein "measure" learn-
            ing by conditioning pigeons at Harvard University Psychol-
            ogy Laboratory. The film includes some expositions of
            the theory of the teaching machines, suggesting that all
            learning is dependent upon reward as a means of rein-
            forcement of the learned response.

801. LEARNING DISCRIMINATION AND SKILLS
      McGraw-Hill 1956 10 min. b/w C/a
      From the Psychology Series
            This film illustrates that fundamental principles of stimu-
            lus discrimination and response differentiation are essen-
            tially the same in any organism. It details how humans
            and animals can learn skills gradually through various
            reinforcements.

802. PIAGET'S DEVELOPMENT THEORY (PARTS I, II, III)
      University of California 1967-72 17-27 min. color
            This filmed series examines stages of the development of
            learning: Part I, "Conservation"; Part II, "Classifica-
            tion"; Part III, "Formal Thought."

803. PRAGMATIC THEORY
      University of Utah 1966 27 min. b/w C/a
      From the Introduction to Philosophy Series
            This film discusses the metaphysical implications of prag-
            matic learning. As exemplified in the thoughts of Charles
            Peirce and John Dewey, it regards the learning process
            as an intelligent basis of investigation and research.

804. PRAGMATISM
      University of Utah 1966 27 min. b/w C/a
      From the Introduction to Philosophy Series
            This film presents philosophical theories, with major at-
            tention given to the John Dewey theory of pragmatism.
            Examined is its influence upon education and learning.

805. PRINCIPLES OF LEARNING, THE
      United States Army National Audiovisual Center 23 min.
      b/w
            The viewer learns specific principles of learning: motiva-
            tion, objective doing, realism, background, appreciation
            and the importance of understanding.

806. PSYCHICS, SAINTS AND SCIENTISTS
      Modern Talking Picture Service 1972 33 min. color
            Narrated by Dr. Thelma Moss of UCLA's Institute of
            Neuropsychiatry, this film explores various phases of psy-
            chic research: telepathy, mind over matter and biofeed-
            back.

807. PSYCHOLOGY SERIES
National Educational Television CRM Films 1963- color C
See individual title listings
The series includes: 1. The Brain and Behavior; 2.
Common Fallacies about Group Differences; 3. Conflict;
4. Controlling Behavior through Reinforcement; 5. Devel-
opment of Individual Differences; 6. Learning Discrimi-
nation and Skills; 7. Perception; 8. Reinforcement in
Learning and Extinction.

808. REINFORCEMENT IN LEARNING AND EXTINCTION
McGraw-Hill 1956 8 min. b/w c/a
From the Psychology Series
Demonstrations are of reinforced behavior; non-rein-
forced behavior is "extinguished." Written and produced
in collaboration with the department of psychology at Yale
and Harvard.

809. SEARCH AND RESEARCH: PSYCHOLOGY IN PERSPECTIVE
Psychological Films 30 min. b/w
An overview film in the field of psychology, the focus is
on the relationships between three forces of learning:
experimental, psychoanalytic and existential or humanistic.

810. SPLIT BRAIN
Indiana University 1967 13 min. b/w
Dr. R. W. Sperry of Cal. Tech "splits" the brain hem-
ispheres to test the independence of each half of the
brain. The theory relates to the independence of each
half, with its own memory and knowledge systems.

811. STAGES OF INSTRUCTION (PARTS I, II, III)
United States Army National Audiovisual Center 1956
Pt. I: 10 min.; Pt. II: 12 min.; Pt. III: 12 min. b/w
The importance of doing, of measuring effectiveness, of
selecting and organizing, of presentations are all related
to different levels of learning instruction. The application, preparation, presentation are all examined.

LISTENING

812. ARE YOU LISTENING?
Strauss Perennial 1966 12 min. b/w C/a
This film explores five major areas of non-listening.
For a more effective communication program, it focuses
on the diagnosis of the causes. Its aim is to provide a
firm basis for discussing non-listening effects, and to encourage people to judge the significance of effective listening.

813.   CAN I TALK TO YOU DAD?
        Teleketics 1972 60-second spot announcement color s/c
        Meant to stimulate the awareness of others of communi-
        cation, this film stresses listening as the essence of
        communication. A teenage boy goes to extremes to jolt
        his father into listening. Only when it is "too late" does
        the father realize he has withheld something vital from
        their relationship.

814.   EFFECTIVE LISTENING
        McGraw-Hill Centron 1959 15 min. b/w s/c/a
        From the Speech Series
        This film stresses the importance of effective listening
        in the communication process. It is a broad analysis of
        major obstacles to effective listening, with suggestions as
        to how individuals can overcome them.

815.   LISTEN, PLEASE
        Coronet 1951 14 min. b/w C/a
        Listening games are demonstrated by children playing:
        how to concentrate on sounds and how to visualize sounds.

816.   LISTENING
        Roundtable 14 min. color
        This film is a case study which examines a typical day of
        a middle manager who does not listen. Exposed are the
        problems and conflicts of stressful situations as a result
        of the non-listening habits.

817.   LISTENING: THE INPUT PART OF COMMUNICATION
        Rank Production Roundtable 1972 14 min. color
        Dramatized in this film are poor listening habits and how
        to correct them. "Input" communication is offered as
        the panacea to open the doors that block solutions.

818.   LISTENING SKILLS: AN INTRODUCTION
        Coronet 1965 11 min. b/w and color s/c
        Images presented suggest a stream of consciousness to il-
        lustrate vividly what may be going through one's mind
        with what "should" be going through one's mind while lis-
        tening.

819.   MAKING YOURSELF UNDERSTOOD
        Encyclopaedia Britannica 1963 14 min. b/w vt/vc s/c/a
        Collaborator: Cyril O. Houle, University of Chicago.
        With the stress on the achievement of listening for more
        effective communication, this film examines basic process
        factors involved. It analyzes the significance of recogniz-
        ing these elements in both criticism and evaluation. Five
        communication elements are suggested: who, what, to
        whom, how and with what effect.

820. MESSAGE TO NO ONE, A
Champion Oklahoma State 1960 25 min. color s/c/a
This film emphasizes the necessity of listening to others
and of being conscious of one's surroundings. Dramatized are the consequences of not listening in a family
setting.

821. MOM, WHY WON'T YOU LISTEN?
Churchill 1971 13 min. color s/a
Using encounter-group and role-playing techniques to deal
with the problem, this film discusses the importance of
timing and approach.

822. OBSTRUCTIONS TO CRITICAL LISTENING AND READING
University of Iowa 1959 30 min. b/w C
This film explores how individuals can become more analytical and perceptive in their reception of communication. It suggests that undue respect is given the printed
word and that listening obstructions must be eliminated.

823. TASK OF THE LISTENER, THE
National Educational Television Indiana University 1956
30 min. b/w c/a
The self-concept theory is explored and the necessity for
training oneself to be a non-evaluative listener in a controversial discussion/dialogue is emphasized. By developing the availability of "non-evaluation," listening communication and problem-solving can become simplified.

824. YOUR AUDIENCE, BLESS 'EM
U. S. Department of Agriculture National Audiovisual Center
1 min. color any age
This brief film examines one aspect of audience communication. In graphic fashion it introduces some concerns
and challenges of the conventional listening audience.

MASS MEDIA

Advertising

825. AD-LAND REVISITED
National Educational Television Indiana University 1961
29 min. b/w s/c/a
An analysis film shows advertising's twentieth-century du-
al function, as mirror and molder of our culture. Mon-
tages and special effects illustrate message fluencies.
Strategies examined are familiar slogans, jingles, testi-
monials and media endorsements.

826. ADVERTISING
      Business Education Films   27 min.   b/w s/c/a
            This film explains the role of advertising in our econo-
            my, our daily lives.   Shown are methods to stimulate
            production, create jobs and demand for new products.

827. ADVERTISING QUESTION, THE
      Business Education Films   National Audiovisual Center   1967
      14 min.   color
            The values and techniques of advertising are discussed
            and some business examples are shown to emphasize per-
            tinent points.   The film is designed to correct some of
            the misconceptions toward advertising.

828. ADVERTISING '66
      American Oil   1965   38 min.   color
            The American Oil Company's 1966 advertising program
            is explained.   The different phases include several spe-
            cific messages intended for various media.   An analysis
            of advertising influence is incorporated in the film.

829. AUTHENTIC INTERVIEW
      University of California   1974   9 min.   b/w
            An ad agency making a car commercial decided to depict
            an "authentic" interview.   The plan was to allow an actu-
            al new car owner to speak candidly.   The result is an
            "exposé of American values and the absurdity of the
            American Dream."

830. BEHIND THE TYPE
      Pennsylvania Newspaper Publishing Association   1957   15 min.
      b/w s/a
            This film explores the editorial, advertising, broadcast-
            ing, public relations opportunities, stressing the need for
            advanced research.

831. BRAND NAMES AND LABELING GAMES
      Benchmark   1973   9 min.   color
            Commentator and satirist demonstrate that expensive
            brand-name products are identical to less-expensive,
            less-advertised products.

832. CALENDAR GAME, THE
      Business Education Films   14 min.   color
            The need for advertising planning and budgeting is empha-
            sized.   Explained are methods of choosing media and di-
            rect advertising and plans for specific promotions.

833. COMMERCIAL: ANXIETY IN COMMERCIALS
      San Francisco State   1968   13 min.   color s/c/a
            Commercials that appeal to human anxieties, agitate
            them and exploit them are illustrated.   A class adver-
            tising technique, many symbols of life in the late sixties
            are exhibited.

834.   COMMERCIAL: KIDDIE COMMERCIALS
       San Francisco State   1968   13 min.   color   s/c/a
           Illustrated are the perennial sales messages to/for chil-
           dren.   Demonstrated primarily for the Saturday morning
           audience, they are designed to "persuade mothers to buy
           prescribed products advertised."

835.   COMMERCIAL: MONEY COMMERCIALS
       San Francisco State   1968   13 min.   color   s/c/a
           The thrust of these messages is that Americans all de-
           sire happiness and equate happiness with the acquisition
           and/or saving of money.   Hucksters suggest ways to use
           the money "saved."

836.   COMMERCIALS: MARLBORO TV COMMERCIALS
       San Francisco State   1968   5 min.   color   s/c/a
           Message sellers present different views of ranching today
           in "Marlboro Country."   These commercials relate the
           product to the American preoccupation with the out-of-
           doors, using techniques that combine psychology, journal-
           ism and broadcasting strategies.

837.   COMMERCIALS, ASSORTED, #1
       San Francisco State   1968   13 min.   color   s/c/a
           This visual collage of commercials exposes the viewer to
           an unending sequence of advertising messages.   Via these
           television spot announcements media students can analyze
           products that: clear skin blemishes, sell the United
           States Navy, and market cigarettes, Swedish automobiles
           and soft drinks.

838.   COMMERCIALS, ASSORTED, #2
       San Francisco State   1968   13 min.   color   s/c/a
           More commercials are synthesized into a mini-message
           center.   Product strategies include those from cigarette
           companies, coffee manufacturers, breath-fresheners and
           more soft drink "peddlers."

839.   COMMERCIALS, ASSORTED, #3
       San Francisco State   1968   13 min.   color   s/c/a
           Messages to convince the consumer that their products
           "make life better" include those from beer commercials,
           diet drinks and hair groom hucksters.

840.   COMMERCIALS, ASSORTED, #4
       San Francisco State   1968   11 min.   color
           The viewer is bombarded with more persuasion.   Fea-
           tured are Professor Irwin Corey's attempt to explain
           "uncola," gypsies discovering a "better" smoke, and how
           a decongestant buffers specific pollens.

841. CONSUMER POWER: ADVERTISING
      Bailey Film Associates 1971 22 min. color s/c/a
            The film presents carefully prepared persuasive devices
            used to sell goods, services, ideas. Ralph Nader, con-
            sumer advocate, and advertising executive Ted Factor
            discuss the effect of advertising on our daily lives. Ex-
            amined is the "over-kill" strategy of selling and the ques-
            tion of how "necessary" advertising is to our free-enter-
            prise economy.

842. CONSUMER'S REPORT
      Canyon Cinema Corporative 1968 8 min. color
            Made from "recycled" television commercials and set to
            an electronic music sound track, this film reinvestigates
            American social values via television imagery and super-
            market strategies.

843. CREATION, THE
      Film-Maker's Cooperative 1970 1 min. color
            This brief statement concerns the faith man places in
            radio and television commercials as a type of "religion."

844. EFFECTIVE WRITING: LEARNING FROM ADVERTISING
      LANGUAGE
      Coronet 1971 11 min. b/w and color
            This film examines advertising language techniques and
            their application to writing and speaking.

845. FOLLOW UP, THE
      Business Education Films 13 min. color
            The focus is on the follow-up on advertisements and pro-
            motions, such as radio commercials. Examined are
            customers' reactions to store advertisements and opin-
            ions for subsequent promotions.

846. HAROLD AND CYNTHIA
      Strawbridge 1970 10 min. b/w and color
            Harold and Cynthia, two "vulnerable" people, become so
            intimidated by Madison Avenue messages on "how to
            live" that they have trouble communicating with each oth-
            er.

847. HE COULDN'T TAKE IT
      Film-Maker's Cooperative 1969 11 min. b/w
            In this satire, Ted Bailey attempts to live quietly with-
            out the interruptions of media (war news on the radio,
            music, commercials and stock market reports). Enticed
            out of his home, he becomes persuaded to race for a
            "bonus" of trading stamps. While accelerating, he loses
            his life. His desired serenity finally comes "without the
            interruption of more media."

848.   LASTING MEDIUM, THE
        Modern Talking Picture Service   (Free Loan Film)   1972
        15 min.   color   s/c
                Viewers go "behind the scenes" to see how "Specialty Ad-
                vertising" successfully helps advertisers achieve promo-
                tional objectives.   The film includes typical examples of
                a myriad of specialties available to advertisers.

849.   MARKETING MONTAGE
        University of Wisconsin   1970   6 min.   color
                This film presents a rapid-fire history of marketing,
                from prehistoric times to the present.   More than 350
                stills are used.   The survey suggests the enormous im-
                pact of contemporary advertising.

850.   NEW FORCE
        Mass Media Associates   1971   1 min.   color
                The viewer sees a television "sales pitch," ridiculing the pre-
                occupation with violence.   Filmed like a spot announce-
                ment, the camera follows speeding cars, war scenes and
                crime while a narrator "sells" the theme of violence as
                a commercial.

851.   PLAIN MAN'S GUIDE TO ADVERTISING, THE
        McGraw-Hill   1962   14 min.   b/w
                Robert Godfrey, Britain's leading producer of animated
                commercials, lampoons some of those television commer-
                cials.   Combining animation with live-action film, he ex-
                plores the art of spot announcement commercials.

852.   POST NO BILLS
        Mass Media Associates   1970   9 min.   color
                An exploitation of commitment, this film is a satirical
                analogy of our modern media.   It tells about a man who
                wages a personal war against billboards and what happens
                to him in the process.

853.   PUBLIC RELATIONS
        March of Time   1948   17 min.   b/w   s/C/a
                The history of public relations work in America is exam-
                ined.   Illustrations include phases associated with modern
                business.   Some leaders in the field are presented.

854.   TELEVISION COMMERCIALS
        Mass Media Associates   1963   20 min. each   b/w and color
                Live and special effects exemplify commercial samplings,
                which include:
                I: A compilation of thirteen separate subjects in black
                     and white;
                II: Animation--compilation of eighteen separate subjects
                     in color and black and white;
                III: Sixteen subjects in color, black and white, live and
                     animation.

855. TV COMMERCIALS
      KGW-TV 1970 10 min. color s/c/a
            Miscellaneous television commercials are spliced together.
            Included are commercials on gas, wine, hair coloring,
            cars, soup, cigarettes, cereals, others.

856. VERY NICE, VERY NICE
      University of Michigan 1967 7 min. b/w c/a
            This film illustrates, with still pictures from magazines,
            newspapers and television, the messages behind which
            men hide their anxieties.

                              Broadcasting

857. BEHIND YOUR RADIO DIAL
      National Broadcasting Company 1948 24 min. b/w c/a
            This film takes the viewer "behind-the-scenes" of NBC
            radio/television studios in New York and Hollywood to
            visit rehearsals and meet prominent personalities.

858. CABLE TV, PUBLIC ACCESS AND PEOPLE
      Mass Media Associates 1974 28 min. color
            The motivation of individuals and organizations toward the
            creative exploitation of public access is the reason behind
            this film recording of actual experiences of participants
            in a public access workshop.

859. CAREERS IN BROADCAST NEWS
      National Television News   Modern Film Rentals 1967 10
      min. color s/c
            This film examines the objectives of broadcast news per-
            sonnel. It shows, in addition, the chaotic and exciting
            nature of news reporting.

860. CHANGE!!!!!
      Northern Virginia Educational Television (WNVT) 1972
      19 min. color
      From Know What I Mean Series: #5
            Instructor Victor Kryston asks questions concerning the
            potential change of messages by specific media. Ques-
            tions relative to the definition of literacy concern the im-
            pact of radio, television, tapes and films in contrast
            with books. "If the Revolutionary War had been televised,
            would it have been a different event?"

861. COMMUNICATION IN THE MODERN WORLD
      Coronet 1958 11 min. b/w s/c/a
            This film defends the significance of communication in
            the local, national and international community. It re-
            views the historical development of communication media,
            examining the place of books, broadcasting, television,
            films in contemporary society.

862. COMMUNICATION REVOLUTION
University of Ohio   7 min.   b/w   s/c/a
A montage of scenes shows the variety of messages and
media that assault the senses of man.   The focus is on
messages from radio, film, advertising.

863. COMMUNICATIONS REVOLUTION, THE
Ohio State University   for Office of Education   1966   22 min.
b/w   c/a
From the Communication and New Educational Media Series
Edgar Dale, Marshall McLuhan, Gilbert Seldes and I.
Keith Tyler discuss the impact of the information explosion and communication mass media on Western Civiliza-
tion.   Questions concern the distribution of power through
a redistribution of information and the need for discrimination in media teaching.   Dr. McLuhan talks of "cool"
and "hot" media, of a global culture made possible by
radio.

864. CRITICUS
Mass Media Associates   1971   10 min.   color
This animated film comments on the power of communications media over public images, particularly in terms
of the conflict of editorialism and the censor.

865. DO-IT-YOURSELF TV PRODUCTION KIT, THE
Cornell University   1972   23-27 min. each   b/w
In three segments, Director John Hershberger tells the
story of television: why it is used; commercial versus
public stations and cable; dimensions of graphics.   He
concludes with practical methods for evaluation and promotion.

866. DOES IT MATTER WHAT YOU THINK?
Verity British Information Service   McGraw-Hill   1945
15 min.   b/w   s/c/a
This film reviews mass media and the exchange of opinions as contributors to public opinion.   Stressed is the
necessity for individual responsibility of each person to
analyze this information to maximize effective decisions.

867. EUROPA RADIO*
Mass Media Associates   1931   11 min.   b/w
A rare film introduces the world to radio, with scenes
in various countries and languages and covering a single
day from sign-on exercises to sign-off time.

868. EXITS AND ENTRANCES
Mass Media Associates   Time-Life   March of Time   color
Short vignettes of early radio shows: Jack Benny, Amos
and Andy, others in the days of the WPA.

869.   FEDERAL COMMUNICATIONS COMMISSION
       McGraw-Hill 15 min. b/w s/c
              This film describes the functions of each of the four bur-
              eaus of the Federal Communications Commission: the
              Safety and Special Radio Service, Field Engineering and
              Monitoring, Common Carrier and Broadcast Services.

870.   FRONTIERS OF NEWS*
       Associated Press 1963 11 min. b/w
              This film is composed of some 200 news photos of front-
              page events for the year 1963. Chief among illustrations
              are: United States fighting in Vietnam, suicide of the
              monks, coronation of Pope Paul, earthquake in Yugoslavia
              and the assassination and funeral services of President
              Kennedy. Television headlines supplant the usual narra-
              tion and the film is accompanied by a musical score.

871.   HISTORY OF TELEVISION, THE
       Pyramind 1971 12 min. color s/c/a
              This Charles Braverman cinema-collage of famous tele-
              vision programs and events encompasses episodes from
              1948 to 1971. Production is by the same company that
              did the "instant American history capsule" for the Smoth-
              ers' Brothers commercials.

872.   INDEPENDENT COMMERCIAL RADIO STATION
       United States Information Agency National Audiovisual Center
       1952 18 min. b/w
              This film illustrates the day-by-day operation of a local
              commercial radio station in the United States.

873.   IS EVERYBODY LISTENING?
       Mass Media Associates 20 min. b/w
              Radio audience habits from comedy to quiz and soap opera
              shows are sampled and analyzed by Hooper Audience An-
              alysis and John Crosby of the New York Herald Tribune.

874.   JOURNALISM--MIRROR, MIRROR ON THE WORLD
       National Educational Television Indiana University 1968
       52 min. s/c/a
              This news reporting analysis compares the coverage of a
              peace demonstration by five news services. The news
              story as developed by each source is presented. The ap-
              proach used and content covered are defended by reporters
              and editors representing media news services. A journal-
              ism professor comments on story deficiencies.

875.   MAKING OF A LIVE TV SHOW
       Pyramid A Charles Braverman Production 1971 16 min.
       color s/c/a
              This explanatory film sneaks behind the scenes of the 1971
              Emmy Award show on the National Broadcasting Company

network.   Included are the planning sessions, rehearsals,
actual broadcasts and the direction simultaneously.

876. MARSHALL McLUHAN: PICNIC IN SPACE
University-at-large   Northern Illinois University   29 min.
color s/c/a
   A "kaleidoscope" of the McLuhan views on communication,
   this film introduces the Canadian media expert as he and
   his friends meet for a picnic.   It is described as a
   "psychedelic feast made up of his thoughts on space, people and the routine of our daily lives."

877. MEDIA: MASSAGING THE MIND
University of California   1972   23 min.   color
   The social effects of media changes are examined by edi-
   tors and commentators.   Electronic image-making as
   well as future media use are both explored.

878. MEDIUM IS THE MASSAGE, YOU KNOW
National Film Board of Canada   1971   24 min.   color
   The medium is television and those "massaged" are the
   listening audience.   Most of the film takes place in a
   Vancouver, Canada class, where students use facilities
   to express their own television "creativity."

879. NEWS STORY
University of California   34 min.   color
   This film illustrates how problems of research, filming,
   editing and presentation affect the objectivity and credibility of a television news story.   All facets of the development of the story are followed.

880. ON THE ROAD WITH CHARLES KURALT
CBS News   Bailey Film Associates   27 min.   color
   The viewer is taken on a tour of the back roads and
   small towns of America to share sights and sounds with
   television newsman Charles Kuralt.

881. QUESTION OF TELEVISION VIOLENCE, THE
National Film Board of Canada   56 min.   color s/c/a
   This documentary examines testimony of the Surgeon General, consumer and parent groups, social scientists and
   representatives concerning the correlation between violence on the screen and violence in real life.

882. RADIO BROADCASTING TODAY
March of Time   1948   19 min.   b/w s/c/a
   A survey and appraisal of radio broadcasting in the United
   States is presented.   Excerpts are from specific pro-
   grams.   The role of the Federal Communications Com-
   mission is explained.

883.   STORY OF BROADCASTING, THE
       Radio Corporation of America 1956 26 min. b/w
       A history of television, this film is introduced with an
       interview of General Sarnoff about the early days of tele-
       vision. Presented then is a short description of how
       television programs are produced, showing the progress
       in production and techniques.

884.   TELEVISION: A POLITICAL MACHINE
       National Educational Television Indiana University 1968
       14 min. b/w s/c/a
       Using the Indiana presidential campaign as a backdrop,
       this film examines the role of television in electoral poli-
       tics. It considers the candidate as a television person-
       ality, the role of newscasts and the character of paid po-
       litical announcements that resemble news reports.

885.   TELEVISION: HOW IT WORKS
       Coronet 10 min. b/w s/c/a
       The layman is introduced to the fundamentals of televi-
       sion broadcasting and reception, from transmission of
       electronic beams to the image on the television screen.

886.   TELEVISION: LINE BY LINE
       International Film Bureau 1970 11 min. color
       Using animation, the film explains the principles of tele-
       vision. A special English version explains the electrical
       energy demonstrations and the picture tube receptions.

887.   TELEVISION AND POLITICS
       Bailey Film Associates 1971 26 min. color
       This film examines many campaign commercials that use
       "Madison Avenue" techniques to package and sell politi-
       cians. CBS Newsman Mike Wallace questions politicians
       and prominent image-makers on their use of media to in-
       fluence the voter.

888.   TELEVISION AROUND THE WORLD
       BBC-TV Robeck 1967 87 min. b/w s/c
       A comprehensive study of the impact of television on the
       lives of the people of the world, this film studies ways
       that television is used in Egypt, Poland, Nigeria, Italy,
       Thailand, Brazil, Russia, Japan and the United States.
       Examples of television use include objectives for educa-
       tion, culture, entertainment, propaganda.

889.   TELEVISION DIRECTING (PARTS I, II, III)
       National Educational Television 1958 each part: 30 min.
       b/w
       Desirable and undesirable production techniques with at-
       tendant problems are presented. Fundamentals for the
       interview and panel discussion programs are reviewed.

890. TELEVISION INTERVIEW, A
Film-Maker's Cooperative   13 min.   b/w
Stan Vanderbeek presents an exercise in "discontinuous
imagery and graphic possibilities" of videotape.   He illustrates an electric-collage interview "with himself."   The
interview covers computer art, movie drome theatres
and the new language of image.

891. TELEVISION REPORTER, THE
Mass Media Associates   1974   25 min.   color
John C. Schultz explores the tasks of television's messen-
gers of broadcast journalism.   Spending a working day
with WNBC-TV's Bob Teague, Schultz portrays the complexities a TV journalist encounters in preparing a news
broadcast.

892. TELEVISION SERVES IT COMMUNITY
Film Associates   Michigan State University   13 min.   color
s/a
Planning, production and transmission of television programs are all examined.   Rehearsals, remote pick-ups,
helicopter coverage focus on the community aspect.

893. THAT THE PEOPLE SHALL KNOW
Modern Talking Picture Service   (Free Loan Film)   1963
21 min.   b/w
Six top journalists describe their careers in the field of
communication.   Discussed are opportunities, challenges
the field offers.   Narrated by Walter Cronkite.

894. THIS IS MARSHALL McLUHAN: THE MEDIUM IS THE MES-
SAGE (PARTS I, II)
NBC News   McGraw-Hill   1967   53 min.   color
In presenting McLuhan's basic ideas and reactions toward
them, this film alternates between comments by McLuhan
himself and a number of persons who agree or disagree
with him.   The film concentrates on information processing aspects of media and the shaping of our "sensibili-
ties."

895. TOMORROW'S TELEVISION: GET WHAT YOU WANT OR
LIKE WHAT YOU GET
National Educational Television   Indiana University   1961
73 min.   b/w   c/a
This film explores the potential impact of some of the developing television technologies.   Primarily these include
cable television with its struggle against theatre owners,
commercial broadcasters and the telephone company.
Television's alternatives and diversity are explored as
well as the FCC policies in the regulation area.

896.   VTR ST. JACQUES
        National Film Board of Canada 1970 27 min. b/w
            A citizen's committee uses closed-circuit television to re-
            cord people's problems and concerns in a simulated so-
            cial action experiment. Videotape recording techniques
            are justified as effective for promoting action.

897.   WHAT'S HAPPENING TO TELEVISION?
        National Educational Television Indiana University 1967
        60 min. b/w s/c/a
            This film examines a critical array of television program-
            ming material by critics, writers, rating companies and
            the FCC. It is suggested that more viewers write to ex-
            press their opinions of program types.

898.   WHOLE WORLD IS WATCHING, THE
        National Educational Television Indiana University 1969
        55 min. b/w kinescope
            This film discusses bias on television, with participants
            David Brinkley, Walter Cronkite, John Fischer and Sena-
            tor John O. Pastore. Topics range from the 1968
            Democratic convention to restraints imposed upon
            television.

                                    Film

899.   ACTING
        Associated Instructional Service   University of California
        1973 32 min. color
        From the Filmmaking Techniques Series
            This film follows an experienced stage actor's transition
            to motion picture work in order to reveal the differences
            between acting techniques.

900.   AMERICAN FILM
        Indiana University 1968 27 min. color
            Excerpts from feature films of five leading American di-
            rectors are presented. Commentary, by Charlton Hes-
            ton, describes the artistic viewpoint, philosophy and style
            of each director. Included are excerpts of: Zinnemann's
            "High Noon"; Hitchcock's "North By Northwest"; Wyler's
            "Friendly Persuasion"; Kazan's "On the Waterfront";
            Stevens' "Shane."

901.   ART OF THE MOTION PICTURE, THE
        Bailey Film Associates 1970 22 min. color s/c/a
            The basics of motion picture photography are explained
            in this film. Interested practitioners learn all about
            panning, composition, lighting, sound, lenses, animation
            and other techniques.

902. BIRTH OF A NATION, THE
       Mass Media Associates 1915 14 min. b/w silent
          Directed by D. W. Griffith, this is an excerpt from the
          famous battle sequence--a classic of camera placement,
          editing, techniques.

903. ELEMENTS OF THE FILM
       Teleketics 1971 28 min. color
          Professor Edward Fischer of Notre Dame and actress
          Ann Blyth explore basic film terminology and film tech-
          nique. Analyzed are the art of the editor, aesthetic
          awareness and behind-the-scenes perception.

904. EVOLUTION OF THE MOTION PICTURE
       University of Illinois 1940 12 min. b/w s/c
          The development of films is traced from early Egyptian
          attempts in 600 B.C. to sound film as it existed in 1940.

905. EYE HEARS, THE EAR SEES, THE
       Film Board of Canada 1971 59 min. color
          Norman McLaren demonstrates his multiple exposure ef-
          fects, how he makes moving pictures without cameras,
          how he makes music tracks without instruments. The
          film reviews the continuous search for fresh ways to bring
          "magic" to the screen in color, form, film movement,
          music.

906. FILM: THE ART OF THE IMPOSSIBLE
       Learning Corporation of America 1972 27 min. color
          Director Michael Ritchie uses filmclips from "Downhill
          Racer" and "The Candidate" to illustrate his discussion
          of the film-maker's art. He points out elements in each
          which contribute to the total experience of the viewer.

907. FILM ABOUT CINEMATOGRAPHY, A
       International Film Bureau 18 min. color
          This film introduces the various techniques of using cine-
          matic film equipment. Throughout the film, the point is
          made that the cinematographer's primary function is to
          realize on film the intentions of the director.

908. FILM ABOUT FILM EDITING, A
       International Film Bureau 15 min. color
          This film enables the viewer to see how the various edit-
          ing techniques work in the film as a whole. Each of the
          techniques is demonstrated with sequences from an estab-
          lished film being edited.

909. FILM ABOUT FILMMAKING, A
       International Film Bureau 17 min. color
          A director illustrates how he and friends made a film us-
          ing means available to any student film-maker. Situa-
          tions encountered are those in both scripted and spontaneous
          filmmaking formats.

910. FILM AS AN ART
      Teleketics 1971 28 min. color s/c/a
      Notre Dame Professor Edward Fischer and actress Jayne
      Meadows discuss filmic art: the use of harmonious edit-
      ing, background music and aesthetic techniques. Film
      clips are shown from "Marty" and "Nanook of the North"
      as demonstration materials.

911. FILM CLUB
      Film-Maker's Cooperative 1968 28 min.
      Award Winner
      Puerto Rican teenagers at a storefront film workshop on
      the New York east side create their own films and exhibit
      them.

912. FILM FIRSTS: PART I*
      San Francisco State 1963 25 min. b/w c/a
      This film surveys the stories of film's earliest days. Il-
      lustrated are many production methods, ideas, techniques
      now "taken for granted," ranging from the first time the
      camera moved to the screen's first "talkie."

913. FILM FIRSTS: PART II*
      San Francisco State 1963 25 min. b/w c/a
      Part II spotlights achievements of a quarter of a century
      of great film pioneers--Edwin S. Porter, George Melies,
      Thomas H. Ince and D. W. Griffith. The years stressed
      --prior to 1914--examine the introduction of technical in-
      novations and photographic "trickery" to the screen.

914. FILM TACTICS
      United States Navy National Audiovisual Center 1945
      22 min. b/w
      This film emphasizes through dramatized episodes how
      training films should and should not be used by Navy in-
      structors.

915. FIRST FLICKERS*
      National Broadcasting Corporation Educational Film Library
      Association 1971 27 min. b/w s/c/a
      This film illustrates some of the sixteen-millimeter re-
      productions of paper prints of the earliest copyrighted
      films preserved in the Library of Congress. There are
      short reenactments of actual events and natural disasters,
      scene-by-scene comparisons of the Great Train Robbery
      and its counterfeit, and rescues by Rover. Much other
      early film footage is offered.

916. FLICKS I*
      National Educational Television 27 min. b/w s/c/a
      The evolution of motion pictures from a simple shadow
      on a wall to modern movies is traced. Sequences from
      such early films as "The Great Train Robbery" and "In-

tolerance" as well as famous personalities of the past including Al Jolson, Lon Chaney, and Laurel and Hardy
are shown.

917.   FLICKS II*
       National Educational Television 27 min. b/w s/c/a
          This film traces the history of animated cartoons from
          1892 picture sequences through the invention of movie
          film. Sequences from Walt Disney's "Skeleton Dance"--
          the first sound cartoon, the development of Mutt and
          Jeff, and early works of other animators are shown.

918.   FOIBLES
       Learning Corporation of America 1971 17 min. color
       s/c/a
          For film study classes, five animated segments, all pro-
          duced in Eastern Europe, expose man's foibles. In dif-
          ferent styles of animation, man is shown variously as
          callous, clumsy, comic, perverse. Titles include "As-
          sistance," "Curiosity," "Parade," "The Abominable
          One," and "Behind the Bars."

919.   FRONTLINE CAMERAS, 1935-1965*
       Mass Media Associates 1965 27 min. b/w
          Willard Van Dyke presents a compilation film using As-
          sociated Press wirephotos covering contemporary history
          and creating a concerned reflection of the world's prob-
          lems.

920.   GRAMMAR OF FILM, THE
       Center of Mass Communication 1972 30 min. color
          John Schultz explains the new set of symbols used by
          television journalists to enable them to tell a story ef-
          fectively with pictures. He highlights the use of con-
          trasting elements and sequences to dramatize a film
          story and bring it to life.

921.   HISTORY OF CINEMA, THE
       Contemporary Brandon 1958 9 min. b/w and color
          This British cartoon satire on the history of film devel-
          opment emphasizes that, although technical progress has
          been made, film content has not matured simultaneously.
          "The curved screen does not make slapstick any more
          or less slapstick."

922.   HISTORY OF THE MOTION PICTURE, THE--A SERIES*
       Mass Media Associates 1962 27 min. each b/w
          This series is a study of the silent movie era with nar-
          rated briefs scrutinizing background information. Titles
          include: America; The Americano; Black Pirate; Blood
          and Sand; Dr. Jekyll and Mr. Hyde; Dracula; The Eagle;
          The Fall of Babylon (Intolerance); Film Firsts, Part I;
          Film Firsts, Part II; Fun Factory; Garden of Eden; The

General; Girls in Danger; Hunchback of Notre Dame; The
Lost World Revisited; Orphans of the Storm, Part I;
Orphans of the Storm, Part II.

923. HISTORY OF THE MOTION PICTURES, THE
Film-Maker's Cooperative   10 min.   b/w
Producer Stan Vanderbeek, in a hasty history of films,
compresses diverse styles and profiles motion pictures,
commencing with "The Kiss" and concluding with a God-
ard film.

924. INTERPRETATIONS AND VALUES
University of California   1964   9 min.   b/w
Outstanding examples of film editing techniques are shown
in their entirety--from script order to final assembly.

925. LANGUAGE OF THE FILM
OFM Productions   28 min.   color
This is the second in the OFM series on motion picture
"art." As a learning theory approach to the development
of the vocation, it illustrates camera use as "functional
conveyance of a message."

926. LANGUAGE OF THE SILENT CINEMA, THE (PARTS I, II)
Mass Media Associates   1973   Pt. I: 100 min.;   Pt. II:
90 min.   b/w
Filmed excerpts from countless silent films are used to
illustrate the syntax of the silent cinema.

927. MAKING A SOUND FILM
International Film Bureau   14 min.   color
This film explains some of the procedures in blending
music, dialogue, editing.

928. MAKING OF A DOCUMENTARY
Carousel   1973   23 min.   color
This film reviews the complete production history of a
one-hour filmed documentary. It explains many production problems, focusing on the ethical and practical difficulties of editing, approach, style, philosophies.

929. MAKING OF A MOVIE, THE
Mass Media Associates   1957   23 min.   b/w
Narrated by Patrick Barr, this is a documentary on the
making of Otto Preminger's 1957 film, "Saint Joan."
This brief account explains the process of filmmaking, the
Preminger methods of production, introduces actress Jean
Seberg.

930. MARCH OF THE MOVIES, THE*
Contemporary   35 min.   b/w   kinescope
This presentation of a television interview includes John
Daly and Gloria Swanson and Conrad Nagle. A cutting

from a 1939 "March of Time" documentary is viewed on
film.   Scenes from "The Jazz Singer," "Birth of a Nation," others are shown.

931.   MARCH OF TIME, THE*
       National Archives 1939 to completion of series
            Classic examples of journalism reporting, "March of
            Time" newsreels are deposited in the National Archives.
            Subjects of the 1939 period stress national defense and
            war.

932.   MARCH OF TIME, THE--A SERIES*
       Time-Life   20 min.   each b/w vt/vc
            The March of Time developed its own film format and es-
            poused definite viewpoints on controversial subjects.   This
            series contains specifics on various incidents, on themes
            of the periods, as well as the original versions of the
            programs on radio and films.

933.   MOVIES
       WTTW   University of California 1963 29 min. b/w
            Twentieth-century movies are examined for clues to
            changes and constancies in American taste.   Sequences
            from films include those of Edison, Hart, Sennett, Chap-
            lin, Griffith.

934.   MOVIES LEARN TO TALK
       McGraw-Hill 1960 27 min. b/w
            The history of film production techniques is documented.
            The viewer sees footage from many films, both silent and
            sound, each with unique innovations.

935.   MOVIES MARCH ON*
       Museum of Modern Art   Mass Media Associates   Time-Life
       1939 22 min. b/w vt/vc
            This filmed documentary is a complete résumé of Ameri-
            can film history from the invention to 1939.   It includes
            much of the specific work of the Mass Media Associates,
            illustrating with views of production methods, containing
            excerpts from many famous American films.

936.   MOVIES MOVE PEOPLE
       Eastman Kodak Modern Talking Picture Service (Free Loan
       Film) 26 min. color
            This film demonstrates how film can assist with business
            communication.   The commentary concerns a series of
            films-within-the-film covering the gamut of business needs
            from training salesmen to image-building.

937.   MOVIES' STORY
       University of California 1970 26 min. b/w
            The history of film from 1895 to 1915 is examined, be-
            ginning with Edison's first experiments and concluding

with Chaplin's early films. The focus is on the work of
Melies, Porter, Griffith and Chaplin.

938.   NATURE OF THE FILM MEDIUM, THE
       Teleketics 1971 28 min. b/w s/c/a
       Professor Edward Fischer, Notre Dame, and actress
       Ruth Hussey explore the unique method of film communi-
       cation. To continue the Teleketics lesson on visual lan-
       guage, the film offers excerpts from "Citizen Kane" and
       "Requiem of a Heavyweight."

939.   ONE MAN'S SHOW
       Film-Maker's Cooperative 1965 62 min. b/w and color
       The frenzied and mechanical American life is caught in
       a McLuhan's-eye view of linear editing. The message is
       a montage of a rock dance, subway trance, all responding
       to the music of the "Mothers of Invention."

940.   ORIGINS OF THE MOTION PICTURE
       United States Navy National Audiovisual Center 1955 20
       min. b/w
       The development and arts of the motion picture are shown
       from the earliest suggestions of Leonardo Da Vinci to the
       perfected sound motion picture of Thomas Edison.

941.   PATHE NEWSREEL, THE*
       Mass Media Associates 1917-1932 20 min. b/w silent
       This series offers coverage from Pathé's beginnings to
       conclusion. From "Wilson Signs Declaration of War" to
       "Billy Sunday Cures Depression," its distinct genre for
       Cinema emerged.

942.   POTEMKIN*
       San Francisco State 1925 67 min. b/w C/a silent
       Regarded by many as the most important film in the his-
       tory of the silent cinema and the greatest work of the
       Russian director S. Eisenstein, this film contains the fam-
       ous mutiny scene, subsequent massacre. The film is a
       recreation of the abortive revolution of 1905 and the Czar-
       ist repression that followed. (Sound was added in 1951.)

943.   PRACTICAL FILM MAKING
       Encyclopaedia Britannica 19 min. color vt/vc
       A staff of professionals is interviewed and filmed at work
       making a low budget feature film. "Before" and "after"
       scenes from the feature motion picture being produced
       are used to illustrate the countless details of film making.

944.   RHETORIC OF THE MOVIE
       Eastman Kodak b/w silent
       For those interested in verbal-visual parallels, this film
       attempts to compare English grammar with elements of
       filmic structure. Six films are explored, illustrating a

"simple movie utterance," a "simple movie sentence,"
complicated movie sentences, varying the point of view,
making movie sense, and movie paragraphs.

945.   SCREEN DIRECTOR
       Indiana University 1951 8 min. b/w
       From the Behind the Scenes Series
          This film explains the work of the director of a Holly-
          wood feature film, showing that familiarity with a variety
          of jobs is required in order to make the best use of
          available resources and personnel.

946.   SCREEN PLAY
       Pyramid 1972 14 min. color
          A basic introduction to film scriptwriting, this documen-
          tary examines modern trends, and illustrates a finished
          film segment showing relation of script to visual image.

947.   SCREEN WRITER
       Indiana University 1949 9 min. b/w
          The importance of the screenwriter is discussed.   Ideas
          expressed must be in terms of visual imagery.

948.   SHORT HISTORY OF ANIMATION, A--A SERIES
       Mass Media Associates 60 min. b/w
          This collection, covering from 1879 to 1933, brings to-
          gether representative early animated cartoons to demon-
          strate the fluency of the art of animation.   Films include
          "Animated Pictures"; "Drame Chez les Tantoches";
          "Gertie the Dinosaur"; "Mutt and Jeff"; "Newman's Laugh-
          o-Gram"; "Felix the Cat"; "Steamboat Willie"; "Mad Dog";
          "Carmen."

949.   SIX FILMMAKERS IN SEARCH OF A WEDDING
       Pyramid 1972 14 min. color
          Six different approaches to filming and recording a wed-
          ding are shown.   Included is a live-action portrait, pixi-
          lation, animation of photo cutouts, a "home movie,"
          straight documentary with lip-synchronization, a sequence
          of color stills taken by the official photographer.

950.   STRUCTURE OF THE NEWS FILM STORY, THE
       Center of Mass Communication 1971 20 min.   color
          Using a 1971 CBS Newsfilm report from Morton Dean in
          Vietnam, this film examines exactly how a news film
          story is put together.   Concepts involved are shown as
          they happen, thereby eliminating the need for verbal ex-
          planations.

951.   THREE COLLOQUIES
       Grove Press 17 min. color
          This film deals with both how movies work and how they
          are made.   The first "colloquy" is an "imitation" of

pedagogic films; the second "colloquy" challenges the idea
of cinéma vérité. The last section, the most radical in
technique and theory, presents optical distortions and
Moog synthesizer controls.

952.   UNDERSTANDING MOVIES
       Teaching Film Custodians McGraw-Hill 1951 15 min. b/w
       This film is designed to serve as an introduction or sur-
       vey for the study of standards for film appreciation.
       Presented are the study of film techniques of some MGM
       films: "Tennessee Johnson," "The Good Earth," "Treas-
       ure Island," "David Copperfield," and "Romeo and Juli-
       et."

953.   VISUAL LANGUAGE OF THE FILM
       Teleketics 1971 28 min. b/w s/c/a
       Dr. Edward Fischer of Notre Dame and actress Ann Blyth
       discuss the alphabet and grammar of filmic language, the
       psychology of camera angles, the effects of various meth-
       ods of lighting, and expression of the nature of the medi-
       um.

954.   "WHAT DID YOU THINK OF THE MOVIE?" MOVIE, THE
       American Film Institute Time-Life 1974 15 min. color
       vt/vc s/c/a
       This satire of movie criticism covers the complete range
       of responses to the question in its title. It catches peo-
       ple on the street and organizes them into rhythmic, the-
       matic patterns that show how little substance there is to
       most people's opinions about films they've seen.

955.   WHEN COMEDY WAS KING (PARTS I, II)*
       Film Center Brandon 81 min. total b/w s/c/a
       The viewer diagnoses "seeable" humor in terms of nos-
       talgia of the great all-time comics of the silent film era.
       Illustrations of their special brand of comedy are given
       by Chaplin, Keaton and Mack Sennett.

956.   YOUNG FILM-MAKERS, THE
       Fordham University Brandon 1971 32 min. b/w
       Probing the attitudes and filming methods of the "media
       generation," this film comments on students attending the
       Young Film-Maker's Conference at Fordham University.
       It follows two separate and very different crews of film-
       makers as they conceive and film their own "instant
       movies."

957.   ZIKKARON
       International Film Bureau 1973 6 min. color
       This is a poetic production that blends "ideas, color, mo-
       tion and sound" to form an "intellectual" experience for
       the viewer. Moving images were produced by moving
       about tiny slivers cut from lineoleum tiles on a black-lit
       animation board.

MOVEMENTS

Civil Rights

958. ABRAHAM LINCOLN: A BACKGROUND STUDY
      Coronet 1951 17 min. color s/c/a
            Illustrated are the writings and speeches of Lincoln in re-
            lation to the civil rights issues of the times.

959. ABRAHAM LINCOLN: A STUDY IN GREATNESS (PARTS I,
      II, III)
      Francis Raymond Line 18 min. each color s/c/a
            This three-part study of Lincoln's philosophy consists of:
            I: Lincoln's Youth; II: The Illinois Years; III: The War
            Years.

960. ABRAHAM LINCOLN AND THE EMANCIPATION PROCLAMA-
      TION
      Project 7, Inc. American Educational Films 20 min. color
      Award: CINE Golden Eagle Award
            This film examines the Lincoln dilemma concerning the
            issue of Negro slavery. As President he "felt it his duty
            to uphold the constitution, in spite of his strong personal
            feelings against slavery."

961. AIN'T WE GOT A RIGHT
      Mass Media Associates 1972 44 min. b/w
            An improvised morality play format illustrates the entire
            ministry of Martin Luther King, from the beginning of his
            Montgomery residence to his assassination. Music and
            dialogue are the fundamental film elements.

962. ALL THE WAY HOME
      Crowell, Collier, Macmillan 1957 30 min. b/w
            This dramatic film examines the reactions of a commu-
            nity when a black family indicates interest in purchasing
            property in their neighborhood.

963. ANGELA, LIKE IT IS*
      National Educational Television (WABC-TV) American Docu-
      mentary Films 1971 60 min. b/w
            After her arrest in 1970, Angela Davis speaks from pris-
            on. In the interview which follows, she replies to ques-
            tions asked by a survey of the people of Harlem. A tele-
            vision panel discussion follows.

964. ANGRY VOICES OF WATTS
      National Broadcasting Company 1966 56 min. b/w
            The workshop and performance of groups are shown in
            juxtaposition against a background of newsreel footage
            taken during the riot. There are also scenes of Watts
            one year later.

965.   AUTOBIOGRAPHY OF MISS JANE PITTMAN, THE
       Learning Corporation of America   1974   116 min.   color
       Awards: Nine Emmies
           This is the television adaptation of Ernest Gaines' novel
           about the tenacity and courage of a black woman from
           her childhood as a slave to her march for civil rights at
           the age of 110. Generally considered one of the finest
           American television films, it shows the suffering, harass-
           ment and oppression faced by black people as well as the
           emergence of black pride, dignity, identity.

966.   BILL OF RIGHTS IN ACTION, THE: EQUAL OPPORTUNITY
       Bailey Film Associates   22 min.   color
           This is a filmed scenario of the argument of supervisory
           promotion based on past discrimination. A black factory
           worker is promoted over a white, even though the white
           has seniority. The case is argued in depth before an
           arbitrator and the film is left open-ended.

967.   BLACK PANTHER (OFF THE PIG)
       San Francisco Newsreel   Canyon Cinema   15 min.   b/w
           The Black Panther Party is shown training itself "in
           struggle, for struggle." Interviews are shown with Huey
           P. Newton and Eldridge Cleaver. Bobby Seale presents
           a ten-point program.

968.   BLACK POWER: WE'RE GOING TO SURVIVE AMERICA
       Henny   Mass Media Associates   Film-Maker's Cooperative
       1968   14 min.   color
       Award: San Francisco Film Festival
           This is a filmed speech by Stokely Carmichael, given on
           the birthday of Huey Newton. The title is the theme:
           concern "not with political and economical matters but
           just plain survival." Interest is manifested in preserva-
           tion of the black race, in terms of its cultural and an-
           cestral roots.

969.   BLACK POWER CONCEPT
       Wayne State University   15 min.   b/w   s/c/a   kinescope
           Reverend F. Cleague contends that Black Power is a re-
           sponse to a world that "black people did not make and in-
           to which they are forbidden entry."

970.   CHILDREN WERE WATCHING, THE
       Time-Life   1974   30 min.   b/w   vt/vc
           This is a drama of a six-year-old black girl who enters
           the first integrated school in New Orleans. There was no
           script for any of the film and no rehearsals. It is told
           from the child's point of view, unfolding as a film essay.

971.   CIVIL DISORDER: THE KERNER REPORT (PARTS I, II, III)
       National Educational Television   Indiana University   1968
       27 min. each   b/w

This documentary analyzes the Kerner Report in terms of the symptoms and possible future effects of racism in this country. Goals of the black movements are discussed; examples illustrate attempts to promote racial harmony.

972. CIVIL RIGHTS MOVEMENT--HISTORIC ROOTS
Encyclopaedia Britannica 1967 17 min. b/w vt/vc s/c/a
The film raises the question: Where, when and why has the civil rights movement come into being to challenge the old order? Answers begin with a review of the slave trade and abolitionist protest. The film covers the evolution of Lincoln's role in the movement, ending with the Emancipation Proclamation.

973. CIVIL RIGHTS MOVEMENT SERIES
Film Institute University of California 1966 17-27 min. b/w
This is a five-part series adapted from the three-hour NBC News Special, "The Civil Rights Revolution of 1963." Segments include: "Historic Roots"; "Personal View"; "South"; "North"; "Mississippi Summer Project."

974. CIVIL RIGHTS MOVEMENTS: THE PERSONAL VIEW
National Educational Television Indiana University 22 min. b/w
A general overview is presented of social conditions as they exist for blacks and whites. Personal experiences are related to portray fear, hate and suspicion. Stereotype analysis and faulty image-making are examined.

975. CONFRONTED
National Educational Television Indiana University 1963 60 min. b/w
White northerners react to black advances in education, employment, housing.

976. FREE AT LAST
National Educational Television Indiana University 1965 30 min. b/w
From the History of the Negro People Series
The American black history is traced from emancipation to the end of World War II. Illustrated are views of Frederick Douglass, Booker T. Washington, W. E. B. DuBois and Marcus Garvey.

977. HERITAGE OF SLAVERY, THE
CBS News Bailey Film Associates 1968 53 min. color s/c/a
From the Of Black America Series
Slavery is examined, as are established attitudes that still persist today. CBS reporter George Foster inter-

views descendants of plantation owners, and black activists, and demonstrates parallels between attitudes then and now.

978.   HUEY!*
       American Documentary Films 1968 33 min. b/w
              The Black Panther Rally in Oakland, California celebrates imprisoned Huey Newton's birthday, with speeches by leaders of the black liberation.   Included are speeches by Eldridge Cleaver, Stokely Carmichael, H. Rap Brown, James Foreman and Bobby Seale.   Illustrated are changes initiated by the party movement and reflected since that time.

979.   I HAVE A DREAM: THE LIFE OF MARTIN LUTHER KING
       CBS News Bailey Film Associates 1968 35 min. b/w
              The forces and life of Martin Luther King are told in terms of his leadership of his people.   Actual news footage examines philosophies and ideas he exemplified.   The film highlights his crusades, arrests, speeches.

980.   INTERVIEW WITH BRUCE GORDON, A
       McGraw-Hill 1964 17 min. b/w
       Award: New York Film Festival (1964)
              Bruce Gordon, a 22-year-old organizer for the Student Nonviolent Coordinating Committee, is interviewed in Selma, Alabama during the height of a drive to register blacks of this community.

981.   IVANHOE DONALDSON
       Crowell, Collier, Macmillan 1964 57 min. b/w
       Award: Mannheim, Germany, Festival
              The first full-length documentary feature on the civil rights workers in crucial areas of the Deep South shows their actual experiences.   A field secretary of the Student Nonviolent Coordinating Committee and his colleagues attempt voter registration in Virginia and Alabama.   Also featured are Council on Racial Equality registration volunteers.

982.   K'MA MAN
       Yale University McGraw-Hill 20 min. b/w
       Awards: CINE plus three film festivals
              With simple images, Peter Rosen documents the personal and ideological struggle for freedom and manhood of black militant John Barber.   After years of nonviolence, John Barber and his fellow black intellectuals are converted to black militancy.

983.   LISTEN, WHITEY
       American Documentary Films 1968 30 min. b/w
              Filmed in the ghetto black areas of Washington, D.C., this shows the aftermath of the assassination of Martin Luther King.   Interviews are shown with black leaders

from all segments of the community and concern is directed as to where the blacks will move. Street scenes show the National Guard and the protestors.

984. MALCOLM X
Carousel 1971 23 min. color
Malcolm's lifetime biography includes his honor student days in junior high school, his class presidency in high school, the frenetic days of drugs in Detroit, Boston, Harlem, and experiences up until the time of his murder.

985. MARTIN LUTHER KING
Time-Life 1972 30 min. b/w vt/vc s/c/a
In this filmed interview, Martin Luther King is shown as a philosophical, religious man with deep convictions about civil rights.

986. MARTIN LUTHER KING: A MAN OF PEACE
San Francisco State 1965 26 min. b/w
Dr. King discusses his faith in man's moral obligation to resist evil in a moral way, which he views as a "combination judeo-christian non-violent method."

987. MARTIN LUTHER KING: FROM MONTGOMERY TO MEMPHIS
Film Associates Bailey Film Associates 1969 27 min
b/w and color
The life work of Martin Luther King is reviewed, with focus on racial injustice, his peace prize and final assessment of his contributions.

988. MARTIN LUTHER KING: THE MAN AND THE MARCH
National Educational Television Indiana University 1968
83 min. b/w
The story of the Poor People's March is told in this documentary. Dr. King confers with aides, speaks at rallies, visits schools and travels for support of the march.

989. MESSENGER FROM VIOLET DRIVE
National Educational Television Indiana University 29 min.
b/w
An interview with Elijah Muhammad, leader of the Black Muslims. He discusses the philosophy of total separation of blacks and whites in America. Also reviewed are the origins of blacks and Caucasian races, the prophecy of the destruction of America, and his mission as the "last messenger from Allah to the American Negro."

990. MISSING PAGES
Fisk University Perennial 14 min. color
Film images reveal students' conceptions of case histories of former slaves. Their experiences were told to a Fisk University social scientist in the thirties. The film's aim

is to associate today's Black Freedom Movement with the
initiative started by Harriet Tubman in the 1850's.

991. NEGRO, THE
National Educational Television   Indiana University   1967
30 min.   b/w
Elijah Muhammad of the Black Muslims, Daniel Watts,
editor of Liberator magazine, and Jimmy Garrett from
CORE express opinions on "Freedom Now." The film
depicts their hopes, emotions, thoughts, frustrations.

992. NEW MOOD
National Educational Television   Indiana University   1965
30 min.   b/w s/c/a
This film reviews the civil rights struggle of the past
decade and traces the impact of the new militancy on
both white and black Americans. It reviews the implications of the 1956 Supreme Court decision repudiating
the doctrine of "separate but equal" facilities in schools
and elsewhere.

993. ONE MORE RIVER TO CROSS
American Documentary Films   1970   24 min.   color
This film reflects the quiet of southwest Georgia and the
black majority's struggle to gain political rights there.

994. OUR BASIC CIVIL RIGHTS
Coronet   1950   14 min.   b/w
Fundamental civil rights and a detailed study of liberties
are presented.   Civil rights are defined in the legal
sense.   A courtroom sequence illustrates how rights are
interrelated and why they must be protected and extended.

995. PANTHERS, THE
American Broadcasting Company   26 min.   b/w
A filmed version of conversation with Julian Bond, Reverend Andrew Young, Cecil Poole and David Hilliard presents their responses to questions received from sectors
of society.

996. PIECE OF THE ACTION, A
National Broadcasting Company   1968   17 min.   color
A case history is told of Detroit, where 43 Americans
were killed and 386 injured during rioting.   The riot-
generated response came from industry-and-government
spawned programs for workers.

997. REMEDY FOR A RIOT
CBS News   Associated Instructional Films   1968   27 min.
b/w
This special network documentary explores the entire subject of racism in terms of the dignity of the black man:
his pressures, needs, fulfillment.

998. REQUIEM
      Mass Media Associates 1968 4 min. color
          A single cinematic tribute to Martin Luther King, this
          "art film" shows the nonverbal communication--the faces
          --of the King followers.

999. RESTRICTED NEIGHBORHOOD
      Teleketics 1971 60-second spot announcement
          When a white couple wants to live in an "unrestricted"
          neighborhood, there is resultant dissension, and they re-
          fuse to consummate the transaction.

1000. RIGHT NOW!
      Brandon 29 min. color
          This documentary explores the procedures and methods
          of blacks in Savannah, Georgia to register and vote.

1001. SEGREGATION: NORTHERN STYLE
      Associated Instructional Materials 31 min. b/w
          Applications by blacks for homes in New Jersey are re-
          fused. Microphones eavesdrop on conversations concern-
          ing integration and the frustrations involved.

1002. SIGNIFICANCE OF MALCOLM X
      Holt, Rinehart and Winston 27 min. b/w s/c/a
          Malcolm X is presented biographically with special empha-
          sis on his influence as a black leader after he became a
          follower of Elijah Mohammed.

1003. SIT-IN
      McGraw-Hill Contemporary 1961 54 min. b/w
      From the NBC White Paper Series
          The first lunch counter sit-in on May 10, 1960 in Nash-
          ville, Tennessee, is documented. What follows is histor-
          ic: black students attend workshops; white sympathizers
          are abused by neighbors.

1004. SLAVERY
      National Educational Television Indiana University 1965
      30 min. b/w s/c/a
          Based on the actual testimony of former slaves, this film
          tells the story of their experiences in the "old South."
          "The liberation of slaves" by Yankee troops is recalled.
          Negro spirituals are used to provide background.

1005. SLAVERY: THE BLACK MAN AND THE MAN
      Silvermine Films, Inc. 22 min. color
          In live scenes on inner-city streets, a young black "per-
          ceives himself, his past and what he must resolve."
          Vivid graphics of slavery are fused with daily activities.

1006. SOME ARE MORE EQUAL THAN OTHERS
       CBS News   Associated Instructional Films   1971   40 min.
       b/w   s/c/a
              This film considers the legal treatment of minorities,
              the bail system and discriminatory jury selections. Eric
              Sevareid narrates.

1007. STILL A BROTHER
       United States Army   McGraw-Hill   1967   90 min.   b/w
              The crises of middleclass American blacks are explored.
              Several points of view are presented including those rang-
              ing from Robert Johnson, editor of Jet, to Dr. Nathan
              Wright, Black Power organizer.

1008. TRIAL: THE CITY AND COUNTY OF DENVER VERSUS
       LAUREN R. WATSON SERIES
       National Educational Television   b/w   four parts
              This film series was the first television broadcast of an
              actual courtroom trial.   Lauren Watson is former Minis-
              ter of Defense of the Black Panther Party in Denver. He
              charges continuous police harassment culminating in his
              arrest.

1009. TRIBUTE TO MALCOLM X
       National Educational Television   Indiana University   1970
       15 min.   b/w   s/c/a
              This film reports the influence of Malcolm X upon the
              present Black Liberation Movement. It reviews his life
              as recollected in an interview with his widow, Betty Sha-
              bazz.

1010. TUMULT, TURMOIL AND TURBULENCE
       National Broadcasting Company   1969   12 min.   b/w
              The transition from the civil rights movement to the more
              militant emphasis is examined.   Changes are contrasted:
              from Birmingham in 1963 to Cornell University in 1969.

1011. WE SHALL OVERCOME
       Crowell, Collier, Macmillan Brandon 1965 10 min. b/w
              Hundreds of words, songs, speeches and interviews are
              capsulized in this documentary showing the mass move-
              ment for racial equality.   Scenes range from the Birming-
              ham bombings and sit-ins to Klansmen meetings.

                                    Peace

1012. ALL WE ARE SAYING
       Mass Media Associates   1970   17 min.   color
              A film digest is presented of November, 1969 Washington
              Peace Moratorium events.   Inspirational concepts are
              stressed, with the focus on the participation of the older
              generation.   The highlight is the roll call of the Vietnam
              dead.

1013. AND ANOTHER FAMILY FOR PEACE
       University of California 1971 32 min. b/w
           Cinéma-vérité portraits--largely interviews--illustrate
           opinions of five middle American families opposed to the
           Vietnam war. Restrained and nonideological, the film ex-
           amines personal family reasons for opposition.

1014. ANTI-WAR PROTEST
       Intext 1970 15 min. b/w
           Comparisons are offered between the anti-war protests of
           World War II and those of Vietnam. Basic questions are
           raised concerning individual rights and responsibilities
           versus a need for national unity and stability.

1015. BATTLE OF CHICAGO
       University of California 1969 23 min. b/w
           This film attempts to study the causes of the 1968 Demo-
           cratic convention Chicago protests. It is a composite of
           recorded sounds, marches, subsequent brutality and ar-
           rests, and in-depth interviews with the black community
           members.

1016. BUT WHAT DO WE DO?
       Henny 1969 23 min. color
           This is the true story of how one Stanford research an-
           alyst working on military projects became conscientiously
           opposed to his work, resigned from his job and joined the
           Peace Corps.

1017. CHICAGO CONSPIRACY TRIAL, THE
       BBC-TV Time-Life 1972 2.5 hours b/w vt/vc s/c/a
           This documentary dramatizes one of the most important
           political trials of the century. Recreated is the atmos-
           phere and setting of the actual trial, wherein the principals
           are charged with "conspiracy to incite riot." Every word
           of the 23,000-page official court transcript is adapted in
           script form. The principal actors are all American.

1018. DIARY OF A STUDENT REVOLUTION
       Indiana University 1969 55 min. b/w
           This film examines the confrontation between student ac-
           tivists and University of Connecticut administrators over
           on-campus recruiting by war-related industries. It ques-
           tions whether the administration's "repressive" action of
           handling arrests was the appropriate response.

1019. DR. SPOCK AND HIS BABIES
       Herman Engle American Documentary Films 1970 27 min.
       b/w vt/vc
       Award winner
           A brief history of the political development of Dr. Benja-
           min Spock's career is presented. Included are speeches
           at numerous rallies and lectures plus the March of Death in
           Washington, 1969.

1020. IN THE NAME OF PEACE
       American World Films 1970 29 min. color
       This conservative documentary is about the New Mobili-
       zation Committee to end the Vietnam War and its Novem-
       ber, 1969 anti-war demonstration in Washington.

1021. MARCH ON THE PENTAGON
       Film-Maker's Cooperative Canyon Cinema 1967 23 min.
       b/w
       The 100,000-"people-march" to Washington on October
       21, 1967, is documented in terms of the faces and lan-
       guage of those involved.

1022. MARCH ON WASHINGTON: BONUS MARCH
       Intext 1970 17 min. color s/c/a
       Bonus marches are examined in detail. Those surveyed
       are from World War I veterans in 1932, together with
       the responses of Congress and the military.

1023. MARCH ON WASHINGTON: RESURRECTION CITY
       Intext 1970 17 min. color s/c/a
       Presented is the "city" that was created to dramatize the
       plight of the poor in Washington, D.C. in March, 1968.
       Comments from protest leaders provoke reactions from
       government officials.

1024. MY COUNTRY RIGHT OR WRONG?
       Learning Corporation of America 1972 15 min. color
       From "Summertree," starring Jack Warden and Michael Doug-
       las
       From the Searching for Values Series
       Rejection of the Vietnam War and social pressures force
       a crisis in life of a university student, impelling him to
       make crucial decisions about his values and future. Dia-
       logue with his father centers on the question of whether
       he "should concede to authority or follow what he thinks
       is right."

1025. NOT JUST THE YOUNG
       Charney American Documentary Films 1969 22 min. color
       Buses traveling to and from the huge peace demonstration
       in Washington, D.C., November, 1969, provide the set-
       ting for a forum to discuss national policy. Parents of
       today's political activists examine the war, economic
       pressures at home and techniques of protest.

1026. PEACE PICKETS ARRESTED FOR DISTURBING THE PEACE*
       Film-Maker's Cooperative Canyon Cinema 1968 9 min.
       color
       Joan Baez captures the "spirit" of the crowd as she
       speaks of nonviolent revolution from the steps of the Oak-
       land Induction Center and, again, in Santa Rita prison.
       The film concludes with planned reunion scenes of re-

leased prisoners and awaiting friends.

1027. PEACEMAKER
Teleketics 1972 8 min. color
This is an allegorical film dealing with the struggle necessary for a man who wills peace by his life and, if need
be, by his death. Appropriate for discussion of the lives
of Martin Luther King, Hammarskjold, Gandhi.

1028. PEACEMEAL
Film-Maker's Cooperative 1968 8 min. color
Awards: Belgium, International, CINE Film Festivals
Feelings and motions of the march on the United Nations
are captured in a montage of "hippies, students, civil
rights activists, elderly citizens, others."

1029. PENTAGON PAPERS AND THE AMERICAN REVOLUTION,
THE
American Documentary Films 1972 54 min. b/w
The dialogue is with Daniel Ellsberg, indicted by the
United States government for releasing "secret" Pentagon
Papers in a study of the war in Southeast Asia. Similari-
ties of the philosophy of both the Vietnam War and the
War of Independence are illustrated. Photographed foot-
age includes Dr. Ellsberg plus associates. The primary
issue raised concerns the validity of a "conscientious act
of political rebellion."

1030. PENTAGON PROTEST
Film-Maker's Cooperative Canyon Cinema 1968 14 min.
b/w
A short documentary of the protest in 1967 at the Pentagon is presented. The film is dominated by a Dick Gregory speech at that demonstration.

1031. PROTEST ON THE CAMPUS: COLUMBIA UNIVERSITY--1968
Intext 1970 15 min. b/w
The pros and cons of the student and faculty viewpoints
are examined as symptoms of a nationwide protest. The
film raises a variety of issues for discussion, particularly the impact of the Vietnam confrontation.

1032. QUIET PROTESTOR, THE
Intext 1970 15 min. color s/c/a
The Quaker philosophy is explored, including: American
aid to Russia in 1920; women organizing boycotts against
supermarkets; Germans risking lives to cross over to
West Germany.

1033. RESISTANCE, THE
Henny 1968 23 min. color
Sequences record speeches and capture the vitality of the
Resistance, anti-draft, anti-Vietnam organization whose

members are dedicated to refusing military service.
Speeches, marches, battle scenes are presented, from
Joan Baez to Martin Luther King.

1034. SAUL ALINSKY WENT TO WAR
National Film Board of Canada   1969   57 min.   b/w   s/c/a
The film presents a portrait of Saul Alinsky, a white man
who "hires" himself to the oppressed, instructs them in
the art of protest and sends them to "battle."

1035. SEMESTER OF DISCONTENT
University of California   1968   60 min.   b/w
This is a composite examination of the issues behind the
waves of unrest that permeated American universities in
the late 1960s.   The primary concern, the Vietnam war,
is argued on campuses from Berkeley to Princeton, by
administrators, students.

1036. SOCIAL REVOLUTION
Encyclopaedia Britannica   1952   17 min.   b/w   vt/vc   s/C/a
From the Political Science Series
The "Social Revolution" traces changes during the past two
hundred years.   Constructive and peaceful methods as well
as destructive methods are examined.

1037. SONS AND DAUGHTERS (PARTS I, II)
American Documentary Films   1966   90 min.   b/w   s/c/a
American youth protest in their first major demonstration
against the Vietnam War, the draft and military training
during the international days of protest in 1956.   Featured
are many personalities, from Jerry Rubin to General H.
Hester.   Music is by "The Grateful Dead."

1038. THEIR CHOICE WAS FREEDOM
Department of Defense   National Audiovisual Center   1966
26 min.   b/w
Those who fled communism to seek freedom tell their
story.   True stories highlight three such defectors: a
member of a Chinese embassy in Stockholm; a Russian
seaman who jumps ship; a Russian security officer in Vi-
enna.

1039. TRIAL OF THE CATONSVILLE NINE, THE
Cinema V   Mass Media Associates   1972   85 min.   color
An adaptation of the play, this film tells the story of
Father Daniel Berrigan and Father Philip Berrigan who,
with seven others, were prosecuted in 1968 in a federal
court for napalming 378 1-A draft board files.   Uses the
courtroom as a forum.   The defendants were found guilty.
Awaiting appeal, Daniel Berrigan wrote the original play
based on the actual transcript of the trial.   Major roles
in the film are by the original New York play cast.

1040.   VIETNAM DIALOGUE
        American Documentary Films   1968   40 min.   b/w
                David Schoenbrun gives a speech after his 1968 return
                from the Vietnam Peace talks in Paris.   He makes sug-
                gestions for the possible solution of the conflict.

10 41.   WHEN LOSERS BECOME WINNERS
        National Film Board of Canada   1969   14 min.   b/w
                The sixties, for American politics, was "the decade of
                growing youth participation."   The film examines the polit-
                ical destinies of the younger participants in terms of the
                Vietnam conflict.

1042.   YIPPIE!!
        American Documentary Films   1968   15 min.   b/w
                This is a filmed response to the statements of Chicago
                Mayor R. J. Daley on the 1968 Democratic Convention.
                With "marginal control" by Abbie Hoffman and Jerry Rub-
                in, this is a filmed farce, combining the "brutality" of
                the Chicago police with an orgy scene from D. W. Grif-
                fith's "Intolerance."

                                    Women

1043.   AFTER THE VOTE: NOTES FROM DOWN UNDER
        Kreps (A Canadian Production)   University of California   1971
        23 min.   b/w
                This film examines the current status of women.   It con-
                siders the suffrage movement, the socialization into "sub-
                missive and subordinate" roles, job discrimination and
                lack of opportunities for advancement.

1044.   ALL MY BABIES
        Center for Mass Communication   1953   55 min.   b/w
        Award Winner
                This is an instructional film concerning the history of
                midwife roles in Georgia.

1045.   AMERICAN PARADE: WE THE WOMEN
        Bailey Film Associates   1975   29 min.   color
                This film is an introduction to the American women's
                movement, emphasizing the growing importance of the
                need for equality.   It is narrated by Mary Tyler Moore.

1046.   AMERICAN WOMAN IN THE TWENTIETH CENTURY (PARTS
        I, II)
        Wolper   1964   58 min.   b/w
                The changing role of the American woman is surveyed
                from the days of the Gibson girl through the Flapper Per-
                iod and Rosie the Riveter status to the woman of the six-
                ties.

1047. ... AND AIN'T I A WOMAN?
University of California   Mass Media Associates   30 min.
color
Reverend Peggy Howland is interviewed concerning femin-
ism in the Episcopal Church.   The thrust is on the
"awareness of the subtle and overt ways in which women
experience the predominance of male attitudes and language in our churches."

1048. ... AND EVERYTHING NICE
Bailey Film Associates   1974   20 min.   color
The film explores the life of a married woman in her
mid-thirties as she joins a women's conscious-raising
group.   Discussed are "growing up in a male-oriented
world and the fears felt by women who attempt to change
their lives."   Scenes of the group are intercut with commentary by feminist Gloria Steinem.

1049. AND WHO ARE YOU?
University of California   1966   30 min.   b/w
From the Choice: Challenge for Modern Woman Series
Hubert Coffee and Marya Mannes lead a discussion of the
discovery of one's inner self and the possible conflicts of
maintaining one's individuality.   The panel affords general information on the opportunities for women, women's
effectiveness in their "chosen role" and the developing
changing attitudes.

1050. ANYTHING THEY WANT TO BE
University of California   1974   8 min.   color
This film explores sex role stereotypes in intellectual and
career-oriented activities.   It illustrates two themes: the
low level of competence expected of girls in both academic and vocational problem-solving tasks and the subtle
manner in which girls' career aspirations are channeled.

1051. ANYTHING YOU WANT TO BE
New Day Films   8 min.   b/w
This film identifies the conventional self-images instilled
in women.   A high school girl is shown being continuous-
ly frustrated as she tries to make independent choices regarding her future.   At every step, the alternatives to
the traditional female role seem to disappear and the
girl's aspirations are squelched.

1052. ARE YOU THE ONE?
Brigham Young University   University of California   1969
24 min.   color
A short drama illustrates that marital success is largely
determined by the partners' perception of marital roles.

1053. ASSERTIVE TRAINING FOR WOMEN (PARTS I, II, III)
American Personnel and Guidance Association   17-20 min.
color
These three films encourage women to defend their legiti-
mate interpersonal rights.   Assertion is distinguished
from aggression which involves violating others' rights.

1054. AUTOBIOGRAPHY OF A WOMAN
University of California   20 min.   color
This imagistic film visualizes the forces that have kept
women in their "place." It is set in a fictional turn-of-
the-century background.   A young woman discovers her
own potential, only to be locked up.   The film deals with
her fantasies.

1055. BACK TO SCHOOL, BACK TO WORK
University of California   1973   20 min.   color
The common forms of opposition faced by wives and
mothers who wish to return to school or to work are examined.   Divided into ten vignettes, the film depicts opposition from female friends as well as from husbands.

1056. BARBARA
University of California   14 min.   b/w
Barbara wakes one morning to find herself literally "para-
lyzed" in the midst of her nuclear family.   Her husband
continually rejects and mocks her needs.   Finally, the
repressed resentments build into violence.

1057. BIOGRAPHY OF SUSAN B. ANTHONY
Washington D.C. Public Library   1951   19 min.   b/w
This film covers the entire campaign for women's suf-
frage.

1058. BLACK WOMAN
National Educational Television   Indiana University   1971
52 min.   b/w
This film examines the role and problems of black women
in America.   It includes interviews and discussions with
many prominent blacks, from Lena Horne to LeRoi Jones,
poet.

1059. CAROLINE
McGraw-Hill   28 min.   b/w
To the public she is the pleasant handler of everyone's
complaints at the telephone office.   But behind her calm
exterior, the film reveals doubts about her domestic
world of husband and child.

1060. CEILING, THE
Impact Films   1962   40 min.   b/w
Czech film with English subtitles
This is a drama about a young woman who discovers she

has set herself a low "ceiling" of attainment by dropping
out of school to become a fashion model.

1061. CHOICE: CHALLENGE FOR MODERN WOMEN SERIES
University of California 1967 30 min. each b/w kinescope
Twelve discussion programs are designed to help women
arrive at reasoned choices as they make decisions af-
fecting themselves, their families and society in the mid-
sixties. The panel program titles are: 1. "And Who
Are You?" with Hubert Coffey and Marya Mannes; 2.
"What Is a Woman?" with Keith Berwick and Margaret
Mead; 3. "The Principle That Counts" with Ethel Alpen-
fels, Herbert Fingarette and Joan Lasko; 4. "Marriage
or Mirage?" with Alexander Rosen and Gertrude Sack-
heim; 5. "The Family Affair" with Joan Lasko and Edgar
Winans; 6. "The Unlonely Women" with Richard Farson
and Eve Merriam; 7. "Where Does All the Money Go?"
with Frances Feldman and Bruce McKim; 8. "Wages of
Work" with Mary Keyserling; 9. "The Time of Your
Life" with Eva Schindler-Rainman and Paul Sheats; 10.
"Who Wants Freedom?" with Elisabeth Mann Borgese and
Richard Lichtman. 11. "Is Personal Growth Selfish?"
12. "What Is the Shape of Tomorrow?"

1062. COMING OUT
University of California 11 min. b/w
This is a process film of the Berkeley Feminist Film
Collective. It reflects the stages of women's "alienation
from men."

1063. CRISIS: WOMEN IN HIGHER EDUCATION
University of Maine 1971 color 30 min.
This film covers a wide range of speakers and concerned
women who raise questions and voice opinions about the
national problem concerning women in higher education.

1064. DADDY DON'T BE SILLY--A CASE FOR EQUAL RIGHTS
Indiana University 1974 27 min. color
The Equal Rights Amendment is examined: its history
and the effects its ratification may have on the lives of
women and men. The focus is on the experiences of
three individuals who were discriminated against on the
basis of their sex. An analysis is made of how the ERA
would have prevented such discrimination.

1065. DOLL'S HOUSE (PARTS I, II)
University of California 1968 Pt. I: 33 min.; Pt. II:
27 min. color
Scenes from one of Ibsen's best known plays, The Doll's
House, are set in a modern suburban home. As the
story develops, Nora's illusions about herself and her
family are destroyed. Professor Norris Houghton, Vas-
sar, does the commentary. The substance of this play,

first produced in 1879, is still contemporary.

1066. 51%
       Drucker   Time-Life   1972   26 min.   color   vt/vc
       Three dramatized episodes portray different aspects of
       prejudice and discrimination against women in a manage-
       ment position. The main thrust of the film "is not equal-
       ity, but quality." The conclusion states that "To deny
       women upward mobility is neither fair, legal, nor good
       business."

1067. FROM 3 A. M. TO 10 P. M.
       McGraw-Hill   1967   15 min.   b/w
       This Yugoslav documentary is a tribute to the working
       housewife. It follows a woman through her workday from
       dawn to dusk; when factory work ends, work at home be-
       gins.

1068. GENESIS
       University of California   17 min.   b/w
       This film centers on the Women's Movement in Boston
       but also refers to personal issues raised within the move-
       ment across the country. Interviews with women and
       their children highlight the authenticity.

1069. GOODBYE IN THE MIRROR
       Impact Films   1964   80 min.   b/w
       A dramatic feature filmed on location in Rome, this film
       is centered around the adventures and illusions of three
       girls living abroad. It explores their restless nature and
       their person-involvements in assuming the "role" of wom-
       en.

1070. GROWING UP FEMALE: AS SIX BECOME ONE
       American Documentary Films   1971   60 min.   b/w
       This documentary investigates the social forces that shape
       self-conceptions of women. Examined are the nursery
       school, high school, parents, family, guidance counselor,
       work and marriage. The story is told through the lives
       of six women, "some wealthy, some poor, some black,
       some white." The stress is on the "continuing pressures
       that help keep a woman 'locked in' a role throughout life."

1071. HAPPY MOTHER'S DAY
       University of California   1964   26 min.   b/w
       This is a documentary about Mary Ann Fischer of Aber-
       deen, South Dakota, who became the mother of quintup-
       lets. The film shows the aftermath, from beauty treat-
       ments to quint souvenirs. The stress is on the "exploita-
       tion" of motherhood.

1072. HELEN KELLER AND HER TEACHER
       University of California 1969 27 min. color
           This film explores the relationship between Helen Keller,
           both blind and deaf, and her teacher, Anne Sullivan, and
           how they learned to communicate using only the sense of
           touch.

1073. HOW TO MAKE A WOMAN
       Polymorph University of California 1972 58 min. color
           This film is an adaptation of a feminist play that symboli-
           cally depicts the difficulties facing a woman who wants to
           create her own identity in a male-supremacist society.
           It shows how two men use "typical" manipulative strate-
           gems and "put-downs" to mold a pair of women into vari-
           ous submissive roles, such as "happy housewife," "nag-
           ging shrew," others.

1074. HUMAN IMAGE, THE: MASCULINITY/FEMININITY
       Bailey Film Associates 1974 15 min. color s/c/a
           Live-action and animated dramatizations challenge beliefs
           in sexual roles. The conclusion: the viewer is asked to
           consider the relationship of being human to being a man
           or a woman.

1075. I AM SOMEBODY
       Contemporary McGraw-Hill 1970 18 min. color
           This sympathetic documentary concerns the successful
           strike by non-professional hospital workers, almost all of
           them black women, in Charleston, South Carolina.

1076. INSIDE THE LADIES' HOME JOURNAL
       Janet Gardner American Documentary Films 15 min. b/w
           On March 18, 1970, 200 Women's Liberation Movement
           women entered the offices of the editor of the Ladies'
           Home Journal with demands. Urged were day care centers
           for magazine employees, minimum weekly wages and an
           end to the philosophy of the magazine: "the perception of
           women in the female perspective only."

1077. JOYCE AT 34
       New Day Films 28 min. color
           The camera follows Joyce as she copes with the reality
           of caring for her new baby while pursuing her career as
           a filmmaker. The pressures, delights, doubts, conflicts
           and compromises she experiences are examined.

1078. MARGARET MEAD
       University of California 1960 30 min. b/w
           Celebrated anthropologist Margaret Mead brings her under-
           standing of primitive cultures to a lively discussion of the
           place of women in modern life, the role of the individual.

1079. MARGARET SANGER
McGraw-Hill 1972 15 min. b/w
    This historical documentary examines the emancipation of
    women and, in particular, the "persecution" of Margaret
    Sanger who played a significant role in the development
    of family planning philosophies. Narrated by Katharine
    Hepburn.

1080. MARIANA
United Nations McGraw-Hill 1971 29 min. color
    This film is concerned with the quality of life for wom-
    en, not only in another cultural group but in another
    country as well. A young woman who is actively work-
    ing for women's rights and social change in Chile, Mari-
    ana is shown in her work at a day-care center, inspect-
    ing working conditions in a factory, in recreation.

1081. MASCULINE OR FEMININE: YOUR ROLE IN SOCIETY
Coronet 19 min. b/w and color s/c/a
    This in-depth study of today's changing roles and attitudes
    expresses questions concerning man's role in the home
    and woman's role in business. Examined are viewpoints
    on many levels and on various aspects of male-female
    relationships.

1082. MODERN WOMEN: THE UNEASY LIFE
National Educational Television Indiana University 1964
60 min. b/w s/c/a
    The inner feelings of college-educated women about their
    various roles are examined. Interviewed are: women
    who live traditional roles of the mother and housewife;
    those who combine roles of career woman and housewife;
    and professional career woman. Candidly discussed are
    their frustrations and dissatisfactions, plus the attitudes
    of the men in their life toward educated women.

1083. MOTHERS ARE PEOPLE
National Film Board of Canada 1974 7 min. color
    An articulate Jamaican woman discusses the problems of
    working mothers who are unable to use facilities of day-
    care centers.

1084. NEVER UNDERESTIMATE THE POWER OF A WOMAN
University of Wisconsin 1971 15 min. color
    The growing need for and effect of women in industry and
    in skilled professions are estimated. Reviewed are per-
    sonnel problems in positions where traditionally women
    have been few in number.

1085. OTHER WOMEN, OTHER WORK
Churchill Boston University 20 min. color s/a
    This film presents vignettes of a number of unusual wom-
    en who hope to "change attitudes toward suitable 'woman's
    work'."

1086. RADCLIFFE BLUES
       American Documentary Films   23 min.   b/w
              A Radcliffe student discusses the process of her radicali-
              zation, particularly her identification with the conditions
              of women in this country.

1087. SALT OF THE EARTH
       American Documentary Films   94 min.   b/w
              This film illustrates how a miners' strike involves the
              participation of the workers' wives.   The film explores
              the "changing consciousness of the women."

1088. SCHMEERGUNTZ
       Nelson   University of California   1964   15 min.   b/w
              This "pioneering" women's film anticipated the feminist
              movement of the seventies.   It contrasts the romantic,
              stereotyped "glamour girl" ideal prevalent in the media,
              advertising and beauty contests, with the more typical
              aspects of women's role--pregnancy, child care, house-
              cleaning, routine.

1089. SISTERS
       Women's Film Cooperative   21 min.   color
              Two sisters on a symbolic journey recall childhood events
              that led to the status of their conflicting female roles.

1090. SOCIAL CHANGE AND THE AMERICAN WOMAN
       Films, Inc.   19 min.   b/w
              The film explores the traditional role of American women
              in the innocent years of the early 20th century.   Social
              changes that have affected American women are viewed:
              legal emancipation, educational, economic opportunities.

1091. SOMETHING DIFFERENT
       Impact Films   1963   80 min.   b/w
       A Czech film with English subtitles
              This film follows a quest for meaning in life by two very
              different women.   Though their lives are not interrelated,
              Vera, a harried, middleaged housewife, and Eva, a cham-
              pion gymnast, reflect complementary aspects of modern
              woman's role.   Eva Bosakova, Olympian Gold Medalist,
              portrays herself in the film.

1092.   SOMETIMES I WONDER WHO I AM
       New Day Films   1972   4 min.   b/w
              This is a brief, succinct study of the conflict felt by a
              young housewife who dreams of the career she could have
              had.

1093. SUSAN B. ANTHONY IS TRIED FOR VOTING
       CBS-TV   McGraw-Hill   1955   27 min.   b/w   s/c/a
       From the You Are There Series
              Susan B. Anthony's fight for women's suffrage is recalled

in terms of the trial and the famous speech that championed the cause and won her freedom.

1094. TAKE THIS WOMAN
University of California 1971 27 min. color
This film illustrates the problems of numbers of women who have fought to obtain unusual or prestigious jobs. The discrimination realities are examined. (With Joan Dempsey Klein, Aileen Hernandez, Yvonne Brathwaite.)

1095. THEY ALSO SERVE
Mass Media Associates 1940 8 min. b/w
The heroine of this simple study is an "average" housewife of England in the days when such women quietly assumed all the burdens of daily living in order to free soldiers and defense workers for their jobs.

1096. THIS IS NO TIME FOR ROMANCE
McGraw-Hill 28 min. color
This film suggests that, for some women, marriage may not end their dreams of romance.

1097. THREE LIVES
Impact Films 1970 70 min. color
Produced by Kate Millett
Three women are interviewed about their respective lives: an older woman, a young artist, a housewife.

1098. TO BE A WOMAN
Billy Budd 27 min. color
Several young women discuss their feelings on the meaning of femininity, stereotypes about females and womanhood. Accompanied by Peter Max-type cartoons.

1099. TO BE YOUNG, GIFTED AND BLACK
Brandon Indiana University 1972 90 min. color
This is the film adaptation of the Broadway play about the life and early death of Lorraine Hansberry, the young black woman who wrote A Raisin in the Sun. It traces her development as a "person and as an artist" and recreates several significant incidents in her life that shaped her thinking.

1100. TROUBLE WITH WOMEN, THE
McGraw-Hill 1959 7 min. b/w
This is a discussion film about the pros and cons of women factory workers. Viewers are asked to take an objective look at the role of the woman factory worker in industry.

1101. VERONICA
University of California 1970 27 min. color
Veronica Glover, a black student leader, tells about her

struggle for self-awareness in the face of pressures from
both black and white students.

1102. VIRGINIA WOOLF: THE MOMENT WHOLE
       University of California 1972 27 min. color
          Selected passages from Virginia Woolf's writings convey
          her concept of woman and articulate the problems and
          pressures of being a woman writer.

1103. WE ARE WOMAN
       Motivational Media 1974 29 min. color
          This film makes a strong case for individual rights and
          what this should/would mean for men. The film is de-
          signed to de-polarize both sexes regarding woman's non-
          traditionalist concept of herself. Narrated by Helen Red-
          dy.

1104. WHAT IS A WOMAN?
       University of California 1966 30 min. b/w
       From the Choice: Challenge for Modern Women Series
          Speakers examine criteria for feminine and masculine
          "traits" as prescribed by society and confused by chang-
          ing patterns. Opportunities for continuing education are
          illustrated as well as development of attitudes that in-
          crease women's effectiveness in their "chosen" roles.

1105. WHAT IS THE SHAPE OF TOMORROW?
       Women's Film Cooperative 27 min. b/w
          Jeanne Noble, psychologist, and Rabbi Alfred Gottschalk,
          Dean, Hebrew Union College, discuss variations in per-
          sonal standards, beliefs and values, spiritual, moral and
          interpersonal sources of strength; and women's power in
          shaping the world of tomorrow.

1106. WHO WANTS FREEDOM?
       University of California 1966 30 min. b/w
       From the Choice: Challenge for Modern Women Series
          Women's chosen roles are discussed in terms of the cur-
          rent conflicts in definition.

1107. WINDY DAY
       Women's Film Cooperative 17 min. color
          This cartoon illustrates two sisters acting out their fanta-
          sies. They perceive women as brides and mothers only.
          It therefore seems natural to them that their fantasy mar-
          riages are followed immediately by old age and death.

1108. WISHFULFILMING
       Women's Film Cooperative 14 min. b/w
          This film explores the process of working "collectively"
          to make a film about women.

1109. WOMAN IN THAT JOB?, A
Department of Labor   National Audiovisual Center   1971
30 min.   color
Directed toward employers, their affirmative action plans,
this film shows them exactly how to re-engineer positions
to encourage women to apply.   It also discusses the "bias" involved in upward mobility on the job.

1110. WOMAN'S FILM, THE
San Francisco Newsreel   45 min.   b/w
Made by an all-woman crew, this film stresses the reality of the day-to-day lives of poor and working-class
women, including blacks and chicanas.   Their increased
awareness led them to become involved in the women's
movement.

1111. WOMAN'S PLACE
Xerox   University of California   1973   52 min.   color
This film traces the influences that create and perpetuate
the "traditional" role of women, including children's
books and toys, film clips and advertising.   It focuses on
examples of how women are questioning and attempting to
change their roles.

1112. WOMAN'S PLACE?
American Association of University Women   30 min.   b/w
This condensation of Frankly Female, a television show
narrated by Betty Groebli, includes a panel discussion by
six women on the status of women.

1113. WOMEN: THE EMERGING RESOURCE
Women's Film Cooperative   1972   7 hours of film and vt
color
The complete program with six sessions includes role
playing, individual participation, group discussions and
team presentations.   The goal is to demonstrate techniques for counseling women and managers to learn how
to design and implement action programs required by law.

1114. WOMEN: THE HAND THAT CRADLES THE ROCK
Women's Film Cooperative   University of California   1971
23 min.   color
This film examines the possibility that today's Women's
Liberation Movement may be a forerunner of a total re-
constitution of women's role in society.

1115. WOMEN, AMEN!
University of California   1973   15 min.   color
This film examines the impact of the women's movement
on churches in the United States.   It shows a young woman activist who organizes consciousness-raising groups,
reforms worship services and finally enters a seminary.

1116. WOMEN EMERGING: COMPARING CULTURAL EXPECTA-
       TIONS
       University of California 1975 27 min. b/w
            This is a documentary of the experiences of a multicul-
            tural women's class at Agora, an experimental school
            within Berkeley High School in Berkeley, California. It
            presents four days to illustrate some of the key issues
            addressed to the class, including differences and similar-
            ities of women of various cultures and the friendship po-
            tential among the women.

1117. WOMEN GET THE VOTE
       CBS McGraw-Hill 27 min. b/w
       From the 20th Century Series
            Using historic footage, this film covers the difficult years
            of the first woman's rights to vote movement, the cam-
            paign and the final triumph.

1118. WOMEN IN A CHANGING WORLD
       University of California 1975 48 min. color
            This film demonstrates that traditional women's roles are
            being challenged by new opportunities as a result of edu-
            cation, family planning and pressures for economic, so-
            cial, political equality.

1119. WOMEN IN COMMUNICATIONS
       Bailey Film Associates 15 min. b/w
            Three articulate young women offer some insight into
            communications careers. Briefings in filmmaking, news-
            reporting and broadcasting are given by: Emiko Omori,
            freelance cinematographer; Carol Pogash, San Francisco
            Examiner reporter; Kathy Gori, KMPC, Los Angeles disc
            jockey.

1120. WOMEN IN PRISON
       Carousel 1974 54 min. color
            This is a revealing survey of conditions in three women's
            prisons in Los Angeles, California, Alderson, West Vir-
            ginia and Marysville, Ohio. Stereotyped, sex-role behav-
            ior is expected of the women while in prison.

1121. WOMEN ON THE MARCH: STRUGGLE FOR EQUAL RIGHTS
       (PARTS I, II)
       National Film Board of Canada McGraw-Hill 1958 30 min.
       b/w
            The struggle for the franchise and other rights is record-
            ed from the beginning of the movement, in the twenties,
            to the status of women in 1958. Both parts treat the
            struggle, the protest and achievements in various fields.

1122. WOMEN TALKING
       Women's Film Cooperative 1971 80 min. b/w
            Featured are conversations with leading personalities in

the forefront of the women's liberation movement. They
relate experiences that contribute to a greater awareness
of women's social "oppression." Housewives contrast
their responsibilities with those of working women.

1123. WOMEN UP IN ARMS
McGraw-Hill   28 min.   b/w
In this study of Moslem women, contrasts are made of
the conflicting lifestyles of three generations.

1124. WOMEN UP THE CAREER LADDER
University of California at Los Angeles   1972   30 min.   b/w
This film provides a springboard for discussion to help
women employees recognize, understand and cope with issues involved in moving up the career ladder.

1125. WOMEN'S FILM
Women's Cooperative   50 min.   b/w
This is an insightful documentary about the heart of the
Women's Movement. Women of different races, back-
grounds, jobs, talk about their lives and participate in
different activities.

1126. WOMEN'S LIB--FROM WHAT? FOR WHAT?
Association-Sterling Films   30 min.   b/w
Marya Mannes, writer and television personality, moderates a panel concerned with job discrimination, the vote,
child care, the black woman, media.

1127. WOMEN'S LIBERATION
ABC Media   1972   23 min.   color
The Women's Movement is surveyed on university campuses, in cities, in corporations and in "the minds of men
and women today." Broad coverage is presented of what
women want and the rhetoric of the plan to get it. Views
range from those of Betty Friedan to those of Senator
Birch Bayh.

1128. WOMEN'S RIGHTS IN THE U.S.--AN INFORMAL HISTORY
University of California   1974   27 min.   color
This film emphasizes the origins of the women's movement in the abolitionist movement and the long struggle
for the vote. Personalities spotlighted are Jane Addams,
Susan B. Anthony, Lucy Stone, Elizabeth Cady Stanton,
others.

1129. WOO WHO? MAY WILSON
New Day Films   1969   33 min.   color
A 63-year-old former "wife-housekeeper-cook-mother"
tells her story. After her husband left her, she moved
to New York City from the country and began creating a
new life in which her hobby, art, became central to her
life.

1130. 'X' FACTOR, THE: WOMEN AS PEOPLE--A SERIES
       (PARTS I, II)
       Cornell University 1970 Each part: 28 min. b/w vt/vc
           Part I presents the objective status and measurable facts
           about women in the United States. Part II deals with the
           image of women, how this image affects attitudes both
           toward self and others. The series brings out some of
           the underlying causes of growing female unrest.

1131. YOU DON'T HAVE TO BUY THE WAR, MRS. SMITH
       Impact Films 1970 30 min. b/w
           Bess Myerson, Commissioner of Consumer Affairs for
           New York City, calls upon each of us to examine govern-
           ment policies by a re-examination of our own individual
           concepts and priorities.

                              NONVERBAL

1132. ART OF SILENCE, THE: PANTOMIMES WITH MARCEL
       MARCEAU
       Encyclopaedia Britannica from 8-17 min. each color vt/vc
           This series of thirteen films deals with the meaning of
           mime: "The Language of the Heart"; "Bip as a Skater";
           "The Painter"; "Bip at a Society Party"; "The Sideshow";
           "Bip Hunts Butterflies"; "The Creation of the World";
           "Youth, Maturity, Old Age"; "The Maskmaker"; "Bip as
           a Soldier"; "The Dream"; "The Hands"; "Cage."

1133. COMMUNICATION CASEBOOK: THE CASE OF THE SILENT
       YELL IV
       Strauss 1956 2 min. b/w C
       From "The Inner Man Steps Out"
           Communication is examined in terms of nonverbal signals
           and unspoken attitudes.

1134. INVISIBLE WALLS
       University of California 1969 12 min. b/w s/c/a
           This film illustrates the dependence of American social
           interaction upon nonverbal communication. The film
           focuses on "invisible barriers" erected by individuals.

1135. IRONY
       Bailey Film Associates 4 min. color
           These stories comment on a different aspect of "irony."
           By analyzing each plot, viewers determine the limits nec-
           essary to achieve irony in a nonverbal narrative form.

1136. KINESICS
       Pennsylvania State University 1964 73 min.
           Raymond L. Birdwhistell, Eastern Pennsylvania Psychi-
           atric Institute, delivers a lecture about a "system of

categorizing and defining facial expressions, gestures,
posturing in terms of communicative meaning."

1137. LITTLE BLUE APRON
Bailey Film Associates 1967 8 min. color s/c/a
Made in Czechoslovakia No narration
The meaning of this story is contingent upon the viewer's
interpretation of the symbols used. The film chronicles
the adventures of a white paper bird and a little blue apron. Some believe the story is a form of protest.

1138. LOOKING FOR ME
University of California 29 min. b/w s/c/a
Janet Adler presents a film about body awareness and
body language. If other communication methods fail,
methods of nonverbal communication are suggested.

1139. LOUDER THAN WORDS
Northern Virginia Educational Television (WNVT) 1971
17 min. color
From Know What I Mean Series: #4
This film suggests that glances, postures, gestures are
all "culture-shaped" and often speak more eloquently
than words. Body language meanings are explored and
compared.

1140. MATRIX III
Museum of Modern Art 1972 9 min. color
This computer-art film by John Whitney, Sr. is a visual
study in symbolism. Patterns evoke meanings for the
viewer, contingent upon each person's experience. An
abstract film; "pure form tells its own story from beginning to end."

1141. MIME OF MARCEL MARCEAU, THE
Learning Corporation of America 23 min. color
This film follows the great French pantomimist at work
both on-stage and behind the scenes. We watch Marcel
Marceau before an audience, giving a seemingly effort-
less performance that runs the gamut from comedy to
tragedy.

1142. NONVERBAL COMMUNICATION
Veterans Administration National Audiovisual Center 1952
27 min. b/w
This film discusses the recognition of clues of nonverbal
communication. Suggestions are offered in which these
clues can be used in interview situations to obtain information and, if necessary, to further therapy.

1143. SMILE, THE
Teleketics 1971 30-second spot announcement
This brief "public service" announcement suggests "man's

countenance portrays many messages to others." It questions man's reactions to facial expressions and the effectiveness of body language.

1144.   STAINED GLASS: A PHOTOGRAPHIC ESSAY
        Bailey Film Associates   1971   8 min.   color   s/c/a
        No narration
            In this essay of nonverbal communication, a craftsman
            makes a stained glass work of art to express his love of
            beauty.   Students of language and composition may interpret his inspiration and perception.

1145.   TOUCHING
        Psychological Films   35 min.   color   vt/vc
            This filmed conversation with Dr. Ashley Montagu, sociologist and anthropologist, develops the case that touching is necessary for human life.   From cuddling the infant to the importance of touching in current encounter therapy, the psychological impact of touching is illustrated.

                    PARLIAMENTARY PROCEDURE

1146.   CONDUCTING A MEETING
        McGraw-Hill   1952   11 min.   b/w   s/c/a
        From the Speech Series
            This film demonstrates basic parliamentary procedures
            which contribute to a successful and efficient meeting.
            The prescribed order of business is explained.   Good
            communication habits are stressed.

1147.   HOW TO CONDUCT A MEETING
        Centron   1970   12 min.   color   s/c/a
        From the Art of Communication Series   (A revised version
        of Speech: Conducting a Meeting)
            This film dramatizes the correct way to conduct a meeting.   The viewer learns the outlines of order of business,
            how motions are made, restated, discussed and amended,
            as well as how to take votes.   The camera acts as a
            participant and instructor and takes the viewer through
            steps of a complete meeting.   Shown are rules of appropriate conduct, disagreements and conflict.

1148.   MR. CHAIRMAN   (THE FUNDAMENTALS OF PARLIAMENTARY LAW)
        Encyclopaedia Britannica   1960   13 min.   color   vt/vc   s/c/a
            This film explores a series of dramatic episodes showing
            organized groups, how discussions can be conducted, and
            how the rules of democratic action can be applied efficiently.

1149. PARLIAMENTARY PROCEDURE
       National Film Board of Canada 1955 22 min. s/c/a
              Illustrated are the rules of parliamentary procedure which
              facilitate the orderly conduct of a meeting. The com-
              mentator joins the meeting and, in an informal manner,
              explains functions of the chairman, motion presentation,
              amendment, point of order and point of information.

1150. PARLIAMENTARY PROCEDURE
       Coronet 1952 11 min. b/w s/c/a
              Explained and interpreted are scenes from a representa-
              tive meeting to exemplify clarity, with the order of busi-
              ness and rules followed by parliamentary procedure. Or-
              der of business, committee reports, amendments, voting
              are all considered.

1151. PARLIAMENTARY PROCEDURES IN ACTION
       Coronet 1965 17 min. b/w and color s/c/a
       Second Edition
              Events of an actual meeting are presented. There are
              parallel explanations of key concepts: duties of officers,
              order of the agenda, committee activities, types of mo-
              tions, subsidiary and privilege.

                              PERCEPTION

1152. ADVENTURES OF AN ASTERISK
       Storyboard Michigan State University 10 min. color c/a
              Animated drawings depict man (symbolized by the figure
              *) as he matures from childhood to adulthood. Unable to re-
              act freely to the world, the adult neither sees nor finds
              pleasure in new things until, through his own child, he
              has "a new rebirth."

1153. AMERICAN IMAGE, THE
       McGraw-Hill 54 min. color
              This film portrays America as seen through the eyes of
              its artists from colonial times to the present. Assist-
              ance is provided by the resources of the Whitney Museum
              of American Art in New York.

1154. CHILD OF THE FUTURE
       National Film Board of Canada McGraw-Hill 1965 59 min.
              b/w
       Host Narrator: Marshall McLuhan
              The viewer learns of technical advances and the subse-
              quent changes in education. The theory and practice of
              visual perception are presented by leading authorities in
              the field, including Dr. Jerome Bruner of Harvard Uni-
              versity.

1155. COMMUNICATION CASEBOOK: THE CASE OF THE WRONG-
WAY WAVE-LENGTH II
Strauss 1956 2 min. b/w C
From "The Inner Man Steps Out"
    Demonstrates the necessity for the study of individual dif-
    ferences in order to realize maximum communication.

1156. CRITIC, THE
Learning Corporation of America 1963 4 min. color any
age
Academy Award Winner, 1963
    This film is a spoof on the audience as well as on the of-
    ferings in today's theatre. It ridicules both "art" that
    is really a hoax and people who mistake their ignorance
    for wit and wisdom. The film analyzes perceptive mo-
    tives of the audience.

1157. CRITICAL THINKING: MAKING SURE OF THE FACTS
Coronet 11 min. b/w and color s/c
Participant: Robert S. Fox, Director, University School of
Education, University of Michigan
Second edition of "How to Judge Facts"
    The discussion concerns facts about a particular situation.
    Topics include those dealing with reading, researching,
    analyzing and television viewing. Suggestions offered in-
    volve: checking primary eyewitness accounts, checking
    sources of information, and assessing skills and knowledge
    of the source.

1158. DEMONSTRATIONS IN PERCEPTION
United States Navy National Audiovisual Center 1951
26 min. b/w
    Using apparatus developed by the Institute for Associated
    Research at the National Institute of Health, this film of-
    fers demonstrations of perceptual phenomena at Princeton
    University.

1159. EXPERIENCE AS GIVE AND TAKE
National Educational Television Indiana University 1956
30 min. b/w c/a
From the Language in Action Series
    Dr. S. I. Hayakawa demonstrates illusory perceptions and
    resultant miscommunication. He concludes: "two people
    can give totally different reports of the same experience.
    At this point, the primary challenge of communication be-
    gins."

1160. EYE OF THE BEHOLDER
Stuart Reynolds 1955 27 min. b/w and color s/c/a
    This film on perception dramatizes the fact that "no two
    people perceive the same thing the same way." It
    stresses the importance of two-way communication, the
    value of empathy, the significance of projection and of
    misjudging others.

1161. FIDELITY OF REPORT
Oregon State Cooperative Extension 1946 6 min. b/w
silent
    In order to measure the accuracy of both observation and
    report, the events of a street robbery are dramatized.
    A questionnaire is circulated concerning the recall of
    events. There is a robbery repetition and another ques-
    tionnaire for recall.

1162. FILMBLOCK I
Mark Adrian Canyon Cinema 1957-65 b/w and color
20 min.
    Black Movie (1957)
    This is a study concerning the effects of different colors
    presented in rhythmic proportion. The purpose is to il-
    lustrate visual effects of the color "red" as different from
    the semantic effects of the spoken word "red." The en-
    tire film consists of a random-generated sequence of dif-
    ferent colors, accompanied by varied names of colors,
    occurring in sequences.

    Text I (1964)
    A computer-generated film, the program contains the fol-
    lowing condition: from a lexical storage there should be
    drawn four words at random, which are understandable
    in English as well as in German. The words are ran-
    domly-distributed as to size, length of projection and
    place on the screen. The film's aim is "to show differ-
    ent associations aroused by purely randomly-generated
    word combinations."

    Text II (1964)
    A computer-generated film, with a program of permuta-
    tion, presents two rows of letters. One contains eight,
    the other nine members, permuted, resulting in different
    combinations of two-letter units on the screen. Occasion-
    ally, the permutation yields semantically meaningful
    words.

1163. IS IT ALWAYS RIGHT TO BE RIGHT?
Bosustow/King Screen Didactic 1970 8 min. color s/c/a
Award Winner
    Orson Welles narrates this animated film parable about
    the "land where men always were right." Focus is on
    contemporary society's problems: generation gaps, ra-
    cial conflict, poverty. The story moves from stalemate
    to the declaration that "you may be right--I may be
    wrong." The film interlaces animation with live-action
    and concludes with "hope and challenge."

1164. JUNKYARD
Bailey Film Associates 1971 10 min. color s/c/a
No narration
    The junkyard appears at first glance to be a depository

of wreckage and endless corrosion. On a closer examination, however, the viewer realizes that the junkyard
may also be perceived as a world of rugged yet delicate
beauty. Moods shift and, finally, the junkyard becomes
a place of inspiration replete with changing shapes, col-
ors, moods.

1165. MAN WHO HAD TO SING, THE
Zagreb Films   Mass Media Associates   1971   10 min.   color
Award Winner
      A luckless Charlie Brown-type character, a little "sing-
      ing man," gets misunderstood throughout a lifetime of
      animated adventures. None of the agitation he causes is
      intentional but, nevertheless, he is never understood, and
      is the Everyman figure personified.

1166. MAN WHO KNOWS IT ALL, THE
National Educational Television   Indiana University   1955
30 min.   b/w   s/c/a
From the Talking Sense Series
      The late Dr. Irving Lee considers the consequences of an
      attitude evident in many people: the disease of "allness."
      "Allness" is evident in one who perceives what he knows
      or says about a thing is all that can be said. He sug-
      gests that mental growth is inhibited when this attitude ex-
      ists.

1167. MEANINGS ARE IN PEOPLE
Bureau of National Affairs   1965   24 min.   color
From the Berlo Effective Communication Series
      Dr. David Berlo analyzes the "conveyor belt" view of di-
      rect communication: "I told you what to do." He sug-
      gests that meanings are in people, rather than in words.
      Showing some "misunderstandings," he presents a reen-
      actment of what was "said" and what was "thought" and
      "implied" by several managers and subordinates in a typ-
      ical work situation. His conclusion is that "communica-
      tion is the main tool in working with people."

1168. MIND THE GAP
Northern Virginia Educational Television   (WNVT)   1972
19:28 min.   color
From Know What I Mean Series: #3
      Instructor Victor Kryston examines language perception
      problems, explaining that eyes, ears and mind act as both
      censors and sensors of information processing. Students
      experiment with methods for overcoming gaps in commun-
      ication.

1169. MISCOMMUNICATIONS
Mass Media Associates   1972   5 min.   color   animation
      Four brief cartoons are each followed by a play-on-words
      parody of a moral, all having to do with confusion in

terms between individuals confronting each other. The
film is conceived as a "series of satirical probes into the
mine-field of human relations." Morals animated include:
when communicating, be credible; when cooperating, communicate first; when communicating, be precise; when
communicating, be persistent.

1170. PERCEPTION
McGraw-Hill National Institute of Mental Health 1957
17 min. b/w C/a
From the Psychology Series
By showing activities of a group of college students spending an evening in a "common room," this film illustrates
basic principles of perception. It details perceptual con-
stancy, attention, expectancy or set and perception as an
organizing process.

1171. PERCEPTION AND COMMUNICATION
Ohio State University for the Office of Education National
Audiovisual Center 1967 32 min. b/w and color C/a
From the Communication Theory and New Educational Media
Series
Third in the series, this film shows examples of how hu-
man perception affects the individual's concept of reality
and the communication process. Two major theories of
perception are introduced: the cognitive and the transac-
tional, each illustrated in six segments.

1172. PERCEPTION OF WORDS
George Washington University 1968 12 min. b/w silent
This laboratory film studies the influence of word usage
frequency on perception. In different order for a total of
sixty trials, words of varied frequencies are projected
four times. Each successive time of projection the word
list is changed to make the words easier to use. Students write guesses before new trials warn of the next
word. Data computed show whether frequency of usage
influences perceptual accuracy.

1173. SAME BUT DIFFERENT
Associated Instructional Films Mass Media Associates 1971
4 min. color
In this satirical film, two people in an imaginary abstract
society learn interesting things about society's expected
roles. Percy is the conformist and Sidney is the would-
be non-conformist. Each questions his role and arrives
at different answers. According to one, "if you want to
be out of the run, stay the same and let all change about
you. So, you end up the different one." The other
learns: "It's perfectly all right to be different provided
you stay the same."

1174. STILL?
      Time-Life 1974 14 min. b/w and color vt/vc
            This film is concerned with how we perceive things and
            also of our memory of that perception. The latter is ac-
            complished by reconstructing childlike sensory experi-
            ences. By flipping back and forth between black and
            white and color, the film suggests a "world wavering be-
            tween the present and the past."

1175. THEORIES OF PERCEPTION
      University of Ohio 5 min. b/w s/c/a
            Dr. Kenneth Norberg defines the relation of perception to
            education. He introduces the fact that there are many
            theories of perception, relating many of these theories to
            applications in industry training programs, intercultural
            programs and programs for the culturally-deprived.

1176. UP IS DOWN
      Pyramid National Audiovisual Center 1969 6 min. color
            An animated fable tells the story of a boy who sees
            things "differently." Examined are the themes of intol-
            erance, conformity and the generation gap.

1177. VISUAL PERCEPTION
      ETC University of Hawaii 1959 19 min. color s/c/a
      From the Horizons of Science Series
            Dr. Hadley Cantril at the Democratic Center at Prince-
            ton University discusses his investigations on the effects
            of some of our assumptions of what we perceive as re-
            lated to experience, preconception.

1178. WAY I SEE IT, THE
      Roundtable 23 min. b/w and color
            When two people perceive the same thing differently the
            "difference" can lead to failure in job assignments and a
            complete breakdown in communication and subsequent re-
            lationships. This open-end film examines perceptual dif-
            ferences and their effects.

1179. WHAT IS A GOOD OBSERVER?
      National Educational Television (WOL-TV) Indiana University
      30 min. b/w
      From the Talking Sense Series
            The late Irving Lee analyzes the difference between a
            good and a bad observer. He explains how observation
            is made, generally, in terms of similarities: yet aware-
            ness of differences is the "mark of the mature mind."

1180. WORLD TO PERCEIVE, A
      National Educational Television Indiana University 1963
      28 min. b/w s/c/a
      From the Focus on Behavior Series
            This film presents the results of specialists' research

on the role of perception in handling and processing information from one's environment. Analyzed is the question of how personalities affect perception.

PERSUASION

1181. ATTITUDE CHANGE
University of Utah   1963   29 min.   b/w   C/a
From the Human Relations Series
This film discusses the popular theory that it is "relatively simple" to change an opinion or attitude. Factors
and qualities necessary to actuate, modify and influence
changes in attitude are detailed.

1182. ATTITUDE FORMATION
University of Utah   1963   29 min.   b/w   C/a
From the Human Relations Series
Sources of the attainment of attitudes are analyzed, as
are the forces that help determine attitudes and the opin-
ions of individuals relative to these forces.

1183. ATTITUDES
Oregon State University   29 min.   b/w   kinescope   c/a
This filmed lecture discusses three crucial attitude areas
important to a supervisor in terms of their formation and
possible change.

1184. BRAINWASHING (PARTS I, II)
CBS-TV News   Associated Films   Each segment: 26 min.
b/w   c/a
From the Twentieth Century Series
Former prisoners of the communists reminisce about
brainwashing techniques and their resistance to them.
They conclude that brainwashing is a combination of "con-
ditioning and suggestion."

1185. BRAINWASHING OF JOHN HAYES, THE
Readers' Digest   1955   27 min.   b/w   s/c/a
This film explains the story of the Reverend John Hayes,
missionary and teacher in China, who found himself sub-
jected to communist brainwashing tortures. He describes
his resistance "to break[ing] under the strain" and his
ability to use his court trial as a sounding board for his
ideas.

1186. CASE HISTORY OF A RUMOR, THE (PARTS I, II)
CBS News   Carousel   1963   26 min. each part   b/w   s/C/a
From CBS Reports Series
This CBS documentary describes the events which took
place following the rumor that the anti-communist mili-
tary maneuver (Operation Water Moccasin) was a "foreign

plot to occupy Georgia and eventually all of the country."
The rumor resulted from "prejudice, political ignorance,
suspicion and created a climate of hostility and extremism."

1187.   CREATIVE ATTITUDE
General Motors (Free Loan Film) 27 min. color s/c
This film on motivation outlines methods to spark new
ideas, recognizing that advanced ideas are often stifled
by ridicule. It suggests that barriers of conventional
thinking should be penetrated and one "should project into the realm of the new and unknown."

1188.   EFFECTIVE PERSUASION
McGraw-Hill 1969 10 min. color s/c/a
From the Oral Communication Series
The viewer learns how effective oral persuasion can be.
The emphasis is on clear organization, simplicity, solid
argument, understanding of relevant strategies, audience
analysis and multi-sensory stimuli. Recorded segments
are shown from speeches by Churchill, Adlai Stevenson,
John F. Kennedy and Martin Luther King.

1189.   EXPERIMENTAL NEUROSES BY CONTROL OF EMOTIONS
Psychological Films 30 min. b/w
This film examines research in which attempts are made
to produce analogues of phobic reactions. It is useful in
discussion of attitude change, hypnosis and conditioning.

1190.   HYPNOTIC BEHAVIOR
Crowell, Collier, Macmillan 27 min. b/w c/a
Dr. Lester S. Beck observes hypnosis through a motion
picture camera. Demonstrated are trance, eye and arm
catalepsy, insensibility to pain, post-hypnotic amnesia
and post-hypnotic suggestion.

1191.   PEOPLE DON'T RESIST CHANGE
Bureau of National Affairs 22 min. b/w
Allan H. Morgensen suggests that the businessman must
involve people closest to the problem to persuade them
to change.

1192.   POWER OF EMOTION IN SPEECH, THE
McGraw-Hill 1969 15 min. color s/c/a
From the Oral Communication Series
The film's message is that speeches which appeal to emotions must have clear and definite purpose, simple language and substantial proof. Specific established speeches
of persuasion are analyzed for purpose, nature of appeals
and reasons for success. Included are Marc Antony's
"Funeral Oration" to exemplify persuasive speech strategies.

1193. PROPAGANDA TECHNIQUES
Coronet 1949 11 min. b/w s/c/a
This film demonstrates seven basic methods of recog-
nized and established propaganda techniques and encourages the adaptation of a judicious, critical attitude toward these methods. .

1194. PUBLIC OPINION
Encyclopaedia Britannica 1948 11 min. b/w vt/vc s/c/a
From the Political Science and Economics Series
Public opinion is analyzed through its various stages:
tension, diagnosis, prescription, debate and action. Its
course, environmental factors and influence are also examined.

1195. RUMOR
Crowell, Collier, Macmillan Columbia 1972 6 min.
Animated
Cartoonist Robert Osborn traces the development of a
rumor as it spreads. Questions posed include: Can a
rumor be brought under control? How can it be prevented?

1196. SOCIAL PSYCHOLOGY
CRM Films 1971 34 min. color vt/vc c/a
From the Psychology Today Series
Award Winner
This film demonstrates the social comparison theory, il-
lustrating how attitudes are formed and changed. It theo-
rizes on the nature of racial prejudice. Appearing are
four psychologists, other specialists.

1197. TRIAL BY COMMITTEE
Teamsters Union San Francisco State 1966 33 min. b/w
c/a
Produced for the Missouri-Kansas Conference of Teamsters, this film reports on the investigation of the team-
ster's union by the McClellan Committee. It is considered a propaganda film in that it "illustrates several ques-
tionable methods of persuasion in its denunciation of procedures of the congressional investigation."

1198. TRUTH AND THE DRAGON
Perennial 1969 11 min. color s/a
This animated film emphasizes the several ways to recognize the guises of propaganda. It stresses the need for
careful listening, researching and separating fact from
fiction. The film concludes that "truth doesn't absorb itself into everyone."

1199. UNCONSCIOUS MOTIVATION
Crowell, Collier, Macmillan 1949 27 min. b/w s/c
Influences of which we are unaware often determine our

everyday actions. In this film a young man and woman
are subjects in a hypnotic suggestion experiment. The
part unconscious motivation plays in human behavior is
shown, with psychological techniques for detecting repressed ideas and beneficial release.

•

POLITICAL

Campaigns

1200. AGE OF KENNEDY (PARTS I, II)
       National Broadcasting Corporation 1967 Pt. I: 23 min.;
       Pt. II: 54 min. b/w s/c/a
           The major events and policies of JFK's presidency are
           all analyzed. These include the campaigns, the Bay of
           Pigs, Peace Corps, Alliance for Progress, as well as
           other history-making decisions of his administration.
           Part I illustrates the early years of his life; Part II sur-
           veys the presidential period.

1201. AGNEW
       Milner-Fenwick United States Information Agency 1970
       15 min. color
       Award: CINE Golden Eagle Award
           Using as a framework the former Vice President's visit
           to seven countries, the film comments on Agnew's activi-
           ties before he became Vice President. It focuses on his
           campaign against racial discrimination and aid to educa-
           tion while Governor of Maryland.

1202. ALL THE KING'S MEN
       Audio/Brandon 109 min. b/w
       Starring Broderick Crawford, Joanne Dru, John Ireland,
       Mercedes McCambridge, John Derek
           Based on the Pulitzer Prize novel of Robert Penn Warren,
           this film is the story of a corrupt administration, a pow-
           er-hungry governor, the campaign and repercussions.

1203. CAMPAIGN
       Coronet University of California 1973 20 min. b/w
           This is a documentary of Democrat Kathy O'Neill's un-
           successful effort to unseat a Republican incumbent in the
           1972 California State Senate election. Interviews provide
           portraits of the candidate and her key staff members as
           well as day-to-day coverage of campaign activities.

1204. CAMPAIGN: AMERICAN STYLE
       CBS News Bailey Film Associates 1968 39 min. color
           An in-depth exploration of a campaign typifies the tech-
           niques of most major United States elections today, in-
           cluding public opinion sampling and image-making.

1205. "CHECKERS" SPEECH*
National Broadcasting Company 1952 30 min. b/w s/c/a
    In defense of a fund contributed to his campaign, Richard
Nixon addresses a national television audience. In this
media "classic," he refers to his wife and to his dog,
Checkers.

1206. CHICAGO: THE SEASONS CHANGE
American Civil Liberties Union American Documentary Films
1968 45 min. b/w
    The ACLU presents the case of political repression which
reigned both inside and outside the Convention Hall. As-
sembled immediately after the events surrounding the
Democratic Convention in Chicago in 1968, this film re-
lives the events through the eyes of the delegates, demonstrators, political leaders, candidates, reporters and by-
standers.

1207. CONVENTIONS: THE LAND AROUND US
American Documentary Films 1970 68 min. b/w
    Using song and film loops, this film presents the televi-
sion convention speeches and confrontations of young and
old. It features the conflicts for the year 1968 between
the rigid social systems and the birth of "new creative
forces."

1208. CONVENTIONS--THE PROCESS IN CRISIS
Metromedia Films Inc. 1970 23 min. c/a
From "The Making of the President, 1968"
    At the Republican Convention in Miami, Nixon is the ap-
parent favorite but there are strategies for Rockefeller
and Reagan. Nixon appeal to middle America and to the
"silent majority."

1209. DEATH OF PRESIDENT KENNEDY, THE
Holt 1964 22 min. b/w s/C/a
    This film reviews the life of the late President, through
his personal and professional crises, from the campaigns
to the funeral procession.

1210. FROM PRECINCT TO PRESIDENT (PARTS I, II)
CBS-TV 1958 27 min. each c/a
From the See It Now Series
    Four days of wide-ranging conversation on a variety of
subjects are exchanged between former President Harry
Truman and Edward R. Murrow.

1211. HARRY TRUMAN (PARTS I, II)
McGraw-Hill 26 min. b/w
From the Biography Series
Award Winner
    The early days, the campaigns, the presidency are all
examined.

1212.   HECKLERS, THE
        Time-Life 35 min. b/w s/c/a vt/vc
             In filming of actual meetings with leading British politi-
             cians and "sincere" hecklers in action. The freedom of
             interchange between the heckler and politician has led to
             the observation that true political "dialogue" exists in
             England.

1213.   HOW BRITAIN VOTES
        British Information Service b/w s/c/a
             This film explores the selection of a candidate, the work
             of his local agents (canvassing, polling), the reopening of
             Parliament and the preparation for the next election.

1214.   HOW WE ELECT OUR REPRESENTATIVES
        Coronet 1964 11 min. color
        Revised edition
             This film stresses the full story of a typical election-
             registration, the primary elections, the campaign, the
             general election and the counting of the ballots. Pointed
             out is the importance of being informed on candidates and
             issues. Discussed also is the impact of television on
             elections, plus ballot mark instructions and operating pro-
             cedures for voting machines.

1215.   HUBERT HUMPHREY: NEW MAN ON CAMPUS
        National Educational Television Indiana University 59 min
        b/w
             Hubert Humphrey, former Vice President, meets with his
             first students as a professor at Macalester College in St.
             Paul, Minnesota, lecturing and participating in a question-
             and-answer session. Some of the topics discussed are
             students' rights, violence, Vietnam, racial problems and
             Chicago during the 1968 Democratic Convention.

1216.   HUNDRED DAYS
        Films, Inc. 1966 b/w
        Narration by Arthur Kennedy; Words of FDR spoken by
        Charlton Heston
             This film considers the effect and long-term political re-
             actions of 100 days' legislation of the Franklin Roosevelt
             administration. Still photos and newsreel footage of pov-
             erty and unemployment during these days are highlights.

1217.   I NEVER FORGET A FACE
        Teaching Film Custodians 11 min. b/w
             This film analyzes the 1920 presidential conventions and
             campaigns, particularly the issue of women's suffrage.

1218.   INAUGURATION OF JOHN F. KENNEDY--36TH PRESIDENT
        OF THE UNITED STATES
        United States Information Agency National Audiovisual Center
        1961 18 min. color
             This is a documentary of the inauguration of the late

President John Kennedy. It contains the final campaign
strategies, the inaugural address and statements concerning the Peace Corps plans.

1219. J. F. KENNEDY'S LAST MESSAGE TO LABOR*
American Federation of Labor   1969   30 min.   b/w   C/a
Introduced by George Meany, President Kennedy delivers
a message to the AFL-CIO Convention (one week prior to
his assassination). The speech reviews the labor movement in campaign format. The theme is "right to work,"
with "education is the key."

1220. JOHN F. KENNEDY--YEARS OF LIGHTNING, DAYS OF
DRUMS
United States Information Agency   Embassy Films, Inc.   1965
90 min.   b/w
The presidency of John F. Kennedy is reviewed: his cam-
paigns, his programs of the Alliance for Progress, Peace
Corps, space exploration.

1221. JOHN FITZGERALD KENNEDY--THE MAN AND THE PRESI-
DENT*
United World Films   1963   9 min.   b/w
From the News Parade Series
This film presents still photos and newsreel shots of the
highlights of the public and private life of John F. Kennedy during the last years of his presidency. It covers
his campaign, his inauguration in 1961, his family life,
his quest for peace and domestic stability, his assassination and the tributes paid from all over the world.

1222. KENNEDY: WHAT IS REMEMBERED IS NEVER LOST
Encyclopaedia Britannica   1966   23 min.   b/w   vt/vc   s/c/a
This memorial, a tribute to the late President, simulates
the march of the funeral caisson through Washington to
Arlington. As the camera passes the major sites of his
administration, his own words, his campaign messages,
and correspondents' comments reveal the issues facing the
administration at that time.

1223. KENNEDY-NIXON DEBATES (I, II, III, IV)*
CBS-TV   1959   60 min. each   b/w   kinescopes   c/a
The two candidates of 1960 discuss national problems, foreign policy and other campaign issues. Questions are ad-
dressed to them from a panel of journalists.

1224. MAKING OF THE PRESIDENT, THE: 1960 (Parts I, II)*
Xerox Wolper   1964   Pt. I: 42 min.; Pt. II: 42 min.
b/w   s/c/a
Based on the Theodore White best-seller, this film follows the primary campaigns of 1960, the nominating convention and the daily campaigning. Forces are analyzed
which shape the destiny of the two candidates, such as
the unanticipated events and the orderly transfer of power.

The conclusion highlights the Kennedy inaugural address.

1225. MAKING OF THE PRESIDENT, THE: 1964*
Xerox Wolper 1965 79 min. b/w s/c/a
This film describes the 1964 political convention and campaigns. It begins with the assassination of President Kennedy and ends with the election of Lyndon Baines Johnson.

1226. MAKING OF THE PRESIDENT, THE: 1968 (PARTS I, II, III)*
Xerox Wolper 83 min. b/w s/c/a
This film describes the paths of candidates Richard Nixon, Eugene McCarthy and George Romney. Also reviewed is the entry into the race by Robert Kennedy and the withdrawal of Lyndon Johnson. Included in the coverage are the assassinations of Dr. Martin Luther King, Jr. and Robert Kennedy, as well as the riots in Chicago during the convention. The conclusion highlights the defeat of Hubert Humphrey by Richard Nixon.

1227. MOST IMPORTANT CAMPAIGN IN THE WORLD, THE
National Association of Manufacturers 18 min. b/w s/c/a
The significance of constructive campaigning is emphasized in this film. Discussed are three activities fundamental to good campaigning: 1. An acceptable candidate who is a sincere and capable citizen; 2. A dedicated manager who can organize and draw out voters; 3. Contributors to sustain required finances.

1228. MOST IMPORTANT PRECINCT IN THE WORLD, THE
National Association of Manufacturers 16 min. b/w s/c/a
A precinct is defined as a geographical area and a unit within any national party organization. The film discusses the responsibility of the precinct committeeman who directs campaign activities. It outlines methods committeemen use to stimulate voting by all precinct members.

1229. NORTH CAROLINA'S TRIBUTE TO PRESIDENT JOHN FITZGERALD KENNEDY
National Film Board of Canada 1964 28 min. b/w s/c/a
This film documents ceremonies honoring President Kennedy at Chapel Hill, North Carolina, on May 17, 1964. It includes addresses by Dr. Billy Graham, Luther Hodges, Governor Sanford, Arthur Smith, Mrs. Rose Kennedy, Edward Kennedy.

1230. PEOPLE'S RIGHT TO KNOW: POLICE VERSUS REPORTERS
University of California 1969 14 min. b/w
This documentary tells of photographer's experiences at the Democratic Convention in Chicago in 1968. It exposes events via news film, including police "harassment" and people in the streets.

1231. POLITICAL PROTEST: THE SPLINTER GROUPS
Intext   1970   16 min.   color
This film considers third party politics by focusing on
the candidacy of George C. Wallace and his American In-
dependence Party in 1968.   Also included are Theodore
Roosevelt and other "splinter group" elections.

1232. POLITICAL PROTEST WITHIN THE PARTY
Intext   1970   15 min.   b/w
The 1968 Democratic candidates for nomination for Presi-
dent are discussed, with emphasis on Senator Eugene Mc-
Carthy's attempts to change the direction of that party.

1233. POLITICS IN ACTION
University of Iowa   1967   41 min.   color   s/c/a
One state election's bipartisan case study of political procedures is illustrated.   The film begins with the precinct
caucus, follows through the county, district and state conventions, pre-primary campaigning, primary election,
general election campaign, and closes with voting returns
on election night.

1234. PRESIDENTIAL ELECTIONS
Encyclopaedia Britannica   1952   14 min.   b/w   vt/vc   s/C/a
From the American Democracy Series
This film details the process of electing a president,
stressing that it is the most "significant" event in American political life.   Animated drawings and photographic
material record previous campaigns.   The film describes
the structure and strategy of campaign organizations and
the major political moves involved in the nomination and
election of a president.

1235. PRIMARIES I: CHALLENGE TO A PRESIDENT
Metromedia Films, Inc.   1970   20 min.   s/c/a
From "The Making of the President, 1968"
President Johnson speaks on the issues of Vietnam and
enters the New Hampshire primary.   After the primary,
Senator Robert Kennedy decides to run.   Subsequently,
Johnson announces plans for deescalating the war and an-
nounces that he will not seek reelection.

1236. PRIMARIES II: THE DEMOCRATS: A PARTY IN TRANSI-
TION
Metromedia Films, Inc.   1970   20 min.   s/c/a
From "The Making of the President, 1968"
Senators Humphrey, Kennedy and McCarthy seek the Pres-
idency.   The film traces their respective campaigns.

1237. PRIMARY: HUMPHREY VERSUS KENNEDY
Time-Life   54 min.   b/w   vt/vc   s/c/a
This is a behind-the-scenes close-up of the now historical
Wisconsin primary contest between Senators Humphrey

and Kennedy. Their entire campaign entourages are examined.

1238. RIGHT TO DISSENT: A PRESS CONFERENCE
University of California 1969 8 min.   b/w
This film focuses on the press conference held by organizers of demonstrations at the 1968 Democratic Convention in Chicago. Footage of the campaign protestors and demonstration marches is included.

1239. ROBERT KENNEDY REMEMBERED
Robert Kennedy Memorial Fund 1968 29 min.   b/w
This film memorial to Senator Robert F. Kennedy is concerned with the quality of his life rather than the facts of his death. It reflects the "intensity, accomplishments as a public servant, his campaigns, and his private citizen contributions."

1240. THOUSAND DAYS, A
Mass Media Associates 1964 27 min.   b/w
The presidential career of John F. Kennedy is commemorated--from his illustrious campaigns to the assassination. Credits include the space innovations, the Peace Corps, several breakthroughs in both domestic and foreign relations. Richard Basehart narrates.

1241. TRUE STORY OF AN ELECTION (PARTS I, II)
Dimension Churchill 1963 57 min.   color s/c/a
A documentary tells of the actual election campaign in which a Republican and a Democrat are vying for election to Congress.

1242. VISUAL ENCYCLOPEDIA OF AMERICAN HISTORY IN THE
20TH CENTURY, THE--A SERIES*
Association 1972 5 min. segments b/w vt/vc
This complete and comprehensive review of events during the years 1893 through the nineteen sixties includes some outstanding political campaign events including: 1901-1906: McKinley Inauguration, Teddy Roosevelt Elected President; 1913-1915: Woodrow Wilson Inaugurated; 1916: Republican Campaign and Convention; Democratic Campaign and Convention; 1917: Woodrow Wilson Reelected; 1919: President Wilson campaigns; 1920-1921: Harding and Coolidge Campaigns; 1922-1923: Suffrage Campaign; 1924: Campaigns and Conventions; 1928-1929: Democratic and Republican Conventions/Campaigns; 1932: The Hoover-Roosevelt Campaigns; 1936: Roosevelt versus Landon; 1940: Party Campaigns/Conventions; 1944: Roosevelt versus Dewey Campaigns; 1948-49: Truman Political Upset; 1952: Eisenhower-Nixon versus Stevenson-Sparkman Campaigns; 1956: Republican/Democratic Campaigns; 1960: Kennedy-Johnson versus Nixon Campaigns; 1964: The Johnson Win; 1968: Chicago Con-

vention/Presidential Campaigns; 1969: Nixon's Inaugural.

1243. WHO IN '68?
ABC-TV 1967 51 min. color
This film provides a prospectus of the convention activities centering around the choice of presidential candidates for the 1968 election. Possible G. O. P. candidates include: Romney, Nixon, Rockefeller and Percy. Each man outlines some of his political views regarding national policies. Democratic candidates include: Johnson, Robert Kennedy, Wallace, Humphrey.

1244. WHOLE WORLD IS WATCHING, THE
Mass Media Associates 1968 18 min. color
This film explores the scenes of violence and disorder occurring at the Democratic National Convention in Chicago in 1968. It visually outlines major events, characterizing some of the major attitudes and forces at work there. Rock music and pictorial news contrast the "solemn vigilance" of the younger generation.

1245. WORLD OF JULIAN BOND, THE
National Educational Television Indiana University 11 min. b/w
Reviewed is the recent career of Julian Bond, member of the Georgia State Legislature and the first black man to be nominated for the vice presidency at a Democratic National Convention. Scenes show him campaigning in New York and then returning to his political duties in Atlanta. Produced by black filmmakers to acquaint students with black America.

The System

1246. ADVISE AND CONSENT
McGraw-Hill Audio Film Center 1962 139 min. b/w
Directed by Otto Preminger; starring Franchot Tone, Henry Fonda, Charles Laughton
Allen Drury's Pulitzer Prize novel of Washington politics examines our Congressional system. The focus is on the power struggles and on the effects of investigations on the personal lives of those involved.

1247. AMERICAN PARADE, THE: POWER AND THE PRESIDENCY
Bailey Film Associates 27 min. b/w
In this film, narrated by George C. Scott, we learn how Washington, Jackson, Polk, Lincoln, McKinley and Roosevelt used public pressure and personal character to gradually increase the power of the presidency.

1248. AMERICAN POLITICAL BEHAVIOR SERIES
Irving Lesser Enterprises   b/w   c/a
This series focuses on the classification of information
for voting behavior analysis.   The lessons are demonstration exercises on teaching of political science.

1249. BALLOTS THAT FLY
Department of Defense   National Audiovisual Center   1964
9 min.   color
Information and background is provided for the absentee
ballot program of the Armed Forces.   The film shows
proper procedure for completing and sending in these ballots.

1250. BEFORE THE MOUNTAIN WAS MOVED
Robert Sharpe   1971   58 min.   color
This film portrays grass-roots politics in Appalachia.   A
group of small farmers and miners form a delegation to
the West Virginia state capitol to petition the legislature
and effect the passage of laws restricting strip mining.

1251. BELONGING TO THE GROUP
University of Minnesota   15 min.   b/w   s/c/a
The meaning of respect is analyzed, with an explanation
of its relation to life in a democracy.

1252. BEYOND THREE DOORS
Western Electric   26 min.   color   s/c/a
The viewer is shown the story of three people who decide
to take an active part in public affairs.   The film shows
the accomplishments of one individual who decides to become "involved."

1253. CHARACTERISTICS OF THE ELECTORATE
Boston University   21 min.   b/w   s/c/a
Claude Robinson, Chairman of the Opinion Research Corporation, analyzes the character of the electorate relative
to party membership, percentage, who votes, age, occupation and response to various types of appeals.

1254. CHARGE AND COUNTERCHARGE
Appleton-Century-Crofts   1968   43 min.   b/w
This film traces the career of Senator Joseph McCarthy
and analyzes his techniques and role in the political life
of America of the fifties.   There are scenes from many
committee sessions.

1255. CITIZEN KANE
Time-Life   120 min.   b/w   vt/vc   s/c/a
Directed and written by Orson Welles, this is a study of
the corruption of power, of Charles Foster Kane, a newspaper tycoon, with parallels to the life of William Randolph Hearst.   Success and power are depicted as empty,
sterile and meaningless.

1256. CLASSIFYING INFORMATION ABOUT VOTER BEHAVIOR
University of Indiana   1970   27 min.   b/w   c/a
From the American Political Behavior Series
   A political science lesson is used to demonstrate the
   process of classifying information about descriptions of
   various factions of the voting population.

1257. COMMUNICATION IN GOVERNMENT
Michigan State University   2 min.   b/w   s/c/a
   Taken from a televised Presidential press conference held
   by John F. Kennedy, this film briefly illuminates the importance of keeping a free and open press forum.

1258. CONSTITUTION AND THE RIGHT TO VOTE, THE
National Educational Television   Indiana University   1957
30 min.   b/w   s/c/a
From the Constitution in Action Series
   Lawsuits are explained which attacked the constitution-
   ality of the Texas "white primary." It traces the role of
   the Fourteenth Amendment as it relates to labor struggles.

1259. CONVERSATION AT THE WHITE HOUSE
AFL-CIO   Boston University   1973   30 min.   color   s/a
   President Lyndon Johnson and AFL-CIO President George
   Meany discuss social legislation enacted during the John-
   son Administration and the goals still to be reached.

1260. DEMAGOGUES AND DO-GOODERS
Time-Life   b/w   vt/vc
From the March of Time Series
   The voices of Huey Long, Gerald L. K. Smith, Father
   Coughlin and Father Divine in this composite of social
   conditions during the depression.

1261. ELECTORATE TIDES OF THE FUTURE
Boston University   22 min.   b/w   s/c/a
   Samuel Lubell, author and analyst, discusses forces
   which bring about changes in the electorate.

1262. FAILURE IN THE TWO-PARTY SYSTEM
Granada   American Documentary Films   1968   27 min.   b/w
   New politicians meet the old party machine bosses. The
   film dramatizes how entrenched power maneuvers the
   country machinery as it packs committees for delegate
   selection and threatens voters economically.

1263. FUNCTIONS OF CONGRESS
Columbia University   McGraw-Hill   1961   29 min.   b/w
s/c/a
   This lecture explores ways in which internal and external
   factors cause a decline in the position of Congress. Functions are outlined which Congress can carry out in the
   contemporary world.

1264. GETTING INTO LOCAL POLITICS
      Modern Learning Aids   20 min.   b/w   s/c/a
      Dr. Norton Long, Professor of Political Science, North-
      western University, analyzes political participation at the
      local level.

1265. HOW OUR TWO-PARTY SYSTEM OPERATES
      Modern Learning Aids   1960   20 min.   b/w
      From the Building Political Leadership Series
      Pictured is the growth of political parties in America,
      with descriptions of the structure of the major parties
      and laws controlling the organization and activities of po-
      litical parties.

1266. MAKING INFERENCES FROM STATISTICAL DATA
      Irving Lesser   Indiana University   22 min.   b/w   vt   c/a
      This film analyzes how students can use statistical data
      to infer political party preparation.   Also examined is the
      effect of education, age, occupation and race on choices
      between political parties.

1267. MAN AND THE STATE: HAMILTON AND JEFFERSON ON
      DEMOCRACY
      Bailey Film Associates   27 min.   b/w
      The main points of controversy between Alexander Hamil-
      ton and Thomas Jefferson are discussed: how strong
      should the Federal government be?   Should the Constitu-
      tion be loosely or strictly interpreted?

1268. MATTER OF CONSCIENCE: ETHICS IN GOVERNMENT
      ABC-TV   1969   51 min.   color   s/C/a
      In response to inquiries instigated by the National Bureau
      of Ethics, various Congressmen express their ideas re-
      garding three areas of question: 1. The need for high
      salaries for Congressmen;   2. The necessity for private
      groups to provide extra money for Congressmen while
      campaigning;   3. Lobbying.

1269. MEETING, THE
      National Film Board of Canada   9 min.   b/w
      This discussion film is designed to raise questions about
      how much support elected groups should be entitled to
      from the electorate.

1270. MOST IMPORTANT POLITICIAN IN THE WORLD, THE
      National Association of Manufacturers   15 min.   b/w   s/c
      "Mr. Citizen" is characterized as the most important poli-
      tician.   The film defines a political party, relating the
      system to United States history.   It illustrates the unity
      of strength and purpose of each party within the precinct.
      In addition, it suggests ways for raising campaign funds,
      particularly on a precinct basis.

1271. MURROW ON "REPORT ON McCARTHY"
       CBS-TV 1965 28 min. b/w
       From the See It Now Series
           In March, 1965, CBS-TV broadcaster Edward R. Morrow
           reports on Senator Joseph McCarthy, Jr., Wisconsin Sen-
           ator. Through the Senator's own words and pictures,
           Murrow attacks "McCarthyism" and "smear techniques"
           involving "guilt by association" as demagoguery. The
           film illustrates the misuse of "half-truths" and the con-
           gressional investigation to intimidate victims in an al-
           leged fight to weed communists from office.

1272. POLITICAL PARTIES
       Coronet 1947 11 min. b/w s/c/a
           This film explores the relationship of political parties to
           the individual. It illustrates the work of party mechanics
           and explains the relationship of local party activities to
           national issues. In addition, it discusses democratic vot-
           ing procedures.

1273. POLITICAL PARTIES
       Encyclopaedia Britannica 1952 18 min. b/w vt/vc s/c/a
           Political party organization and operation are explained,
           emphasizing the role of the opposition party. The film
           dramatizes a series of situations illustrating how the
           parties give citizens an opportunity to participate in gov-
           ernment by nominating men and promoting programs.

1274. POLITICIAN, OR VOTE FOR ME, THE
       Film-Maker's Cooperative 7 min. b/w any age
           In this political satire, a politician delivers a speech in
           downtown Los Angeles. He becomes incoherent and then
           paranoid as the crowd becomes more and more hostile
           toward him. He "escapes" into his imagination where he
           murders his ego and jumps into the lake screaming "vote
           for me."

1275. POLITICS: THE OUTER FRINGE
       National Broadcasting Company 51 min. b/w C/a
           The meaning of "left wing" and "right wing" movements
           is analyzed. Also discussed are activities by various
           groups of the populace in opposition to theories and gov-
           ernmental interpretations of the constitution.

1276. POLITICS CAN BECOME A HABIT
       Associated Instructional Films 27 min. b/w
           This film encourages active personal involvement in solv-
           ing social problems as the responsibility of each individ-
           ual citizen. A teacher joins a demonstration against city
           officials after she learns of the laxity with which the city
           enforces health and safety laws.

1277. POLITICS FILM, THE
       Crowell, Collier, Macmillan 27 min. color
              This film presents some contemporary problems in the
              form of conversations with emerging 18-year-old voters.
              Narrated by Peter Falk.

1278. POLITICS, POWER AND THE PUBLIC GOOD
       Learning Corporation of America 20 min. b/w
       From the Searching for Values Series
              Specially edited from Columbia Studio's "All the King's
              Men," this film portrays long-term politician Governor
              Stark (Broderick Crawford), proud of "getting things done
              for the people," ruthlessly fighting to retain his office
              with unethical tactics.

1279. POLLSTERS AND POLITICS
       Associated Films 1963 26 min. b/w
       From the 20th Century Series
              Polling as a tool of political campaigning is surveyed.
              The film documents its uses for Governor Sanders' 1962
              campaign in Georgia. The discussion includes comments
              by Gallup, Roper, Harris pollsters.

1280. POWERS OF THE PRESIDENCY: ARMED INTERVENTION
       Bailey Film Associates 23 min. color
              In this film, the President must choose a course of ac-
              tion in an international crisis and he must do so quickly
              on the basis of swiftly changing and often conflicting in-
              formation.

1281. PRESIDENCY: THE SEARCH FOR A CANDIDATE
       Encyclopaedia Britannica 1970 29 min. b/w vt/vc s/c/a
              This film examines the choice of a candidate for the na-
              •tion's highest office. Analyzed are the variety of ways by
              which a candidate can become the party choice, how poli-
              tics is "the art of the possible," and how compromise is
              essential in the decision-making process in a democracy.

1282. PRESIDENT, THE
       Encyclopaedia Britannica 17 min. b/w vt/vc s/c
              Dramatic major historical events are illustrated to dem-
              onstrate the present power and influence of the President.
              The responsibility and scope of today's Chief Executive's
              powers are analyzed.

1283. PRESIDENT OF THE UNITED STATES: TOO MUCH POWER?
       Encyclopaedia Britannica 1972 27 min. b/w and color
       vt/vc
              This film explains presidential power and the numerous
              "checkpoints" upon this power. The history of the presi-
              dency is explored through film clips and etchings. The
              use of power by Lincoln, Jefferson, the Roosevelts,
              Truman, Kennedy, and others, is analyzed.

1284. PRESSURE GROUPS
       Encyclopaedia Britannica 1952 22 min. b/w vt/vc s/c/a
       Pressure groups and their methodology are revealed. The
       contention is that they "are a necessary instrument for
       decision-making in a democracy."

1285. PRESSURE GROUPS IN ACTION
       Modern Learning Aids 1960 20 min. b/w s/c/a
       From the Government and Public Affairs Series
       Dr. Marbury Ogle, Professor of Government, Purdue Uni-
       versity, defends the need for pressure groups in our dem-
       ocratic political system.

1286. PROBLEM METHOD, PART I: DEFINING THE PROBLEM
       AND GATHERING INFORMATION
       McGraw-Hill 1955 18 min. b/w
       From the Teacher Education Series
       A study is made of the problems of pressure groups in a
       democracy. Examined are principles and techniques of
       gathering and organizing information.

1287. PROBLEM METHOD, PART II: USING THE INFORMATION
       TO SOLVE THE PROBLEM
       McGraw-Hill 1955 17 min. b/w
       From the Teacher Education Series
       Viewers learn the functions and limitations of pressure
       groups in terms of their application to local situations.

1288. PROFESSION OF POLITICS, THE
       Ideas 1966 29 min. b/w s/c/a
       From a series of interviews with Democratic and Republi-
       can leaders, congressmen, assemblymen and university
       students, viewers gain insight into the functioning of poli-
       tics as structured within the framework of political parties.

1289. PUBLIC OPINION IN A DEMOCRACY
       Coronet 1950 11 min. b/w s/C/a
       This film discusses the significance of public opinion and
       illustrates how it is formed and determined for a mean-
       ingful community issue.

1290. RELIGION AND POLITICS
       Holt 26 min. b/w s/C
       Dr. C. Eric Lincoln explores the role of ministers in the
       social protest of black Americans in urban ghettos during
       the period of 1945-1954. Also discussed is the effect of
       two wars, the NAACP, and other factors in shaping politi-
       cal ideologies.

1291. RIGHT TAKES OVER, THE
       National Educational Television Indiana University 30 min.
       b/w s/c/a
       One man's thinking dominates "the minds of" the people

in a town and controls their right to self-expression.

1292. ROLE OF THE CONGRESSMAN
Centron 1971 23 min. color s/c/a
Various tasks of a member of the U.S. House of Representatives are reviewed: lawmaker, ombudsman, political educator, campaigner, investigator, consultant.

1293. SMEAR: THE GAME OF DIRTY POLITICS
Crowell, Collier, Macmillan 26 min. b/w s/c/a
From CBS' Twentieth Century Series
This film suggests that "all is not always as it seems" during political campaigns. It takes a close look at the technique of "the big lie." Some of the most famous smears of past presidential campaigns are explored.

1294. SOME PEOPLE STAYED HOME
Paramount Teaching Film Custodians 9 min. b/w s/c
Excerpt from the motion picture, "The Great McGinty"
The corrupt practices of a city political machine are satirized. Candidates are elected by recruiting vagrants to vote in place of citizens who neglect their responsibility to vote on election day.

1295. SPECIAL ABOUT VOTER BEHAVIOR
Indiana University 1970 27 min. b/w C/a
This political science lesson divides the class into subgroups of voter populations and discusses how each group will vote.

1296. STAR SPANGLED EXTREMISTS
Carousel Associated Instructional Films 28 min. b/w
The birth, development and history of extremists are examined in a study of the "radical right." Detailed are illustrations of how movements can be started by small but vocal groups.

1297. STATE POLITICAL ORGANIZATION AND LEGISLATIVE PROCEDURES
Boston University 18 min. b/w
This film discusses local and state political organizations and presents details of state legislative procedures typical of all states except Nebraska.

1298. TRUMAN AND THE USES OF POWER
Learning Corporation of America 18 min. b/w
How President Truman enlarged the power of the executive branch of the government is the subject. His handling of domestic issues is examined: McCarthyism, Civil Rights Legislation.

1299. UNDER THE JUGGERNAUT
Time-Life 9 min. color vt/vc

The theme of this film is political assassination. It is a "kaleidoscope" of images of Malcolm X, Martin Luther King, John and Robert Kennedy, Lee Harvey Oswald, others.

1300. UNITED STATES CONGRESS, THE: OF, BY AND FOR THE PEOPLE
Encyclopaedia Britannica 1972 27 min. color vt/vc
Viewers learn of the responsibilities of law-makers. The film examines day-to-day work of a Congressman and a Senator, visiting meetings, hearings, briefings. Hubert Humphrey comments on the historical and constitutional developments.

1301. VOTE, THE
Department of Defense National Audiovisual Center 10 min. b/w
Actor E. G. Marshall narrates this essay on how service personnel obtained the right to vote and methods of absentee ballots cast in the 1964 election.

1302. WARREN YEARS, THE: GREAT DECISIONS
National Educational Television Indiana University 1969 27 min. b/w
Major Supreme Court rulings are discussed in the areas of desegregation, civil rights and criminal procedures. Both allied and critical evaluations are presented by former Justice Arthur Goldberg and former Attorney General Ramsey Clark.

1303. WARREN YEARS, THE: PROFILE OF EARL WARREN
National Educational Television Indiana University 1969 27 min. b/w s/c
The political career and personal philosophy of Earl Warren are examined.

1304. WILLIAM BUCKLEY
Indiana University 30 min. b/w
This film presents the views of the editor of National Review, a conservative publication. He states his opinions on a variety of political subjects from voters' beliefs to government "threats."

PROCESS/THEORY

1305. COMMUNICATION CASEBOOK, THE: THE CASE OF THE CHAIN REACTION, III
Strauss 1956 2 min. b/w C
From "The Inner Man Steps Out"
This film demonstrates the significance of sensitivity

to the emotional reactions of others, and suggests that the
long-range consequence of communication is a process-
transmission from one to another.

1306.   COMMUNICATION CASEBOOK, THE: THE CASE OF THE
        TUNED-OUT MIND, I
        Strauss   1956   2 min.   b/w   C
        From "The Inner Man Steps Out"
            The two-way nature of all communication is explained.   Il-
            lustrations suggest that profitable exchanges can only occur
            when both parties are receptive and respectful of what each
            offers.

1307.   COMMUNICATION CHANNELS
        University of Utah   1963   29 min.   b/w   C/a
        From the Human Relations Series: #25
            Analysis of available methods for sending messages.

1308.   COMMUNICATION FEEDBACK
        Bureau of National Affairs   1965   24 min.   b/w and color   c/a
        From the Berlo Effective Communication Series
            David Berlo examines problems which arise when changes
            are made in an organizational system.   Showing the use and
            misuse of feedback, he suggests that effective communica-
            tion is impossible if feedback is ignored.

1309.   COMMUNICATION THEORY
        Prism   Modern Learning Aids   1966   27 min.   b/w
        From the Mr. Wizard Series
            The viewer is introduced to the basic units of many com-
            munication systems.   One simple computer system dem-
            onstrates the process wherein a dot may be used to form
            pictures and codes to present letters and eventually sound.

1310.   COMMUNICATION THEORY AND THE NEW EDUCATIONAL
        MEDIA SERIES
        Ohio State University for the U.S. Office of Education   1966
        b/w   c
        See individual title listings
            This series provides a repertory of materials for those in-
            terested in the interpretation and articulation of theory, re-
            search in communication, learning theory, perception and
            instructional technology.   Titles include: 1. The Informa-
            tion Explosion (34 min.); 2. The Process of Communica-
            tion (46 min.); 3. Perception and Communication (32 min.);
            4. The Teacher and Technology (49 min); 5. Communica-
            tion Revolution (22 min.); 7. Music Research (17 min.);
            8. Teaching Machines and Sidney Pressey (12 min.).

1311.   COMMUNICATIONS
        Northeastern University   20 min.   b/w
            This film deals with the importance of communication.
            Examples presented illustrate both "formal" and "infor-

mal" lines of communication plus additional aspects of
communication theory and practice.

1312. COMMUNICATIONS INPUT
University of Utah 1963 29 min. b/w C/a
From the Human Relations Series: #24
The sources of messages and how they are formulated
are discussed in this film.

1313. COMMUNICATIONS MODEL, A
University of Utah 1963 29 min. b/w C/a
From the Human Relations Series: #23
This film attempts to look at the problems involved in
communication by first defining the problem.

1314. COMMUNICATIONS MODEL, A
National Educational Television Indiana University 1967
30 min. b/w C/a
From the English Fact and Fancy Series
Mr. James Bostain investigates way in which a message
is delivered, the signaling systems of speech, para-
speech, kinesics, writing. He analyzes the different
ways a message can be perceived and/or received. The
film explores the roles of the perceiver and demonstrates
that efficient message delivery must take every possible
step to keep the perceiver's attention.

1315. COMMUNICATIONS OUTPUT
University of Utah 1963 29 min. b/w C/a
From the Human Relations Series
This film discusses the necessary forces "put in" and
"taken out" of communications. It illustrates the fact
that, although messages may end up in the "right" place,
they may still have no effect.

1316. COMMUNICATIONS PRIMER, A
Eames Classroom Film 1954 22 min. color s/c/a
This introductory film demonstrates various aspects of
communication. By introducing theories, it offers a
broad concept of what communication represents and how
it is utilized in many of life's situations. Technical data
for the film comes from specialists Shannon, Weiner and
von Neumann.

1317. CRITICAL EVALUATION
Coronet 1972 11 min. b/w and color s/c
Emphasizes the necessity to understand, question and
judge communicative efforts. Stress is given to the receiver's role in the communication process.

1318. INFORMATION PROCESSING
CRM Time-Life 1971 28 min. color vt/vc s/c/a
Dr. Donald Norman, University of California Psychology

Consultant, and David Steinberg host this film which isolates and analyzes how people process information at a noisy, crowded cocktail party. Demonstrated theory in includes: information reception, language processing, storage, strategies, mnemonics, retrieval and problem solving.

1319. INTRODUCTION TO FEEDBACK, AN
       IBM Encyclopaedia Britannica 1960 11 min. color vt/vc
       s/C
       Using animation and action photography, this film introduces the subject of communication feedback. It illustrates the control of feedback processes by explaining the presence of oscillation in any given situation. Discussed also are plotting a course, measuring performance and corrective measures.

1320. MAKING YOURSELF UNDERSTOOD
       Encyclopaedia Britannica 1963 14 min. b/w vt/vc s/c/a
       This film is an introduction to communication theory. The significance of these elements is stressed: the speaker, the audience, the message. In illustrative episodes, the viewer learns how signs, signals and symbols transmit meaning.

1321. MISSED SIGNALS IN EXTENSION
       National Agricultural Project Michigan State University
       11 min. b/w c/a
       A series of one to two-minute action situations are demonstrated in which less than perfect communication takes place.

1322. NATURE OF COMMUNICATIONS, THE
       University of Iowa 1959 30 min. b/w C
       As a broad introduction to communication study, this film offers fundamental illustrations of basic elements of the communication process.

1323. PROCESS OF COMMUNICATION, THE
       Ohio State University for the Office of Education National
       Audiovisual Center 1967 46 min. b/w and color C/a
       From the Communication Theory and New Educational Media
       Series
       This film demonstrates the theory and methods of the communication process. Beginning with an animated theoretical model, it follows sequences detailing the theory by examples drawn from communication networks in educational, industrial, military and research settings. Military models are shown at the Command and General Staff College at Ft. Leavenworth; school administrative training models at Ohio State University; teacher training with the Kersh simulator at Oregon State, and the computer-based systems from the University of Illinois.

1324. PROCESS OF COMMUNICATION, THE (IN SPANISH)
This is the same film as above.

1325. ROADBLOCKS TO COMMUNICATION
National Educational Television (WGBH-TV) Indiana University 1963 30 min. b/w
From the Dynamics of Leadership Series
This film explores the concept of "feedback" as one method of communication improvement. It distinguishes between understandings and disagreements and explains the use of "watchdog" reaction and audience panels.

1326. TEACHER AS A MODEL OF COMMUNICATION
University of Ohio Michigan State University 3 min. b/w s/c/a
Dr. George Gubner ties together the major elements and issues in the communication process. The emphasis is on the professional teacher and his responsibility and role in the process.

1327. WHAT'S IN A PLAY: DRAMATIC ACTION
Bailey Film Associates 1971 17 min. color s/c/a
Stressing communication processes, this film views theatre as a form of communication. Questions asked are: What's in a play? How does it engage our interest? The organization of dramatic action is analyzed in terms of the listener: the audience.

PUBLIC SPEAKING

1328. ART OF COMMUNICATION SERIES, THE
Centron 1969 Each: 27 min. color s/c/a
See individual program listings:
1. Communication by Voice and Action (Delivery)
2. How to Conduct a Meeting (Parliamentary Procedure)
3. Microphone Speaking (Delivery)
4. Reporting and Explaining (Public Speaking)
5. Stage Fright--What You Can Do About It (Delivery)

1329. BUILDING AN OUTLINE
Coronet 10 min. b/w s/c/a
This film teaches that clear thinking, economical expenditure of time and effective communication with others result from orderly planning. Outlining is merely writing down that organization.

1330. CONCEPTS OF PURPOSE
University of Iowa 1959 30 min. b/w C
For classroom speech application, this film concentrates on effective objectives related to speaking and writing. Explicated is the relationship between choice of purpose

and the organization, unity and selection of supporting material. The stress is on the need for a coherent, well-defined purpose in any communication.

1331. DESCRIBING AN INCIDENT
Coronet 11 min. b/w s/a
This film effectively contrasts two descriptions of the same incident, stressing clarity, completeness and significant details.

1332. FRAMEWORK OF IDEAS
University of Iowa 1959 25 min. b/w c
With a pronounced emphasis on class needs, this film stresses the necessity for organization in writing. The "structural" organization approach is suggested: introduction, body and conclusion.

1333. FUNDAMENTALS OF PUBLIC SPEAKING, THE
Coronet Business Education Films 1950, revised 1969
14 min. b/w and color s/c/a
Collaborator: Dr. Carl Dallinger, Speech Department, Northern Illinois University
From the Language in Action Series
The second edition explains how to analyze speech situations: the planning, delivery and effective evaluation. Using public speaking in everyday situations, it examines communication in terms of the speech, the speaker and the audience. Stressed are preliminary research, organization of material, practice and audience analysis.

1334. IDEAS IN COMMUNICATION
University of Iowa 1959 30 min. b/w c
The function of this film is the exploration of the potential sources of ideas for effective speaking and writing. Frequently these sources emanate from a combination of the communicator's experience supplemented by research, reading and other methods of investigation.

1335. OPENING SPEECH, THE
National Film Board of Canada International Film Bureau
1960 8 min. b/w any age
Award Winner
This animated film, also known as "Norman McLaren's Opening Speech," creates a satirical situation wherein a microphone becomes a source of frustration. While the speaker is attempting to deliver a welcoming speech, the film shows the microphone as it comes to "life," exhibiting temper, reluctance, shrewdness.

1336. ORATOR, THE
Trick Studio, Prague McGraw-Hill 1962 11 min. color
Awards: Bergamo Film Festival, Oberhausen; Karlovy Vary Awards

A cartoon-like puppet film directs its satirical barbs at loquacious speakers whose words are often meaningless. A man prepares a speech at home and practices the presentation before his wife. On the basis of her reaction, he presumes the speech to be a success. Instead of a dialogue, words are visualized by strings of letters spewing out of the speaker's mouth. The audience is bored during the actual speech delivery.

1337. ORIGINAL ORATORY--CRITICISM AND DEMONSTRATION
University of Iowa 1969 29 min. b/w s/c
Professor Robert Kemp, University of Iowa, and students of forensics discuss the nature and background of "original oratory." He also describes related material, organization and structure. Students deliver an original oration, identifying respective techniques.

1338. PLANNING A SPEECH
McGraw-Hill 1968 15 min. color s/c/a
From the Oral Communication Series
Viewers learn how to choose a topic and how to organize content according to the nature of the material. Stressed is the importance of the speech presentation, that it be simultaneously informative and interesting. The use of notes in place of a full-written speech is recommended to encourage naturalness.

1339. PLANNING YOUR TALK
McGraw-Hill 1951 12 min. b/w s/c/a
From the Speech Series
This film focuses on the combination of planning and organization of a talk. Detailing significant points for speech planning, the blueprint should include the need for 1) attention of the audience; 2) giving examples; 3) presenting facts, reasons; 4) conclusions or suggested action.

1340. PROCESS OF REVISION
University of Iowa 1959 30 min. b/w C
Viewers learn techniques for improving a manuscript. Suggestions include editing or expanding ideas, better selection of materials, and elimination of mechanical and spelling errors.

1341. REPORTING AND EXPLAINING
Centron 1970 14 min. color s/c/a
This film treats a basic kind of verbal communication: reporting and explaining. Emphasizing the use of guidelines for achieving clarity and interest, it suggests several examples from information speeches. Suggestions include: being specific, organizing by ideas, utilizing visual aids and speaking in simple terms.

1342. RESEARCH TECHNIQUES
       University of Iowa 1959 30 min. b/w C
              The film analyzes the significance of research, investiga-
              tion, preliminary reading, narrowing subjects, note-tak-
              ing, outlining, synthesizing and evaluating and preparing
              manuscripts.

1343. RESEARCHING A TOPIC
       McGraw-Hill 1968 11 min. color s/c/a
       From the Oral Communication Series
              This film focuses on the significance of thorough research
              and effective interview techniques. It specifies steps for
              speech preparation: selecting a topic, obtaining primary
              source information, compiling references and bibliogra-
              phy, and using visual aids.

1344. SPEECH PREPARATION
       C-B Educational Films University of California 1958
       14 min. b/w s/c/a
              With classroom and conference situations this film sum-
              marizes the basic steps in speech preparation. Funda-
              mental procedures are related to contemporary content
              so that they will appear more relevant.

1345. WHY STUDY SPEECH?
       McGraw-Hill 1955 11 min. b/w s/c
              The discussion concerns the study of speech techniques,
              the significance of these techniques to the student now and
              later in life. Some of the fundamental activities involved
              in an introduction to speech are examined.

1346. YOUR FIRST SPEECH
       Bailey Film Associates 1960 11 min. b/w s/c/a
              Preparation and presentation procedures are shown for
              the first speech given before an audience. Effective
              speeches are organized into three major divisions. Addi-
              tional pointers on style and delivery are presented.

                            RHETORICAL TOPICS

                             History/Criticism

1347. ARISTOTLE AND THE SCIENTIFIC METHOD
       Coronet 1959 15 min. s/c
              The ideologies of Aristotle are stressed as they are re-
              lated to the development of the scientific method. Depart-
              ing from Plato's ideas, the film relates observances Aris-
              totle made based on his own observations. Explained are
              classification of data, performance with experiments and
              generalizations.

1348. ARISTOTLE'S ETHICS: THE THEORY OF HAPPINESS
       Encyclopaedia Britannica 1962 30 min. color vt/vc s/c
       From the Encylopaedia Britannica Humanities Series
            Mortimer Adler interprets the philosophical problems of
            Aristotle's theory of happiness. Defined is the meaning
            of happiness, its contribution to the "good life." The
            film maintains that the pursuit of happiness must be "co-
            operative, not competitive."

1349. ASSASSINATION OF JULIUS CAESAR
       McGraw-Hill 1955 24 min. b/w s/c/a
       From the You Are There Series
            Walter Cronkite narrates the events leading to the "Ides
            of March," and the prophecy that Julius Caesar would be
            killed on March 15, 44 B.C. The film shows the politi-
            cal climate of that day and gives insight to this turning
            point in history.

1350. COMMUNICATION WHICH EVALUATES AND CRITICIZES
       University of Iowa 1959 30 min. b/w C
            The viewer learns the necessity for developing coherent,
            relevant and objective standards for general evaluation in
            both critical writing and speaking. In addition, the film
            establishes a rationale for the common use and values of
            effective criticism.

1351. DEATH OF SOCRATES, THE
       Columbia Broadcasting System Time-Life 1955 27 min.
       b/w vt/vc s/c/a
            Socrates died in 399 B.C., refusing to renounce his be-
            liefs. The film illustrates the Athenian laws concerning
            the "necessity for death" rather than life and the stifling
            of freedom of discourse.

1352. GALILEO: THE CHALLENGE OF REASON
       Learning Corporation of America 1970 26 min. color
       Award Winner
            This film is the story of the man and humanist as well
            as the founder of modern experimental science. Because
            of his unorthodox beliefs he was brought before the in-
            quisition.

1353. GOOD NIGHT, SOCRATES
       McGraw-Hill 35 min. b/w
            This documentary illustrates the death of a tradition.
            Greek traditions in a community fade away or are assimi-
            lated into an American city.

1354. GREAT AMERICAN SPEECHES
       Oxford 1972 15 min. each color s/c/a
            Through the use of contemporary art and modern graph-
            ics each speaker is placed in the "appropriate time and
            setting." Each speech is delivered by a noted actor.

The three presented are: 1. Patrick Henry's "Liberty or
Death" speech (featuring Barry Sullivan); 2. Washington's
"Farewell Address" (featuring William Shatner); 3. Lin-
coln's "Gettysburg Address" (featuring Charlton Heston).

1355. GREEKS, THE: IN SEARCH OF MEANING
Learning Corporation of America 1972 26 min. color
s/c/a
Problems with which the Greeks wrestled are dramatized:
freedom, license, law, the meaning of life. Philosophies
of Aristophanes, Socrates, other followers are examined.

1356. HISTORIAN SERIES, THE: INDUCTIVE TEACHING OF THE
HISTORIAN'S METHOD OF INQUIRY
Holt 1966 27-30 min. each b/w kinescope
Inductive techniques stress acquisition of critical thinking
skills. Program titles are: 1. How the Historian Classi-
fies Information; 2. How the Historian Proves Hypothe-
ses; 3. How the Historian Asks Questions; 4. How the
Historian Decides What Is Fact; 5. How the Historian
Deals with Mind Set.

1357. HISTORICAL METHOD OF INQUIRY: ANSWERING QUESTIONS
Holt 1966 30 min. b/w
Professor F. Fenton stresses the methodological approach
when analyzing the causes of the Reformation. A historian must ask questions to get answers. Specific applicability to questions versus general applicability is discussed.

1358. HISTORICAL METHOD OF INQUIRY: CLASSIFYING INFOR-
MATION
Holt 1966 30 min. b/w
Professor Fenton presents and explains the historical
method of classifying information. The class discussion
revolves around the historian's definition of frame of reference.

1359. HISTORICAL METHOD OF INQUIRY: DEALING WITH THE
MIND
Holt 1966 30 min. b/w
Discussing perceptual differences, this film suggests in-
terpretation depends on different frames of reference.
One tends to evaluate on the basis of mind set. "Mind
set determines to some degree the facts that are selected
for report."

1360. HISTORICAL METHOD OF INQUIRY: DECIDING WHAT IS
FACT
Holt 1966 30 min. b/w
The essential points made are: there is a need for a
historian to see and appreciate other frames of reference;
he must "test" their truths and tell what is accurate.

1361. HISTORICAL METHOD OF INQUIRY: PROVING HYPOTHESES
       Holt 1966 30 min. b/w
              Dr. Fenton explains the inductive approach to history.
              The historian's view is analyzed.

1362. NEED FOR GREEK PHILOSOPHY, THE: PLATO AND
       ARISTOTLE
       University of Utah 1962 19 min. b/w
       From the Christian Philosophy Series: #6
              The views of Plato and Aristotle are discussed. Empha-
              sized is the relevance of Christian thought as the philo-
              sophical framework for the expression of ideas, nature of
              man and nature of God.

1363. PLATO'S APOLOGY: THE LIFE AND TEACHING OF SOC-
       RATES
       Encyclopaedia Britannica 1962 24 min. color vt/vc s/c/a
       From the Humanities Series: #6
              Mortimer Adler reveals the character of Socrates. He is
              interpreted as a man who inspired, then outraged his
              citizen peers; as a teacher who taught by asking, rather
              than telling; and, finally, as a philosopher who disturbed
              the complacency of men's minds.

1364. PLATO'S DRINKING PARTY
       Time-Life 40 min. b/w vt/vc s/c/a
              The contemporary setting gives the viewer a clear pic-
              ture of Socrates, Aristophanes, Agathen and Alcibiades.
              Leo McKern plays Socrates, for whom "absolute love is
              the philosophy of resounding truth."

1365. RESOLVE OF PATRICK HENRY, THE
       CBS McGraw-Hill 1956 28 min. b/w s/c/a
       From the You Are There Series
              March 23, 1775 is reconstructed, when Patrick Henry's
              famous speech in Richmond, Virginia sways the Virginia
              Convention in favor of establishing the proposed state
              militia, a major event in the growing rebellion of the col-
              onies.

1366. SOCRATIC VIEW OF PHILOSOPHY
       University of Utah 1966 27 min. b/w C/a
       From the Introduction to Philosophy Series: #2
              Socrates' questioning techniques are examined. In terms
              of achieving piety and belief, the Socratic dialogue is ex-
              plored.

1367. TRIAL OF SOCRATES, THE
       Bailey Film Associates 1972 29 min. color c/a
              This film reviews the trial and death of Socrates. Dia-
              logue is drawn from Plato, Xenophon, Aristophanes, as
              well as other Greek "personalities."

1368. YOU ARE THERE--A SERIES
       CBS Bailey Film Associates 22 min. each color
           CBS news correspondent Walter Cronkite is anchorman as
           top correspondents interview the famous and infamous, re-
           creating a series of "eye-witness" enactments of some of
           the most significant events of rhetorical history: 1. "Co-
           lumbus and Isabella"; 2. "The Fall of Troy"; 3. "Gali-
           leo and the Universe"; 4. "Harriet Tubman and the Under-
           ground Railroad"; 5. "Lewis and Clark and the Great Di-
           vide"; 6. "The Mystery of Amelia Earhart"; 7. "The
           Nomination of Abraham Lincoln"; 8. "The Ordeal of a
           President"; 9. "Paul Revere's Ride"; 10. "The Record
           Ride of the Pony Express"; 11. "Siege of the Alamo";
           12. "The Torment of Joan of Arc"; 13. "The Treason of
           Benedict Arnold"; 14. "The Trial of Susan B. Anthony";
           15. "The Vision of Dr. Koch."

                                Philosophic

1369. ALBERT SCHWEITZER
       University of Utah 1962 29 min. b/w
       From the Christian Philosophy Series: #22
           Albert Schweitzer's life and theories are analyzed, includ-
           ing their influence on contemporary philosophic and re-
           ligious logic.

1370. ANIMAL FARM (PARTS I, II)
       McGraw-Hill Part I: 37 min.; Part II: 38 min. color
       s/c/a
           George Orwell's famous fable is illustrated, showing the
           domestic animals revolting against the cruel farmer. Ex-
           changing one form of tyranny for another, they then find
           themselves taken over by the pigs.

1371. ANSWERING SOVIET PROPAGANDA
       United States Information Agency 14 min. b/w s/c/a
           Charles T. Vetter, training officer with the USIA and the
           Peace Corps, illustrates communist propaganda tech-
           niques.

1372. ARNOLD TOYNBEE
       National Broadcasting Company Encyclopaedia Britannica
       1958 28 min. b/w vt/vc s/c/a
       From the Wisdom Series
           British historian Arnold Toynbee, author of the ten-volume
           study of history, discusses the experiences that have in-
           fluenced his work. Described are his research, his writ-
           ing and his philosophy of historical causation.

1373. BERTRAND RUSSELL
       Encyclopaedia Britannica 1958 28 min. b/w vt/vc s/c/a

From the Wisdom Series
Bertrand Russell, philosopher, mathematician, winner of Nobel Prize for literature, reviews eighty years of changing beliefs and philosophies.

1374. BERTRAND RUSSELL DISCUSSES HAPPINESS
Coronet 1961 14 min. b/w s/c/a
Bertrand Russell discusses mankind's future in these three segments: Russell discusses philosophy; Russell discusses power; Russell discusses the role of the individual.

1375. CHALLENGE OF IDEAS, THE
National Audiovisual Center 1961 30 min. b/w s/a
Contrasted is the ideological struggle between the free world and the communist bloc. Described are objectives and techniques used by the USSR to influence peoples of the world. Narrator is the late Edward R. Murrow with Lowell Thomas, Helen Hayes, others.

1376. CHESS GAME, THE
Centron 1972 9 min. color s/c/a
Produced by a Harvard graduate student, this symbolic wordless discussion film analyzes revolution in terms of deceit, forces, cruelty and/or "position holding."

1377. CHINA: A HOLE IN THE BAMBOO CURTAIN
University of California b/w
This film points out improvements in China since the revolution, particularly in the widespread availability of special services.

1378. CHINA: ONE QUARTER OF HUMANITY
Edgar Snow American Documentary Films 1968 74 min. color
This film, edited by China correspondent, Edgar Snow, is a feature documentary about the people of China, based on three decades of news/analysis footage.

1379. CHINA: RISE OF COMMUNIST POWER, 1941-1967
Metromedia Films, Inc. 1967 29 min. b/w s/c/a
Theodore White examines the control of the mainland of China in a documentary.

1380. CHINA UNDER COMMUNISM (1st edition)
Encyclopaedia Britannica 1959 23 min. color vt/vc s/c
Allegedly free to photograph "anything," author John Strohm in 1958 became the "first" American newsman to be allowed within communist-held China. The film reviews the regime's method of forcing radical departures from the traditional oriental patterns of living.

1381. CHINA UNDER COMMUNISM (2nd, 3rd editions)
      Encyclopaedia Britannica 1962 30 min. color vt/vc s/c/a
          More of Mr. John Strohm's documentary film updates the
          "unrestricted" travel footage. Included are interviews
          from scores of refugees.

1382. COMMUNISM
      Department of Defense National Audiovisual Center 1967
      30 min. b/w
          The objective of this film is to present the basic philoso-
          phy of communism in terms of its purpose, strengths and
          weaknesses.

1383. COMMUNISM: DEFENSE DEPARTMENT FILMS
      Defense Department, National Audiovisual Center b/w
          A series of films relate specifically to the philosophy of
          Communism. Titles include: "Challenge of Ideas" (31
          min.); "Communism" (30 min.); "Communism: Blue-
          print for Conquest" (33 min.); "Communist Europe" (19
          min.); "Communist Target: Youth" (19 min.); "Commu-
          ist Weapons of Allure" (36 min.); "Freedom and You"
          (53 min.); "Road to the Wall" (35 min.); "Third Chal-
          lenge" (45 min.).

1384. COMMUNISM: THE SOVIET MODEL
      National Educational Television 28 min. b/w s/c/a
          The historical development of the present Russian system
          is presented. The entire philosophy is detailed from the
          relationship of the State to the free market pressures.

1385. COMMUNIST ACCENT ON YOUTH
      Pepperdine College 1961 30 min. b/w s/c/a
      From the Crisis for America Series
          This film contrasts philosophies of socialist communism
          with those of a free republic.

1386. COMMUNIST CHINA
      McGraw-Hill 1965 23 min. b/w s/c
          The land of the people of Communist China in 1965 is pre-
          sented in terms of resources, both human and material.
          Modern and traditional philosophies are contrasted in Pe-
          king and Shanghai.

1387. CONFRONTATION (PARTS I, II, III)
      National Broadcasting Company 1969 81 min. total color
      s/c/a
          A crisis of "society in conflict" is typified in a case study
          of a strike at San Francisco State College. A minor inci-
          dent escalates until it involves most segments of the city.
          Action and reaction of leaders and followers are docu-
          mented.

1388. CONVERSATIONS WITH ERIC HOFFER SERIES
CBS   Indiana University   National Educational Television
b/w
The author-philosopher converses about: "The Role of
the Weak"; "Man's Struggle for Uniqueness"; "Reading and
Writing"; "The Nature of Man"; "From the Cradle to
Skid Row."

1389. DAG HAMMARSKJOLD
CBS Encyclopaedia Britannica 1965 27 min. b/w vt/vc
s/c/a
Accomplishments as a mediator are reviewed in this an-
alysis of the career of the Swedish General of the United
Nations from 1953 until his death in the Congo in 1961.
His negotiation successes are all reviewed.

1390. DIALECTICAL MATERIALISM INTERPRETED
Learning Corporation of America 1971 4 min. color
any age
With animated graphics, the essence of Marxian theory is
explained as a segment within the film "Marxism, The
Theory That Split a World."

1391. ELECTRONIC LABYRINTH
University of Southern California 1970 17 min. color
Documentary footage suggests a dreamlike world of 1984
and 2001 where science seeks to dominate men, attempting through experimentation to "dehumanize him." The
hero, THX 1138, escapes from the "labyrinth," reaffirm-
ing humanistic man's ability to endure.

1392. END OF CONFLICT
National Educational Television Indiana University 29 min.
b/w
Spiritual-leader Krishnamurti discusses discontent resulting from comparisons of what we are with an idea of
what we should be. To end the conflict, he suggests "we
must become totally attentive to and aware of our present environment without interference from memory and
past experience."

1393. ERIC HOFFER: THE PASSIONATE STATE OF MIND
CBS Mass Media Associates 1967 54 min. b/w
Based on the Eric Hoffer books, this film analyzes the
ordeal of change and the related "passionate state of
mind."   With CBS newsman Eric Sevareid, Eric Hoffer
reviews the Vietnam War, drugs, Red China and race riots.

1394. EXISTENTIALISM
University of Utah 1966 29 min. b/w C/a
From the Introduction to Philosophy Series: #5
The ethical theories of philosophers are explored, par-

ticularly those of Nietzsche, who taught existentialist
moral philosophy as man's search "for the highest good."

1395. FACE OF RED CHINA, THE (PARTS I, II)
McGraw-Hill 1958 56 min. total b/w c/a
Photographed in 1958, this film reports on conditions at
that time in Communist China. It explains the system,
recreation, labor, military training.

1396. FREEDOM AND YOU
Defense Department National Audiovisual Center 1962
53 min. b/w
An American citizen suddenly finds his town taken over
by communists in this feature film, narrated by Jack
Webb.

1397. FUTURE SHOCK
Continental McGraw-Hill 1972 42 min. color
An imaginative documentation of the rapid social and tech-
nological changes now taking place. The viewer is also
exposed to all the problems arising in adapting to these
changes. (Based on the book by Alvin Toffler.)

1398. FUTURISTS, THE
McGraw-Hill 1967 27 min. color
Man's future is seen by leaders in science, sociology and
government. Walter Cronkite elicits opinions, viewpoints
and speculations about what man is doing to himself. In-
terviewees are many, including Isaac Asimov and R.
Buckminster Fuller.

1399. GENERATION GAP, THE: ITS CAUSES AND EFFECTS
National Catholic Office for Radio-Television Associated
Films 30 min. b/w
Analyzed are some of America's most pressing contempo-
rary inter-generation issues.

1400. HOW DO THINGS LOOK?
McGraw-Hill 27 min. color
Ecumenism, the roles of science, art and the humanities,
and the place of democracy are topics discussed in this
panel conversation. Five eminent thinkers in fields of
education, international relations, religion and philosophy,
arts and bio-medicine predict events and attitudes of the
21st century. Included are: Robert Hutchins, noted educator, and Lord Peter Ritchie-Calder, University of Edin-
burgh.

1401. HUMAN IMAGE, THE: WHAT IS THE GOOD LIFE?
Bailey Film Associates 17 min. b/w
This film searches for definitions and finds many different answers. The contrasts reflect the diversity of the
individuals and commitments in America.

1402. HUMANITIES: A SEARCH FOR MEANING
       McGraw-Hill 29 min. color
              Analyzed are attempts to answer timeless questions con-
              cerning man's hopes, goals, purpose in life. Creative
              activity is stressed as a method of communicating con-
              temporary meanings.

1403. I AM ALSO A YOU
       Pyramid 1970 14 min. color s/c/a
              An attempt to bridge "the people gap," this film tries to
              show the similarities between people, generations, differ-
              ent points of view. Quotations are used from Buddha,
              the Bible, the Talmud, Disraeli and other sources.

1404. INSIDE RED CHINA (PARTS I, II)
       CBS Audio/Brandon 1972 51 min. color
              Robert Cohen's documentary of life under Mao presents
              contemporary news analysis of life in the Republic of
              China.

1405. JOY OF ACHIEVEMENT, THE
       Dana 1974 14 min. color
              "A Values Perspective" film, this documentary uses
              quotes from people throughout history who have been rec-
              ognized as positive achievers: Thomas Jefferson, Thom-
              as Edison, Helen Keller, Franklin D. Roosevelt. Lou
              Rawls sings background music.

1406. LOOK AT COMMUNISM
       National Educational Television 1955 15 min. b/w c/a
              According to this film, socialism is necessary before
              communism can take over. Discussed are three elements
              of communism: 1. dialectic materialism; 2. economic
              determinism; 3. atheism.

1407. MACHIAVELLI ON POLITICAL POWER
       Bailey Film Associates 27 min. color
              Machiavelli's ideas on the philosophy of values and poli-
              tics of his day.

1408. MAO'S CHINA
       Audio/Brandon Crowell, Collier, Macmillan 1972 77 min.
       color s/c/a
              This film portrays life in the large urban areas as well
              as on the collective farms. It is the "first" major docu-
              mentary about life in the People's Republic of China, re-
              cording effects of the cultural revolution. It was chosen
              for screening at the White House prior to former Presi-
              dent Nixon's trip to China.

1409. MARX WAS HERE
       Time-Life 40 min. color vt/vc s/c/a
              This film traces the history of Marx's connections with

England, from his arrival as a political refugee through
years of suffering in Soho to the comparative prosperity
of his later life in Hempstead. It reconstructs his
friendships, problems he faced.

1410.   MARXISM: THEORY THAT SPLIT A WORLD
Learning Corporation of America 1971 27 min. color
The principles of "Dialectical Materialism" are illustrated, stressing the flaws in Marxian theory: the con-
tradiction between his hope and the reality of the day.

1411.   MEDITATION: YOGA, T'AI CHI AND OTHER SPIRITUAL
TRIPS
University of California 1973 23 min. color
This film examines the growing popularity of traditional
Eastern philosophy and religion. It visits a school of
Hatha yoga, shows a t'ai chi master and his students,
and includes interviews with writers Colin Wilson and
Alan Watts.

1412.   NATURE OF MAN, THE
National Educational Television Indiana University 20 min.
b/w
Eric Hoffer presents an extended dialogue about man's
weaknesses and how they relate to the total processes of
"learning to become human."

1413.   NOBODY WAVED GOODBYE
National Film Board of Canada Crowell, Collier, Macmillan
80 min. b/w
Award Winner
This film traces the relationship of two teenagers in their
first rejections of law and convention. In search for "human values in an impersonal society," they rebel against
standards of their parents and middle-class society. The
film explores in depth the social and personal attitudes
of "two adolescents who cannot communicate with society."

1414.   PAST, PRESENT AND FUTURE
National Educational Television 20 min. b/w
Professor Dan Bell, Columbia University, discusses labor and values with former Vice President Hubert Humphrey. The discussion continues with an example of student radical philosophy.

1415.   PEOPLE OF "PEOPLE'S CHINA"
University of California 1975 53 min. b/w
This film contains numerous interviews with various Chinese who reflect the commitment of contemporary Chinese
philosophy.

1416. PEOPLE UNDER COMMUNISM TODAY
CBS News   34 min.   b/w   s/c/a
From CBS Reports Series
> From the program "East Europe: Satellites Out of Or-
bit," this film examines two contrasting satellite nations
in the post-Khrushchev era--Czechoslovakia and Yugoslavia. Illustrated are "westerning" trends, restrictions
on freedoms and contrasts with the two countries and the
rest of Europe.

1417. PROFESSOR LETTVIN TUNED IN
Public Broadcasting Indiana University 90 min.   b/w
> Before an audience of students, Dr. Jerome Lettvin talks
of "disengagement from society through drug use or other
means." He answers questions, reminds students that
they will inherit the world and they will "need judgment
uncontaminated by any judgment-destroyer in order to
deal with problems competently."

1418. QUESTION, THE
McGraw-Hill 1969 10 min. color
Award Winner
> According to this British cartoon, a little man searches
for life's answers in politics, money, psychology, religion and war. Sooner or later none of these places provides the satisfying answers. The question, "What is
life all about?" is only meaningful and answerable when
"we are able to relate to someone else."

1419. QUESTION OF VIOLENCE, THE
National Educational Television Indiana University 59 min.
b/w
> This film analyzes the historical, social and psychologi-
cal factors which underlie violence in contemporary life.
The history of violence is traced from encounters with
Indians to present-day upheavals. Mass media responsibilities relative to violence are also examined.

1420. RED CHINA
BBC-TV Time-Life 1971 50 min.   color vt/vc s/c/a
> This documentary portrays China as a monolithic society
with one leader: Mao Tse-tung. Many scenes illustrat-
ing contemporary Chinese life are shown, with evidences
of hostile anti-American propaganda.

1421. RED DETACHMENT OF WOMEN
American Documentary Films 1972 90 min.   b/w
> The revolutionary ballet, now available to American audi-
ences, explains the story of a young woman who escapes
enslavement of federal landlords to join a group of revo-
lutionaries.

1422. REFLECTIONS IN SPACE
Screen Gems 1970 27 min. b/w s/c/a
This film expresses the impact that space exploration has
upon all creative arts in the curriculum areas: journalism, history, cinematography and music. Starring are:
William Buckley, Archibald Macleish, James Wyeth, others.

1423. RIOT MAKERS
University of California 1971 29 min. color
This is a conservative attempt to demonstrate that riots
are primarily the result of work done by well-trained agitators.

1424. ROCK IN THE ROAD
Bailey Film Associates 1971 6 min. color no narration
Award Winner
This animated film presents a brief story to symbolize
moral and ethical values. A man trips over a rock and
plunges into a hole. As he emerges, he discovers someone else coming, replaces the rock and hides. The second man also falls into the hole and, in turn, sets up the
accident for the third; the third does similarly for the
fourth. Finally, the fourth man removes the rock, fills
the hole and goes away happy.

1425. SHANGHAI: THE NEW CHINA
Bailey Film Associates 35 min. b/w s/c/a
This film affords a rare opportunity to witness politicians
discussing the past and future. Also offered are many interviews with citizens who talk of the changes in their own
lives since the revolution.

1426. SILENT MAJORITY, THE
Creative Film Society 4 min. b/w
Award: CINE Golden Eagle Award
This is a political satire about the "older generation" which
lives in MacArthur Park, Los Angeles, California.

1427. STRUGGLE IN IRELAND: BERNADETTE DEVLIN
American Documentary Films 1972 30 min. b/w vt
Bernadette Devlin is heard during her tour early in 1971
as she makes a strong plea for the poor and working peoples of all nations. During this appearance in the United
States, she speaks "to unite all peoples against oppression."

1428. TALE OF TODAY, A
Mass Media Associates 1972 10 min. color
Some of the basic points of ideology and idealism that have
spawned communal life styles are explored. The Gebauers,
who made the film, and members of the commune portrayed relate their manifesto to the "philosophies of their
mentor, Thoreau."

1429. THIRD CHALLENGE, THE
U. S. Air Force   National Audiovisual Center   1963   45 min.
color
Communist techniques are portrayed where political parties have been infiltrated by sympathizers and "taken
over."

1430. TRENDS
Learning Corporation of America   1972   9 min.   color
This animated film looks at the evolution of man's ideas
in many areas.   Communication problems are discussed
and the relationship with man's nature is examined.

1431. VIEW OF AMERICA FROM THE 23rd CENTURY
National Educational Television   23 min.   color   s/c/a
John W. Gardner, former Secretary of Health, Education
and Welfare, dramatizes how present institutions might
look when viewed from the perspective of the 23rd century.

1432. VOICES FROM THE RIGHT
Indiana University   1966   30 min.   b/w
People explain what the radical right represents and op-
poses.   Those interviewed include: Dr. Fred Schwartz,
Christian Anti-Communism Crusade; Kent and Phoebe
Courtney, Conservative Society of America; Dr. William
C. Douglass; Elizabeth Linington, John Birch Society
member, others.

1433. WHERE ARE WE GOING?
National Educational Television   29 min.   b/w
Krishnamurti, Indian spiritual leader, examines the world
crisis and expounds the philosophy that "all that is important is what we are and what is--not what we think
should be--and this requires a radical transformation of
the mind."

1434. WHO GOES THERE?--A PRIMER ON COMMUNISM (PARTS
I, II)
McGraw-Hill   1964   Each part: 27 min.   b/w   C/a
The history of socialism is examined.   The men who cre-
ated communism are introduced and their gains and set-
backs appraised.

1435. YEAR OF THE COMMUNES
Association Films   1970   54 min.   color
Filmed entirely on location, narrated by Rod Steiger,
this documentary illustrates lifestyles at nine different
communes in the West.   It contrasts the "straight" and
"hippie" communes, analyzing both successes and failures.   Margaret Mead reviews the film.

1436. YOUNG AMERICANS
       National Educational Television   Indiana University   1965
       60 min.   b/w
              "Youth Culture" is explored with narration and documen-
              tary footage of interviews of young Americans and knowl-
              edgeable experts.

                              Religious

1437. BEHOLD ... ALL THINGS NEW
       Mass Media Associates 1968 27 min.   color
              This is a documentary of the general convention of the
              World Council of Churches at Uppsala, Sweden in 1968.
              Many voices reflect the turmoil, spectacle, challenge that
              permeate the conference.

1438. BROTHER FRANCIS AND SISTER EARTH
       Mass Media Associates 1973   45 min.   b/w
              The philosophy of St. Francis of Assisi serves as the
              essential message in this documentary on the threats to
              human survival.   Some of the "best thinking" done on how
              to approach problems of pollution, waste, nature, en-
              vironment is examined.

1439. BUDDHIST WORLD, THE
       Modern Talking Picture Service   Free Loan Film   11 min.
       color
              Photographed in India, Thailand, Japan and Tibet, this
              film reviews the origins of Buddhism through the life,
              work and philosophy of Gautama Buddha.   The major ten-
              ets of the Buddhist belief are illustrated.

1440. CHALLENGE TO AUTHORITY
       Indiana University 26 min.   b/w
              This documentary provides an inquiry into the opinions of
              various persons, lay and clerical, concerning the Catho-
              lic Church's authority in the lives of its members.

1441. CHESSMASS
       Mass Media Associates 1972 2 min.   color
              This film illustrates a miniature Mass with everybody con-
              cerned portrayed in miniature animation as chesspieces.
              Discussion groups are encouraged to examine the variety
              of perceptions of the symbolism.

1442. CONTEMPORARY CATHOLICISM
       University of Utah 1962 29 min.   b/w
       From the Christian Philosophy Series: #14
              The theory of Neo-Thomism is discussed as outlined by
              Jacques Maritain.   The meaning of "truth" is examined,
              as is the role of the Catholic Church in resolving social
              problems.

1443. CONTEMPORARY LIBERALISM
       University of Utah   1962   29 min.   b/w
       From the Christian Philosophy Series: #25
            Discussed are results of scientific inquiry as they relate
            to theories of William Elbry Channing, exponent of Uni-
            tarianism.

1444. CONTEMPORARY MORMONISM
       University of Utah   1962   29 min.   b/w
       From the Christian Philosophy Series: #30
            The ideology of Mormonism is discussed with questions
            resolved concerning its doctrinal philosophy.

1445. CONTEMPORARY PROTESTANTISM
       University of Utah   1962   29 min.   b/w
       From the Christian Philosophy Series: #18
            This film discusses ways in which Protestant Fundamen-
            talism influenced attitudes toward science, ,social and
            economic problems.   Outlined are the sources of its ap-
            peal.

1446. EVOLUTION, HIGHER CRITICISM AND THE COMPARATIVE
       STUDY OF RELIGION
       University of Utah   1962   29 min.   b/w   C/a
       From the Christian Philosophy Series: #23
            This film reviews the effects of scientific inquiry on re-
            ligious thought.   The study of religions illustrates how
            the theory of evolution has precipitated a more critical
            scrutiny of the Bible.

1447. FOUR RELIGIONS: HINDUISM AND BUDDHISM (PART I)
       National Film Board of Canada   1967   30 min.   b/w
            Part I investigates Hinduism, the chief religion of India
            and "the oldest religion of mankind," and Buddhism, as
            a religion attempting to inspire "human dignity and
            grace."

1448. FOUR RELIGIONS: ISLAM AND CHRISTIANITY (PART II)
       National Film Board of Canada   1967   30 min.   b/w
            Part II explores Islam, the youngest of the great reli-
            gions, and Christianity, both of which draw many of
            their principal beliefs from the Jewish religion.

1449. GREAT CONVERSATION
       American Broadcasting Company   1963   54 min.   b/w   s/c/a
            Delegates to the Third Assembly of the World Council of
            Churches at New Delhi are interviewed.   The film also
            includes visits to a Protestant monastery.   In addition,
            one sequence shows the Pan-Orthodox Conference at
            Rhodes, with a report on the world-wide Ecumenical
            Movement within the Christian Church.

1450. HINDU WORLD, THE
Modern Talking Picture Service   Free Loan Film   11 min.
color
> This historical and cultural survey of Hinduism stresses
> various mental and physical disciplines through which
> Hindus seek eternal union with Brahma.   Also treated are
> the caste system, belief in reincarnation, and the deep
> influence of religion on the Hindu way of life.

1451. IN THE NAME OF ALLAH
Indiana University   1971   76 min.   b/w
> This film examines the culture, vision, history and scrip-
> tures of the Islamic religion by studying varied aspects
> of life in the Moslem community of Fez, Morocco.   It
> emphasizes the teaching of the Koran.

1452. ISLAM
McGraw-Hill   19 min.   b/w
> This is a study of the political, cultural and religious
> nature of the Islamic community.

1453. JESUITS, THE: HATED SOCIETY
BBC-TV   Time-Life   1972   51 min.   color   vt/vc
> The story of the Jesuits, the most "militant order of the
> Roman Catholic Church," is explained, from its founding
> to the present.

1454. JESUS TRIP, THE
Time-Life   35 min.   color   vt/vc   s/c/a
> The "Jesus Freaks" communes are examined.   The group
> believes that the Bible is the only word of truth and the
> only safeguard against an imminent "doomsday."

1455. JUDAISM (PART I)
National Educational Television   Indiana University   1956
30 min.   b/w   kinescope
> Jewish history is examined.   Jewish religious beliefs con-
> cerning rights and responsibilities of man are reviewed.

1456. JUDAISM (PART II)
National Educational Television   Indiana University   1956
30 min.   b/w   kinescope
> The Ten Commandments provide minimum rules needed
> for the Jewish basic concept of ethical and ritualistic law.

1457. LIBERALISM: RELIGION IS TO SATISFY NEEDS
University of Utah   1962   29 min.   b/w   c/a
From the Christian Philosophy Series: #24
> Liberalism is defined as a "basic belief that religion is
> a type of experience giving direction and meaning to life,
> security and importance to social relationships." Stressed
> is the interpretation of experience based on Christian tra-
> ditions.

1458. MAHATMA GANDHI: SILENT REVOLUTION
       International Film Bureau 38 min.   color   s/c/a
              Background material for the study of modern India is pro-
              vided, with analysis of social and economic problems.

1459. MAN OF CONSCIENCE
       CBS News Bailey Film Associates 28 min.   b/w s/c/a
              Pacifist A. J. Muste, Christian minister, teacher,
              leader, civil rights leader, is introduced. Because of
              his expression of his beliefs, he lost his first fulltime
              ministry.

1460. MARTIN LUTHER
       Lutheran Film Association Teaching Film Custodians 29 min.
       b/w
       Award: CINE Golden Eagle Award
              Martin Luther's motivating influences are studied in this
              biography. Reviewed are the creation of his 95 theses
              and the inauguration of the Reformation.

1461. MARTIN LUTHER AND THE PROTESTANT REFORMATION
       Time-Life 30 min.   b/w vt/vc s/c/a
              This film illustrates the philosophy behind the writings of
              Martin Luther. Detailed also is the background for his
              excommunication from the Catholic Church.

1462. MOSLEM WORLD: BEGINNINGS AND GROWTH
       Modern Talking Picture Service 1972 11 min.   color
              This film reviews the Mohammedan way of life, intercul-
              tural influences, and its impact on western life.

1463. NONVIOLENT PROTEST: GANDHI AND KING, TEACHER
       AND PUPIL
       Intext 1970 15 min.   b/w
              The philosophy of nonviolent civil disobedience of Mahat-
              ma Gandhi and Martin Luther King are compared. Film
              clips of actual speeches and activities of these leaders
              are shown. Discussion topics concern the effectiveness
              of nonviolent protest as a method of gaining desirable
              ends.

1464. PAUL J. TILLICH (PARTS I, II, III, IV)
       National Educational Television Indiana University
       Each: 29 min.   b/w
              These four segments deal with: Part I: a discussion of
              the Tillich philosophy concerning religion; Part II: moral-
              ity versus moralism; Part III: psychotherapy as it re-
              lates to religion; Part IV: religious education.

1465. PREACHER, THE
       Mass Media Associates 1972 1 min.   color
       Award Winner
              A late-night television sermonette is viewed by a beer-

drinking viewer. The impact of the sermon is negligible,
prompting much controversy as to the film's intent.

1466. PROTEST AND COMMUNICATION
BBC Time-Life 60 min. color vt/vc
From the Civilisation Series: #6
Sir Kenneth Clark comments on creative expression at the
close of the 15th century. It is described as an age of
doubting and hesitation. Spurred on by questions, the
Reformation and the new faith, Protestanism "smashes
graven images of the Roman Catholic Church."

1467. QUESTION OF METHOD, A
International Film Bureau 6 min. color
A conflict is presented between an instructor and parents
concerning the right of the instructor to encourage doubt
of religious truths that parents have taught their children
to accept on faith.

1468. RELIGIOUS FREEDOM: AMERICA'S BEGINNINGS
Coronet 14 min. b/w and color s/c/a
Collaborator: Sydney E. Ahlstrom, Yale University
Religious intolerance in Europe during the 1600s was one
of the forces that drove men to America. The forces be-
hind the initiation of the Constitution and the Bill of
Rights are examined.

1469. ROMAN CATHOLICISM: PROOFS FOR GOD'S EXISTENCE
University of Utah 1962 29 min. b/w C/a
From the Christian Philosophy Series: #10
Roman Catholicism history is presented in brief, with
methods for analysis of "proof" of God's existence. The
film sketches the life and influence of St. Thomas Aqui-
nas, his methodology of analysis and proofs of God's existence.

1470. SERMON ON THE MOUNT NOW
Mass Media Associates 1972 19 min. color
This is a reading of the Sermon on the Mount accompanied by a mélange of images, most of them vérité scenes,
reflecting upon the look and "feel" of contemporary life.
The film's objective is for the viewer to relate the Sermon's message to present-day immediacy.

1471. SON OF MAN
Time-Life 96 min. b/w vt/vc
This controversial drama is about Jesus, the man. The
question asked is "Am I Indeed the Messiah?"

1472. ULTIMATE TRIP, THE
National Broadcasting Company 1970 32 min. color
The "Jesus Freak" evangelical group tells its story.

1473. UNKNOWN GOD, THE
       Modern Talking Picture Service   Free Loan Film   29 min.
       color
              The Apostle Paul relates to Timothy his controversies
              with the heathen philosophers of Athens, and that he was
              there to present the true God, whom they acknowledge to
              be unknown to them.

1474. VATICAN, THE
       Time-Life   52 min.   color   vt/vc   s/a
              Photographed are rarely seen departments of the Holy See.

1475. WHAT IS RELIGIOUS FREEDOM?
       University of Utah   1957   29 min.   b/w   C/a
       From the Great Issues in Religion Series
              A discussion by Sterling McMurrin, Waldemer P. Read
              and William Mulder considers the constitutional back-
              grounds of civil action and social relationship in terms
              of religious freedom.

1476. ZEN IN RYOKO-IN
       Macmillan   71 min.   color
              This film interprets in full the complete experience of
              Zen meditation as part of the Buddhist participation.

                                    War

1477. AFTERMATH OF WORLD WAR I
       McGraw-Hill   1962   27 min.   b/w   s/c
              Factors are presented which resulted in the political in-
              stability, national rivalry and social unrest after World
              War I.

1478. ALL-STAR BOND RALLY*
       United States Training Film   National Audiovisual Center
       17 min.   b/w   s/c/a
              An all-star cast entertains to promote the World War II
              bond effort.   The film contains almost every established
              entertainer of the World War II period who contributed to
              "selling" bonds.

1479. AMERICAN REVOLUTION: 1770-1783--A CONVERSATION
       WITH LORD NORTH
       Bailey Film Associates   1974   33 min.   color   s/c/a
              Peter Ustinov and Eric Sevareid are featured in this first
              part of a series of interviews on personalities and issues
              of the American Revolution.

1480. AMERICAN TIME CAPSULE
       Braverman Pyramid   1969   3 min.   color   s/c/a   vt/vc
              With flash-frame technique, two hundred years of Ameri-
              can history is condensed.   Beginning with shots from the

Revolutionary War, the images whiz by until current
world conflicts come into view. The frequency of war
"flashes" suggests that much of the history of this country has been violent.

1481. AMERICA'S CRITICS ABROAD
Defense Department   National Audiovisual Center   1965
20 min.   b/w
This film drama comprises a series of vignettes showing
how American personnel overseas can counter criticism
and answer questions about life in the United States.   Its
objective is to convince the serviceman that "it is his
responsibility to be directly informed."

1482. ANATOMY OF AGGRESSION, THE
United States Information Agency   National Audiovisual Center   1961   29 min.   b/w
Communist activities are viewed during the past fifteen
years, with stress on the conflicts between democracy
and totalitarianism.

1483. ANATOMY OF VIOLENCE
National Educational Television   Indiana University   1968
30 min.   b/w   c/a
A Congress on the Dialectics of Liberation was held in
London to explore the relationship of violence to social
reform.   Speakers included Professor H. Marcuse, University of California, Paul Goodman, Stokely Carmichael
and Allan Ginsburg.

1484. AND THEY WERE FIVE
Macmillan   9 min.   color
This film makes a transition from five young boys playing, to five grown men--all of whom die on the battlefield.

1485. ANDERSON PLATOON
McGraw-Hill   Contemporary   Mass Media Associates   1968
65 min.   b/w
Awards: Academy Award plus many others
This film reviews a day in the life of an American army
platoon stationed in the central highlands in Vietnam, in
late 1966.   It captures the "spirit of camaraderie, humor,
homesickness, stoicism and determination."

1486. ARES CONTRE ATLAS (MARS VERSUS ATLAS)
Crowell, Collier, Macmillan   Brandon   1967   8 min.   color
Award: Grand Prix   1967 at Annecy
In five episodes, the absurdity of war is demonstrated in
this animated film.   Episodes show the ironies of war;
e.g., a plant is destroyed by its own bombs.

1487. BATTLE, THE
Mass Media Associates 1971 5 min. color
Awards: 1971 Oberhausen Film Festival; London, New York
awards
> The internal workings of the body in a young vigorous
> soldier are animated to simulate a massive war. The
> war is carried to every part of the "corpus, reeking de-
> struction." Finally, amid all the ruins, the bugler blows
> "taps," and the camera reveals a bent old man.

1488. BATTLE OF BRITAIN*
United States Army National Audiovisual Center 1943
54 min. b/w s/c/a
From the Why We Fight Series; Directed by Frank Capra
> This film illustrates how the British fought back from
> the German terror tactics. The blitzes on London, fire
> bombings, conversations with the British, are all part of
> the film.

1489. BLACK G.I.
National Educational Television Indiana University 1970
55 min. b/w
> The role of blacks in past wars is briefly traced. Focus
> is on the Vietnam War and the disproportionate percentage
> of frontline black troops and casualties. There are inter-
> views with testimony that whites taught some Vietnamese
> to call blacks "nigger."

1490. BLACK SOLDIER
CBS News Bailey Film Associates 1968 26 min. b/w
> Bill Cosby narrates the history of black Americans in the
> Armed Forces. Rare silent footage plus paintings and
> cartoons show their participation in World Wars I and II,
> the Korean War and the Vietnam conflict.

1491. CAMERA GOES ALONG, THE
Mass Media Associates 1936 12 min. b/w
> Sequences provide an illustration of Nazi propaganda meth-
> ods. Parades, mass formations, other methods were de-
> signed for the impact of the camera and not necessarily
> for the spectators.

1492. CHAOS AND CONFLICT
Indiana University 1968 30 min. b/w
> This film reviews the many wars since World War II,
> raising the question of arms trade and the responsibility
> of major powers. Both internal insurgencies and wars in-
> volving international intervention are covered.

1493. CHESS GAME, THE
Centron 7 min. color s/c/a
> A board and chess players are used to make a statement
> about revolution and the difficulty of changing the funda-
> mental patterns of society.

1494. CHILDREN'S GAMES
       Mass Media Associates   10 min.   b/w
           Children "playing" at war is the theme of this film.

1495. CHRISTIANS AT WAR
       Time-Life   52 min.   color   vt/vc   s/c/a
           This is a filmed examination of the sporadic violence by
           both Protestant and Catholic terrorists which continues in
           Northern Ireland.

1496. CIVIL WAR (PARTS I, II)
       Learning Corporation of America   1972   27 min. each   color
       s/c
           The dialogue in these films is taken verbatim from letters,
           speeches, periodicals and diaries of the period.   Part I
           concerns the "Anguish of Emancipation," while Part II ex-
           amines the "Promise of Reconstruction."

1497. CIVIL WAR: ITS BACKGROUND AND CAUSES
       McGraw-Hill   16 min.   color
           The development of different economic lines of the north
           and south is traced and reflected in the politics and con-
           flict of the period.

1498. CIVILISATION
       Museum of Modern Art   1916   b/w   silent
           Propaganda for the pacifist camp in American public opin-
           ion at that time, this film renders ideas and sentiments
           of anti-war feeling.

1499. CODE, THE
       United States Air Force   National Audiovisual Center   1959
       27 min.   b/w
           This visual presentation of the United States fighting man's
           "Code," narrated by Jack Webb, covers the themes of sur-
           render, capture, escape and conduct as a prisoner of war.

1500. CODE AND YOU, THE
       United States Navy   National Audiovisual Center   1953
       27 min.   b/w
           The major points of the uniform code of military justice
           are examined as it is interpreted by the United States
           Armed Forces.

1501. CONSTITUTION AND MILITARY POWER, THE
       National Educational Television   Indiana University   1957
       30 min.   b/w   s/c/a
       From the Constitution in Action Series
           Two court cases involving military-civilian relations in
           wartime are analyzed.   The film shows the relationship of
           the constitution to issues of military-civilian relationships
           during wartime.

1502. DECEMBER 7, 1941*
CBS   McGraw-Hill   1956   25 min.   b/w
      The Japanese surprise attack on Pearl Harbor is shown
      as it triggered American entry into World War II.

1503. DIVIDE AND CONQUER
Office of War Information   Brandon   1943   60 min.   b/w
s/c/a
      Shown are Nazi techniques of spreading hate and fear,
      distrust and confusion.   The propaganda devices of Hit-
      ler are illustrated, as are the espionage systems used
      to destroy the morale of the French people.

1504. FABLE-SAFE
Crowell, Collier, Macmillan   1972   9 min.   color
      In an animated story set to folk music, the subject of
      war is approached lightly with a missile race that has
      reached its stage of superoverkill.   "The juxtaposition of
      the light approach with the serious subject causes im-
      pact."

1505. FELLOW AMERICANS*
Office of Emergency Management   National Audiovisual Center
10 min.   b/w
      Narrated by James Stewart, this is an elegy to men
      killed at Pearl Harbor.   It is recognized as a "master-
      piece of wartime documentary."

1506. FREEDOM'S FINEST HOUR
McGraw-Hill   54 min.   color
‣ Awards: CINE Golden Eagle, other
      Ronald Reagan narrates this film about the Revolutionary
      War, with the assistance of some of the ballads and art
      works of that period.

1507. FRIENDS AND FOES
National Broadcasting Company   1969   156 min.   b/w   s/c/a
      This film surveys American involvement in the interna-
      tional confrontations of the sixties.   Described are crises
      from Berlin to Vietnam, emphasizing the need to resolve
      future problems "before they develop."

1508. GERMAN-AMERICAN BUNDISTS*
Thorne   4 min.   b/w   any age
      Bundist youth camps, meetings and conferences are the
      "target" for the distribution of literature.   Featured is
      American Bund Fuehrer Fritz Kuhn at a mass rally in
      Madison Square Garden, which is interrupted by violence.

1509. GIVE ME LIBERTY!
Brandon   20 min.   b/w
      A background is presented of the period in which Patrick
      Henry, with his famous speech, stirred American colon-
      ists to resist British tyranny.

1510. GOOD TIMES, WONDERFUL TIMES
       American Documentary Films 1965 70 min. b/w
            Footage of the past two world wars is interspersed with
            the cant of cocktail chatter to illustrate the hypocrisy of
            world conflict. The combat documentary footage took
            two years to collect from the archives of London, Mos-
            cow, Tokyo.

1511. GOODBYE, BILLY: AMERICA GOES TO WAR, 1917-1918
       Coronet 1971 27 min. b/w
            To create the experience of a culture at war, this film
            shows the patriotism, fervor, ritual that inspired and
            "justified" American participation.

1512. GREAT WAR, THE (PARTS I, II)
       McGraw-Hill 52 min. b/w
            The events leading to the outbreak of World War I are
            dramatized to present an account of its progress, from
            Germany's invasion of Belgium through her surrender to
            the Allied forces.

1513. "H" BOMB OVER US
       Crowell, Collier, Macmillan 10 min. color s/a
            Using technical film methods, this animated film points
            up the scientific findings on the potency of the H-bomb
            danger. A graphic portrayal shows the impact of a 1-
            megaton H-bomb warhead on Los Angeles, California.
            No program of solutions is presented, but the subject is
            left open for discussion. The text is taken from a study
            published by the Center for the Study of Democratic Insti-
            tutions, Santa Barbara, California.

1514. HAPPY BIRTHDAY FELISA
       Mass Media Associates 10 min. color
            From fast-cutting montages, the viewer sees the film-
            maker's daughter's fifth birthday party while the parents
            are discussing "current events." Each candle on the
            cake symbolizes another war, another "agony."

1515. HAT, THE: IS THIS WAR NECESSARY
       Mass Media Associates 1967 28 min. color s/c/a
       animation
            Two soldiers patrolling a border keep hostile eyes on
            each other. The hat of one falls off into enemy terri-
            tory. Whose hat is it now? Arguments turn into
            threats and soon a full-scale international crisis begins.

1516. HITLER: ANATOMY OF A DICTATORSHIP
       Learning Corporation of America 1972 23 min. b/w
       Consultant: Dr. James Shenton, Department of History,
       Columbia University
            This documentary covers Hitler's career from his emer-
            gence on the political scene in 1923 to the end of World

War II. The mistakes in judgment which led to Hitler's ascendancy are analyzed.

1517. HITLER: THE FALL OF THE THIRD REICH (PART II)
Wolper McGraw-Hill 1963 26 min. b/w
From the Biography Series
> The early German victories in World War II are analyzed, as is the "turn of the tide," when allied victories toppled Nazi power and brought about Hitler's suicide.

1518. HITLER: THE RISE TO POWER (PART I)
Wolper McGraw-Hill 1963 27 min. b/w
From the Biography Series
> This film examines the boyhood and early life of Hitler. Included is his part in forming and leading the national socialist party to power in 1933 and events which led to the beginning of World War II in 1939.

1519. HOW TO KILL
Benchmark 11 min. color s/c/a
> The sanctity conflict--holiness of life and devastation of war--is examined.

1520. I MISS YOU SO
Macmillan 8 min. b/w s/c/a
> A soldier's wife writes him a touching letter which serves to illustrate the contrasts between her ordinary, workday world and his battlefront days.

1521. IN A REVOLUTIONARY WORLD
KRMA 29 min. b/w s/c/a
> The United States' lack of participation in the League of Nations is reviewed, including the neutrality acts of the thirties, foreign aid after wars, and the extent and character of our participation in Indo-China and Korea.

1522. INTEGRATION IN THE MILITARY
Brandon 26 min. b/w
From the 20th Century Series
> A documentary on the racial integration of the American military, this film shows not only how it was established and to what degree, but also how it is working and how individual rights are protected.

1523. INTERVIEWS WITH MAI LAI VETERANS
Contemporary Crowell, Collier, Macmillan 1970 22 min. color
Award: Best Documentary Short (Academy Award) of 1970
> Five Mai Lai veterans are interviewed in their homes and offices. Reviewed are their individual stories, telling where they were and what they were doing that day of March 16, 1968. The film records how "ordinary young men are brutalized by war and are made to perform violent acts without thinking."

1524. INVASION--NAZI VERSION*
       Audio/Brandon 1955 18 min. b/w
            An actual Nazi newsreel intended for German audiences
            attempts to explain the Normandy invasion. The news-
            reel is shown intact except for English translation and
            explanation of the German narration.

1525. IT CAN'T LAST*
       Office of War Information   National Audiovisual Center
       1944 20 min. b/w
            This film, written for the United States Navy by Archi-
            bald MacLeish, illustrates actual efforts of troops in war
            in contrast to a civilian's idea of what is occurring.

1526. JAPANESE RELOCATION*
       Office of War Information National Audiovisual Center 1943
       9 min. b/w s/c/a
            Shown is the mass migration of 100,000 people of Japa-
            nese descent from the West Coast to states far enough in-
            land to "secure us from the threat of immediate inva-
            sion." Specifics cover from the first registration of all
            Japanese until the final settlement was accomplished.

1527. KEEPING INFORMED
       National Audiovisual Center 20 min. b/w
            This film explains the origin, development and use of
            communications media for keeping our Armed Forces in-
            formed of their role in attaining the "nation's objectives."

1528. KENNEDY VERSUS KHRUSHCHEV
       Wolper 1965 b/w s/c
       From the Men in Crisis Series
            The verbal confrontation between two world leaders over
            the Cuban Missile Crisis is reviewed. The film shows
            how Kennedy's stand forced Khrushchev to dismantle the
            Cuban missile sites.

1529. KNOW YOUR ALLY: BRITAIN*
       National Audiovisual Center 1944 42 min. b/w
            First of a World War II series to deal with peoples with
            whom we fight and "with whom we stand or fall," the
            film includes a study of English mores.

1530. KNOW YOUR ENEMY: THE VIETCONG*
       National Audiovisual Center 20 min. b/w
            This film contains the Central Office for South Vietnam
            propaganda newsreels of the Viet Cong, captured by ele-
            ments of the 173rd Airborne Brigade during "Operation
            Junction City" in Tay Ninh Province.

1531. KOREAN ARMISTICE
       National Audiovisual Center 27 min. b/w
            This film describes the workings of the Korean Armistice

Agreement and what it requires of the United States to
maintain it.

1532. LAND WITHOUT JOY
American Documentary Films 1968 27 min. b/w c/a
This British documentary focuses on Saigon during the
Tet offensive. In interviews with American military,
reasons are stated for the destructive response to the VC
attacks.

1533. LANGUAGE OF FACES
McGraw-Hill 1961 17 min. b/w
Award Winner; Directed by John Korty
This anti-war statement of the American Friends Service
Committee reviews the contrasts in our society: children
singing during bomb drills, people watching military pa-
rades.

1534. LAST REFLECTIONS OF A WAR
Mass Media Associates 44 min. b/w
A dramatized view is presented of the involvement in
Vietnam by the late Bernard Fall.

1535. LIBERATION OF NAZI CONCENTRATION CAMPS*
Thorne 5 min. b/w any age
This film portrays conditions discovered at various concentration camps by the arriving Allied troops and Red
Cross personnel. Atrocities and gas chambers are
viewed. The producer suggests that this film be handled
with "discretion" since much of the content is shocking.

1536. LISTEN TO BRITAIN
McGraw-Hill 1942 19 min. b/w
Made as a British wartime propaganda example of the
lyric documentary, this film illustrates the sights and
sounds of one day in Britain in World War II. Without
any voice commentary, the images are linked with contrasting, complementary sounds.

1537. LIVING (VIVRE)
McGraw-Hill 8 min. b/w
The impression left behind by war on its witnesses is
conveyed in these selected newsreel excerpts of faces.

1538. MEIN KAMPF*
Sweden McGraw-Hill 1960 117 min. b/w
Directed by Edward Leiser
Using contemporary newsreel footage, this documentary
traces the rise and fall of the Third Reich.

1539.	MEMORANDUM
		National Film Board of Canada McGraw-Hill 1966 58 min.
		b/w
		Award: San Francisco Film Festival, Best Documentary
			In flashbacks through the mind of a survivor, this docu-
			mentary probes the phenomenon of Nazi concentration
			camps.

1540.	MEMORIAL
		Mass Media Associates 1972 10 min. color
			This is an elegiac film recalling what it was like to fight
			and die on the Somme in the summer and autumn of 1916.

1541.	MILITARY JUSTICE
		Defense Department National Audiovisual Center 1954 94
		min. b/w
			A dramatic portrayal is enacted of general courtmartial
			proceedings under the Uniform Code of Military Justice
			as established by Public Law 506.

1542.	MINISTER OF HATE
		McGraw-Hill 1961 27 min. b/w s/c/a
		From the 20th Century Series
			Shown are the techniques of mass thought control created
			by Nazi Joseph Goebbels. Documented with historical
			film footage, the effect of totalitarian control of commun-
			ications on a society is demonstrated. The film illus-
			trates how Goebbels gained complete control of the media,
			using it as a weapon to enforce an image of Hitler.

1543.	MOCKINGBIRD
		Brandon Macmillan 1963 39 min. b/w s/c/a
			In this adaptation to film of the classic short story by
			Ambrose Bierce, a Union Army man accidentally shoots
			his Confederate Army twin brother. Standing night guard,
			he sees an indistinct moving figure in the distance and
			fires. The shock causes the soldier to desert.

1544.	MORALITY OF WAR: CONSCIENCE VERSUS AUTHORITY--
		TRIAL BY FIRE
		Association Sterling Free Loan Film 27 min. color and
		b/w
			This film suggests that a "just war cannot be fought by
			unjust means." A combat pilot is ordered to bomb a vil-
			lage hiding guerrillas. He refuses to fly the mission and
			faces court martial. His commanding officer and family
			try to persuade him to change his mind. He wavers but
			persists. The audience is left to decide whether or not
			he acted "rightly."

1545.	MUNICH CONFERENCE, THE*
		Thorne 4 min. b/w any age
			Newspapers announce Hitler's demands for the Sudeten-

land; Mussolini, Hitler, Chamberlain and Daladier arrive
at Munich and sign the Munich Accord. Chamberlain returns to London and makes the "peace in our time"
speech at the airport. The film ends with the German
invasion and occupation of Czechoslovakia.

1546. MY COUNTRY--RIGHT OR WRONG?
Learning Corporation of America 15 min. color
Rejections of the Vietnam War and crucial decisions about
the draft incite discussions between Jerry and his father
concerning patriotic duty.

1547. NAME, RANK AND SERVICE NUMBER
National Audiovisual Center 1965 23 min. b/w
This film enacts the true story of two American officers
captured by communists. It pictures their perseverance
under duress and shows how servicemen who live by the
Armed Forces code of conduct "find inner strength to resist enemy pressure and torture."

1548. NEGRO SOLDIER
War Department 1944 40 min. b/w
Frank Capra, supervisor
World War II documentary footage shows a minister
preaching the history of blacks in the United States,
stressing their participation in World War II. Langston
Hughes hailed the film as "the most remarkable Negro
film ever flashed on the American screen."

1549. NIGHT AND FOG
Mass Media Associates 1962 35 min. color
A commentary on man's inhumanity to man is presented
in French, with English subtitles. Black and white sequences filmed by the Nazis inside their own concentration camps are matched against the color and contrasts
of the same camps today.

1550. NO VIETNAMESE EVER CALLED ME NIGGER
American Documentary Films 1969 68 min. b/w
To state the relationship between racism at home and
abroad, this film of the Harlem Fall Mob March in 1967
lets the "street people" speak about black ghetto life and
the relationship between racism and the Vietnam War.
Interviews are shown with three black Vietnam veterans.

1551. NOTE FROM ABOVE
Mass Media Associates 1970 2 min. color animation
Awards: Winner, Oberhausen Film Festival, 3 other awards
This satire on conventional religion and war concerns several notes dropped by a "divine presence." One says,
"thou shalt kill." And shots are exchanged. A final note
reads, "should have read 'thou shalt not kill'; sorry--my
mistake." Unfortunately, there is no one alive to pick up

the note and read it. "In a word, truth to be 'revealed' must be affirmed in human experience."

1552. OFFSPRING
Brandon Crowell, Collier, Macmillan 1968 5 min. color
A montage of newsreels, stills and live-action footage juxtaposes a healthy American child singing peacefully with the starving and inured young of other countries. Musical accompaniment is "Where Have All the Flowers Gone?"

1553. 1000 CRANES: THE CHILDREN OF HIROSHIMA
Brandon Crowell, Collier, Macmillan 24 min. b/w s/c/a
This film links the ancient Japanese belief that "the folding of 1000 paper cranes will protect one illness" to the heritage of the children of Hiroshima. Visits to survivors of the bombing and to leaders of the "Folded Crane Club" provide the basis for an "open plea" for all people to work for peace.

1554. OPENING OF THE NUREMBERG TRIALS, THE
Thorne 1971 5 min. b/w s/c/a
The German war crimes trials begin in Nuremberg, Germany. Justice Lawrence listens to the defendants' pleas. Goering responds and is rebuked by the court. The other defendants make their pleas. The prosecution begins its case.

1555. OVER THERE--1914-1918
McGraw-Hill 1963 90 min. b/w
German and French newsreels, official army films, suppressed and contraband films, propaganda productions and films shot by amateur photographers all present one of the most complete wide-range accounts of World War I.

1556. PERFECT TRIBUTE, THE
Metro Goldwyn Mayer 1935 20 min. b/w (Restricted to class use)
In this story by Mary Shipman Andrews, viewers see the background to the delivery of the Gettysburg Address. The film describes the circumstances of its writing, revealing Lincoln's "spirit and his attitude toward the defeated South." Recounted is his initial speech to a wounded Confederate soldier.

1557. POTSDAM CONFERENCE, THE*
Thorne 4 min. b/w any age
There are scenes of confederate sessions and dialogue of Churchill. Attlee, Truman, Stalin and Eden.

1558. PRELUDE TO WAR*
War Department   Museum of Modern Art   1942 53 min.   b/w
From the Why We Fight Series; Directed by Frank Capra
Depicted are events leading to World War II during the
period from 1931 to 1938. The rise of fascism, Nazi
and Japanese imperialism are all examined.

1559. PRISONER OF WAR
Crowell, Collier, Macmillan   52 min.   b/w   s/c/a
Americans who were prisoners in Korea during the war
there are subjects of this film, which deals with their
treatment by the enemy and their reactions to it.

1560. REASON WHY, THE
Bailey Film Associates   14 min.   color   s/c/a
In this one-act allegory starring Eli Wallach and Robert
Ryan, questions are dramatized concerning the impulses
of man toward war, violence, murder. Written by Arthur
Miller, who recalls, "I wanted to put down facts--the
way we're made..."

1561-1600. [No entry]

1601. REBUTTAL OF THE SELLING OF THE PENTAGON, THE
CBS News   Associated Instructional Films   1971   23 min.
color
This CBS film's message is a response to the original
program charges by members of the government. The
objectors include former Vice President Spiro Agnew and
former Secretary of Defense Melvin Laird. The film was
telecast the same night as the rebroadcast of "The Selling of the Pentagon." The President of CBS News responds on behalf of the network.

1602. RED, WHITE AND BLACK
CBS News   Carousel   1970   19 min.   s/c/a
From the CBS' Sixty Minutes Series
Racial violence is examined among United States troops.
The situation in Germany is reviewed with both factions
expressing views. The United States High Command de-
clined to comment on charges that the "G.I. justice is
prejudicial toward the whites."

1603. RISE AND FALL OF NAZI GERMANY, THE*
March of Time   McGraw-Hill   1947   17 min.   b/w   s/c/a
This documentary film records Hitler's conquests and de-
feats, beginning with the Saar plebiscite in 1935. It
shows how Hitler led the Third Reich to domination over
fifteen countries, the defeat and occupation of Germany,
and the problems which faced the Allied Control Commission.

1604. RISE OF ADOLPH HITLER, THE
      Columbia Broadcasting System 1955 27 min. b/w
      From the You Are There Series
          The film reenacts events of September 9, 1936 at Nurem-
          berg, Germany, just six months after Nazi troops marched
          into the demilitarized Rhineland.

1605. RISE OF THE NAZI PARTY, THE*
      Thorne 5 min. b/w any age
          The Nazi rise to power is shown against the background
          of German inflation and unemployment. Hitler is in-
          stalled as Chancellor and Nazi violence smothers opposi-
          tion. The film ends with a montage of Hitler in various
          public appearances.

1606. RUMOURS OF WAR
      Time-Life 60 min. color vt/vc s/c/a
          This film is a behind-the-scenes view of man's power to
          destroy all humanity. A look is taken at war in terms
          of the slow nuclear arms race. Missile scenes and at-
          tempts for nuclear arms treaties are illustrated.

1607. SELLING OF THE PENTAGON, THE
      CBS News Carousel 1971 53 min. color s/c/a
      Award Winner
          This documentary focuses on several major areas of the
          Pentagon's public relations activities. It challenges de-
          fense expenditures, VIP junkets, pro-war speeches and
          service recruiting methods. Propaganda films suggest
          that policies are "slanted" and "selective."

1608. SPEAK OUT ON WAR
      Common Cause American Documentary Films 1971 30 min.
      b/w
          The people's lobby presents a panel discussion on the
          urgency for complete United States troop withdrawal from
          Indochina by December, 1971. The panel represents a
          broad constituency within the country of labor, business,
          university students, blacks and a "growing number of Vi-
          etnam veterans."

1609. STORY OF AN UNKNOWN SOLDIER, OR HOW THEY ENDED
      THE KELLOGG-BRIAND PACT AND ENDED WAR FOR ALL
      TIME
      American Documentary Films 10 min. b/w
          This satire is about man's efforts in the twentieth century
          to end war forever through treaties, pacts and edicts. It
          shows newsreel footage of all European diplomats and
          heads-of-state, with eloquent commentary on the function
          and problems of state diplomacy.

1610. SUFFER LITTLE CHILDREN
       National Broadcasting Company 1972 53 min. color
       s/c/a
            This film examines the effects of violence on the children
            in Northern Ireland. It focuses on the pervasive hatred
            that has developed between Catholic and Protestant groups
            and what that hostility is doing to their children as a
            "breeding ground" of bigotry.

1611. TEN DAYS THAT SHOOK THE WORLD*
       Mass Media Associates 1928 67 min. b/w silent s/c/a
       Directed by Sergei Eisenstein
            Made as part of the tenth anniversary of the October Rev-
            olution of 1917, the subject matter is treated as part of
            a political cartoon. The classic film commemorates the
            Bolshevik Revolution, depicting the historical forces set
            in motion by the overthrow of Czar Nicholas II in 1917.

1612. THESE ARE THE MEN
       Office of War Information   11 min.   b/w s/c/a
            The influence of Nazi leaders on the minds of the youth
            of Germany is illustrated. The scenes include Hitler,
            Goebbels, Goering and Hess.

1613. THIRD WORLD WAR, THE
       Cuba American Documentary Films 1970 90 min. b/w
            Roberto Retamar, one of Cuba's and Latin America's
            leading poets, created this feature-length documentary.
            It explains the significance of the Indochina War for the
            national liberation struggles challenging people of Asia,
            Africa, Latin America.

1614. THIS IS THE CODE: CONDUCT BEFORE THE ENEMY
       United States Navy National Audiovisual Center 11 min.
       b/w
       From This Is the Code Series
            This Navy film analyzes the code of military justice con-
            cerned with conduct before the enemy, treatment of pris-
            oners, conduct as a prisoner, including anti-persuasion
            strategies.

1615. TIME AND FORTUNE: VIETNAM NEWSREEL
       Filmmaker's Cooperative 4 min. color
       Directed by Jonas Mekas
            An interview with the War Minister of Lapland concerning
            the war in Vietnam presents a few practical suggestions,
            among them the advice to turn over the conduct of the
            war to the "Mafia."

1616. TIME OF THE LOCUST
       Peter Gessner Audio/Brandon Mass Media Associates 1966
       12 min. b/w s/c/a
            As Lyndon Baines Johnson delivers a war policy speech

on Vietnam, there is a juxtaposition of sound and images
to visuals of battlefield atrocities.

1617. TIME OUT OF WAR
McGraw-Hill 1954 22 min. b/w
Award: Academy Award; 1st prize, Venice Film Festival
A documentary of a lull in the fighting during the Civil
War shows two Union soldiers and a Confederate Army
man "taking time out from war," exchanging conversa-
tion.

1618. TO END THE WAR
American Documentary Films 1969 30 min. b/w
A television panel analyzes the American petition for
Congress to end the involvement in Vietnam. Explaining
the reasons for their support of the Hatfield-McGovern
amendment to cut off all war funds are Senators Hatfield,
Church, Goodell and McGovern.

1619. TOTAL WAR
National Film Board of Canada   Learning Corporation of
America 27 min. b/w
This film shows how war reaches all of humanity. A
World War II survey, it traces the discontent of Germans
in the thirties and their acceptance of Hitler; the "rape"
of Austria; the defeat of the French; and England's heroic
struggle for survival.

1620. TOYS
National Film Board of Canada   Mass Media Associates
1967 8 min. color
Awards: Cannes International Film Festival
This film shows the contrasts of children and war toys,
placed together in a store window scene. You see the
children pressed against the store glass, with "reflections
of mingling images." Eventually, the sounds of the de-
lighted children are spoiled by the war toys "coming to
life."

1621. TOYS ON A FIELD OF BLUE
Brandon Crowell, Collier, Macmillan 20 min. b/w s/c/a
No narration
Minus dialogue, this film makes a humanistic appeal for
brotherhood. A "statement" of irony shows a lonely old
war veteran who recalls his own war experiences as children play war games.

1622. TRIAL AT NUREMBERG
CBS News McGraw-Hill 27 min. b/w
From the 20th Century Series
This film documents the trials of the top twenty-one
Nazis charged with crimes against peace, war crimes
and crimes against humanity. Both American and Rus-

sian films are used to illustrate this eleven-month trial.

1623. TRIUMPH OF THE WILL*
Museum of Modern Art   1932-35   120 min.   b/w
This Nazi propaganda film "documents" the Nazi party
conference at Nuremberg in 1934 to present a glimpse of
Hitler, Goebbels, Himmler and other Nazi leaders.   It
contains significant oratorical warnings to other nations.
(No English titles.)   The same film is available with Eng-
lish titles in an abbreviated forty-minute length.

1624. TRUE GLORY, THE*
Office of War Information   Museum of Modern Art   1945
85 min.   b/w
Viewers see a cross-section of wartime life, with messages of hundreds of battle pictures that reflect the action.

1625. VARIATIONS ON A THEME
Brandon   1962   11 min.   b/w   c/a
A statement against war, this film shows the "glorifica-
tion of wartime experiences" and the complacency of a
"comfortable" society oblivious to the rebirth of militar-
ism.   In three parts, "Objectivity," "Shocked," "Shriek-
ing," the messages are delivered.

1626. VIETNAM: HOW DID WE GET IN, HOW DO WE GET OUT?
American Documentary Films   1967   33 min.   b/w
David Schoenbrun, journalist/historian and eyewitness to
our Vietnam involvement since its inception, analyzes the
United States commitment to Indochina.   His audience is
a group of San Francisco businessmen.

1627. VIETNAM--JOURNAL OF A WAR
Time-Life   53 min.   b/w   vt/vc   s/c/a
BBC television reporters filmed Vietnam--its people, soldiers, the entire war--to give American viewers a perspective from another country's news interpreters.

1628. VIETNAM AND BEYOND
SANE   American Documentary Films   1970   45 min.   b/w
CBS correspondents in Indochina for twenty-five years
present plans for withdrawal of our troops in a message
to the American people.

1629. WAR
Ideal   Mass Media Associates   22 min.   color   s/a
This statement on the "abhorrence of war" reviews the
violence from the beginning of mankind to the dropping of
the hydrogen bomb.   Futility is depicted through a montage
of paintings, stills, newsreel clips.   A single voice-over
represents the "eternal soldier."   To provoke discussions
on the alternatives to war, this film attempts to portray
"man's inhumanity to war."

1630. WAR COMES HOME
       Knight   American Documentary Films   1970   30 min.   b/w
              A perceptive look at the effect of the Indochina war on
              returning veterans and their families. One G.I. tells of
              "being ordered to kill for no apparent reason"; a career
              officer explains his resentment of anti-war groups.

1631. WAR COMES TO AMERICA*
       War Department   Museum of Modern Art   1945   67 min.
       b/w
       From the Why America Fights Series; directed by Frank
       Capra
              A brief history of the United States provides a background
              for the events of 1931-1941, leading to the impact of
              World War II.   American public opinion is analyzed and
              its response to these pressures is illustrated.   Mr. Cap-
              ra considers this film "one of the most graphic visual
              histories of the United States ever made."

1632. WAR GAME, THE
       McGraw-Hill   1966   49 min.   b/w
              An attempt is made to show what would happen to Great
              Britain in the event of a nuclear attack.   Information is
              furnished by "experts in nuclear defense."   The overall
              reaction of the general public is complete panic.

1633. WAR GAMES
       Teleketics   60-second spot announcement   color
              A symbolic analogy of conflict shows a bridge game be-
              tween two couples.   The hostess makes the wrong bid.
              Nothing is said until the visiting couple returns home.
              Then the couple argue--with sounds of realistic warfare.
              Their children are surprised to discover the violence of
              war in their own home.

1634. WHEN JOHNNY COMES MARCHING HOME
       American Broadcasting Company   42 min.   color
              This documentary surveys the areas of unemployment and
              civilian bias and the resultant plight of the veterans re-
              turning home.

1635. WHO INVITED US?
       National Educational Television   Indiana University   1970
       60 min.   b/w
              This film documents the network of 2,270 foreign mili-
              tary installations currently held by the United States, in-
              cluding 340 designated as "major bases."   The history of
              these bases is examined, as well as the continuing cost
              to the taxpayers for their lease and maintenance.

1636. WORLD WAR I: THE VERSAILLES CONFERENCE
       Thorne   4 min.   b/w   any age
              A panoramic view of the palace, the arrival of President

and Mrs. Woodrow Wilson, and Clemenceau speaking to
delegates are all presented. The film also includes various conference proceedings with the "big Four"--Lloyd
George, Orlando, Clemenceau and Wilson.

1637. WORLD WAR I: UNITED STATES HOME FRONT CARTOONS
       Thorne 3 min. b/w
           Composed of four cartoons, this film intends that Ameri-
           cans do their "bit" for the war effort. Using animation,
           appeals are made to "fight," maintain victory," "pay
           our debts," "finish the job," and "purchase Liberty
           Bonds."

1638. YALTA CONFERENCE*
       Thorne 4 min. b/w any age
           Scenes of Yalta and the palace are shown with Eden,
           Churchill and Stalin in conversation. Various conference
           sessions are shown.

       NOTE: Thousands of feet of film are deposited in the Nation-
           al Archives related to the subject of wartime motion pic-
           tures. Defense Department films, newsreel service
           films, Signal Corps, State Department films are all avail-
           able. In addition, there are captured enemy films, and
           films on relocation of the enemy within the United States.
           The Museum of Modern Art (New York) also has an ex-
           tensive collection of war films.

1639. [No entry]

                              THERAPY

                             Individual

1640. A TO B
       University of California 1974 35 min. color
           This is a dramatic portrait of a young woman in transi-
           tion "between two worlds"--that of a child ruled by adult
           parents and teachers and that of an independent young
           woman among her peers. The depiction of the emerging
           sense of self-identity is the core of the film.

1641. AGE OF ANXIETY
       Macmillan 52 min. b/w
       From the Twentieth Century Series
           A survey of the treatment of mental illness, this film
           is told in the words of the Menninger brothers, co-
           founders of the Menninger Foundation, a non-profit or-
           ganization for the study of mental problems, their diag-
           nosis and prevention.

1642.   AS SICK AS THEY SAY I AM
        University of California   1967   35 min.   b/w   kinescope
             This is an unedited interview with a 24-year-old patient
             in a psychiatric ward of a county hospital.   Intended for
             use in teaching dysfunctional aspects of social work.

1643.   BROKEN BRIDGE, THE
        Time-Life   35 min.   color   vt/vc   c/a
             This study shows the methods used by American therapist,
             Irene Kassorla, to restore communication between autistic
             children and the outside world.

1644.   CHILDREN IN CONFLICT: A TALK WITH IRENE
        Grove Press   20 min.   b/w
             This film in a series witnesses a conversation between a
             staff worker and a young patient.   Through the skill and
             warmth of the social workers, the patient is encouraged
             to express her feelings.

1645.   CLIENT-CENTERED THERAPY (PART I):   A FIRST INTER-
        VIEW
        Pennsylvania State University   1952   31 min.   C
             The film shows the initial interview between psychologist
             Dr. Carl Rogers and a client, a female graduate student
             who is bothered by social isolation.   It includes an intro-
             duction, summary and occasional explanatory comment by
             a therapist.

1646.   CLIENT-CENTERED THERAPY (PART II):   THERAPY IN
        PROCESS
        Pennsylvania State University   1952   30 min.   C
             The viewer sees an essentially continuous record of an in-
             terview between Dr. Rogers and a client, a middle-aged
             woman who has difficulty communicating with her daughter
             and husband.

1647.   COME OUT, COME OUT, WHOEVER YOU ARE
        Indiana University   1971   39 min.   b/w
             This film traces the communication problems of nine
             long-term patients who have become so dependent upon
             their hospital that they do not want to be released.   A
             special type of "confrontation" therapy is attempted, with
             positive results: one man who had not spoken for 23
             years expresses himself.

1648.   COMMUNICATION CONCEPT AND SKILL
        Video Nursing, Inc.   1968   44 min.   b/w
             This film details how basic communication concepts are
             utilized by nurses to understand and maximize skills in
             therapy.

1649. COUNSELING--A CRITICAL INCIDENT
       National Institute of Mental Health   National Audiovisual Cen-
       ter   1971   8 min.   color
            A pastoral counselor is confronted by a distraught mother
            who has discovered that her daughter smokes marijuana.

1650. COUNSELING: ITS TOOLS AND TECHNIQUES
       Mahnke   1950   23 min.   b/w   s/a
            This film illustrates how a well-trained counselor works,
            uses skills, techniques. Included are interviewing, test-
            ing, questionnaires, films.

1651. COUNSELOR, THE
       National Audiovisual Center   15 min.   color
            A look at the workday of a Neighborhood Youth Corps
            counselor, this film shows how the counselor builds a re-
            lationship of trust, understanding and mutual care that
            helps youth mature and develop intrapersonal communica-
            tion.

1652. CRISIS
       University of California   1972   27 min.   color
            This is a training film designed to show general audiences
            typical parole agents' activities involving counseling of
            parolees. After each episode shown, a freeze frame per-
            mits the audience to discuss the effects of the handling of
            issues and attitudes.

1653. DEPRESSION: A STUDY IN ABNORMAL BEHAVIOR
       Time-Life   1972   26 min.   color   vt/vc   s/c/a
            This film follows a young housewife-teacher through the
            course of a depressive illness. It discusses the many
            and often conflicting approaches, theories, criteria, thera-
            pies and treatments relating to this type of behavior.
            The current trend, this film concludes, is to blend differ-
            ent approaches and therapies in an attempt to offer more
            individual help.

1654. DOING CASEWORK
       Indiana University   20 min.   b/w
            Problem-solving that must take place between client and
            caseworker is discussed. The steps of problem-solving
            are outlined.

1655. ESCAPE TO NOWHERE
       University of California   1968   27 min.   color
            A girl who has a drug addiction problem talks about the
            aimlessness of her wanderings. Imaginatively produced
            and designed, this film is pertinent for opening communi-
            cation channels between parents, children, teachers and
            students.

1656. FRONTIERS OF PSYCHIATRY ON CAMERA: COMMUNICA-
TION PROBLEMS AND PROGRESS
Roche Films   b/w   20 min.
In this filmed interview, Henry W. Brosin, past president of the Psychiatric Association, explores the basis
of science, the interest in communication of emotional
expression. He discusses, in addition, the use of the
computer in psychiatry.

1657. LOWEN AND BIOENERGETIC THERAPY
Psychological Films, Inc.   48 min.   color
Dr. Alexander Lowen describes and demonstrates his work
with bioenergetic therapy, a theory that the "unconscious"
really exists in the muscle constrictions of the body.
His view is that therapy requires working with the body
as opposed to "mind."

1658. MAGIC MIRROR OF ALOYSE
Columbia University National Institute of Mental Health   1965
color   26 min.
A 77-year-old schizophrenic, Aloyse, can only communicate through pictures. The film illustrates how her pictures explain some of the mechanisms of her psychosis.
It describes her life and analyzes the characteristics of
her "picture communication."

1659. NEUROTIC BEHAVIOR: A PSYCHODYNAMIC VIEW
Time-Life   19 min.   color   vt/vc   s/c/a
This film reviews the life of Peter, a 19-year-old university sophomore, showing how his behavior is linked to
anxiety from without and childhood memories from within.
Behavior is shown to be the interplay between dynamic
mental forces, both conscious and unconscious. What determines neurotic behavior is how a person deals with
anxiety.

1660. ONE DAY A WEEK
Mass Media Associates   35 min.   b/w
This film illustrates the actual experiences of one com-
munity psychiatrist on his visit to the Rodman Job Corps
Center in New Bedford, Massachusetts. There he offers
mental health consultation to the staff and the Center.

1661. PROBLEM OF ACCEPTANCE
New York University University of California   1970   47 min.
b/w
This is a psychodramatic exploration of a 17-year-old
homosexual woman's feelings of self-rejection. Introductory and closing comments are by psychiatrist Ira Pauly.

1662. PROBLEMS, PURPOSE AND PROGRESS
Indiana University   30 min.   b/w
Thomas D. Hunt compares goals that caseworkers may

examine.   Communication therapy problems are reviewed.

1663. PROGRAMMED INSTRUCTION IN MEDICAL INTERVIEWING--
A SERIES
Wayne State University   20 min. each   b/w   kinescopes   c/a
A series of twelve films cover test questions, patient and
doctor analysis and present suggestions for improvement.

1664. PSYCHIATRIC INTERVIEW SERIES
University of California   1967   10-30 min.   color
Sixteen spontaneous psychiatric interview films can be
used to discuss communication problems and the develop-
ment of identity.   UCLA doctors Robert L. Stoller and
Robert H. Geertsma are the authors.   Titles range from
"Evaluation for Diagnosis" to "Problems in Gender Iden-
tity. "

1665. PSYCHOANALYSIS
Indiana University   30 min.   b/w
Two Chicago psychoanalysts enact episodes from several
analytic sessions.   Explanations are given for the changes
in patients' attitudes.

1666. PSYCHOTHERAPEUTIC INTERVIEWING--INTRODUCTION
Veterans Administration   National Audiovisual Center   1950
11 min.   b/w
This film explains the basic principles of the doctor-
patient relationship and the structure and goals of the
psychotherapeutic interview.

1667. PSYCHOTHERAPEUTIC INTERVIEWING--METHOD OF PRO-
CEDURE
Veterans Administration   National Audiovisual Center   1950
32 min.   b/w
An interview between patient and psychiatrist is analyzed
in terms of the principles and methods employed.   Emphasized is the doctor-patient-relationship-planning in terms
of goals, focusing upon relevant topics.

1668. PSYCHOTHERAPEUTIC INTERVIEWING, PART IV
Veterans Administration   National Audiovisual Center
This film focuses on the clues involved in interview situations for the purpose of communicating therapeutic information.   Interviews are unrehearsed.

1669. PSYCHOTHERAPY, NUMBER 1: THE COUNSELOR
University of Wisconsin   1960   27 min.   b/w   c/a
Dr. Carl Rogers considers how a therapist best relates
to his clients.   He stresses the necessity for honest listening, showing compassion, accepting rather than judging.

1670. PSYCHOTHERAPY, NUMBER 2: THE CLIENT
       University of Wisconsin 1960 27 min. b/w c/a
            The viewer shares with Dr. Carl Rogers, psychologist
            and psychotherapist, the explanation of the process that
            goes on with a client during successful psychotherapy.
            Shown is a portion of an actual therapeutic session with
            a follow-up interview with the client.

1671. RECOGNITION AND THE MANAGEMENT OF ANXIETY
       Wyeth National Institute of Health 1965
       28 min. b/w c/a
            Discussed is the use of psychotherapy in the treatment of
            anxiety. Illustrated through interviews are symptoms of
            anxiety experienced before, during and after treatment
            and the patterns anxiety follows.

1672. REINFORCEMENT THERAPY
       National Mental Health Institute 1966 45 min. b/w
            This is a film about research on behavior modification
            through reward reinforcement learning. Demonstrating
            the effectiveness of this procedure on emotionally-dis-
            turbed children and adults, this film focuses on communi-
            cation problems.

1673. ROLE PLAYING IN GUIDANCE
       University of California International Film Board 1953
       14 min. b/w c/a
            This film dramatizes the action techniques of guidance.
            Illustrated are how a role-playing situation is introduced,
            how it is conducted and the potential effectiveness of the
            training.

1674. ROLE PLAYING IN HUMAN RELATIONS
       National Institute of Mental Health 1949 27 min. b/w
            This film examines the techniques of role-playing for
            gaining insight into human relation and communication
            problems.

1675. ROLLO MAY AND THE HUMAN ENCOUNTER (PARTS I, II)
       Psychology Films, Inc. 1970 Each part: 20 min. color
            Examined in these films are: Part I: Self-Self Encoun-
            ter and Self-Other Encounter; Part II: Manipulation and
            Human Encounter; Four Elements of Human Encounter
            (Empathy, Eros, Friendship and Agape).

1676. SEARCH AND RESEARCH: PSYCHOLOGY IN PERSPECTIVE
       Psychology Films, Inc. 1963 30 min. b/w c/a
            This film tells the story of a young lady seeking psycho-
            therapy and describes the experimental, psychoanalytic
            and humanistic psychological approaches to treatment.
            Three psychologists, Dr. Carl Rogers, Dr. Harry Har-
            low and Dr. Rollo May, participate.

1677. THREE APPROACHES TO PSYCHOTHERAPY (PARTS I, II,
       III)
       Psychology Films, Inc. Pat. I: 48 min.; Pt. II: 32 min.;
       Pt. III: 37 min.; b/w and color c/a
            Part I: Dr. Carl Rogers describes the process of client-
            centered therapy, conducts an interview with a patient
            and gives a summation of the effectiveness of the ses-
            sion.
            Part II: Dr. Frederick Perls describes Gestalt Therapy,
            conducts an interview with a patient and gives a summa-
            tion of the session.
            Part III: Dr. Albert Ellis describes the process of ra-
            tional-emotive psychotherapy, conducts an interview with
            a patient and gives evaluation of therapy sessions with
            three specialists.

1678. TO BE SOMEBODY
       Women's Film Cooperative 1971 color 29 min.
            This is an unrehearsed and unstaged documentary on the
            progress of a young Mexican-American woman who is
            searching for work in an unfamiliar world. She seeks
            aid at a local training program for youths where, with
            the aid of a counselor, she begins to resolve her con-
            flicts through communication.

                              Group

1679. ACTIVITY GROUP THERAPY
       Center for Mass Communication 1950 56 min. b/w
            Based on the work of psychoanalyst Samuel Slavson, this
            film follows the day-to-day and long-term events in the
            development of a group of emotionally-disturbed and so-
            cially-maladjusted boys who are in group therapy.

1680. ACTUALIZATION GROUP, THE--A SERIES
       Psychology Films 1972 45 min. each b/w
            In these behavioral films, Dr. E. Shostrom illustrates
            authentic, unrehearsed psychological group therapy.
            Originating on KHJ-TV in Los Angeles, there are seven
            films in the series: 1. Risking Being Ourselves; 2.
            Freedom and Actualization; 3. Aggression, Actualiza-
            tion; 4. Manipulation and Actualization; 5. Divorce from
            Parents; 6. Self-disclosure; 7. From Deadness to
            Aliveness.

1681. ACTUALIZATION THERAPY: AN INTEGRATION OF
       ROGERS, PERLS AND ELLIS
       Psychological Films, Inc. 27 min. color
            Sequences from the film series, "Three Approaches to
            Psychotherapy," are shown, illustrating the work of
            Rogers, Perls and Ellis. After these film clips are
            shown, each of the therapy styles is analyzed. Actuali-

zation Therapy attempts to integrate each of these into a "working unity."

1682. BEHAVIOR MODIFICATION: TEACHING LANGUAGE TO PSYCHOTIC CHILDREN
Prentice 1969 45 min. color
This film examines methods of teaching psychotic children the functional use of speech, utilizing the war and punishment techniques. It shows a program where the children are taught to understand the meaning of words and to comprehend ideas based on external stimuli.

1683. CASEWORK IN PUBLIC WELFARE SERIES
Indiana University Each: 30 min. b/w
Thomas D. Hunt, American Public Welfare Association, presents a series of sixteen films designed to assist in the training of public welfare personnel. The goal is to help the client help himself. If casework is to be successful, the caseworker must have "interest in the client and his problems."

1684. CHILDREN IN CONFLICT: GROUP THERAPY
Grove Press 60 min. b/w
This film reproduces the social, psychological and interpersonal aspects of a group session of the staff members of a child-care treatment center. In this context, group therapy is a method of self-discovery which helps the individual effect positive changes in himself.

1685. CIRCLE OF LOVE
McGraw-Hill CBS News 27 min. color
From the 21st Century Series
Observed in this film is an "Encounter Group," created as a means of improving interpersonal understanding and relationships. Methods and problems involved in the use of group techniques are illustrated.

1686. CONVERSATION WITH CARL ROGERS, A--A SERIES
Psychological Films, Inc. b/w
In this film series Dr. Rogers comments on a variety of subjects, including his current thinking on client-centered therapy, on humanistic psychology and his close affinity for a phenomenological approach to human beings.

1687. DIALOGUES: DR. CARL ROGERS (PARTS I, II)
Associated Instructional Films Crowell, Collier, Macmillan 1971 Each segment: 50 min. color c
Part I, Dr. Carl Rogers discusses motivation, perception, learning, the self. He reviews his development of client-centered therapy and his reactions to encounter groups, their strengths and weaknesses. In Part II, he examines important issues facing contemporary psychology and his major contributions.

1688. DISTANT DRUMMER--BRIDGE FROM NO PLACE
       Airlie   National Audiovisual Center   23 min.   color   s/c/a
              New approaches to addiction therapy by the National Insti-
              tute of Mental Health and private group centers such as
              Synanon and Daytop Village stress communication encoun-
              ter approaches.

1689. EAGLEVILLE: YOU'RE NOT ALONE
       University of California   1971   52 min.   color
              This is a cinéma-vérité record of the intensive group
              therapy program at Eagleville, a suburban Philadelphia
              hospital where alcoholic and drug abusers, under the
              guidance of enthusiastic therapists, learn to deal with
              their emotions and feelings.

1690. ENCOUNTER: TO MAKE A START
       Psychological Films, Inc.   32 min.   b/w
              This is a documentary film of an unique confrontation be-
              tween police and young radicals. It reviews a day-long
              workshop-encounter session: talking, arguing, learning
              body awareness and sensitivity exercises.

1691. GAMES FUTURISTS PLAY
       McGraw-Hill   1969   26 min.   color   c/a
       From CBS' 21st Century Series
              This film introduces new games man is now "playing" to
              prepare himself for the world of tomorrow.   Some of the
              methods of his search for knowledge for answers to so-
              cial problems are projected concerns.   Role-playing is
              recommended as "fundamental" for future strategies.

1692. GAMES PEOPLE PLAY: THE PRACTICE   (PART TWO)
       National Educational Television   Indiana University   1967
       30 min.   b/w   s/c/a
       From the Spectrum Psychology Series
              Dr. Eric Berne focuses on the distinctions between con-
              cepts of interaction and concepts of transaction.   At his
              clinic in Carmel, California, he explores assumptions and
              displays specific games.

1693. GAMES PEOPLE PLAY: THE THEORY (PART ONE)
       National Educational Television   Indiana University   1967
       30 min.   b/w   s/c/a
              Dr. Eric Berne, psychiatrist-author, is concerned with
              his theory of transactional analysis. Explained is the
              terminology of "game," "script," "ego," and "transac-
              tional."

1694. GESTALT SERIES
       University of California   1969   Each: 24-27 min.   color
              The Gestalt Therapy method, using a spontaneously se-
              lected and unrehearsed group, is explained by Dr. Fred-
              erick Perls.   Titles include: "What is Gestalt?";

"Everything Is Aware Process"; "Marriage"; "Madeline's
Dream"; "Memory and Pride"; "Philosophy of the Obvi-
ous"; "Awareness"; "Gestalt Prayer."

1695. GROUP THERAPY
Grove Press 1968 2 parts: 60 min. total b/w C/a
In this series of films from "Warrandale," a group session is reproduced for the purpose of analyzing social
and psychological aspects of interpersonal relationships.
Encouraged are open exchanges of feelings, recognition
of fear, rejection and anxiety. Analysis is made of resistance to the process of change.

1696. HOUSE ON THE BEACH
Indiana University 1968 60 min. b/w
This is a film about Synanon House, the rehabilitation
community in Santa Monica, California for former nar-
cotics addicts. It includes scenes of encounter sessions
during which members attempt to shatter one another's
rationalizations and illusions.

1697. HUMAN POTENTIAL MOVEMENT: JOURNAL TO THE CEN-
TER OF THE SELF
University of California 1972 23 min. color
Dr. William Schultz of the Essalen Institute follows the
development of a six-hour talk group session. Demon-
strated are techniques for release of one's aggressions.
Stressed are aspects of the movement that seek to foster
openness and trust.

1698. I'M O.K.
University of California 1973 33 min. color
This chronicle of the Stockton Community Parole Center's
intensive treatment survival program pilot study records
the physical and psychological rigors of a 26-day survival
program for delinquent boys. Physical skills are learned
as well as transactional analysis group therapy.

1699. I'M O.K.--YOU'RE O.K.: CAN T. A. FREE THE CHILD IN
US?
University of California 1974 23 min. color
This introduction to the principles of transactional analysis reviews its basic theses concerning the existence in
each person of a child, a stern parent and a mature
adult. It shows a group session in demonstration with
therapeutic methods. Commentary is by Dr. Thomas A.
Harris, psychiatrist and author of I'm O.K.--You're O.K.

1700. IMPROVISED DRAMA (PARTS I, II)
Eastern Michigan University Time-Life 30 min. ea. b/w
vt/vc s/c/a
John Hodgson, drama lecturer, leads groups of students
in imaginary situations, acting out solutions to various
types of problem-situations.

1701. IN THE NOW
      Psychological Films   45 min.   b/w
          Three selected sessions concern working with a "dream,"
          an incident of the recent past, and a current interaction
          --all in the "here and now."

1702. INTERSTAFF COMMUNICATION
      New York University   42 min.   b/w
      From the Psychodrama in Group Processes Series
          Produced by Dr. Ira Pauley, this film demonstrates the
          use of psychodrama techniques to facilitate interstaff com-
          munication. It is a condensation of a two-hour spontane-
          ous workshop session. The central theme concerns a
          work-centered problem by a psychiatrist in charge of a
          psychiatrist unit at the University of Oregon Medical
          School.

1703. INTERVIEW WITH DR. ERICH FROMM (PARTS I, II)
      Crowell, Collier, Macmillan 50 min. each b/w
          Part I: Dr. Fromm discusses productive and non-pro-
          ductive character orientations and discusses escape mech-
          anisms as therapy. Part II: Dr. Fromm's approach to
          psychotherapy is explained; included are theories and tech-
          niques, plans for future work.

1704. INTRODUCTION TO PSYCHODRAMA
      Therapeutic   1951   27 min.   b/w
          Supplemented by an explanatory narration by a psychiatric
          consultant, this film demonstrates the function of thera-
          peutic theatre and several psychodrama techniques.

1705. JOURNEY INTO SELF
      Pennsylvania State University 1968   47 min.   b/w c/a
      Nominated for an Academy Award
          Drs. Carl Rogers and Richard Farson lead an intensive
          basic encounter group session. Eight strangers from all
          over the country assemble for interviews, with the film
          highlighting emotional moments of their interaction.

1706. LEARNING TO LIVE--A SERIES
      Jeffrey Weber Mass Media Associates 1974 30 min. each
      color
          The thrust of this series is that personal growth and re-
          warding relationships can be gained through transactional
          analysis. The eight-films include: 1. "Ego States"; 2.
          "Transactions"; 3. "Strokes"; 4. "Time Structures";
          5. "Feelings"; 6. "Games"; 7. "Acquiring Life 'Scripts";
          8. "Changing Life Scripts."

1707. LISTENING
      University of California 1971 30 min. color
          Excerpts are shown from the 1971 conference of the In-
          ternational Association of Hotlines at Asilomar, California,

to provide an overview of concepts involved in crisis intervention by telephone. The film features noted psychologist Dr. Carl Rogers as the principal speaker.

1708. MEETING
University of California   30 min.   b/w
This film depicts various obstacles to honest communication that hamper effective collaboration in a community
drug prevention program.

1709. NEED FOR DIALOGUE, THE
University of California, 1970 30 min.   color   vt
From Drugs: The Children Are Choosing Series
From a seven-part series, the search for communication
is stressed in a day-long conference in which San Francisco Bay Area students, psychiatrists, ministers, administrators and instructors participate.

1710. NEW TRUCK DILEMMA, THE
Bureau of National Affairs   24 min.   color
Diverse films show group role-playing experiences as ex-
amples of the case-study method of film use.

1711. ONE APPROACH: STORY OF THE RENAISSANCE PROJECT
University of California 1972   32 min.   color
Renaissance House is shown.   It is a therapeutic community run by ex-addicts in New Rochelle, New York,
where "selected" drug users live for a year while they
reeducate themselves in needs and values.   Encounter
group sessions are the formal outlet for pressures.

1712. PLACE TO MEET--A WAY TO UNDERSTAND
Cornell University 1972   27 min.   b/w   vt/vc
Dr. Urie Bronfenbrenner explains this documentary about
two groups of children: one from a slum area school
and one from middle income.   The goal is for each child
to have the opportunity to maximize his potential development.

1713. ROLE-PLAYING IN HUMAN RELATIONS TRAINING
National Education Association 1949   27 min.   b/w   C/a
Illustrated and explained are the uses of role-playing
techniques in analyzing problems of human relations.
Shown is a group in "Group Development" as they enact
simple incidents involving various role-playing techniques.
The film covers skills required and studies problems of
gaining insights uncovering interpersonal relationships,
perceptions.

1714. SESSION WITH COLLEGE STUDENTS, A
Psychological Films   30 min.   b/w
This film shows Dr. Frederick Perls demonstrating meth-
ods of Gestalt Therapy to the university students.   He

explains the expression of the meaning of dreams, and
the existential theory of the "here-and-now-living."

1715. SOCIAL GROUP WORK
University of Minnesota 1967 30 min. b/w s/c
From the Adolescent Girls in Conflict Series
An institution for delinquent girls is examined. The
treatment concerns the resolution of communication problems. In a live group session, the girls exchange dialogue.

1716. STORY OF N.T.L., THE
National Training Laboratory 1960 12 min. b/w C/a
The philosophy of the National Training Laboratory's activities is explained. Illustrated are a T-group (sensitivity training group) and other activities in a typical day
at the National Education Association's teacher laboratory.

1717. TRANSACTIONAL ANALYSIS
CRM 1974 30 min. color
This film introduces the use of transactional analysis in
management. It illustrates the reasons for people's actions in organizations and demonstrates how to promote
productive employee behavior.

1718. WARM-UP TO PSYCHODRAMA
University of California 1968 30 min. b/w
This documentary focuses on spontaneous, unrehearsed
behavior in a college class in sociodrama and role-playing in education. Employing nonverbal and psychodramatic techniques, the group confronts one of the members
who has been "perceived" as "turning off" the participation of others.

1719. WARRANDALE
Grove Press 1972 105 min. b/w
Warrandale is a Canadian residential treatment center for
emotionally-disturbed children. The therapy approach encourages the "expressions of even the most violent and
destructive feelings." The stress is on open communication and release of inner hostility.

1720. WHAT CAN WE DO?
University of California 30 min. color
From the Drug Abuse Series
"Open communication" between adults and the young, "non-
threatening" discussions, student-teacher conferences, encounter sessions are illustrated. "Unbiased communication is essential to any effective education program. All
sides of the controversy must be aired."

PART II

VIDEOTAPES/VIDEOCASSETTES

VIDEOTAPES/VIDEOCASSETTES

ARGUMENT

1721. EVALUATING AN ARGUMENT (VT)
CHITVC WTTW-TV Great Plains Instructional Television
45 min. 2-inch C
From the English Composition Series

1722. EXAMINE EVIDENCE, REASONING LOGIC (VT)
CHITVC WTTW-TV Great Plains Instructional Television
45 min. 2-inch C
From the English Composition Series

1723. LOGIC AS CALCULATION--THOMAS HOBBES (PARTS I, II)
(VT)
CHITVC WTTW-TV Great Plains Instructional Television
45 min. 2-inch C
From the Logic Series

1724. LOGIC AS DIALECTIC--PLATO (PARTS I, II, III) (VT)
CHITVC WTTW-TV Great Plains Instructional Television
45 min. 2-inch C
From the Logic Series

1725. LOGIC AS PROBLEM-SOLVING--DEWEY (VT)
CHITVC WTTW-TV Great Plains Instructional Television
45 min. 2-inch C
From the Logic Series

1726. SCOPES "MONKEY TRIAL" (1925) (VC)
Brodart
Visual Encyclopedia of American History Series

BUSINESS/ORGANIZATIONAL

1727. ADVANCED CONCEPTS AND TECHNIQUES IN SUPERVISORY
PRACTICE--A SERIES (VT)
Telstar
Instructor: John Farley, Howard Mold, College of St. Thom-
as, St. Paul, Minnesota
    This series presents a perspective of the supervisor's

267

responsibilities.   Program titles include: 1. A Point of
View for Supervision;   2. Management of Work--Manage-
ment of Objectives;   3. Management of Work--Problem
Analysis;   4. Management of Men--Evaluative-Appraisal
Process;   5. Management of Men--Staffing and Hiring
Process;   6. Management of Relations and Situations--
Modification of the Work Force;   7. Management of Re-
lations and Situations;   8. Management of Ideas--Com-
munication;   9. Management of Ideas--Supervisory Prob-
lem-Solving Process;   10. Developing the Individual and
Strengthening the Organization.

1728.   ART OF HANDLING GRIEVANCES, THE (VT)
        American Video Network   VCI   30 min.   color
        This animated course is designed to explain the actions
        a supervisor must take to insure "quick and just" solu-
        tions to grievances.

1729.   BUSINESS, BEHAVIORISM AND THE BOTTOM LINE (VT/VC)
        CRM   Time-Life   20 min.   color   F
        See entry number 118.

1730.   CHALLENGE OF ORGANIZATION, THE   (VT)
        Republic Steel Corporation   29 min.   2-inch   b/w   c/a
        Organization charts are discussed with explanations of
        the chain of command, communication departmental insul-
        ation, corporate and departmental objectives.   "Tight"
        organizational approaches are compared.

1731.   COMMUNICATING SUCCESSFULLY (VT)
        Time-Life   2-inch   color   F
        See individual title listings
        This is a multi-media course for the business executive
        who wants his ideas to be "bought" as well as understood.
        Three divisions exist within the course: How to Make a
        More Effective Speech; How to Conduct a More Produc-
        tive Meeting; How to Give a More Persuasive Presenta-
        tion.

1732.   COMMUNICATIONS IN THE OFFICE (VT)
        Great Plains Instructional Television   30 min.   2-inch   b/w
        s/c/a
        From the Office Career Training Series
        Stressed is the need for a command of the English lan-
        guage for effective office communication.

1733.   CONTROLLING TURNOVER AND ABSENTEEISM (VT)
        Telstar
        Instructor: Dr. George D. Heaton, human relations specialist
        This series is designed to help supervisors reduce turn-
        over by proper application of human relations skills.
        Sessions include: 1. Using Stimuli to Influence Behavior;
        2. Stimuli Which Reduce Turnover; 3. Four Factors in

Behavior; 4. Suggestions about Correcting and Criticizing
People; 5. A Study in the Many Things Which Influence
Human Behavior; 6. How to Discipline to Improve Atten-
dance and Reduce Turnover; 7. Understanding Frustra-
tion and Its Effect on Absenteeism and Turnover; 8.
Summary.

1734. DELEGATE--DON'T ABDICATE (VC)
National Educational Media, Inc. VCI 12 min. color F
From the Professional Management Program Series
This is the story of Harry Andrews, a manager who
prides himself on his ability to delegate. Realistic delegation goals are recommended as are communication
goals to subordinates; sharing background thinking and
problems; giving definite instructions; checking progress
regularly; remaining accessible.

1735. EFFECTIVE EXECUTIVE, THE (VT/VC)
Time-Life Five 25-min. programs color F
See entry number 57.

1736. EFFECTIVE ORGANIZATION, THE (VT/VC)
Time-Life Six 30-min. programs color F
See entry number 59.

1737. GAMES EDUCATORS PLAY (VT/VC)
Cornell University 25 min. b/w
This program acquaints the viewer with the development
of business management games in which teams of players
from industries attempt to predict consequences of "plays"
in areas of commerce.

1738. GOOD GOODIES (VT)
Time-Life 5 min. color
This program demonstrates how oversell can destroy a
product or firm, while "honest" advertising can attract
and persuade customers, consumers, clients.

1739. HANDLING COMPLAINTS (VC)
National Education Media, Inc., VCI 14 min. color F
This dramatic presentation revolves around customers'
complaints. Basic principles are suggested for resolving
conflicts.

1740. HANDLING TELEPHONE COMMUNICATIONS (VT)
Great Plains Instructional Television 30 min. 2-inch b/w
s/a
The basic principles of good telephone usage are noted,
particularly as they apply to use in the business world.
Standard complaints about inefficiency of office communication are illustrated.

1741.   HOW TO CONDUCT A MORE PRODUCTIVE MEETING   (VT)
        Time-Life   25 min.   color   F
             This lesson gives techniques needed to conduct business
             meetings which bring positive results.   Stressed are:
             listening, language, concentration.

1742.   HOW TO GIVE A MORE PERSUASIVE PRESENTATION   (VT)
        Time-Life   25 min.   color   F
             This lesson shows the viewer how to sell the subject that
             he knows so well to people who may not have much time
             to listen.   Audiovisual aids are encouraged to use as per-
             suasive materials.

1743.   HOW TO MAKE A MORE EFFECTIVE SPEECH   (VT)
        Time-Life   25 min.   color   F
             Two sets of techniques are taught: how to prepare and
             how to write a speech.   Suggestions include: how to
             "size-up" audiences, define objectives, research facts,
             organize material, deliver.

1744.   HUMAN SIDE OF SELLING, THE   (VC)
        Video Educators Inc.   VCI   color
             Ben Kain presents a ten-program course including: Be-
             lievability; Telephone Selling; Closing; Objections; other
             effective techniques.

1745.   MANAGEMENT: A JOINT VENTURE--A SERIES   (VT)
        Telstar
        Instructor: Francis W. Hayes, Assistant General Manager,
        Russell-Miller Company
             This course presents key functions of management illus-
             trated as the "Management Wheel."   Each of these func-
             tions is a spoke in the wheel, including the hub, which is
             the people (or staff), and the rim, which makes the wheel
             work.   That rim is communication.   Titles include: 1.
             Concept of Change; 2. Planning; 3. Staffing; 4. Organ-
             izing; 5. Directing; 6. Controlling; 7. Innovating and
             Coordinating; 8. Communicating.

1746.   MANAGEMENT AND THE FUTURE (VT)
        Republic Steel Corporation   29 min.   2-inch   b/w   c/a
             The challenges of future management problems are out-
             lined.

1747.   MANAGEMENT BY OBJECTIVES   (VT)
        Time-Life   Six 24-min. programs   color   F
             See entry number 74.

1748.   MANAGEMENT BY OBJECTIVES   (VT)
        Telstar
        Instructor: Dr. George S. Odiorne, Director, Bureau of Indus-
        trial Relations, Business Administration, University of Michigan,
        Ann Arbor, Michigan.
             This course is designed to enable an individual to install

the philosophy of the series into his own work situation.
For all levels of management. Lesson titles include:
1. Establishing Performance Criteria; 2. Clarification
of Job Responsibilities and How Performance Is Meas-
ured; 3. Organizational Goal Planning Requirements; 4.
Problem Solving by Objectives; 5. Innovation by Objectives; 6. Requirements for Using Principles; Methods.

1749. MANAGEMENT THEORY: INTERACTION   (VT)
Time-Life   Eight 25-min. programs   color   F
These eight films record and analyze a variety of "interactions, " with the aim of helping managers examine and
improve their own interactive skills.   Titles include:
1. Interaction (Overview); 2. Selection Interview (Round
One); 3. Selection Interview (Round Two); 4. Selection
Interview (Round Three); 5. Interview with the Boss;
6. Buyer versus Seller; 7. Territorial Rights; 8. Meeting in Progress.

1750. MANAGERIAL DECISION-MAKING   (VT)
Republic Steel Corporation   29 min.   2-inch   b/w   c/a
Critical management decisions are examined and sugges-
tions are presented for their improvement.

1751. MANAGER'S ROLE IN PUBLIC AFFAIRS, THE   (VT)
Republic Steel Corporation   29 min.   2-inch   b/w   c/a
From the Modern Management Methods Series
Business/government relations are sketched with empha-
sis on the vital role of today's business manager in pub-
lic affairs.

1752. MANAGING AND COMMUNICATING BY OBJECTIVES   (VT)
Republic Steel Corporation   29 min.   2-inch   b/w   c/a
From the Modern Management Methods Series
Illustrated is how to combine overall organizational re-
sults with a sound human relations philosophy.

1753. MODERN MANAGEMENT METHODS--A SERIES (PART I)
(VT)
Republic Steel Corporation   each: 29 min.   2-inch   b/w
c/a
Titles include: Challenge of Organization; Changing Management Patterns; Long-Range Planning; Manager's Role
in Public Affairs;   Managing and Communicating by Objectives; New developments in Human Relations; New Dimensions in Organizations.

1754. MODERN MANAGEMENT METHODS--A SERIES (PART II)
(VT)
Republic Steel Corporation   each: 29 min.   2-inch   b/w   c/a
Titles include: Introductory Statistics for Management;
Management and the Computer; Management and the Fu-
ture; Managerial Decision-making; others.

1755. MODERN SUPERVISORY PRACTICE (VT)
       Telstar
       Instructors: John Farley and Howard Mold
           Course sessions include: 1. The Supervisor--Leader of
           the Team; 2. The Supervisor--His Responsibility; 3.
           The Supervisor's Problem in Leadership; 4. Supervisor's
           Role in Cost Reduction; 5. Supervisor's Responsibility
           for Human Relations; 6. Supervisor and Time Manage-
           ment; 7. Supervisor and Decision-Making; 8. Supervisor
           as the Coach; 10. Supervisor and Self-development.

1756. MOTIVATION TO WORK (VT)
       Time-Life Five 25-min. programs color
           Frederick Herzberg's famous "motivation-hygiene" theory
           probes the problems of increasing efficiency in business
           and industry. Titles include: 1. Modern Meaning of Ef-
           ficiency; 2. KITA, or What Have You Done for Me Late-
           ly?; 3. Job Enrichment in Action; 4. Building a Climate
           for Individual Growth; 5. The ABC Man: Manager in
           Mid-Career.

1757. NEW DIMENSIONS IN ORGANIZATIONAL COMMUNICATIONS
       (VT)
       Republic Steel Corporation 29 min. 2-inch b/w c/a
       From the Modern Management Methods Series
           The process of communication is explained in terms of
           its effectiveness for management in organizations.

1758. PROFESSIONAL MANAGEMENT PROGRAM SERIES (VC)
       National Educational Media, Inc. VCI color F
           This series focuses on the needs of today's management
           and supervisory personnel. Titles include: The Super-
           visor--Motivating through Insight; Eye of the Supervisor;
           Discipline--A Matter of Judgment; The Training Memor-
           andum; Increasing Productivity; Flight Plan; Delegate,
           Don't Abdicate; Time Game; Manager and the Law.

1759. PROFESSIONAL SALESMAN, THE (VC)
       Video Communications, Inc.
           Titles include: Selling with Visuals; Communications; A
           Sharper Focus; Using Psychology in Selling.

1760. PSYCHOLOGICAL ASPECTS OF SUPERVISION: A SERIES
       (VT)
       Telstar
       Instructor: Francis Hayes
           Human reactions in supervisory relationships are studied.
           Titles include: The Supervisor's Job; Why We Behave
           as We Do; Cooperation; Techniques of Delegation; Disci-
           pline; Effective Communication; Problem-Solving; Training
           Employees; Counseling.

1761. RIOTS AND CROWD CONTROL: ANATOMY OF ANGER
(VT/VC)
Woroner, for Motorola   30 min.
The trainee is shown how grievances can be reconciled
through understanding and how crowds can be controlled.
It is aimed at law enforcement training programs.

1762. SECRETARIAL SKILLS--A SERIES   (VC)
Video Communications, Inc.
This series includes the following programs concerning
communication: 3. Let's Communicate; 5. Let's Com-
municate by Telephone; 7. Let's Communicate with the
Superior; 8. Let's Communicate with the Future.

1763. SUCCESS IN SUPERVISION--A SERIES   (VT)
Department of Agriculture   WETA-TV   each: 30 min.
Designed for supervisory professional positions; titles
include: 4. Communication; Talking and Listening; 5.
Communication: Writing and Reading; 6. Motivation;
others.

1764. SUCCESSFUL PERSUASION   (VC)
National Educational Media, Inc.   VCI   14 min.   color   F
This program presents a basic analysis of the art of persuasion and sales for people in all facets of business. It
deals with psychological encounters that underlie every
transaction in which one is trying to convince the other
to agree or accept.

1765. SUPERVISOR, THE--MOTIVATING THROUGH INSIGHT   (VC)
National Educational Media, Inc.   VCI   11 min.   color   F
A chess game is used to illustrate important aspects of
motivation. Insight into human emotions and myths involved are discussed.

1766. SUPERVISORY LEADERSHIP   (VT)
Telstar
Instructor: Dr. George D. Heaton, human relations consult-
ant
This course presents basic human relations tasks and
skills of supervision. Titles include: 1. Fundamental
Duties of the Supervisor; 2. Attitudes of People; 3. The
"I" Pattern of Behavior; 4. Levels of Human Needs; 5.
Improving Skills of Communication; 6. Improving Skills
of Listening; 7. Group Participation; 8. Basic Skills of
Effective Leadership.

1767. SUPERVISORY SELF-DEVELOPMENT   (VT)
Telstar
Instructor: Dr. George D. Heaton, human relations consultant
This series is based on the premise that the individual
supervisor can only succeed in assigned responsibilities
when he has learned to establish specific personal and

job-related goals, assess obstacles in front of goals, and attack specific problems. Programs range from Goal-setting to How to Motivate Others.

1768. TELEPHONE MANNERS (VC)
National Educational Media, Inc. VCI 10 min. color F
This program on telephone usage concerns courtesy. It is recommended for: supervisors, secretaries, reception-ists, salesmen, managers.

1769. TOTAL LEARNING EXPERIENCE, THE (VT)
Time-Life nine programs color 20-27 min. each
In a self-contained training program directed by the re-search and findings of six outstanding behavioral scien-tists--Argyris, Gellerman, Herzberg, Likert, McClelland, McGregor--this series stresses current management con-cepts related to the productive use of human resources. Programs include: 1. Strategy for Productive Behavior; 2. Motivation through Job Enrichment; 3. The Self-Moti-vated Achiever; 4. Understanding Motivation; 5. and 6. Theory X and Theory Y: The World of Douglas Mc-Gregor; 7. Human Nature and Organizational Realities; 8. The Management of Human Assets; 9. Motivation in Perspective.

1770. TOUGH-MINDED MANAGEMENT (VT)
Time-Life five 25 min. programs color
In this series, Joe Batten dramatizes and defines his prin-ciple of "toughmindedness." Titles include: 1. Manage-ment by Example; 2. Man in the Mirror; 3. The Fully Functioning Organization; 4. The Fully Functioning Society; 5. The Fully Functioning Individual.

1771. TRAINING MEMORANDUM, THE (VC)
National Educational Media, Inc. VCI 10 min. color F
A young supervisor has a fantasy-experience while resist-ing enlisting in a special course called "How to Train." Based on the Dickens classic, A Christmas Carol, the program utilizes a "ghost" who teaches the supervisor the values of training. Modern methods and philosophy are illustrated, examined.

1772. YOU ARE THERE AT THE BARGAINING TABLE (VT/VC)
American Medical Association Encyclopaedia Britannica
1955 50 min. b/w F s/c/a
See entry number 115.

1773. YOU, THE SUPERVISOR--A SERIES (VC)
Video Communications, Inc.
Program titles include: Interviewing and Selecting; Orien-tation and Training; Counseling; Leadership.

CROSS-CULTURAL

1774.   AFRICA AND THE BLACK HERITAGE   (VC)
        Video Communications, Inc.
            The series includes the history, customs and potential of
            black Africa.

1775.   AFRICAN ANTHOLOGY--A SERIES   (VT)
        National Instructional Television   fifteen 20-min. lessons
        Instructor: Joyce McPhillips, University of Michigan
            The viewer is introduced to Africa through its literature,
            people and customs.   Programs include: 4. Story of
            Protest; 15. Protest Literature and Literature of Revolu-
            tion.

1776.   AMERICANS FROM AFRICA: A HISTORY   (VT)
        Central Virginia Educational Television   (WCVE-TV)   Great
        Plains Instructional Television
        Instructor: Dr. Edgar Toppin, Professor of History, Virginia
        State College
            The series' aim is to develop better understanding among
            students by increasing their awareness of the part that all
            Americans have played in the making of this country.
            Titles include: African Beginnings; Slave Trade; Slavery;
            Black Men in the American Revolution; Resistance; Black
            Codes; Disfranchisement; NAACP; Desegregation; Mili-
            tancy; Black Power, others.

1777.   ARMCHAIR ANTHROPOLOGY: FAMILIES OF MAN   (VC)
        Video Communications, Inc.
            This series offers insights into typical families among
            various cultures around the world.   The series ranges
            from peoples whose "preservation of traditional beliefs
            has made them difficult to assimilate into modern life to
            groups whose flexibilities of values has allowed for social
            changes."   Titles include: Modern Mayan (14 min.);
            Woman of Chamula (14 min.); Amazon Family (19 min.);
            Peiping Family (21 min.); Sampan Family (16 min.);
            Yugoslav Farm Family (14 min.); Black Forest Family
            (14 min.); Life around Titicaca (14 min.).

1778.   BLACK AWARENESS   (VC)
        Video Communications, Inc.
            The series includes: Edge of the Arena, Portrait in
            Black, 14th Generation Americans; A Man named Charlie
            Smith.

1779.   BLACK FRONTIER   (VC)
        National Instructional Television   four 59-min programs   color
        F
        Great Plains Instructional Television
            Program titles include: 1. New American; 2. Cowherders;
            3. Buffalo Soldiers; 4. Exodusters.   William Marshall

hosts this series about black history in the early American west.

1780. CULTURE SHOCK: A HISTORICAL SURVEY OF SOCIETIES IN TRANSITION (VC)
Video Communications, Inc.
The series surveys Turkey, Tropical Africa, Israel, Poland, South America and Yugoslavia.

1781. CULTURES AND CONTINENTS (VT)
New York State Education Department   28 min.   s/c/a
This series studies various societies around the world by examining cultures of these societies.   The first four programs deal with the African continent; the last five with South America.

1782. FAMILIES OF THE WORLD (VT/VC)
Great Plains Instructional Television   five 30-min. lessons color
The changing role of the family in five representative countries of the developing world is recorded.   Program titles are: 1. India; 2. Zambia; 3. Thailand; 4. Turkey; 5. Costa Rica.

1783. FIRST U.N. MEETING (VC)
Video Communications, Inc.
Time Line Series

1784. GHETTO POLITICS (VT)
Cornell University   33 min.   1970
Using a game designed by Gertrude Fish, eight students attempt to bridge the gap between theory and practice in seeking solutions for public problems of poverty in New York's lower East Side.   Students are able to apply communication techniques and to learn something about decision-making.

1785. HOME OF THE BRAVE (VT/VC)
Time-Life   3 min.   color
The rise and fall of the American Indian Empire is capsulized in a brief collage of the events of five centuries.

1786. IMAGES (VT)
National Instructional Television   20 min.   b/w
This videotape presents non-verbally eleven different scenes dealing with racial and socio-economic differences. It encourages free interpretation of these realistic or symbolic encounters.

1787. ODYSSEY IN BLACK (VT)
KLVS (Las Vegas) National Instructional Television
Great Plains Instructional Television 1971 fourteen 30-min.
programs
Award: Broadcast Media Award from San Francisco State
College
The series takes the viewer from African origins of the
black race through the Civil War to today's "Black Revo-
lution." Titles include: Origins; Slavery; Crisis; War;
The Black's Role; Aftermath of War; Disappointment;
Post-Reconstruction; World War I; Harlem; Depression;
War Years; Education; The "Black Revolution."

1788. ONE NATION, INDIVISIBLE--SERIES (VT)
National Educational Television five 30-min. programs
Racial conflict is discussed in terms of social and eco-
nomic situations of black Americans.

1789. PEOPLE (VT)
WETA National Instructional Television ten 20-min. lessons
s/c
Instructor: Brenda Hopkins, Catholic University
The differences of ethnic and racial groups are analyzed,
including tensions, bigotries, hatred. Lessons include:
3. Images; 6. Prejudice; 8. Unchartered Freedoms;
9. Where Is the Race?

1790. PREJUDICE (VT)
National Instructional Television 20 min. b/w
This videotape presents scenes on the effects of prejudice
and negative attitudes and behavior. It describes problems in housing, employment, and relations within and
between groups. Suggestions are made concerning the
value of one-to-one relationships in place of impersonal
categorizations.

1791. SOCIAL SCIENCE, NO. 1--A SERIES (VT)
CHITVC WTTW-TV Great Plains Instructional Television
Each: 45 min. 2-inch C
Francis Gaul presents a series analysis of why man acts,
thinks and feels as he does. Current scientific research
is examined and the significance of groups in human behavior is highlighted. Relevant program titles include:
1. Action Groups; 2. Changing Family; 6. Changing Ethnic Groups; 12. Culture and Personality; 24. Social
Class Influences; 26. Theories of Prejudice; 28. Volun-
tary Groups.

1792. SOCIAL SCIENCE PSYCHOLOGY (VT)
Time-Life 30 min.
Award: International and New York Film Festivals
Prejudice is studied in terms of the actual busing situa-
tion. Insight is offered into how and why the hostility begins.

1793. SOCIOLOGY I (VT)
National Instructional Television
This series presents basic terms of sociology and the so-
ciological view of "men in cultures and groups." It considers institutions, basic intercultural processes and various types of groups.

1794. SOLEDAD BROTHERS' LAWYERS SPEAK TO THE PRESS
(VT)
American Documentary Films 1 hour F
The Soledad brothers' lawyers speak to the press after
the murder of George Jackson at San Quentin.

1795. STOKELY CARMICHAEL (VT)
Northeastern University
Stokely Carmichael is interviewed on the David Frost
program.

1796. WHERE IS THE RACE? (VT)
National Instructional Television 20 min. b/w
This program looks at the many incorrect and humorous
notions about the origins of the races. It introduces
"scientific evidence" pertinent to rational discussion of
race.

1797. WHERE WE STOP, NOBODY KNOWS (VT)
National Instructional Television 20 min. b/w
This videotape shows some of the effects of white racism
on the lives of minority group males and on the racists'
own lives. Conclusions are based on the Kerner Commission Report and the Commission on Civil Rights' book-
let, "Racism and How to Combat It."

DYADIC

1798. IMPROVE CONVERSATION (VT)
CHITVC WTTW-TV Great Plains Instructional Television
45 min. 2-inch b/w C
From the Fundamentals of Speech Series, Unit 5

1799. INTERPERSONAL BEHAVIOR (VT)
National Medical Audiovisual Center 44 min. b/w
This videotape illustrates the evaluation of total interpersonal behavior in an interview. It considers general attitudes, character traits, styles as seen in personality
disorders.

1800. INTERPERSONAL COMPETENCE--A SERIES (VT)
Telstar 47 videotapes none over 30 min.
Instructor: Dr. Joseph C. Bentley, Associate Professor,
Utah University

See individual title listings
The course consists of nine independent units with the
number of tapes in parentheses: Unit I: The Self (11);
II: Communication (14); III: Motivation (3); IV: Help-
ing (5); V: Learning (4); VI: Creativity (2); VII:
Stress (3); VIII: Groups (3); IX: Growth (2).

1801. INTERROGATION I--FIELD (VT/VC)
Woroner Films, for Motorola
The trainee in a police cadet program participates in a
series of events as an observer, including interviewing
witnesses and comparing observations. A police department training film.

1802. ON THE WAY UP (VC)
Video Communications, Inc. six 30-min. programs color
This series devotes each of its segments to one or more
communication concepts. Titles include: 1. Shut Up and
Listen; 2. What's Needed and Wanted; 3. You Versus I;
4. Bridging the Gap; 5. Clean Communication; 6. You're
in Command.

1803. PATIENT INTERVIEW--SCIENCE AND ART (VC)
Video Communications, Inc.
Programs include: Medical Interview; Surgical Interview;
Psychiatric Interview.

EDUCATIONAL TECHNOLOGY

1804. AMPEX COMMUNICATIONS (VT)
Ampex nine 45-min. tapes b/w and color
Today's flexible communication abilities are contrasted
with primitive communication techniques. Unique uses
of videotape in business are explained.

1805. CASE FOR ITV, THE (PART I) (VT)
New York State Education Department 30 min. 2-inch
b/w C
The demands on education are analyzed, with suggestions
for implementation of new methodology relating to instructional television.

1806. CASE FOR ITV, THE (PART II) (VT)
New York State Education Department 30 min. 2-inch
b/w C
Television lesson planning demands organization, clarity,
pace. Exemplified are techniques to be used for specific
instructional enrichment.

1807.   CETO TELEVISION FILMS   (VC/VT)
        Centre for Educational Television (London)   24 presentations:
        22 in b/w and 2 in color   F   s/c/a
            These films now available on videotape and videocassette
            focus on television production training and offer wide and
            varied application on many subjects and at diverse levels.

1808.   ETV AND LIFE LONG EDUCATION   (VT)
        New York State Education Department   WNDT-TV   Great
        Plains Instructional Television   30 min.   2-inch   b/w   C
        From the Communications and Education Series
            The problems of institutional education and the dangers
            of mass media are discussed.   Suggestions are made to
            provide improvement in search for knowledge on educa-
            tional television.

1809.   FOURTH NETWORK, THE   (VC)
        Great Plains Instructional Television   20 min.   color   F
        See entry number 426.

1810.   GET THE PICTURE   (VC)
        Great Plains Instructional Television   12 min.   color   F
            June Dilworth, Director of Broadcasting, KCTS-TV, Uni-
            versity of Washington, details thoroughly the many prob-
            lems that can arise in the final link of any televised in-
            struction chain.

1811.   INSTRUCTIONAL RADIO-TELEVISION   (VC)
        Ampex   39 min.   b/w
            Edited are summaries of a session pertaining to instruc-
            tional radio and television matters developed at the 44th
            annual convention of the National Association of Education-
            al Broadcasters.   Reports include: The Status and Future
            of Educational Technology; Blacks at Decision-Making
            Levels; Rights and Responsibilities of the Television
            Teacher.

1812.   ITV: AN ORGANIZATION   (VT)
        New York State Education Department   WNDT-TV   Great
        Plains Instructional Television   30 min.   2-inch   b/w   C
        From the Communications and Education Series
            A conversation with James Brish, Superintendent of
            Schools, Washington County, Maryland, concerns closed
            circuit television education systems.

1813.   ITV IN HIGHER EDUCATION   (VT)
        New York State Education Department   WNDT-TV   Great
        Plains Instructional Television   30 min.   2-inch   b/w   C
        From the Communications and Education Series
            Higher education techniques for use of instructional tele-

vision, their potential for the future and advantages
and disadvantages are analyzed.

1814. SET-UP, PRODUCTION TECHNIQUES AND PREVENTIVE
MAINTENANCE FOR THE SINGLE-CAMERA   VTR SYSTEM
(VT)
Didactic Systems   27 min.
"Creative" control over equipment is the goal of this les-
son.

1815. TEACHER TELETIPS (VC)
Great Plains Instructional Television   20 min.   color   F
See entry number 444.

1816. TELEVISION TECHNIQUES FOR TEACHERS (VC)
Great Plains Instructional Television   24 min.   color   F
See entry number 455.

1817. TWO UTILIZATION PRESENTATIONS (VT)
Great Plains Instructional Television   I: 28 min.;   II: 47
min.   F
The "two utilization presentations" are "TV In the Classroom" and "Studio Teacher," both explanations of the
unique function of television in the classroom.   These
programs may be used in any situation where there is a
need for a quick background of involved activities prior
to and during a televised lesson.

1818. USING TECHNOLOGY: THE EQUIPMENT (VT/VC)
Great Plains Instructional Television   eight 20-min. programs
b/w
Each of the programs in this series concerns familiariza-
tion with and operational explanations of various types of
audiovisual equipment.   Explanations cover reel-to-reel
tape records, overhead projectors, still projectors, motion picture projectors, special photographic equipment,
radio, television and videotaping.

1819. VTR FEEDBACK (VT)
Didactic Systems   18 min.
The advantages of videotape in the areas of feedback are
illustrated.   Discussed is the planning, preparation, various uses of VTR and demonstrations, with types of equipment and situations illustrated.   One application demonstrated is "role-playing."

1820. VTR PRODUCTION PLANNING (VT)
Didactic Systems   28 min.
This tape explains the production planning process, the
use of videotape (audience analysis, conferences, evaluation, et al.) and demonstrates audio and video techniques.

FREEDOMS

1821. CENSORSHIP AND OBSCENITY (VT)
New York State Education Department 30 min. 2-inch b/w
From the Communications and Education Series
This lesson discusses both prior censorship and punitive censorship and defines the legal implications.

1822. COURTS AND LAWYERS AT WORK (VT)
New York State Education Department 30 min. 2-inch C
Instructor: David Kochery, Professor of Law, State University, New York
Surveyed is the American legal system with particular stress on a layman's understanding of the court operations and legal profession. Programs include: 1. The Right to Trial; 5. Lawyer's Skills; 7. and 8. Professional Ethics; 13 and 14. First Amendment Freedoms; 15. The Law and the Free Press.

1823. FREDERICK DOUGLASS AND AFRO-AMERICANS IN THE ABOLITIONIST MOVEMENT (VT)
WCVE-TV Great Plains Instructional Television 30 min. 2-inch s/c/a
From the Africa: A History Series

1824. FREE PRESS AND FAIR TRIAL (VT)
New York State Education Department 30 min. 2-inch b/w C
From the Communications and Education Series
Discussed is the conflict between the freedom of the press and due process of law. According to this lecture, the media has "aggravated the situation."

1825. FREEDOM OF SPEECH (VT)
New York State Education Department 30 min. 2-inch b/w C
From the Communications and Education Series
The free pursuit of fact and values appears to be a human duty not to be "interpreted," according to this central lesson.

1826. FREEDOM OF THE PRESS (VT)
New York State Education Department 30 min. 2-inch b/w C
From the Communications and Education Series
Analyzed is the question of whether or not freedom of the press and speech are synonymous. The unresolved dilemma is discussed in terms of government sanctions, consumer education.

1827. HERITAGE OF FREEDOM (VC)
Electronic Video Recording 38 min. color
Four portrayals delineate the background of the growth of liberty in the United States.

1828. ORSON WELLES: AMERICAN HERITAGE (VOLUME II) (VC)
Video Center color
From Assortment #7
> Orson Welles portrays the final court summation of Clar-
> ence Darrow, who defended a brilliant black physician ac-
> cused of murder in the early nineteen hundreds.

1829. OUR LIVING BILL OF RIGHTS (VT/VC)
Encyclopaedia Britannica 3 programs: I, II: 23 min.; III:
25 min. F
> These titles are discussed in detail under the appropriate
> category of film listings: I: Freedom to Speak: The
> People of New York versus Irving Feiner; II: Justice un-
> der the Law: The Gideon Case; III: Equality under the
> Law: the Lost Generation of Prince Edward County.

1830. PRIVACY AND THE RIGHT TO KNOW (VT)
New York State Education Department WNDT-TV Great
Plains Instructional Television 30 min. 2-inch C
From the Communications and Education Series
> The struggle between privacy and electronic devices is
> discussed in terms of the increasing problem. Empha-
> sized is the climate of opinion and role of mass media
> as factors in the problem.

1831. RUSH TOWARD FREEDOM--A SERIES (VT)
New York State Education Department 6 programs: 30 min.
each 2-inch s/c/a
> The modern history of the civil rights struggle in the
> United States is presented.

1832. SOCIAL SCIENCE (NO. 2)--A SERIES (VT)
CHITVC WTTW-TV Great Plains Instructional Television
45 min. each program 2-inch C
> Dr. Leon Novar examines the political and economic or-
> ganization of society and the problems of individual free-
> dom. Programs include: Attack on the Supreme Court;
> Capitalism's Big Critic--Karl Marx; Classical Democratic
> Theory, I and II; Conservatism, I, II, III.

GROUP DISCUSSION

1833. COMMUNICATION (VT)
Telstar approx. 30 min.
Instructor: Joseph C. Bentley, Ph.D.
From the Interpersonal Competence series
> This series unit focuses on building relationships with
> others, examines concepts, perceptions, vignettes in
> terms of interpersonal and group dynamics.

1834. COMMUNICATIONS GAP (VT)
       WAST (Albany, N.Y.) Cornell University 29 min.
       This program on the communications gap between genera-
       tions was broadcast in the series, "Table Talk," over
       Channel 13, WAST, Albany, New York. Mrs. Cecelia
       Roland of Albany and Sheryl Harrington of Schenectady,
       New York, discuss some of the underlying causes of mis-
       understanding.

1835. GROUPS (VT)
       Telstar   approx. 30 min.
       Instructor: Joseph C. Bentley, Ph.D.
       From the Interpersonal Competence series
            The focus of these lessons changes to more formal set-
            ting of group interactions. Shown and analyzed are two
            groups which are ineffective for different reasons.
            Teamwork, task roles and group building are discussed,
            as is conflict and constructive criticism.

1836. HOW TO CONDUCT A MEETING (VT)
       Republic Steel Corporation 29 min. 2-inch b/w s/c/a
       From the Understanding Politics Series
            Acceptable parliamentary procedures are illustrated:
            the handling of motions, amendments and other rules for
            conducting a meeting.

1837. HUMAN RELATIONS TODAY--A SERIES (VT)
       CHITVC WTTW-TV Great Plains Instructional Television
       45 min. each 2-inch b/w

1838. IMPROVE PARTICIPATION IN GROUP DISCUSSION (VT)
       CHITVC WTTW-TV Great Plains Instructional Television
       45 min. b/w C
       From the Fundamentals of Speech Series

1839. LEADERSHIP IS (VT)
       Cornell University 33 min. b/w F
            Three parts of this program explore the significance of
            leadership in group situations. Discussed are: leading
            at the right time and at the right place, knowing the sub-
            ject area, and getting along with people.

1840. NEW DEVELOPMENTS IN HUMAN RELATIONS AND LEAD-
       ERSHIP (VT)
       Republic Steel Corporation 29 min. b/w c/a
       From the Modern Management Methods Series (Part I)
            Research in the field of human relations is illustrated
            and explained in terms of attitudes toward people.

INFORMATION SYSTEMS

1841. COMPUTER REVOLUTION (PARTS I, II) (VT)
Modern Talking Picture Service (Free Loan Tape) 30 min.
1-inch c/a
The computer revolution is examined in terms of the challenge and the effects.

1842. INFORMATION SYSTEMS (PARTS I, II, III) (VT)
Time-Life color animation
Three programs define the principles, terminology and objectives of the information systems approach to problem-solving. This series is designed to "further understanding and stimulate discussion among management and employees."

1843. SYSTEMS ANALYSIS AND DESIGN (VT)
Time-Life color animation
This series of videotapes focuses on the concepts of the systems-approach to solving real-life situations. Individual program titles and times are: 1. The Systems Approach (6 min.); 2. Defining Systems Objectives (10 min.); 3. Information Systems Planning (7 min.); 4. Information Systems Analysis (11 min.); 5. Information Systems Design (6 min.); 6. Information Systems Implementation (8 min.); 7. Information Systems Evaluation (5 min.)

1844. UNDERSTANDING COMPUTERS (VT/VC)
Time-Life 30 min. color
The computer "mystique" is unmasked and uses are illustrated for education and business. This is an introductory overview designed to motivate the novice in the field by showing how computers work, what they can and cannot do, how they can serve better.

INTRAPERSONAL

1845. GROWTH (VT)
Telstar 30 min. b/w
Instructor: Dr. Joseph C. Bentley
Three lessons discuss the significance of self change. Lesson one examines nine principles of change. Lesson two reviews the purposes and directions in life. Lesson three makes suggestions concerning the implementation of activities.

1846. JOSHUA IN A BOX (VT)
Time-Life 5 min. color animation
Joshua, confined to a box, attempts to escape. His emotional response to frustration of confinement may be interpreted on many levels.

1847. MOTIVATION (VT)
       Telstar   30 min.   b/w
       Instructor: Dr. Joseph C. Bentley
              Three lessons include: Objectives of Definition and Con-
              cepts of Social Needs; Maslow's Hierarchy of Needs; Re-
              actions to the Same Stimulus.

1848. PERSONALITY AND SOCIAL BEHAVIOR   (VT)
       Telstar   10 lessons b/w
       Instructor: Dr. Joseph C. Bentley
              A good basis for understanding some observable psycho-
              logical problems is presented in lessons: Personality
              Defined; Approaches to Personality; Theories of Person-
              ality; Development and Personality; Assessment of Per-
              sonality; Frustration and Conflict I, Frustration and Con-
              flict II; Conflict and Society; When Behavior Breaks
              Down; Mental Health and Mental Illness.

1849. SELF, THE (VT)
       Telstar   30 min.   11 lessons b/w
       Instructor: Dr. Joseph C. Bentley
              This unit consists of: the accelerated rate of change;
              definition of competency; understanding ourselves; theories
              of conflict; goals of learning; perception; concept of self;
              values and attitudes; self-fulfilling prophecy; self-trust;
              analysis and summary.

1850. SENSATION AND PERCEPTION   (VT)
       Telstar   30 min.   6 lessons b/w
       Instructor: Dr. Joseph C. Bentley
              Lesson titles include: The Nature of Stimuli; Receptors
              of Stimuli; Worlds of Perception; Definition of the Situa-
              tion; Organization in Perception; Attention and Set.

1851. STRESS (VT)
       Telstar   30 min.   3 lessons b/w
       Instructor: Dr. Joseph C. Bentley
              Lessons include: Analysis of Cognitive Skills; Internal
              Defense Mechanisms; Coping with Stress.

                                  LANGUAGE

1852. DIALECTS OF VARIOUS LANGUAGES (DEVELOPMENTS OF
       DIALECTS) (VT)
       National Center for School and College Television 30 min.
       2-inch C
              Settlement and migration factors of language are analyzed,
              including industrialization, urbanization and education.

1853. ENGLISH FACT AND FANCY SERIES   (VT)
       WETA-TV   National Instructional Television   15-30 min. each
       b/w   F   C
       Instructor: James C. Bostain, linguist, communication spe-
       cialist
       Award: Local Emmy from the Academy Award of Television
       Arts and Sciences, 1965
            This series is a more specialized version of the instruc-
            tional programs listed under Films: Language. De-
            signed to help improve teaching by presenting English as
            a social and behavioral phenomenon, the programs relat-
            ing to communication are: 1. Scientists and Advocates;
            2. Language as a Behavioral Phenomenon; 3. Structure
            and Content; 4. Talking and Writing (Systems); 5. Talk-
            ing and Writing (Compares Speech with Writing); 6. Re-
            finements; 7. Dialects, Diversity; 8. English and Latin;
            9. Search for a "Universal Grammar"; 10. Change in
            Language; 11. Meaning; 12. Communication Model; 13.
            Formal English as a "Foreign Language"; 14. Noun Con-
            structions; 15. Verb Constructions.

1854. LANGUAGE AND THOUGHT   (VC)
       Great Plains Instructional Television 15-30 min. each b/w
       F   C
       Instructor: Dr. S. I. Hayakawa, semanticist, San Francisco
       State College
            A much more detailed series of Dr. Hayakawa's seman-
            tic analysis of language is presented than is offered under
            Films: Language. Titles include: 1. Language and Cul-
            ture; 2. Language of Reports; 3. Contexts; 4. Denota-
            tion and Connotation; 5. Phatic communion; 6. Language
            of Social Control; 7. Language of Poetry; 8. Language of
            Science; 9. Advertising and Semantics; 10. Process of
            Abstraction; 11. Semantics of Prejudice; 12. Two-valued
            Orientation; 13. Revision of Vision; 14. Semantics and
            Social Change; 15. Semantics in International Relations.
            Similar to Language in Action Series under Films: Lan-
            guage.

1855. LANGUAGE AS A BEHAVIORAL PHENOMENON   (VT)
       WETA-TV 30 min. 2-inch b/w C
       From the English Fact and Fancy Series
            James Bostain discusses areas to which rational appeals
            are presented in order to defend linguistic preferences.

1856. MEANING (VT)
       WETA-TV 30 min. 2-inch b/w C
       From the English Fact and Fancy Series
            The association between talking and "things" is analyzed.
            The efficiency of language "depends upon the awareness of
            language areas of ambiguity and specialty."

1857. MORE LINGUISTIC APPROACHES   (VT)
       KQED-TV National Instructional Television 2-inch b/w C
       Language "control" approaches are examined.

1858. PHILOSOPHY OF LOGIC AND LANGUAGE, THE (VT)
       State University of New York
            A videotaped address, "Philosophical Progress in Lan-
            guage Theory," is offered by Professor W. O. Quine,
            Harvard University. Response is by Professor Max
            Black, Cornell University.

1859. SPEED READING SYSTEMS   (VC)
       Time-Life 45 min. each color
       Collaborator: Dr. Edward Fry, Director, Reading Center,
       Rutgers University
       Instructor: Dick Cavett
            This is an eight-part course to increase reading, improve
            speech skills, comprehension and vocabulary. Lessons
            include: Comprehension, Vocabulary, Perception and
            Meaning; Rapid Communication. Home assignments are
            included.

1860. SUCCESS THROUGH WORD POWER--A SERIES   (VT)
       Telstar 10-30 min. sessions b/w
       Instructor: James Brown, Professor of Rhetoric, University
       of Minnesota
            Lessons are presented for those desiring the development
            of increased vocabulary effectiveness for speaking, listen-
            ing, reading, writing. Titles include: 1. Words that
            Make the Difference; 2. Words with a Past; 3. Word's
            Best Friend; 4. People Who Became Words; 5. Company
            Words Keep; 6. Winning Ways of Words; 7. Word Sleuth-
            ing; 8. Words that Make Dollars; 9. Words as Passports.

1861. SUMMARY OF UNIT I: LANGUAGE PROPOSITIONS AND
       SYLLOGISMS   (VT)
       CHITVC WTTW-TV 45 min. 2-inch b/w C
       From the Logic Series, Unit I: Language, Propositions,
       Syllogisms

                         LEARNING THEORY

1862. ASPECTS OF BEHAVIOR   (VT/VC)
       Time-Life 30 min. color F C
            See entry number 762.

1863. CONVERSATION WITH B. F. SKINNER, A (VT/VC)
       CRM Films Time-Life 1972 20 min. color F s/c
            See entry number 776.

1864. DEVELOPMENT (VT/VC)
CRM Films 1972 32 min. color F s/c
From the Psychology Today Series
See entry number 777.

1865. EDUCATIONAL PSYCHOLOGY--A SERIES (VT)
CHITVC WTTW-TV Great Plains Instructional Television
45 min. each C
Dr. Bryan Feather focuses on the learning process, modern psychology, investigation tools and qualities desirable in instructors. Titles pertinent to communication concepts include: 5. Basic Processes of Adjustment; 8. Dynamics of the Motivational Process; 10. Interests and Attitudes; 11. Orientation; 23. Social Psychology of Learning; 27. Fields of Psychology and the Instructor; 28. Learning: the Dynamics of Change; 3. Interaction in the Learning Process; 35. Behavioral Objectives for Learning Situations; 36. Conditioning Techniques; 38. Humanistic Psychology.

1866. GENERAL PSYCHOLOGY--A SERIES (VT)
CHITVC WTTW-TV Great Plains Instructional Television
45 min. each 2-inch b/w C/a
Dr. Fred McKinney investigates problems concerning intelligence, individual differences, learning, motivation and perception. Programs relating to communication concepts include: Behavioral Science; Conflict and Adjustment; Emotion; Nature of Learning; Perception; Psychological Motives; Social Motives; Statistics in Psychology; Thinking, Language and Problem-Solving.

1867. INTELLIGENCE AND HUMAN ABILITIES (VT)
Telstar
This unit includes two lessons: 1. The Nature of Intelligence; 2. The Effects of Intelligence. Program number one defines intelligence and presents examples of intelligent behavior. Program number two explains the effort of intelligence in the area of educational achievement.

1868. INTERACTION ANALYSIS (VC)
Ampex 50 min. b/w
Dr. Edmund J. Amidon, Temple University, discusses interaction analysis to demonstrate the methodology used to classify teacher-classroom behavioral patterns and to develop methods for behavioral change.

1869. LEARNING (VT)
Telstar
Instructor: Joseph C. Bentley, Ph. D.
This unit is part of the Interpersonal Competence Series and includes four lessons: classical conditioning; operant conditioning; self-learning; intelligence interpretations.

1870. LEARNING (VT/VC)
       CRM Films Time-Life 30 min. color F C
       Award: CINE Golden Eagle Award
           See entry number 798.

1871. LEARNING AND REINFORCEMENT (VT)
       Learning Incorporated 30 min. 2-inch s/c/a
       From the Learning Theory Series
           This program presents some of the principles which can
           be of significant value to the person interested in devel-
           oping efficient and successful approaches for the applica-
           tion of learning theory to instruction.

1872. PERSONALITY (VT/VC)
       Time-Life 30 min.
           A psychology examination tests a young man who has al-
           ready been examined in interviews by himself, with his
           family and with his girlfriend.

1873. PERSPECTIVES ON LEARNING (VT)
       Learning, Incorporated 30 min. 2-inch s/c/a
       From the Study Skills Series
           The functional relationship between the stimuli and the
           response is explained in terms of maximizing the profit
           from learning efforts.

1874. PSYCHOLOGY (VT)
       Telstar eleven units
       Instructor: Joseph C. Bentley, Ph.D.
           This course is designed to assist the student in learning
           to understand behavior. The eleven units include: the
           science of behavior; the human organism; tools of psy-
           chology; human growth and development; sensation and
           perception; learning; thinking and problem-solving; intelli-
           gence and human abilities; motivation and man; personal-
           ity and social behavior; conflict, adjustment and mental
           health.

1875. PSYCHOLOGY I: THE PRINCIPLES OF BEHAVIOR (VT)
       National Instructional Television 30 min.
       Award Winner
           The behavior of organisms is considered. Behavior cate-
           gories are illustrated: motivation, perception, learning
           techniques. Also treated are principles of behavior re-
           lating to purpose, intentions, goals.

1876. PSYCHOLOGY II: MAN AND HIS MOTIVES (VT)
       National Instructional Television 30 min.
       Award Winner
           The subject of human motivation is discussed. Basic
           theories and research findings are introduced to illustrate
           reasons for man's thoughts and actions.

1877. PSYCHOLOGY TODAY--A SERIES (VT/VC)
      CRM Films Time-Life Videorecord color
           Many of these programs on videotapes and videocassettes
           are listed in detail under individual titles in the film por-
           tion of this study. Program titles include: 1. Aspects
           of Behavior; 2. The Sensory World; 3. Information Proc-
           essing; 4. Learning; 5. Developing; 6. Social Psychol-
           ogy; 7. Personality; 8. Abnormal Behavior.

1878. SIMULATION (VC)
      Ampex 4 min. b/w
           Simulated experiences to prepare students to deal with
           real situations are presented in interaction laboratory con-
           texts using videotape episodes, role-playing, incidents.
           Participants are: Dr. Donald Cruickshank, University of
           Tennessee; Dr. Frank Broadbent.

1879. SKINNER AT M. I. T. (VT)
      Northeastern University
           Dr. B. F. Skinner is interviewed at the Massachusetts
           Institute of Technology concerning his discoveries and fu-
           ture plans.

1880. TOOLS OF PSYCHOLOGY (VT)
      Telstar
           This three-lesson unit with Dr. Joseph Bentley contains
           the following three programs: 1. Measurement in Psy-
           chology; 2. Properties of Tests; 3. Statistics as a Tool.

                              LISTENING

1881. ANALYZE EVERY AUDIENCE (VT)
      WTTW-TV Great Plains Instructional Television 45 min.
      2-inch b/w C
           From the Fundamentals of Speech Series: Unit I

1882. COMMUNICATION: TALKING AND LISTENING (VT)
      Department of Agriculture WETA-TV Great Plains Instruc-
      tional Television 30 min. 2-inch b/w
      From the Success in Supervision Series
           Emphasized is the importance of thinking before speaking.
           The differences between hearing and listening are con-
           trasted as well as the techniques for conveying ideas oral-
           ly.

1883. LISTEN ACCURATELY (VT)
      CHITVC WTTW-TV Great Plains Instructional Television
      45 min. C
      From the Fundamentals of Speech Series: Unit IV

1884.   LISTEN CRITICALLY   (VT)
        CHITVC   WTTW-TV   Great Plains Instructional Television
        45 min.   C
        From the Fundamentals of Speech Series;   Unit IV

1885.   LISTEN TO SOME OF YOUR FELLOW CLASSMATES   (VT)
        CHITVC   WTTW-TV   Great Plains Instructional Television
        45 min.   C
        From the Fundamentals of Speech Series: Unit IV

MASS MEDIA

1886.   BROADCASTING: TELEVISION RIGHT OF ACCESS   (VT)
        New York State Education Department   WNDT-TV   Great
        Plains Instructional Television   30 min.
        From the Communications and Education Series
            The right of television to defend its "freedom of expres-
            sion" is discussed.

1887.   BROADCASTING: THIRTY YEARS RETROSPECT   (VT)
        New York State Education Department   WNDT-TV   Great
        Plains Instructional Television   30 min.   b/w   c/a
            The history of broadcasting is reviewed,   including inci-
            dents of its cultural influence.

1888.   COMMUNICATION AND SOCIETY: A CONVERSATION   (VT)
        New York State Education Department   1968   c/a
        Mr. Charles Siepmann, Professor Emeritus, New York Uni-
        versity, in a conversation with Lord Reith, founder and first
        director-general of BBC
            Lord Reith emphasizes that the exploitation of radio should
            provide a conscious social purpose.   Mr. Siepmann pre-
            sents his own analysis of the Reith concepts.

1889.   COMMUNICATIONS AND EDUCATION--A SERIES   (VT/VC)
        New York State Education Department   WNDT-TV   Great
        Plains Instructional Television   30 min. each   C/a
        Award: Ohio State Instruction Award for Education in Radio-
        Television
            Charles Siepmann, former Chairman of the Department of
            Communication, New York University, discusses communi-
            cation and its relationship to education and society.   Some
            of these titles are described in the film section.   Perti-
            nent communication concepts include: 1. Race against
            Time; 2. Democracy; 3. Communications Revolution; 4.
            Broadcasting; 6. Freedom of Speech; 7. Freedom of the
            Press; 8. Newspapers; 9. Free Press, Fair Trial; 10.
            Broadcasting; 11. Privacy and the Right to Know; 12.
            Censorship; 13. and 14. Propaganda.

1890. COMMUNICATIONS REVOLUTION, THE (VT)
New York State Education Department WNDT-TV Great
Plains Instructional Television 30 min. b/w C/a
From the Communications and Education Series
The characteristics of the "revolution" are analyzed with
emphasis on specialization, growing power of mass media,
new freedom of the press and significance of propaganda.

1891. EARLY ART OF THE CINEMA (VC)
Video Communications, Inc.
A compilation of early film art-forms includes: "The
Cure," "Mabel's Married Life," "Great Train Robbery,"
"Corner in Wheat," "Beast at Bay," "The Eagle,"
"Cruise of the Jasper," "Lost World."

1892. ENVIRONMENT AND DEVELOPMENT OF PUBLIC RELA-
TIONS (VC/VT)
Ampex 27 min. b/w
From the Public Relations Discussion Series
The historical background of public relations is illustrated,
including the pioneers and contemporary personalities.
Participant: Mr. Samuel Friedman, Assistant to the Gen-
eral Manager, Los Angeles Department of Water and
Power, Los Angeles, California.

1893. EXITS AND ENTRANCES (VT/VC)
Time-Life color
See entry number 868.

1894. FILM AND SOCIETY, THE (VT)
New York State Education Department 30 programs 30 min.
each
Director: Peter Schillaci
This series reviews the American film as it creates and
reflects structures in the society. Program titles are:
1. Film and Society; 2. God's Country; 3. Don't Fence
Me In; 4. Fastest Gun in the West; 5. Six-gun Morality;
6. Saddle-sore; 7. Crime Pays; 8. Private Eye; 9. In
the Name of the Law; 10. and 11. Universal Soldier;
12. I Spy; 17. The Haunted Image; 18. Die, Monster;
19. The Mind Boggles; 20. The Infernal Machine; 21.
Song and Dance; 22. Some Are Less Equal; 23. The
Greatest Story Retold; 24. Land of Disney; 25. Dial H
for Hitchcock; 26. Doing America's Thing; others.

1895. FUTURE OF PUBLIC RELATIONS, THE (VT/VC)
Ampex 28 min. b/w
Discussed are accreditation and the professional status of
public relations plus changing personnel qualifications and
the public relations practitioner of the future.

1896. GIVING THE PUBLIC WHAT IT WANTS   (VT)
New York State Education Department   WNDT-TV   Great
Plains Instructional Television   30 min.   2-inch   b/w
From the Communications and Education Series
    Equitable program service should include the widest va-
riety of experiences or attempt to meet television's four
basic needs: entertainment, practical information, knowledge, awareness and experience.

1897. MARCH OF TIME SERIES*   (VC)
Time-Life   20 min. each (4)   color   F
See entry number 932.

1898. MARSHALL McLUHAN: PICNIC IN SPACE   (VT)
University-at-Large   VCI   28 min.   color
See entry number 876.

1899. MASS COMMUNICATIONS: EFFECTS   (VT)
New York State Education Department   WNDT-TV   Great
Plains Instructional Television   30 min.   2-inch   b/w
From the Communications and Education Series

1900. MOVIES MARCH ON   (VC)
Time-Life   22 min.   color   F
See entry number 935.

1901. NATIONAL ASSOCIATION OF EDUCATIONAL BROADCASTERS
CONVENTION   (VC)
Ampex   1969   b/w
   I. Ampex Videotape Highlights: Educational television sum-
maries of sessions pertain to educational television
broadcasting matters.   Participants are: McGeorge Bundy,
Ford Foundation; Lawrence Frymire, Telcom Communications; Frank Pace, Corporation for Public Broadcasting;
Marvin Bowman, University of Kentucky; William Grier,
University of California; Chalmers Marquis, National Association of Educational Broadcasters; Wilbur Cohen, Department of Health, Education, Welfare (45 min.).
  II. Ampex Videotape Highlights: Educational radio excerpts
from summaries of sessions are presented.   Participants
are: McGeorge Bundy; Patricia Swenson, Portland public
schools; Nicholas Johnson, Federal Communications Commission; E. G. Burrow, University of Michigan; Reverend Edward Riddick and Robert Moot, National Association of Broadcasters; Wilbur Cohen (44 min.).
III. Ampex Communications: A survey is presented of communication techniques from primitive times to today's use
of videotape for medical, business, education needs.

1902. NETWORKS AND THE RATING GAME, THE   (VT)
KOGO-TV National Instructional Television   30 min.   color
From the Television Today Series
    The beginnings of networks and the significance of station

affiliation are examined. Some of the advantages of affiliation are reviewed and some of the relevant federal
laws discussed.

1903. PR PROCESS, THE: COMMUNICATING (VT/VC)
Ampex 29 min. b/w
> Communication theories are introduced, including media
> techniques and press relations. Participants: Wallace
> Jamie, Director of Public Relations, Carnation Company;
> Ms. Lois Gaines, Furman Associates.

1904. PR PROCESS, THE: EVALUATING (VT/VC)
Ampex 29 min. b/w
> Pre- and post-testing are discussed as are impact meas-
> urement and feedback to fact-finding. Participant: Mr.
> Joseph La Barbera, Director of Advertising and Publicity,
> Title Insurance and Trust Company.

1905. PR PROCESS, THE: FACT-FINDING (VT/VC)
Ampex 29 min. b/w
> Opinion research is analyzed: when, what kind, how
> much.

1906. PR PROCESS, THE: PLANNING (VT/VC)
Ampex 29 min. b/w
> This program reviews strategy and tactics. Participant:
> Mr. Ty Scroggins, Public Relations Manager, Getty Oil
> Company.

1907. PROFESSIONAL PUBLIC RELATIONS--A SERIES (VT/VC)
Ampex twelve programs 29 min each
Public Relations Society of America
Supervisor: Dr. Kenneth Smith, University of California at
Los Angeles
> This series is designed to prepare members of the Pub-
> lic Relations Society of America for their accreditation
> examination. Titles include: Public Relations, Public
> Opinion, PR Process, others.

1908. PROMOTION, THE: ITS ROLE IN THE TOTAL MARKETING
PROGRAM (VT)
CHITVC WTTW-TV Great Plains Instructional Television
45 min. b/w C
From the Marketing Series

1909. PROMOTIONAL CAMPAIGN, THE (VT)
CHITVC WTTW-TV Great Plains Instructional Television
45 min. b/w C

1910. PUBLIC RELATIONS: WHAT IS IT? WHO IS IT? (VT/VC)
Ampex 27 min. b/w
> Definitions and concepts are presented, including patterns
> of current practice. Participant: Mr. Ray Silvius, Vice

President of Public Relations, Western Air Lines, Inc.

1911. PUBLICS OF PUBLIC RELATIONS, THE   (VT/VC)
Ampex 27 min. b/w
Analyzed are the "publics,"--the general, community, spe-
cial publics. Participant: David Hurford, Director of
Public Relations, Sears Roebuck and Company.

1912. TELEVISION TODAY: A SERIES (VT)
National Instructional Television Time-Life eight 30-min.
programs s/c/a
Host: William Stevens, Jr., President of Time-Life Productions
This series surveys the scope and impact of the broadcasting industry. It is designed to provide a general
background of the organization, legal, commercial creative, communication aspects at work in the television
medium. Program titles are: 1. Tour of a Broadcast
Facility; 2. Television Programming; 3. Networks and
the Rating Game; 4. Which Public? Which Interest?; 5.
They Don't Make Commercials Like They Used To; 6. The
Front Porch Is Steady; 7. What's Going On in the World;
8. The Kids Watch, But....

1913. THAT YOU MAY KNOW (VT)
Indiana University 15 min. each 24 programs b/w s/a
This series is a study of the newspapers, magazines,
films, radio and television as media of mass communication. Program titles range from Behind the Radio Dial to
What Shall We Listen To? and include a survey of media
messages and strategies.

PERSUASION

1914. PERSUASION: APPEAL TO EMOTIONS (VT)
CHITVC WTTW-TV Great Plains Instructional Television
45 min. b/w
From the English Composition Series, Unit IV

1915. PROPAGANDA: INTERNATIONAL AND DOMESTIC (VT)
New York State Education Department WND-TV Great Plains
Instructional Television 30 min. b/w C
From the Communications and Education Series
Reviewed is the international babble of the propagandists,
including domestic and foreign merchandising of political
propaganda.

1916. PROPAGANDA: ITS POWER (VT)
New York State Education Department WND-TV Great Plains
Instructional Television 30 min. b/w C
From the Communications and Education Series

Four outcomes of propaganda are examined: nothing, conversion, precipitation or confirmation. The saturation, repetition and association techniques used by propagandists are related to education's failure "to teach logic."

1917. PROPAGANDA: MEANING AND SIGNIFICANCE (VT)
New York State Education Department WND-TV Great Plains Instructional Television 30 min. b/w C
From the Communications and Education Series
The concerns of propaganda should involve the power it possesses as well as the misuse of the word itself, according to this educational videotape.

1918. PROPAGANDA: SECTION 315 (VT)
New York State Education Department WND-TV Great Plains Instructional Television 30 min. b/w C
From the Communications and Education Series
The equal time provision is analyzed as it relates to the larger social issues of the cost of running for office.

1919. PUBLIC OPINION AND PERSUASION (VT/VC)
Ampex 29 min. b/w
This seminar on definitions of public opinion, principles of persuasion and their interdependence for social significance includes participant: Joseph Roose, Director of Jewish Federations, New York City, N.Y.

POLITICAL

1920. AMERICAN INSTITUTIONS (VT/VC)
Great Plains Instructional Television thirty 30-min. programs color c
This series examines the roles of major American institutions such as government, labor, education, military, religion, and the family and their relationship to the total structure of American society. Titles include: Political Parties; The Presidency; Congress; Congress in Conflict; others.

1921. AMERICAN SYSTEM, THE (VT/VC)
Great Plains Instructional Television 20-25 min. programs b/w
This series was developed to provide understanding of constitutionalism, federal systems, the organization of government on the national level. Titles include: The U.S. Senator; The Executive Branch; State of the Nation; others.

1922. CITIZEN KANE: (VT/VC)
Time-Life 119 min. 2 cassettes b/w F
See entry number 1255.

1923. DEMAGOGUES AND DO-GOODERS   (VC)
       Time-Life   30 min.   color   F
          See entry number 1260.

1924. 51% (VT/VC)
       Drucker   Time-Life   25 min.   color   F
          See entry number 1066.

1925. GETTING INTO LOCAL POLITICS   (VT)
       Republic Steel Corporation   29 min.   2-inch   b/w
       From the Understanding Politics Series
          Advice is given toward helping participatory politicians.
          Analyzed are capabilities needed for involvement.

1926. GOVERNMENT STORY, THE   (VT)
       Westinghouse Group "W"   Telstar   40 programs   30 min. each
       Host: Stephen Horn
          Narrators   E. G. Marshall and Paul Long tell the story
          of a democracy.   The first twenty programs deal with
          Congress; programs twenty-one through thirty-five are on
          the Presidency; thirty-six through forty on the Federal
          Courts group.   Other titles include: 28. Presidential
          Persuaders; 33. The President, Press and Public; 38.
          Framework of Freedom; 40. Supreme Court and Society.

1927. HISTORY MACHINE, THE   (VT)
       University-at-Large   VCI   50 programs   7 min. each
          This is a mammoth perspective of the most important
          events and people of twentieth-century America.   Many
          political events (campaigns, elections, decisions) are in-
          cluded.

1928. HOW TO RUN A POLITICAL CAMPAIGN   (VT)
       Republic Steel Corporation   29 min.   2-inch   b/w   s/c/a
       From the Understanding Politics Series
          Problems of electing a candidate to office are explained.
          Campaigning practices are examined.

1929. IDEOLOGY, INTEREST GROUPS AND POLITICS IN THE
       UNITED STATES   (VT)
       CHITVC   WTTW-TV   Great Plains Instructional Television
       45 min.   b/w   C
       From the Social Science #2 Series

1930. NATIONAL GOVERNMENT   (VC/VT)
       CHITVC   WTTW-TV   Great Plains Instructional Television
       thirty 45-min. lessons   b/w   c
          Television instructor Professor Ward Fleming of Chicago
          City College presents the following political course divi-
          sions: I: Origin of the Republic; II: The Constitution of
          the Republic; III: Branches of Republican Government;
          IV: Popular Political Action in the Republic; V: Govern-
          ing the Republic.

1931. NATIONAL GOVERNMENT, THE--A SERIES (VT)
CHITVC WTTW-TV Great Plains Instructional Television
thirty 45-min lessons b/w c
Dr. Harvey M. Karlen stresses four elements in political science behavior, with an analysis of the nature and
uses of political ideas and the structure and operations
of political institutions. Programs include: 2. Analysis
of Election Returns; 3. Civil Rights; 6. Declaration of
Independents; 15. Party Organization; 22. Public Opinion; 23. Problems Today; others.

1932. NATURE OF THE POLITICAL PROBLEM, THE (VT)
CHITVC WTTW-TV Great Plains Instructional Television
45 min. 2-inch C
From The Man and His State Series

1933. PROBLEM OF CONTROLLING LEADERSHIP IN A DEMOC-
RACY (VT)
CHITVC WTTW-TV Great Plains Instructional Television
45 min. 2-inch C
From the Courts and the Judicial Process Series

1934. PUBLIC RELATIONS IN A DEMOCRACY (VT/VC)
Ampex 25 min. b/w
Government information practices as related to the needs
of the citizen are discussed. Included are topics of persuasive political public relations. Participant: Mr. Kenneth Palmer, Palmer/Larson Communications.

1935. UNDERSTANDING POLITICS--A SERIES (VT)
Republic Steel Corporation 29 min. each s/c/a
Series titles include: Characteristics of the Electorate;
Getting into Local Politics; How to Conduct a Meeting;
How to Run a Political Campaign; Our Two-Party System;
Waging a Political Campaign.

1936. VISUAL ENCYCLOPEDIA OF AMERICAN HISTORY IN THE
TWENTIETH CENTURY, THE (VC)
Bro-Dart F
See entry number 1242.

1937. 'X' FACTOR: WOMEN AS PEOPLE, THE (VT/VC)
Cornell University 1970 2-part series 28 min. each b/w
See entry number 1130.

PROCESS/THEORY

1938. COMMUNICATIONS (VT)
Telstar twenty-four lessons
Instructor: Dr. James Connolly, Associate Professor, Speech
and Theatre Department, Hamline University
Interprets stimulus, perception, thought and response.

Individual units and lesson titles are: Unit I: The Cycle
of Communication (Importance of Communication Cycle,
Stimulus and Perception, Nature of Thought, Response);
Unit II: The Nature of Language (Definition, Problems,
Listening, One-to-one Communication, Task-Centered
Situations, Situational Elements); Unit III: The Use of
Language in Group Situations (Group Communicative Situ-
ations, Major Elements, Problem-Solution Methods, Con-
tributions, Discussion); Unit IV: Thinking (Critical Think-
ing, Reasoning); Unit V: Prepared Discourse (Preparing,
Organizing, Patterns, Support, Presentation, Summary).

1939. COMMUNICATIONS MODEL, A (VT)
WETA-TV National Instructional Television 30 min.
2-inch b/w F
From the English Fact and Fancy Series
See entry number 1313.

1940. DEVELOPING COMMUNICATION SKILLS (VT)
Telstar 1/2- and 1-inch
Instructor: Malcolm E. Shaw, Management Consultant, West-
port, Connecticut
The goal of this series is to improve communication tech-
niques. Titles are: 1. The Communication Process; 2.
Communication Patterns; 3. Resistance to Change; 4.
Choosing Communication Patterns; 5. Listening; 6. Im-
proving Feedback Skills.

1941. INFORMATION PROCESSING (VT/VC)
Time-Life 30 min. color F
Award: CINE Golden Eagle Award
See entry number 1318.

PUBLIC SPEAKING

1942. ENGLISH COMPOSITION: A SERIES (VT)
WTTW-TV Great Plains Instructional Television 45 min.
each C
Dr. John T. Queenan examines the problems of effective
writing, organization of ideas and discourse methodology.
Programs relating to communication are: 1. Acknowledg-
ing Sources in Text; 2. Analysis; the Outline; 4. Choosing a Topic; 7. Analogy; 9. Deductive Reasoning; 11.
Diction; 12. Evaluating Argument; 18. Logical Fallacies;
20. Organization; 21. Persuasion; 28. Writing the Research Paper; 33. Identification and Definition; 36. Classification and Illustration.

1943. EVALUATE MORE OF YOUR FELLOW CLASSMATES (VT)
CHITVC WTTW-TV Great Plains Instructional Television
45 min. b/w C
From the Fundamentals of Speech Series

1944. FUNDAMENTALS OF SPEECH: A SERIES (VT)
CHITVC WTTW-TV Great Plains Instructional Television
45 min. each b/w C
Dr. Robert A. Johnson explains the theory and practice
of oral communication, emphasizing the development of
poise, delivery and organization of ideas. Individual
titles include: 1. Analyze Every Audience; 2. Build a
Useful Outline; 3. Choose Subjects Appropriate; 4. Confidence; 5. Evaluation Standards; 6. Evaluation of Peers;
7. Evidence; 8. Research Materials; 9. Conversation;
10. Oral Reading; 11. Group Discussion; 12. Televised
Speaking; 13. Language; 14. Listening; 15. Listening;
16. Listening; 17. Rehearsals; 18. Sensory Appeals;
19. Review; 20. Review; 21. Material Choices; 22. and
23. Skills; 24. Concepts of Speech; 25. Vision, Sound,
Language; 26. Overall; 27. and 28. Vision: Speech.

1945. IMPROVE ORAL READING (VT)
CHITVC WTTW-TV Great Plains Instructional Television
45 min. 2-inch b/w C
From the Fundamentals of Speech Series

1946. IMPROVE TELEVISED SPEAKING (VT)
CHITVC WTTW-TV Great Plains Instructional Television
45 min. 2-inch b/w C
From the Fundamentals of Speech Series

1947. SPEAKING EFFECTIVELY (VT)
Telstar ten lessons
Instructor: Dr. Ronald M. Brown
Course objectives include the development of a system for
composing and expressing thoughts orally, the provision
of practice materials and guides to develop individual
skills for speaking effectively and the development of self-
confidence in expressing one's thoughts.

1948. SPEECH PREPARATION (VC)
Av-Ed VCI 13 min. b/w F s/c/a
The purpose of this program is to present basic steps in
preparing a speech, applying them to contemporary material so they can be clear and practical for the user.

1949. SUCCESS THROUGH PRACTICAL SPEECHMAKING: A SER-
IES (VT)
Telstar 10 sessions 30-min. each
Instructor: Ronald Brown, Professor Rhetoric, University of
Minnesota
For those who want lessons in effective communication,

this series provides speech skills. Titles are: 1. Knowing What's Involved; 2. Sizing up Situations; 3. Having Something to Say; 4. Getting Behind a Point; 5. Arranging the Parts and the Points; 6. Rehearsing Aloud; 7. Aiming for a Reaction; 8. Commanding Attention; 9. Reacting to Reactions; 10. Evaluating Speakers.

RHETORICAL TOPICS

1950. AMERICA IN THE SIXTIES   (VT/VC)
       Time-Life   29 min.   color   F
              Three short pieces by Charles Braverman depict a decade of war and peace, space exploration and earth days, rock groups and assassinations, elections.   Titles are: Kinestasis 60; The Exiles; Space Place.

1951. AMERICAN TIME CAPSULE   (VT/VC)
       Time-Life   3 min.   color   F
       Award Winner
              See entry number 1480.

1952. CHALLENGE OF MODERN PSYCHIATRY TO RELIGION, THE (VT)
       KUON-TV   Great Plains Instructional Television   30 min.
       2-inch   b/w   c/a
              From the Counseling Center of the New York Federation of Reform Synagogues, Director Rabbi Henry Kagan lectures.

1953. COMMUNISTS, THE--A SERIES   (VT)
       VITA   1967   20 min. each   s/c/a
              The essential knowledge of the growth and development of communism, theory and practice, is presented.

1954. COMMUNISTS, THE--A SERIES   (VT)
       KVI-TV   National Center for School and College Television
       20 min. each (revised edition of entry no. 1953)
              Programs include: Communism in China and the Far East; Communist Empire; Communist Foreign Policy; Communist Leaders; Communist Theory; Origins of Communism; Soviet System.

1955. CONTEMPORARY ISSUES--SERIES 70'S   (VC)
       Great Plains Instructional Television   7 programs   b/w and color   F
              Each program uses a different approach. Titles include: Consent of the Governed; Lock and Bolt Club; First Person Singular; "Got a Minute?"; Just for Kicks; Breathe Deep; Non-Conformity.

1956. EVOLUTION OF COMMUNISM (VT)
CHITVC WTTW-TV Great Plains Instructional Television
45 min. b/w C
From the Social Science #3 Series

1957. FREEDOM AND OBEDIENCE TO LAW: PLATO (VT)
CHITVC WTTW-TV Great Plains Instructional Television
45 min. b/w C
From the Social Science #2 Series

1958. HUMANITIES (VT)
WTTW-TV Great Plains Instructional Television 30 lessons
45 min. each
Instructor: Donald E. Smith, Professor of Humanities, Chicago City College
Unit I concerns Persons, Places and Events (five speeches on love and the wisdom of Socrates); Unit II concentrates on the World of Myth and Legend (Truth-seeker; Sophocles; others); Unit III reviews the Realm of Idea and Speculation (Politics of the state).

1959. HUMANITIES, NO. I--A SERIES (VT)
CHITVC WTTW-TV Great Plains Instructional Television
This series integrates areas of literature, painting, architecture and music for interdisciplinary study. Programs related to communication are: The Drama; Lyric Poetry; Production of the Stage Play; Narrative Poetry.

1960. HUMANITIES, NO. II--A SERIES (VT)
CHITVC WTTW-TV Great Plains Instructional Television
The great issues of today are analyzed with diverse solutions proposed. Issues include: Ethics, Morality.

1961. MAHATMA GANDHI LEADS INDIA IN NONVIOLENT PROTEST (VC)
Bro-Dart
From the Visual History Series

1962. OTHER VIETNAM, THE (VC)
Electronic Video Recording (EVR)
This program shows the Vietnamese engaged in their own self-improvement, as well as with American civilian specialists who work beside them.

1963. PHILOSOPHY OF COMMUNICATIONS AND THE ARTS, THE (VT)
State University of New York b/w
The address on "Philosophy of Communications and the Arts" is given by Professor Richard McKeon, University of Chicago, with Dr. Kenneth Burke, Visiting Professor of Philosophy, Harvard University, responding.

1964. PHILOSOPHY OF EDUCATION--A SERIES (VT)
CHITVC WTTW-TV Great Plains Instructional Television
45 min. each 2-inch c
   This series concerns human versus political, social, economic and ethical experience and focuses on problems of
   education. Programs include: Education and Communism; Education and Political Democracy; Education and
   Social Democracy; Goals of Education.

1965. PHILOSOPHY OF HUMAN RIGHTS, THE (VT)
State University of New York b/w
   The address "Philosophy of Human Rights" is given by
   Sidney Hook, Professor of Philosophy, New York Univer-
   sity. Professor Raymon Aron, University of Paris,
   moderates.

1966. PHILOSOPHY OF RELIGION--A SERIES (VT)
New York State Education Department 28 programs 30 min.
each
Instructor: Professor Dane Gordon, Rochester Institute of
Technology
   Program titles include: Definition of Religion; Contradic-
   tion; Symbols; Empirical Knowledge; Analogy; Religious
   Language; Metaphor; Myth and Allegory; Meaning and Use;
   Evil; Contemporary Theology; Philosophy of Religion.

1967. PHILOSOPHY OF SOCIAL SCIENCE (VT)
State University of New York b/w
   The address "Philosophy of Social Science" is presented
   by Professor H. L. A. Hart, Oxford University. Response is by Professor R. M. Dworkin, Yale University.

1968. PROTEST AND COMMUNICATION (VT/VC)
Time-Life 52 min. color F
See entry number 1466.

1969. RELIGIOUS EXPERIENCE, THE (VC)
Video Center
Part of Assortment #2
   The impact of religion on man is analyzed. Source,
   forms, functions and roles of religion in men's lives are
   illustrated, with supporting commentary ranging from
   Marcus Aurelius to Dag Hammerskjold.

1970. RISE OF ADOLPH HITLER, THE (VC)
Bro-Dart
From the Visual Encyclopedia of American History Series

1971. SELLING OF THE PENTAGON, THE (VT)
CBS News 1971 52 min. color F s/c/a
See entry number 1607.

1972. SIXTIES, THE   (VC)
Time-Life   15 min.   color
Award Winner
> News footage from a paradoxical decade, contrasts the
> divisions in our society and the polarity of our thinking:
> Birmingham and Woodstock; Biafra and Vietnam; Eugene
> McCarthy and Richard Daley.

1973. STRUGGLE IN IRELAND: BERNADETTE DEVLIN   (VT)
American Documentary Films   3 hours   F
See entry number 1427.

1974. STUDENT DISSENT IN PERSPECTIVE   (VT)
New York State Education Department   10 programs   60 min.
each   s/c/a
Instructor: Len Post, New York State Education Department
> The perspective includes racial problems, curriculum de-
> velopment, censorship, school administration, teacher
> methodology, student evaluation, positive action, topics.

1975. TIME MACHINE SERIES, THE   (VC)
Video Communications, Inc.
> A videocassette "History of America in the Twentieth Cen-
> tury," this series contains many speeches, conferences,
> campaigns, election highlights.

1976. TWO OLD MEN: NOAH AND SOCRATES   (VC)
Video Center
From the Miscellaneous Series
> Orson Welles parodies both Noah and Socrates, with read-
> ings and philosophical comments about their concepts.

1977. UNDER THE CLOUDS OF WAR   (VC)
Time-Life   20 min.   color
> Part of the "March of Time" Series, this unit includes a
> fight for peace; Mussolini's invasion of Ethiopia; Hitler's
> march into Austria.

1978. WAY BACK WHEN   (VC)
Video Communications, Inc.
> The series includes, "The War," "American Normalcy,"
> "Heroes," "The Big Bang."

1979. WHAT IS THE GOOD LIFE: ARISTOTLE   (VT)
CHITVC   WTTW-TV   Great Plains Instructional Television
45 min.   2-inch   b/w   C

1980. WHAT IS VIRTUE: ARISTOTLE   (VT)
CHITVC   WTTW-TV   Great Plains Instructional Television
45 min.   2-inch   b/w   C

THERAPY

1981. ADDICTION (VC)
        Video Communications, Inc.
            Some of these titles appear to be pertinent to communica-
            tion concepts. They include: Encounter I, II; and Any-
            body Else Who's Listening (See entry number 642).

1982. COMMUNICATION: CONCEPT AND SKILL (VT)
        Video Nursing WTTW-TV 1968 44 min. 2-inch b/w
        From the Nursing in Psychiatry Series
            Basic concepts of communication are utilized by the nurse
            to understand and to increase skills in therapy.

1983. COMMUNICATION IN THE NURSE-PATIENT RELATIONSHIP
        (VT)
        Video Nursing WTTW-TV 1968 44 min. 2-inch b/w
        From the Nursing in Psychiatry Series
            The application of problem-solving approach in communi-
            cation and the interviewing process between nurse and pa-
            tient is examined.

1984. COUNSELING THE ADOLESCENT (VT/VC)
        Great Plains Instructional Television 10-30 min. programs
        b/w
        Instructor: Dr. Rudolf Dreikurs
            This series is aimed at professionals who spend most of
            their time counseling adolescents. Titles include: 1.
            The Democratic Evolution of Society; 3. Group Discussion
            with Normal Teenagers; 4. Juvenile Delinquency; 10. Case
            Studies.

1985. INTERPRETING BODY LANGUAGE IN EVERYDAY PRACTICE
        (VC)
        Professional Research, Inc VCI 60 min. color
        Instructor: Dr. Gordon Deckert, Chrmn., Dept. of Psychia-
        try and Behavioral Sciences, University of Oklahoma Health
        Sciences Center

1986. NEED FOR DIALOGUE, THE (VT)
        KQED-TV National Instructional Television 30 min. 2-inch
        C
        From the Drugs: Children Are Choosing Series
            See entry number 1709.

1987. TRANSACTIONAL ANALYSIS FOR THE PRACTICING PHYSI-
        CIAN (VC)
        Professional Research, Inc. VCI 60 min. color
        Instructor: Dr. Gordon Deckert, Chrmn., Dept. of Psychia-
        try and Behavioral Sciences, University of Oklahoma Health
        Sciences Center.

PART III

SIMULATIONS/GAMES

SIMULATIONS/GAMES

ARGUMENT

1988. CONFIGURATION
Wff 'n Proof   s/c/a
Players: one
The object of the game is to increase reasoning abilities.

1989. DRUG DEBATE, THE
Didactic Systems   Academic Games   45 min. per debate
s/c/a
Players   6-35
In this structured debate, opposing viewpoints are presented concerning the legalization or prohibition of many
drugs and related products in use today.   Winning or los-
ing the game is determined by the relative effectiveness
in changing the group's opinions about these products.
The purpose is to encourage informative, "reasoned," and
unemotional discussion.   An evaluation "instrument," a
coding system, enables assessment of the effectiveness of
the debate strategies.

1990. GAME OF MODERN LOGIC, THE
Laymen E. Allen   Wff 'n Proof
Teaching logic skills to law students is the object of this
simulation activity.

1991. INNOCENT UNTIL
Abt Games   Games Central   5-11 hours   s/a
Players: 24-32
This is a role-play simulation which recreates the courtroom drama of a trial by jury.   Players express their
feelings on important issues, make key decisions, gain
knowledge of judicial procedures and terminology.   The
case is one of manslaughter; the parts are played by a
judge, attorneys, key participants, witnesses, jury members.

1992. INQUEST
Didactic Systems
Players: 2 or more
Participants practice common and subtle errors in the
process of scientific inquiry.   The goal is to examine

experimental evidence to determine in which of two models the evidence belongs. Examined are observing, measuring, interpreting concepts.

1993. JURY GAME
Social Studies School Service   2-3 hours   s/a
Players: 25-35
The game examines an important aspect of a "fair trial," --the right of an accused person to be judged by an impartial jury. In a role-play simulation of the jury selection process, players explore the nature of prejudice, examine critical thinking skills, question strategies. Players become judges, attorneys, prospective jurors, clerk reporters, observers. The object is to select a jury of 6, 8, 10 or 12 jurors plus one alternate juror, all of whom will render a "fair" verdict in the case.

1994. MOOT
Impact
Players attempt to solve three legal cases during mock trials. Crimes are simulated, the cases are taken to court, theories and practices are applied. Subjects are drugs, delinquency, civil law and juveniles.

1995. QUERIES AND THEORIES
Wff 'n Proof Learning Games Associates   s/c/a
Players: two or more
This is essentially a linguistics game involving argument and the relationship of science and language, "a simulation of the scientific methods and generative grammars." Players use inductive reasoning; gain skills in organizing, analyzing, synthesizing data.

1996. TRIAL
Adult Leisure Products Corporation
Players: 6 or more
For those interested in argument, players assume roles of prosecution, defense, witnesses, judge and jury. A case is tried as it develops from key bits of evidence. The prosecution team invents the case against the accused: the defense team invents "its own side of the story."

1997. TRI-NIM: THE GAME FOR COMPLEAT STRATEGISTS
Wff 'n Proof
Players: 2-3
The fourth "R"--reasoning--is stressed in this analytical game. Using mathematical and strategic implications, players solve problems involving technical decisions.

1998. VERDICT II
Avalon II   s, possibly c

Players debate court cases. Controlled conditions "do not permit much debate training."

1999. WFF 'N PROOF
Wff 'n Proof   s/c
Players: 2-6
A game of "modern logic" which offers practice in abstract thinking. A twenty-one-game kit, the majority deal with symbolic logic opportunities: the rules of inference, logical proofs and the nature of formal systems.

BUSINESS/ORGANIZATIONAL

Management

2000. DECISION GUIDES
Didactic Systems
Players: 4 to 5 teams
This game is designed to help managers clarify philosophies of leadership and of management. Participants resolve problems pertaining to common leadership/management situations and then explore principles applied to arrive at their decisions.

2001. DECISION MAKING
Didactic Systems   approx. 2-1/2 hours
Players: unlimited number of teams; 3-5 players per team
Management decisions involve risk evaluation, development of opportunities, various other management programs. In the course of the game, participants are expected to clarify their philosophy of management and to develop an approach toward continuing personal development. Roles: members of a management team.

2002. EFFECTIVE DELEGATION
Didactic Systems   approximately 3 hours
Players: unlimited number of teams; 3-5 players per team
This exercise provides managers, management trainees and upper-level supervisors with opportunities to exchange ideas on various delegation styles. Roles: department managers.

2003. EFFECTIVE SUPERVISION
Didactic Systems   3 hours
Players: 3-5 per team
This exercise is designed to help supervisors, foremen and managers improve management skills. It attempts to define objectives, set priorities, integrate goals, teach communications with superior and subordinates, examine attitudes toward work groups. Roles: supervisors.

2004. EXECUTIVE DECISION
Didactic Systems
Players: 2-6
   Players purchase raw materials, manufacture goods,
   market them for profit.

2005. EXECUTIVE SIMULATION, THE
Didactic Systems nine 1- 2-hour sessions or 3-day seminar
Players: 3-8 teams per industry; 3 to 5 players per team
   This computerized general management game provides an
   opportunity to give managers an exercise in decision-
   making for finance, production and marketing. It is designed for upper- and middle-level managers.

2006. EXERCISE SUPERVISE
Didactic Systems   2-4 hours
Players: 4-12
   Analyzed are the effects of various leadership "styles" on
   the performance of a task and satisfaction derived from
   performing it. The "styles" include the participatory,
   persuasive and coercive.

2007. GOAL-SETTING GAME, THE
Didactic Systems
Players: 3-man team
   In this game teams compete in achieving or surpassing a
   goal set by top management. It provides an opportunity
   for participants to examine the nature of goal setting,
   procedures for establishing standards with subordinates.

2008. LEADERSHIP GAME, THE
Didactic Systems
   Participants explore the organization structure, leadership and "followship" in that structure. "Supervisors"
   and "subordinates" are teamed up to complete a project.
   Each team competes to complete it. After completion,
   discussion centers on the role of the supervisor in getting
   the work done by delegation to others, the need for planning and how to reduce conflicts and increase communication.

2009. LEADING GROUPS TO BETTER DECISIONS
Didactic Systems   3-1/2 hours
Players: 3-5 per team
   Managers and executives improve skills as conference
   leaders in problem-solving and decision-making situations.
   Decisions involve: defining the problem; premature solu-
   tions; obtaining relevant facts from inferences; participa-
   tion in the group; coping with obstacles; communication.

2010. LOW BIDDER: THE GAME OF MANAGEMENT STRATEGY
Entelek s/a
Players: 2-26
   To teach strategy of selecting jobs on which there are

apt to be relatively few bidders, to estimate personnel problems, to anticipate competition--these are some of the management situations examined in this simulation activity.

2011. MANAGEMENT
Avalon Hill   s/c
Players: 2-4
The neophyte is given an introduction to "realistic employment situations."

2012. MANAGEMENT FOR SUPERVISORS
Didactic Systems   approx. 3 hours
Players: 3-5 per team
For the improvement of management skills by supervisors, decisions involve: objectives, preparing goals, communications with superiors and subordinates, leadership styles. Roles: supervisors.

2013. MANAGEMENT IN A FOREIGN COUNTRY
Didactic Systems   3 hours
Players: 3-5 per team
This exercise is intended to assist with the "sensitization" of managers to the cultural differences prior to assuming positions in a foreign country, and to provide a framework for exploring various approaches to transfer problems.

2014. MANAGEMENT IN GOVERNMENT
Didactic Systems   3-4 hours
Players: 3-5 per team
This is a composite simulation drawing from other exercises. Decisions involve: delegation, motivation, obstacles, communication. Roles: directors.

2015. MANAGEMENT SIMULATION AND SEMINAR
Didactic Systems   s/c
Players: 12-100
Players learn theories and practice. Application of personnel stresses the human side of enterprise, insight through feedback from team members.

2016. MANAGEMENT STYLES PROFILE
Didactic Systems   3 hours
This is a survey feedback analysis designed to help managers increase their overall effectiveness by making them more aware of the total work environment in which they function. Survey questionnaires are used.

2017. MANAGEMENT THROUGH FACE-TO-FACE COMMUNICATION
Didactic Systems   3 hours total
Players: 3-5 per team
This simulation is in two parts. Both provide middle managers the opportunity to practice communication

skills. Decisions in Part I involve perception in differences in meaning, working with abstractions, tailoring
messages to the receivers, separating fact from inferences, handling rumors, improving downward communication. Part II decisions involve giving assignments effectively.

2018. OFFICE MANAGEMENT
Didactic Systems   approx. 3 hours
Players: 3-5 per team
This simulation is a government version of "Management
for Supervisors," adapted to the environment, language
and problems of the Civil Service Commission. Roles:
participants are supervisors responsible for office services in a medium-sized organization.

2019. PROSPER
Didactic Systems   2-3 hours
Players: any multiple of 6 participants
A simulation exercise aims at increasing managers'
awareness of race-related problems in the work environ-
ment.

2020. STYLES OF LEADERSHIP DECISION GAME
Roundtable
Designed to be used with the film "Styles of Leadership,"
this game outlines three major elements to consider in
choosing leadership style. The game enables managers
to practice skills by selecting the most appropriate leadership style based on sixteen situations presented.

2021. SUPERVISORY SKILLS
Didactic Systems   2 hours
Players: 3-5 per team
Supervisors and trainees sharpen their managerial skills.
Decisions concern planning, goals, communication, both
upward and downward. Roles: supervisors.

2022. TRANSACTIONAL ANALYSIS--IMPROVING COMMUNICATIONS
Didactic Systems   3 hours
Players: unlimited number of teams; 3-5 players per team
This simulation covers analysis of and practice with the
three basic ego states. It also includes exercises on
recognizing complementary and crossed transactions, and
approaches for turning crossed transactions into more effective communications.

Negotiation

2023. COLLECTIVE BARGAINING
Didactic Systems   Science Research Associates   s/c
Players simulate the atmosphere and conditions that pre-

vail during negotiation of a new labor contract. Designed primarily for foremen, supervisors and managers to influence relations with members, the exercise dramatizes political and social forces at work. Role-playing: union negotiators, managers.

2024. EXERCISE NEGOTIATIONS
Didactic Systems   2-4 hours
Players˙ 4-12
This exercise examines the extent to which commitment to a group's strategy can seriously limit a negotiator's behavior. To illustrate, the "non-zero sum" nature of a bargaining situation is examined, where both sides can win or lose.

2025. GRIEVANCE HANDLING
Didactic Systems   2 hours
Players: 3-5 players per team
Supervisors and foremen practice handling of grievances. Decisions involve complaints about work overtime, a promotion and other conditions. Roles: recently-appointed supervisors.

2026. GRIEVANCE HANDLING (NON-INDUSTRIAL)
Didactic Systems   approx. 3 hours
Players: 3-5 players per team
Office managers in business, government and institutional organizations develop more thorough approaches to human relations in their department. Decisions involve a search for basic causes and disposition of various grievances and policies for reduction of incidence. Roles: office supervisors.

2027. HANDLING CONFLICT IN MANAGEMENT: CONFLICT AMONG PEERS
Erwin Rausch and Wallace Wohlking   Didactic Systems
2-3 hours
Players: unlimited number of teams; 5 per team
Participants are encouraged to discuss the defensive and other emotional reactions that arise--how to recognize them, how to deal with them, how to turn them toward constructive problem-solving. Roles: participants are supervisors in a factory.

2028. HANDLING CONFLICT IN MANAGEMENT: SUPERIOR/SUB-ORDINATE-GROUP CONFLICT (GAME I)
Didactic Systems   2-3 hours
Players: 4 per team
Decisions involve hostile reactions, dissension, planning strategies, polarized groups, impasses, selecting leadership patterns. Roles: managers.

2029. HANDLING CONFLICT IN MANAGEMENT: SUPERIOR/SUB-
       ORDINATE-GROUP CONFLICT (GAME II)
       Didactic Systems 2-3 hours
       Players: 5 per team
           Basic details are equivalent to Game I (see above).
           Roles are participants playing managers who are also
           proficient technical specialists.

2030. HANDLING CONFLICT IN MANAGEMENT: SUPERIOR/SUB-
       ORDINATE-GROUP CONFLICT (GAME III)
       Didactic Systems approx. 2-1/2 hours
       Players: 5 per team
           Decisions involve confrontation, reactions, defensiveness,
           evasiveness, withdrawal, dealing with hostile responses.
           Roles: participants are managers in a medium-sized
           company.

2031. MARKET NEGOTIATION MANAGEMENT GAME
       Didactic Systems
       Players: any number of teams; 5-8 players per team
           This exercise permits participants to take part in typical
           business negotiations. It illustrates the interdependence
           of firms in a distribution chain. Roles: manufacturers
           and distributors.

2032. SETTLE OR STRIKE
       Abt Associates approx. 8 hours s/c
       Players: 24-32 (6 to 8 teams)
           Each player is exposed to types of information important
           in successful collective bargaining, to practical problems
           that arise at the bargaining table and to strategic prob-
           lems important to both parties in achieving successful
           labor relations. Teams represent union and management
           bargainers.

2033. STRIKE: A SIMULATION OF LATE NINETEENTH CENTURY
       LABOR-MANAGEMENT RELATIONS
       Interact
           Players assume the roles of owners, managers, foremen
           or workers in one group. In the other group, there are
           the unemployed--immigrants, migrants, socialists, an-
           archists. Conflicts of interest occur between these
           groups. Phase I eventually ends in a strike, lockout or
           collective bargaining. In Phase II, players participate in
           contemporary collective bargaining sessions. Techniques
           in the two phases are compared.

2034. UNION ORGANIZING GAME
       Didactic Systems 4-6 hours
       Players: up to 36
           This simulation/training game deals with the subject of
           union organizing--why and how unions develop, employee
           organizing committees, recognition, picketing, etc. It

includes 20 different simulations based on organizing techniques.

Personnel Development

2035. ACADEMIC DEPARTMENT GAME, THE
Didactic Systems
> This game is designed to simulate decisions facing heads of academic departments in a university, such as teaching assignments, promotions, etc. Participants discuss and compare decisions. The exercise is intended as a training aid and not as an evaluative device. Participants may experiment with a variety of objectives.

2036. ACHIEVEMENT GAME, THE
Didactic Systems
> This game is designed to dramatize three principles relating to goal setting: that the high achiever is a moderate risk taker; that a manager must ask for goals that employees perceive as both challenging and attainable; that performance is improved if employees participate in setting goals that affect them or that they must meet.

2037. APPRAISAL BY OBJECTIVES (Coaching and Appraising)
Didactic Systems   approx.   3 hours
Players: 3-5 per team (teams unlimited)
> Practice in evaluating subordinates and coaching them in appraisal interviews is provided. Specific decisions involve: planning for the interview, evaluating objectives with qualitative and quantitative measurements, communicating about personal goals and preparation of a check list for performance appraisal by objectives. Roles: participants are managers in a department with sales-oriented as well as administrative functions.

2038. APPRAISAL GAME, THE
Didactic Systems (Sterling Institute)
> The class is divided into two groups, each with different tasks to complete. The first group must plan and produce a set of cards for mailing while the second group constructs a performance-appraisal sheet on which effectiveness and efficiency are measured. Criteria are established to evaluate progress and performance in meeting goals.

2039. ASSUMPTIONS GAME, THE
Training House   Didactic Systems   about 30 min.
Players: 6-20
> This game exercise is designed to demonstrate the principle of selective perception: that we see and interpret situations according to our own needs, interests, goals, values, past experience. Also examined is the subject

of prejudice, how it influences assumptions and vice
versa.

2040. BUY
Simile II
Players: 15-35
To learn concepts of inventory, sales, advertising, research and development, students role-play members of
a management team who must make decisions to maximize profit for the corporation.

2041. COMMUNICATING FOR RESULTS
Didactic Systems 3 hours total
Players: 3-5 players per team
This is a lower-level version of Managing Through Face-
to-Face Communication. This game provides an opportunity for supervisors to practice communication skills.
In Part I, decisions involve interpreting symbols, applying the "ladder of abstractions," gearing messages to
the receiver, classifying statements and responding to
emotional remarks. In Part II, decisions involve giving
assignments and instructions, handling rumors and "downward communications."

2042. COMMUNICATION
Educational Research s/c
Primarily a business game, it can be applied in the
teaching of communication in organization.

2043. COMMUNICATION GAME, THE
Training House Didactic Systems 60 min.
Players: 4-20 people, working in pairs
The objectives of this game are twofold: to give participants an opportunity to test their ability to explain their
thoughts in writing and to demonstrate that the effectiveness of written communication can be evaluated best on
the basis of results achieved.

2044. COMMUNICATION GAME, THE
Didactic Systems
Barriers to the effective flow of information are examined, as is the role of the employee in the communication process. Two exercises are presented: 1. Participants pass a message by word of mouth; 2. They document a message and deliver it. In the discussion that
follows, the communication process is discussed, with
successes and failures noted. Also highlighted are the
effect of feedback and how it encourages or inhibits communication.

2045. COMMUNICATIONS: PROBLEMS AND OPPORTUNITIES
Didactic Systems approx. 3 hours
Players: 3-5 players per team
The exercise is intended to assist managers with com-

munication problems. Specifically reviewed are: skills
in adapting messages to the needs of the receiver, responses to emotional statements, perception in recognizing inferences; upward communication ability. Roles:
participants are middle managers.

2046. CONFIDENCE BUILDING GAME, THE
Didactic Systems   1-2 hours
The class is divided into half, each given a different set
of tasks to complete which only the other half of the class
can help to perform. The objective is for participants to
recognize and seek help when and as needed, whom to
seek the help from and how to explain the problem or
situation in a way in which the other person can help.

2047. CREATIVITY EXERCISE
Didactic Systems   flexible amount of time
Players: 3-6 per group
Participants explore approaches to creativity. Included
are eighty match-stick puzzle arrangements and solution
sets and a leader's guide.

2048. EDPLAN
Abt Associates
This is a simulation of contemporary educational planning,
with participants playing the roles of instructors, administrators, elected officials, students, parents. Through
meetings of the PTA, School Board, City Council, members try to achieve respective organizational goals within
the prescribed budget.

2049. EMPLOYMENT MARKET
Information Resources   s/c/a
Players: 10-15
Learners become involved with both sides of job hunting:
locating the job, interviewing, training people.

2050. ENTERPRISE
Interact
Participants are divided into groups of bankers, businessmen, brokers, consumers, welfare poor, politicians,
lobbyists. These groups interact with one another, buying
and selling labor, capital and engaging in economic activities.

2051. EXERCISE ATTITUDES
Bernard M. Bass   Didactic Systems   2-4 hours
Players: 4-12
Trainees are encouraged to express and share with others
their concerns. Their expectations about work satisfaction are examined in regard to: material gain, interest,
leadership and procedures.

2052. EXERCISE COMMUNICATION
       Bernard M. Bass   Didactic Systems   2-4 hours
       Players: 4-12
           This role-playing exercise explores the advantages and
           disadvantages of one-way and two-way communication.
           To contrast effective and ineffective communication and
           account for differences, roles are given to observers,
           senders and receivers of communication.

2053. EXERCISE EVALUATION
       Bernard M. Bass   Didactic Systems   2-4 hours
       Players: 4-12
           This exercise provides an opportunity for the trainee to
           express feelings about the trainee program at a time
           when the problems may be dealt with. Trainees compare
           the intuitive with the systematic approach.

2054. EXERCISE OBJECTIVES
       Bernard M. Bass   Didactic Systems   2-4 hours
       Players: 4-12
           To permit examination of perceived organizational goals
           and the effects those perceptions have on decision-making,
           this exercise has as participants, managers of a small
           firm.

2055. EXERCISE ORGANIZATION
       Bernard M. Bass   Didactic Systems   1-4 hours
       Players: 4-12
           Explored are the problems involved in developing and ex-
           ecuting plans in large organizations. The focus is on the
           implication of intergroup competition and rivalry. Roles:
           workers.

2056. EXERCISE SUCCESS
       Bernard M. Bass   Didactic Systems   2-4 hours
       Players: 4-12
           Participants consider important factors for success in
           organizational life.

2057. LIFE CAREER
       Academic Games   1-6 hours
       Players: 2-20
           This exercise simulates certain features of the labor
           market, the "education market," and the "marriage mar-
           ket," as they now function in the United States and as
           projections indicate they may be in the future. During
           each decision period, players plan their schedule of ac-
           tivities for a typical week, allocating time for responsi-
           bilities.

2058. PETER PRINCIPLE GAME, THE
       Uniquity   Social Studies School Service   30 min.-1 hour
       Players: 4

This is a board game based on the principle that in a hierarchy, all people tend to rise to their levels of incompetence. The winner is the last to reach a level of incompetence, not the player who climbs highest. Players declared incompetent can no longer actively play. Based upon the Dr. Laurence Peter book by the same title.

2059. SELECTING EFFECTIVE PEOPLE
Didactic Systems   3 hours
Players: 3-5 per team
Practice includes various selection and interviewing techniques and preparation of procedures for use in future hiring. Roles: participants are managers in a medium-sized company.

2060. SIMULATED COMMUNITY TRAINING GAME
Roy Weston   c
Players: 1-30 in 1-6 teams
The purpose of this simulation activity is to train decision-makers.

2061. TO DEVELOP AND SHARPEN COMMUNICATION SKILLS
Didactic Systems
30-role kit
New employees sharpen skills in human relations and face-to-face communication. Simulations include: discussions between trainees/supervisors, caller/receiver, et al.

2062. WORK ASSIGNMENT
Didactic Systems   approx. 3 hours
Players: 3-5
Supervisors develop better approaches for assigning work to subordinates. Decisions involve: evaluating employee's performance; communicating job assignments to subordinates and reviewing approaches. Roles: supervisors.

2063. WORK GAME, THE
Didactic Systems
This game helps new employees understand what a company is all about. During the game, planned and unplanned obstacles are put in a way of production. On completion, discussion focuses on the need for establishing work standardization, need for supervision, group morale, performance.

2064. WRITING GAME, THE
Didactic Systems
All members of a "department" observe their supervisor role-play with a supervisor of another "department" who has lured his best worker into joining that department. Each observer then writes a memo to the personnel manager from his supervisor's point of view. After exchang-

ing memos across departmental lines and applying "writing inventory criteria," participants receive scored, edit memos and discuss effectiveness.

Sales

2065. MARKET STRATEGY
       Didactic Systems   3 hours
       Players: 3-5 per team
            This exercise is for managers with sales and marketing responsibilities to explore various approaches to more effective market strategy planning. Roles: marketing managers.

2066. PRINCIPLES OF EFFECTIVE SALESMANSHIP
       Didactic Systems   3 hours
       Players: 3-5 per team
            Assistance with the development of presentations shows how their products or services can meet needs. The sales approach, checklist and strategies are all discussed.

2067. SALES GAME
       Didactic Systems   2 hours
       Players: 3-5 players per team
            An executive with sales responsibility can practice campaign management skills. Designed to stimulate "better understanding of the selling process," the game can be played three different ways: "in its entirety in a single day, in installments or through the mail."

2068. SALES PROMOTION
       Didactic Systems   2 hours
       Players: 3-5 per team
            Central opportunities in sales promotion are highlighted. Decisions involve: organizational opportunities; risk evaluation of alternatives; selling the sales promotion activity within the company and methods for measuring promotion function. Roles: newly-appointed sales promotion managers.

2069. SALES STRATEGY
       Didactic Systems   1-2 hours
       Players: 3-5 per team
            Salesmen review and improve skills. Decisions concern planning, prospecting, training and strategies. Roles: newly-appointed district managers.

2070. SALESMANSHIP IN ACTION
       Didactic Systems   1-1/2 hours
       Players: 3-5 players per team
            To improve selling skills, this game presents typical selling situations worked into a schedule. The salesman

learns the importance of planning his time to earn the
maximum sales dollar potential.   Roles: salesmen.

CROSS-CULTURAL

2071. BAFA BAFA
Social Studies School Service   1-2 hours
This is a simulation game on the meaning and characteristics of culture, designed to give participants experience
in observing and interacting with a different culture.
Players are divided into an Alpha and Beta group or "culture." Alpha is a relaxed culture which values personal
contact and intimacy; Beta is an aggressive money-ori-
ented culture which measures worth by how well someone
performs in the marketplace.   Observers from each are
involved and visitors are exchanged.

2072. BALANCE: A SIMULATION OF SHORT-RANGE ECONOMIC-
GOALS VERSUS LONG-RANGE ENVIRONMENTAL GOALS
Interact
Players are divided into families of four members each
and live in Ecopolis, an expanding city with many ecological problems.   Participants study the problems of pollu-
tion, land usage, population problems and decide whether
or not each problem necessitates social action.

2073. BLACK EXPERIENCE, THE
Uniquity
An American history game, this exercise includes a
board designed for 1-4 players.   Each player begins as
a slave and works up to the present, encountering along
the way obstacles and challenges of varying degrees.

2074. BLACK AND WHITES
Psychology Today   1-2 hours or more   s/c
Players: 2-7
Designed to give middle-class white students the feeling
of urban "helplessness," the exercise permits role-identi-
fication and neighborhood involvement.   Players choose
either "black" or "white" roles with the specific object of
buying and controlling property.   The game affords "experiences" in ghetto life, welfare, attempts to buy into
white suburbs, redistribution of wealth, power and
"shakeups" of the status quo.

2075. CITIES GAME, THE
Pyschology Today   one hour or longer
Players: 4-8
To simulate the realities of urban life, this game of urban
tension and negotiations permits "secret deals," economic
"muscle," "vote-buying,"--all to explore the psychology
of power and politics.   There are four power roles:

business, government, slum dwellers and agitators. Each
vies for stronger positions in a city. If the power group
cannot solve its problems, it destroys the city.

2076. COFFEE GAME, THE
Teleketics
A set of three posters makes up an effective simulation
activity for developing a consciousness concerned with
peace and justice. The focus is on the inequalities of the
coffee trade between the United States and the Latin American countries. The wide-ranging complexities of the
problem lead to an awareness of difficulties involved.

2077. COMMUNITY DECISION GAMES
Social Studies School Service   4 games
This series deals with interest groups, value conflicts
and consensus within an urban community. Each game is
designed to help participants anticipate, understand, and
deal with conflicts over community problems. Subjects
range from school problems to budgets and taxes.

2078. CRISIS
Western Behavioral Institute   Simile II   40 min.   s/c/a
Players: 18-36
In this simulation of international conflict, participants
manage affairs of six fictional nations. Challenges include alliances, world police forces, commissions, negotiations.

2079. CULTURE CONTACT
Abt Associates   1-2 hours
Players: 30
This simulation is designed to study the potential for conflict when two very different cultures are brought together. Playing the roles of a trading expedition and a non-
industrial island tribe, participants decide whether the
visiting culture may remain on the island and under what
terms.

2080. DIG
Interact   s/c
Using anthropological techniques, this game concerns the
interrelations of cultural patterns.

2081. DIGNITY
Social Studies School Service
This human relations game seeks to portray the frustrations of people in the ghettos. Its object is to reach a
square called Dignity. To get there, a player tries to
avoid Shanty Town, Housing projects, Skid Row and other unpleasant places. Players encounter setbacks as
well as unanticipated opportunities.

2082. DIPLOMACY
Games Research Interact 2-4 hours s/c
Players: 3-7
Players attempt to gain supremacy over Europe through
negotiations and intrigue. Students assume the roles of
"Great Powers" prior to World War I. Bargaining or
joining military conversations takes place as to rumors
and threats. Written orders are completed in private,
after which all players read them aloud and follow directions.

2083. GAME OF BRINKSMANSHIP, THE
Interact 3-5 hours
Players: 20-45
Two superpowers, the United States and Russia, are involved in several Cold War crises. Players must decide
how to handle each as negotiators are forced into confrontation and must develop proposals for compromise.

2084. GHETTO
Academic Games Didactic Systems 2-4 hours s/a
Players: 7-10
Simulations involve the pressures under which the urban
poor live and the choices that face them. Each player is
given a fictional personal profile. He allocates his time
among several alternatives: work, play, school, crime,
"passing time," and neighborhood improvement.

2085. GRAND STRATEGY
Abt Associates 1-2 hours s/a
Players: 11-30
This is a role-play simulation of international relations
and diplomacy in Europe just prior to the outbreak of
World War I. Players represent heads of state, ministers of war and foreign ministers for ten nations who
negotiate or make war, with changes in strategy caused
by growing participation of the United States and the Russian Revolution. It is designed to develop an understanding of alliances, coalitions, agreements and treaties.

2086. IMPACT
Instructional Simulation s/a
Players: 20-40
This is a group simulation showing selected community
action and problem-solving situations to illustrate how individual and collective actions affect an imaginary community, its institutions, associations, residents. Each
person is supplied with biographical information, member-
ships in various groups and differential involvement in
key community issues based on newspaper analysis.

2087. INTER-COMMUNITY SIMULATION, THE
       Department of Political Science, University of Southern Cali-
       foria c/a
       Players: 6
             Factors are represented and analyzed that effect decision-
             making patterns in multi-county economic development
             districts. The purpose is to investigate bargaining be-
             havior (process) and bargaining results (outcome).

2088. INTERNATIONAL SIMULATION
       Science Research Associates s/c
       Players: 20-36
             A simplified system represents nations and an interna-
             tional organization. Participants are given the experience
             of making decisions in a miniature prototype of the com-
             plicated international world. Simulation activity involves
             trade, forming coalitions, waging war. Each nation is
             given information about its wealth, form of government,
             defense position, population and basic resources. Using
             this information, leaders of each nation plan goals and
             strategies.

2089. LIFE IN ISRAEL
       Creative Studies, Inc. c/a
       Players: 3-20
             Players experience cross-cultural training for absorption
             in Israel.

2090. MYTHIA: A WORLD AFFAIRS SIMULATION
       American Institute for Research s/c/a
       Players: 8-40 (teams of 8)
             Simulation activity objectives include the development of
             "international perceptivity." The aim is to develop co-
             operative attitudes toward international endeavors.

2091. NEW TOWN
       Harwell Association 2 hours or more s/c
       Players: 4 or more (2-5 teams)
             Participants consider political and economic forces in the
             development of urban areas. The "New Town" encour-
             ages players to build a city by buying property for house-
             es, businesses, industries. Each player must weigh per-
             sonal interests against the best interests of the communi-
             ty.

2092. POTLATCH PACKAGE
       Abt Associates s/a
       Players: 30
             This exercise centers on the potlatch ritual, a way of
             life of the Kwakiutl Indians of the Pacific Northwest.
             The social organization is introduced by the game "Open-
             ing the Deck," which uses profile cards to show the kin-
             ship and status forms of the tribe. "Mini-Ethnography

of the Kwatiutl; the Potlatch Game," uses tokens representing trade goods to recreate this social and economic
institution.

2093. SANGA
Interact
Players: 35
> This is a simulation of the Dogon tribe's village life in
> Mali, West Africa. Players role-play a village divided
> into six family units, with each household having speci-
> fied goals to reach which are representative of Dogon life.

2094. SECURITY
Institute of Communication Research   University of Illinois
s/c/a
Players: 20 (2 teams)
> Attempts to show the results of different strategies of
> "graduated and reciprocated initiatives." It demonstrates
> usefulness in tension reduction and concerns specifically
> different international strategies.

2095. SIMULATION: THE DECISION-MAKING MODEL
World Affairs Council of Philadelphia
> Participants play roles of decision-makers for five hypo-
> thetical countries with a wide range of resources. The
> object is to try to improve their nation's domestic and in-
> ternational position. Explained are ways in which poli-
> tics, diplomacy and economics are considered.

2096. SITTE
Western Behavioral Institute Simile II 2-4 hours s/c
Players: 10-35
> Five interest groups attempt to effect changes in a city
> through the use of influence and discussion: business,
> the disenfranchised, government, ad hoc committees, tax-
> payers' associations.

2097. SUNSHINE
Interact
Players: 35
> Players research ways of resolving current racial prob-
> lems. In a simulation of current minority problems in a
> "typical" American city, players are "born" by choosing
> race-identity tags. The class is divided into a mythical
> city with six neighborhoods, with varying degrees of seg-
> regation and integration in housing and schooling. Pre-
> and post-attitude tests on racial "tolerance" are indica-
> tors of the results of the experience.

2098. TELECITY
Applied Simulations International s, possibly c
Players: 25-75
> In the operation of a simulated city, players make deci-

sions concurrently and collaboratively to accomplish self-determined individual and/or group strategies.

2099. THEY SHOOT MARBLES, DON'T THEY
Didactic Systems   2-3 hours
Players: 25-30
During a process of developing an urban community, players are encouraged to experiment with rule-governed behavior, governmental structures, law enforcement policies and problems of wealth distribution.

2100. TRACTS
Instructional Simulations
Players: 20-40
A socio-political simulation, the game illustrates controversy inherent in core city land use. The object of the simulation involves compromise and negotiation. Strategies include political decision-making and land use.

2101. TRANSIT
Instructional Simulations
Players: 20-40
This is an urban transportation and traffic simulation which shows "professional planners" and citizens negotiating concerning freeways, traffic flow, mass transit concepts.

2102. URBAN AMERICA
Social Studies School Service   10 hours   s/a
Players: 20-36
This simulation deals with problems and crises faced by American cities. As residents of four neighborhoods in a small city, players make decisions and elect a city council to deal with problems of low income, busing, environment.

2103. URBAN GAMES
Didactic Systems
Players: one game set;   10 players' manuals
Four priming games are designed to explain the subjects of community issues, rapid transit, industrial part development, regional shopping centers.

2104. WORLD GAME
Teleketics
Players: minimum 25
In this two-stage simulation, key people in five countries struggle for solutions to common problems. Delegates are sent to a world council for consensus solutions.

DYADIC

2105. ABELSON-BAKER INTERVIEW, THE
        Didactic Systems
                The objective of this game is improvement in concepts
                and skills associated with interpersonal communications.

2106. COMPATIBILITY
        Uniquity
        Players: 2-4 couples
                A couple of real life situations in which couples respond
                simultaneously are simulated. Each predicts the response
                of his/her partner.

2107. COUPLES
        Uniquity
                This series of games contains simulations ranging from
                fantasy games to playful imagery. The participants may
                change games as they change partners. For example,
                there are role-playing games where one may be a gypsy
                fortune-teller or a contestant on the 300th hour of a dance
                marathon. Each tries to get the partner to do the work.

2108. IMPROVE INTERPERSONAL COMPETENCE
        Didactic Systems   48 role-play kit
                This kit contains teaching materials for the concepts of
                face-to-face communication, human relations, conflict res-
                olution. It is a "role-playing collection" of organization
                problems: discipline, training, delegation, failures to
                communicate.

2109. INTERVIEWING
        Boston   South End Community Center   s/c
                This game is about job application interviews.

2110. INTERVIEWING
        Didactic Systems
        Players: teams of 4 players
                Practice is provided in interviewing, primarily to select
                applicants for a position. Decisions involve job specifica-
                tions, starting the interview and in-depth interviewing.
                Roles: personnel executives.

2111. JOHN AND GEORGE INTERVIEW, THE
        Didactic Systems
                Participants listen to a tape recording of an interview be-
                tween John, a supervisor, and George, an employee whose
                production has fallen behind. Participants follow the dia-
                logue for subsequent discussion.

FAMILY

2112. FAMILY COMMUNICATION GAMES, THE
       YMCA Training Consultation, Detroit
              This is an experimental model of a training program for
              a "leaders' meeting" of a simulated family.

2113. FAMILY GAME, THE
       CRM Company
              The object of this game is to "refresh contacts between
              members of a family."

2114. F. L. I. P.
       Instructional Simulations   time varies   s/c
       Players: 1-30
              This is a socio-economic simulation with didactic units
              which deal with problems of investment, credit and inter-
              est in terms of changing family goals.   Twenty different
              families are available as units, each illustrating roles of
              size, income, education and socio-economic variables.

2115. GENERATION GAP
       Social Studies School Service   1-1-1/2 hours   s/possibly c
       Players: 4-10
              Interaction is simulated between a parent and an adoles-
              cent with respect to certain issues on which they have
              opposing attitudes.   Conflict is presented within a context
              of rules which reflect "the structure of power and inde-
              pendence in a family."   The purpose is to emphasize that
              "conflicts can be ventilated through communication."

2116. PARENT-CHILD
       Academic Game Associates   Johns Hopkins University
              The relationship between a parent and an adolescent is
              simulated in respect to five issues which are perceived
              differently by both.

FREEDOMS

2117. AMERICAN CONSTITUTIONAL CONVENTION
       Science Research

2118. HANG-UP
       Unitarian Universalist Association   s/c
              In this game, designed to promote empathy and tolerance,
              each player is dealt seven "hang-ups."   To attempt to un-
              derstand white racist attitudes, each player becomes a
              black person or a white person.   Players attempt to re-
              act to the "stress" situations.

2119. LIBERTE
Social Studies School Service   s/c
The aim of this game is to analyze economic, social, political backgrounds of the French Revolution.   Players
are divided into five French socio-economic groups: roy-
alty, clergy, nobles, bourgeoisie and peasants.   Role
identification, daily taxation, tithing, trading and conflict
push factions toward revolution.   Debates before the National Assembly concern the great issues of the Revolution.

2120. MICRO-COMMUNITY
Interact
While players study history, they form their own "micro"
community, in which they organize themselves and take
cooperative actions paralleling material studied.   Players
assume responsibility of government and business, create
rules, and their own "Bill of Rights."

2121. NINE MEN PLUS
William C. Brown Co.   one hour or more   s/c
Players: 3 or more
Players read evidence upon which past Supreme Court decisions concerning speech were based.   Then they act as
justices and decide who won.   There is also opportunity
for players to try to persuade other participants that they
should vote differently.   Points are scored for determining the outcome correctly.

2122. PLEA BARGAINING: A GAME OF CRIMINAL JUSTICE
Social Studies School Service   4 one-hour sessions   s/c
Players: 4-35
In this simulation players view the pressures of limited
time and mounting caseloads on the workings of criminal
justice.   Players take on the roles of public defenders,
district attorneys, judges and defendants within the criminal justice system of a large city.

2123. POWER VERSUS FREEDOM
Social Studies School Service   s/a
A short simulation lasting three or four class periods
asks players to develop a government, solving problems
of group survival.   Solutions lead to the identification of
the elements of government and the values of the society
which formulated the government.

2124. 1787: A SIMULATION GAME OF THE CONSTITUTIONAL
CONVENTION
Social Studies School Service
This game helps players to understand the conflicting in-
terests involved during the creation of the U.S. Constitu-
tion.   The object of the game is to produce a Convention
document which subsequently is compared with the U.S.
Constitution.

2125. YES, BUT NOT HERE
       Macmillan s/possibly c
       Players: 20-40 (45 teams)
            To achieve an understanding of a particular public housing
            problem, participants analyze bias. Teams become
            "sensitive to the conflict of public good and private inter-
            est."

GROUP DISCUSSION

2126. AGENDA: A SIMULATION OF DECISION-MAKING IN A
       CHURCH ASSEMBLY
       Didactic Systems 2-4 hours
       Players: 18-39 participants
            People learn to work together more effectively in large
            groups. Players assume roles of delegates and lobbyists
            at the annual meeting of the highest policy-making body of
            their denomination. Practical skills are offered in nego-
            tiation, confrontation, political strategy, public speaking
            and parliamentary procedure.

2127. CAN OF SQUIRMS
       Contemporary Drama Service all ages
            This discussion-starter game is adaptable either for a
            one-to-one situation or for group discussion. It can be
            used as a teaching tool or played as a competitive game.
            Every package includes game, guide and 100 discussion
            concepts. Ideas and materials for customizing to indi-
            vidual needs are included. There are specific versions
            for college students.

2128. COLLEGE GAME
       Ronald Short, Whitworth College s/c
       Players: 3
            To stimulate discussion areas, this game provides orien-
            tation for freshmen. The goal is to "break down the so-
            cial and emotional barriers between the students and the
            faculty."

2129. CONFRONTATION
       Adult Leisure Products Corporation Creative Communications
       and Research 30 min.-3 hours, 30 min.
       Players: 4 to 7
            Interaction is the concern of this game of "students and
            protestors against the establishment." The theme is
            based on the student protest movement. Students assume
            the roles of either protestors or establishment types. In
            a series of rounds, demands are made, either accepted
            or rejected, with subsequent periods of discussion and
            negotiation. If the latter fails, a "confrontation" may be
            called which could produce either peaceful protest or riot-
            ing. The game can be played either competitively or for
            discussion purposes only.

2130. DEELIE BOBBERS
Didactic Systems   3-4 hours (creativity exercises);   1 hour (simple exercises)
Players: up to 24 participants
An introductory-device construction game enhances the understanding of group processes and group dynamics. The game attempts to increase the ability of the participants to develop unusual and imaginative approaches to problem-solving. Both simple decision-making and creative exercises are included.

2131. HIDDEN AGENDAS
Didactic Systems
Players: 5-participant set
This role-play situation involves five different roles, designed to dramatize the impact of hidden agendas on a small group meeting. The particular situation is a conference between a field manager and his men.

2132. INITIATIVE GAME, THE
Didactic Systems
Participants learn that "initiative is the mark of success." Each is assigned five problems to solve. They discover that as problems become more complex they must take the initiative to work with others to explore efficiently and arrive at a solution. Post-game discussion highlights individual versus group approaches to problem-solving; the need for initiative in arriving at solutions to complex problems, and the importance of contributions from all group members.

INFORMATION SYSTEMS

2133. BEAT THE COMPUTER
CCM Company s/c/a
Players are offered a simulated computer system through which they explore the unknowns of "hardware and software." Using real "programs," problems are solved by moving each set of cards.

2134. COMPUT-A-TUTOR
Didactic Systems flexible time
Players create flow charts, program decisions, become familiar with concepts. Roles: computer programmers.

2135. DATA CALL
Richard R. Johnson, Earlham College, Indiana c
Data Call is a computer-based simulation game for teaching research strategy.

2136. SIMULATION OF A COMPUTER
       North Idaho Jr. College   c
       Players: 1-30
              This simulation exercise is designed to increase under-
              standing of computer functions.

                              LANGUAGE

2137. FOIL
       The Three-M Company   s/possibly c
       Players: 2-4
              In this card game, related to Scrabble, participants are
              dealt cards with letters on them.   Points are scored by
              forming words from the letters.   Words are then scram-
              bled and players attempt to unscramble their opponents'
              words.

2138. ON-WORDS
       Wff 'n Proof   s/c/a
              This game encompasses virtually every conceivable aspect
              of words.   The authors hope it is an incentive for players
              to attend more closely to words and language, to seek in-
              formation and insights.   Letter cubes are shaken by indi-
              vidual players, goals are set, challenges are made.
              Other cubes (Resources, Forbidden, etc.) modify strate-
              gies.

2139. PASSWORD
       Milton Bradley   s/c/a
       Players: 4 to 7
              Several versions of this game exist.   Creative students
              can make up their own adaptations.   Team-playing per-
              mits each to decide which words will be used.   A mem-
              ber of a team is given a word and has a limited amount
              of time to communicate it to his partner without actually
              saying the word.   Points are awarded for correct guesses.

2140. SCRABBLE
       Selchow and Richter   2 hours or more   s/possibly c
       Players: ideally 4
              To sharpen vocabulary, players select randomly-drawn
              tiles.   Points are scored for various strategies involving
              the forming of words in crossword puzzle fashion.

2141. SCRABBLE: SENTENCE CUBE GAME
       Selchow and Richter
              A word game concentrates on the completion of sentences.
              Players roll out twenty-one word cubes and, with a time
              limit, piece them together into meaningful sentences.

2142. VERBAL GAME, THE
       Interact
              Players use standard card game techniques: prefix, root
              and suffix cards. The first person to make words with
              all his cards wins.

LEARNING THEORY

2143. ESP
       Uniquity 2-4 players
              This game helps test perceptive skills and powers of con-
              centration against those of our participants. If you have
              been able to develop extrasensory perception powers you
              may be successful in intercepting the "thought waves" of
              opponents.

2144. INSTRUCTION GAME, THE
       Didactic Systems
              In this game, participants are paired into teacher-learner
              teams. After a few minutes of instruction, roles are re-
              versed for a similar time period. Each "learner" then
              evaluates his "teacher." Thus, each participant, as in-
              structor, gains insight into strengths and weakness in
              face-to-face learning situations.

2145. SYSTEM I
       Instructional Systems Didactic Systems 20-40 min. s/c
       Players: 2-4
              Interaction is the concern of this game which reinforces
              learning of both subject matter content and structure.
              The System I format is based on behavioral learning tasks.
              Since content is controlled by the instructor, the game
              can be used equally well in all subject areas. Teaching
              concepts include "learning tasks at cognitive levels and
              curriculum linkage."

LISTENING

2146. LISTENING GAME, THE
       Didactic Systems
              The objective is to teach that listening is "functionally se-
              lective." Two men (on tape) discuss an issue. Before
              playing the tape, the instructor distributes six different
              sets of instructions to participants (participants believe
              they are receiving the same instructions). All listen to
              the taped conversation and answer the same questions,
              comparing answers. By examining all six sets and the
              four-page script of the taped discussion, participants are
              able to understand how "mental sets" and individual needs
              influence listening.

MASS MEDIA

2147. ADMAN
American Institute of Banking   c/a
   Public relations in banking is illustrated with effective
   advertising strategies designed by competing participants.

2148. INTERMEDIA
University Associates Press, Inc.
   Role-playing represents experiences based on teaching
   techniques in the study of journalism.

2149. MOVIE MOGULS
Research Games
Players: 2-6
   Participants battle other production companies for awards,
   dream up advertising campaigns, buy up contracts, com-
   pete as Hollywood producers.

MOVEMENTS: Women's

2150. FEMALE IMAGES
Instructional Simulation   2-3 hours   c/a
Players: 4-8
   An exercise in social identities, this is a five-part unit.
   It employs the workings of a group who jointly perform
   group-guided tasks in life-skill exercises.   Identities are
   treated as decisions and options in relation to self-ex-
   ploration: recognition, analysis, inquiry (decision-making),
   problem-solving, evaluation and appraisal.   Each step "is
   carefully designed for relevance to women."

2151. HERSTORY
Interact
Players: 35 maximum
   This is a simulation of male and female roles, emphasizing women's circumstances, past and present.   Through
   simulation, role-playing, discussion, players examine
   male-female role expectations.   Groups attack manners,
   marriage, jobs, achievement, nature concepts.   Contributions and hopes are evaluated.

2152. HE-SHE: HIM-HER
Hoi Polloi, Inc.
   An "anti-Women's Movement" exercise; male markers are
   bolts, female markers are wedding rings.   Women try to
   "get out of the kitchen."   Men try to keep them there.

2153. LIB GAME, THE
Creative Communication and Research Uniquity
Players: 4 to a large group
   This is an interaction game in which players take turns

assuming the roles of women involved in the women's liberation movement and of other groups affected by this
movement. A game consists of four rounds of discussion and voting. At the end of four rounds each participant will have played every role.

2154. PROFAIR
Didactic Systems
Players: multiple of 5 participants
Managers and professionals increase their awareness of
roles in the promotion or hindering of equal opportunities
for women at work.

2155. WOMAN AND MAN
Psychology Today 1-2 hours s/c
Players: 2-5
Participants play "as a man or as a woman." Moving
around the game board, players negotiate, debate and attempt to answer questions concerning roles society has
assigned. They can switch roles.

2156. WOMEN IN MANAGEMENT
Didactic Systems approx. 3 hours
Players: unlimited number of teams; 3-5 players per team
Participants deal with decisions concerning clarification
of issues, improving relationships with subordinates,
gaining acceptance of peers, handling business trips, dealing with superiors. Roles: newly-appointed managers
(female).

2157. WOMEN'S LIB
Urban Systems
Players: 4-7
Players discuss, debate, bargain, bribe and decide sig-
nificant women's liberation issues.

2158. WOMEN'S LIBERATION
Social Studies School Service
Part of a series of American Problems
An "Edu-game," #322, part of an innovative discussion-
game exercise.

NONVERBAL

2159. BODY TALK
Psychology Today Games 30 min.-1 hour s/c
Players: 2-10
Somewhat related to the old-time charades, this game of
nonverbal communication rewards participants who attempt
to express and receive emotions successfully without using words. Cards with emotions written on them are
dealt to players. They attempt to communicate these

emotions by using their entire bodies or parts of the
body. The object of the game is to "get rid of" cards
by expressing and receiving emotions effectively.

PERSUASION

2160. OPINION
Selchow and Richter
The object of this game is to make "judgments of fellow
players and convince others of these judgments."

2161. PROPAGANDA GAME, THE
Altatelic Instructional Materials   Wff 'n Proof   s/c
Players: two to four
Players learn professional techniques by listening to examples of propaganda and then try to determine what
technique the speaker is using. Inasmuch as the game
has varied levels of difficulty, players advance as they
increase in proficiency. Propaganda techniques include
public opinion inference, "bandwagon" appeals, faulty analogy, technical jargon, emotional appeals, "out of context" quotes, rationalization.

2162. PUBLIC OPINION
Public Opinion Quarterly   time: several class meetings   s/c
Players: any number
A group process game in which the players are assigned
roles. A complicated system of recording the opinions
of groups and individuals is applied. As the game pro-
gresses, participants may change their opinions on issues.
At the conclusion, "final" opinions are recorded and tal-
lied.

POLITICAL

Campaigns

2163. CAMPAIGN
Instructional Simulations   1-2 hours for each of 4 days
s/c/a
Players: 16-32
Participants become involved with a political simulation
of a state legislative race in a two-party system. Issues,
tactics, strategies, nominating committees, news coverage, vote switching and party workers are all factors af-
fecting the candidate's campaign. Stressed are "behavioral analysis of key campaign factors, campaign processes
and strategy building."

2164. COALITION: THE PRESIDENTIAL ELECTION GAME
Social Studies School Service   6-10 hours
Players: 16 to any number
Four candidates of different political ideologies compete
to form a winning coalition of interest groups, with each
interest group trying to elect the candidate most respon-
sive to its needs and concerns. Following the building of
platforms by each party and extensive campaigning, players hold a general election.

2165. CONVENTION
Games Research, Inc.
Players: 2-6
This game is a contest to win nomination for President
of the United States. Delegates, primaries, caucuses,
demonstrations are all a part of the candidates' activities.

2166. DEKALB POLITICAL SIMULATION
Marshal H. Whithel, Political Science, Rensselaer Polytech-
nic Institute   s/c
Players: 25-72 divided in 7 teams
The object of the game is to teach the actual dynamics of
an election campaign.

2167. DIVISION
Interact
Divided into four factions representing Lincoln, Douglas,
Breckenbridge and Bell, players study fourteen issues di-
viding America during the 1850s.

2168. ELECTION, USA
Education Games, Inc.
Players: 2-4
Players advance or gain votes by their ability to correctly answer questions on the constitution. Based on the
electoral college system, the object of the game is to win
the election by being the first candidate to obtain 270
electoral votes. Questions are categorized according to:
General, Executive, Judicial, Legislative (House of Representatives or Senate).

2169. HAT IN THE RING: THE PRESIDENTIAL NOMINATING
GAME
Social Studies School Service   s/possibly c
Players: 3-8
Players have the experience of trying to win a nomination
for President. Simulating travel from state to state,
players compete with opposing candidates for votes of
1,300 delegates to the National Convention. The game
leads to the Convention, with its caucuses and demonstrations and attempts to obtain delegate votes.

2170. NEXT PRESIDENT, THE
Reiss Associates   2-4 hours or longer   s/c
Players: 2-8
  Candidates are chosen in the primaries.   The election is
  decided by how well you win the party organization, campaign programs and advertising strategies.   Participants
  may play as historical figures or contemporary candidates.

2171. PRESIDENTIAL ELECTION CAMPAIGNS
Science Research

2172. REPUBLICAN NATIONAL NOMINATING CONVENTION
Cedar Rapids Community School District   s/possibly c
  Players are offered a chance to participate in meaningful
  life-like political events and share some of the experience, techniques and strategies of nomination.

2173. SIMPOLIS
Abt Associates   3-1/2 hours   s/a
Players: 30-50
  This is a simulation of a mayoral election, designed to
  introduce players to the major urban problems of trans-
  portation, civil rights, education.   An election is held.

2174. VOTE
Education Research Systems
  Players utilize a computer to investigate voting behavior
  in a variety of campaigns and legislative bodies.

2175. VOTES: A SIMULATION OF ORGANIZING AND RUNNING A
POLITICAL CAMPAIGN
Interact   3 weeks
Players: 25-35
  Simulating candidates, campaign staffs, voters, players
  conduct three-month campaign for president, congress,
  governor or local office.   Committee develops positions
  on key issues to improve their party's images.   Votes determine the winner of the final election.

The System

2176. CONFRONTATION: THE GAME OF PROTESTORS AGAINST
THE ESTABLISHMENT
Social Studies School Service   30 min.-1-1/2 hours
Players: 4-any number
  This game simulates a confrontation between players making change in the system and members of the Establishment.   In a series of rounds, participants make demands
  which are either accepted or rejected or alternate proposals made.   If negotiations fail, a "confrontation" may be
  called which could result in peaceful protest or a riot.

Players learn to understand issues and positions of different sides.

2177. CZAR POWER
Instructional Simulations   s/c/a
Players: 23-40
The basic social class system of Czarist Russia is replicated: the Czar, nobility, civil service, military, clergy, merchants, peasants.   Fourteen major problems present options for social classes.   Winning means gaining rewards that support czarism.

2178. DECISION-MAKING BY CONGRESSIONAL COMMITTEES
Science Research

2179. DEMOCRACY
Didactic Systems   30 min. -4 hours   s/c
Players   6-11
Participants learn of the relationship between the constituent's interests and legislators' actions.   Players assume the roles of legislators: give speeches, debate, negotiate, vote on issues.

2180. DESTINY
Interact
This historical simulation focuses on the American political situation during the period leading to the Spanish American War.

2181. DISUNIA
Interact
Players: 35 maximum
Divided into thirteen states on a new planet in 2087, players struggle with problems Americans became entangled in during the Articles of Confederation.   The simulation culminates in a constitutional convention with representatives.

2182. GOOD SOCIETY EXERCISE, THE
International Relations Program, Syracuse University   s/c
The thrust of this exercise is on communicating and bargaining, political process and urban conflicts.

2183. GRAPHIGRAMES
Social Studies School Service
Each game contains 90 player cards
Five games examine opinion surveys.   Each game contains three statements on which players must register opinions with stick-on labels.   Participants predict how the others will vote and then compare and discuss results of the survey.   Game divisions are: Political Attitudes; Attitudes about the Environment; Attitudes about War and Peace; Attitudes about Citizenship; Do-It-Yourself.

2184. ISLAND: A DEVELOPMENT GAME
       Social Studies School Service   2-5 hours
       Players: 7-24
              This simulation is designed to reflect economic and polit-
              ical conditions in a newly developing subtropical island.
              Players present conflicting political and material inter-
              ests; the island's government, the national labor force,
              a foreign bank, and three foreign companies operating on
              the island.

2185. LIE, CHEAT AND STEAL
       Uniquity
       Players: 6 or less
              This game allows you to decide how honest you want to
              be. It is possible to win by being scrupulously honest
              or by cheating--within the framework of the rules.   One
              wins by accumulating money and buying votes.   There
              are blackmail cards and protection cards to add interest.

2186. METROPOLITICS
       Social Studies School Service   Simile II   1 hour   s/c
       Players: 18-35
              Players assume the roles of citizens of a mythical coun-
              try who attempt to decide among four types of city gov-
              ernment for the study of local metropolitan government.
              Through persuasion and coalition-formation, they propose:
              (a) single county-wide government; (b) two-level approach;
              (c) district approach; (d) neighborhood governments.
              Metropolitan government is stressed.

2187. MR. PRESIDENT
       Minnesota Mining   s/c/a
              Six different games, many with several variations, range
              from identifying photographs of Presidents to answering
              questions from "clue" cards.   Some involve role-playing.
              The object is to understand better achievements of those
              who occupied the Presidency.

2188. NAPOLI
       Western Behavioral Science Institute   Simile II   2-4 hours
       s/c/a
       Players: 15-35
              This simulation permits players to assume roles of legis-
              lators who debate and evaluate national issues.   Their ob-
              ject is to get reelected.   Party, personal, constituent
              conflicts are experienced.

2189. NORTH VERSUS SOUTH
       Social Studies School Service   4-5 hours
       Players: 20-80
              Northern teams of Abolitionists, Free Soilers and Mod-
              erates, and Southern teams of Rebels, Realists and
              Moderates deal with the issues that divided the North

and South prior to the Civil War.   The question of seces-
sion is discussion material.

2190. PARTY CENTRAL
Instructional Simulations   s/possibly c/a
Players: 23-20
The rise, control and political impact of national social-
ism from 1928-1939 in Central Europe are all detailed.
The intent is to "involve players in historical situations
that allow the rise of national socialism."

2191. PLANS
Simile II   3-8 hours   s/c/a
Players: 12-35
Members of six pressure groups make changes in American society.   The six interest groups are: military, civil rights, nationalists, internationalists, business and labor.   Each group has from two to six members and com-
municates with other groups by written messages and in
scheduled conferences.   Players learn about the process
of bargaining, trading and pressuring to affect social
change.

2192. POLITICAL-MILITARY EXERCISE
M.I.T. (Center for International Studies)   c/a
Players: 8-50 in 1-5 teams
The objectives of this simulation include the exposure of
the complexities of real decision-making in foreign policy.
Actual behavioral conditions are simulated.

2193. POLITICAL SIMULATION
Rensselaer Polytechnic Institute   s/c
Players: 21-200 in 7-10 teams
Players learn vicariously some lessons relating to politi-
cal strategies.

2194. PRESSURE: A SIMULATION OF DECISION-MAKING IN LO-
CAL GOVERNMENT
Interact
Players: 35 maximum
Players become citizens in a community beset by local
conflicts and problems: zoning versus personal rights;
cultural and ecological preservation versus economic
goals; school modernization versus tradition and budgets.
Group pressures to influence agencies are examined.

2195. SIMSOC
Free Press   s/possibly c
Players: 20-40
Participants assume roles of citizens in a society under
stress conditions.   Players must actively question the
nature of the social order and examine processes of social conflict and social control.   Objectives are to gain

power and influence society toward one's political concepts.

2196. STATE LEGISLATORS
Macmillan Company   s/c
Players: 18-26   divided into 3 teams
    Experiences are offered in negotiation and strategy-for-
    mation to involve students in the legislative process.
    Exercises expose them to "regional bias" in the legisla-
    tive structure.

2197. STATE SYSTEM EXERCISE
International Relations Program, Syracuse
    Students are introduced to concepts used by statesmen to
    "maintain patterns of stability" in the international politi-
    cal system.   Players negotiate, declare war, bargain for
    peace.

2198. WOODBURY POLITICAL SIMULATION
Little Brown   c
Players: 25-70, divided into 8 teams
    Party organization, with affiliated groups, Republican and
    Democratic campaigners, media and brokers, are all en-
    gaged in a political campaign in the town of Woodbury.

PROCESS/THEORY

2199. HAAR HOOLIM: PERCEPTION GAMES
Adult Leisure Products Corporation   to c
Players: 1 to 6; 15 different games
    Final patterns created are evaluated according to difficulty
    level and offer practice in visualizing the process of ab-
    stract concepts.

2200. INFORMATION
Academic Games   45 min.-2 hours   s/c/a
Players: 8 and up
    This quiz game is used to teach any body of information.
    Constructed as a "frame game," its rules provide a set
    of activities and scoring procedures so that players' suc-
    cess in answering questions about some particular topic
    can be encouraged and recorded.   Topics can be adjusted
    for a wide variety of purposes.

2201. INFORMATION GAME, THE
Didactic Systems
    Communication problems occur when a message is trans-
    mitted from person to person.   In this version, partici-
    pants are given colored blocks, sticks and cardboard
    screens to work behind.   Only one participant is given
    oral instructions concerning what to build with his blocks
    and sticks.   The participant then instructs the man beside

him, who in turn teaches the next, and so on. One by
one, the cardboard screens are removed as the instructor focuses discussion on where communication failed and
why.   The game is repeated with printed instructions for
every other participant, who instructs his neighbor.

2202.   PREDICTION
Unitarian Universalist Association 30-60 min.   s/c
Players: 3-6
The credibility of each participant is challenged as each
rolls a four-colored die.   The game's object is to predict the other player's answer.   Players next draw a
question card to be asked by another player.   Correct
predictions are rewarded with additional spaces and incorrect predictions with backward moves.   Whoever
reaches the end of the game board first, wins.

2203.   PROCESS
Didactic Systems 8 sessions of 2-3 hours each
A program of eight self-instructional exercises provides
a framework in which groups of individuals convene and
deal with interpersonal issues.   The exercise is designed
as an educational experience for those who are "interested in gaining a better understanding of themselves and
the way in which they relate to others."

RHETORICAL TOPICS

Philosophic

2204.   CAMPUS CRISIS GAME
WGBH-TV c/a
Players: 10-12 teams
Players learn an understanding of the causes of campus
protest.

2205.   CONDUCTING PLANNING EXERCISES
Instructional Simulations s/possibly c
Players: 16-36
Players plan and propose alternative solutions to complex
social problems: faculty-student communication; drug
abuse; family relationships.

2206.   COPE: A SIMULATION OF ADAPTING TO CHANGE AND
ANTICIPATING THE FUTURE
Interact
Players: 35 maximum
Living in the city of Technopolis, players live through
five future time periods in the era 2000-2040 A.D., involving computers and human relationships and subsequent
problems.   Other pertinent changes are anticipated with
analysis suggested.

2207. DYNASTY
       Dynasty International   s/c
            In a mythical oriental country, players deal with prob-
            lems of law and order.

2208. ETHICS
       Art Fair
       Players: up to 8
            Ethics is a game of choices. As a player, one is pro-
            jected into situations that range through the spectrum of
            human experience. Faced with difficult decisions, a
            course of action must be selected. The judgments of
            peers must be faced. One explores concepts of morality,
            uses persuasion, inference to score high.

2209. GENERAL AGRICULTURAL FARM SIMULATION
       Pennsylvania State University   s/c
       Players: 1 or more
            Players have experiences parallel to real life and test
            rhetorical principles in "meaningful contexts."

2210. HUMANUS
       Simile II   1-1/2 hours or two 50-min. periods
       Players: 5 or more
            This simulation activity forces both moral and practical
            decisions upon players who participate as members of
            "survival cells," following a wide epidemic. They are
            linked to the outside world, monitored and controlled by
            their "survival computer," Humanus, which communicates
            to them through a voice "printout," a cassette recording.
            Problems concern moral dilemmas, who should survive
            and whether or not to risk contact with other groups.

2211. MICRO SOCIETY
       Real World Learning
            A simulation environment in which players develop con-
            cepts about institutions and patterns of behavior of con-
            temporary American society.

2212. PUZZLE: A SIMULATION ENABLING STUDENTS TO PER-
       FORM THE TASKS OF A BIOGRAPHER-HISTORIAN
            Interact
       Players: 4 teams (35 players, maximum)
            Players search the library for previously "planted" docu-
            ments from historians to piece together subjects' lives
            and "create" original documents. After writing original
            and individual/team biographies, players challenge and
            defend biographical inferences and judgments they have
            made.

2213. SOCIETY TODAY
       Psychology Today

The forces at work in society are explored. Conditions are changing and "no one knows whether disaster or great fortune will develop next." In this game, luck and knowledge of current happenings determine results.

2214. STARPOWER
Simile II   1 to 2 hours   all levels
Players: 18-35
Players build a three-tiered society according to the wealth each player can acquire. Participants move from one level to another of society through trading. The game stimulates discussions about the uses of power. According to the manufacturer, "it is our most popular game," used by institutions from prisons to churches.

2215. VALUES
Social Studies School Service
Players: 3-6
Designed to promote discussion of current local issues, players are challenged by other players as they move along the board. In defense, each player speaks on a topic for sixty seconds, is interviewed for three minutes or chooses to pass. "Right" or "wrong" answers to questions are very rare.

War

2216. BRINKMANSHIP: HOLOCAUST OR COMPROMISE
David Del Porto, Mt. Pleasant   s/possibly c
Players: 25, divided into 2 teams
Players learn of the Cold War crisis between 1945-1967. The two "superpowers" are directly involved. National interests and security and foreign policy become a challenge through direct participation in negotiation.

2217. CONFLICT
Simile II   5-8 periods of 50 min. each
Players: 27-42
Participating as national leaders in a disarmed world in the year 1999, participants test basic mechanisms of Arthur Waskow's disarmament model: 1. The more consensus, the more force; 2. Gradual deterrence; 3. Minimal use of force against minimal targets; 4. Major power veto. Sometimes peace prevails but other times the model fails and war develops.

2218. CONFRONTATION: THE CUBAN MISSILE CRISIS
School Marketing, Inc.

2219. GUNS OR BUTTER
       Simile II   1-2 hours   s/a
       Players: 18-28
            In this simulation of international conflict, players form
            teams to understand how an arms race can be started
            and whether institutions can be changed to promote peace.
            Serving as leaders of nations, players try to increase
            the real wealth of their country, while making certain it
            is secure from attack.   Leaders form alliances, trade,
            defend themselves.

2220. MISSION: A SIMULATION OF OUR INVOLVEMENT IN VIET-
       NAM
       Interact
       Players: 35 maximum
            As members of various factions, players research, then
            argue the viewpoints of Hawks, Doves or Moderates.
            They assume identities: Senators, professors, students,
            military leaders and the President and press secretary.
            Protests, polls contribute.

2221. NUREMBERG: A SIMULATION OF WAR CRIME TRIALS OF
       1945-46
       Social Studies School Service
            Role-playing French, British, American and Russian
            judges, participants witness and recreate the Internation-
            al Military Tribunal held at Nuremberg in 1945.   During
            the mock trial players decide moral issues, legal issues;
            questions are debated, analyzed, resolved.

2222. PEACE: A SIMULATION OF WAR-PEACE ISSUES DURING
       WILSONIAN ERA
       Social Studies School Service
            Players are grouped into five factions: Anglophiles,
            Francophiles, Germanophiles, Idealists and Realists.
            Each group must come up with specific promises for the
            President during the conflict and after at Versailles.
            Players debate views, publish them, attack the opposition.

                              THERAPY

2223. BLINDFOLD GAME, THE
       Didactic Systems (Sterling Institute)
            Designed to develop insight and sensitivity, this game is
            a structured form of T-group or "laboratory" training.
            By placing blindfolds on half the participants and pairing
            them with the other half, the "blind" become dependent
            upon the sighted in order to succeed at three assigned
            tasks.   In follow-up discussion, participants examine the
            extent to which they recognized their dependency and
            sought or gave help.

2224. CYCLE: AN INTERACTION UNIT INTRODUCING THE
STAGES OF THE HUMAN LIFE
Interact 3 weeks
Players: 25-35
    A combination of activities is based on the eight stages of
psychologist Erik Erikson's human life cycle--Infancy,
Childhood (Early), Play Age, School Age, Identity, Young
Adulthood, Mature Age. Players are helped to understand the relationship between behavior and those problems related to a particular stage of life. Through
"problems" and "solutions" seminar groups, players analyze three case studies.

2225. FEEL WHEEL, THE
Psychology Today
    A device developed by a team of psychologists to allevi-
ate tensions in personal encounter, "The Feel Wheel" is
a circle divided into 32 pie-shaped sections. Each has a
different emotion written on it. Players put their "tokens"
on the emotion that they are feeling, "leading to out-in-
the-open" discussion and better understanding.

2226. GAMES PEOPLE PLAY
MASCO The Head Box   s/c/a
Players: 2-8
    The goal of this game is to develop perception in recog-
nizing social action and the consequences. Players have
a variety of roles and are given the opportunity to air
hostilities.

2227. GROUP THERAPY
The Head Box   Uniquity 1 to 2 hours   c, a
Players: 3-8
    Participants randomly draw instructions which direct them
to perform such tasks as describing themselves or telling
each member of the group what one likes about him. The
other players judge his sincerity and he moves backward
or forward accordingly. The player may perform the instructions he receives or choose not to perform them.

2228. INSIGHT
Games Research, Inc. 1 hour or more s/c/a
Players: 2 to 20
    The objective of this game is to evaluate the personality
of the other players and to compare one's self-evaluation
with that of others. Tallies are recorded so that each
player can compare his self-image with those of others.
"Powers of perception" are the primary learning objectives.

2229. INTERACTION
Simulation, Inc.
Players: 2-4
    Participants gain points by traversing "positive attitude"

objects and by betting on directions other players will
choose.

2230. JUVENILE DELINQUENCY GAME
Research Analysis
Players and achievers gain "insight into the values of
others," then begin behavioral change of respective attitudes.

2231. "NOW" COMMUNICATION GAME, THE
Holistic Press   s/c/a
This game is designed to "make participants more clear-
ly aware of their communication needs and to foster expression of these needs to partners or to family." The
results are more open and honest communication. The
game can be placed on the wall to encourage increased
awareness, openness and clarity of needs and communicating them as they occur.

2232. "O.K. GAME," THE
Simco   any age
Players: 2-6
This is a game board version of the transactional analysis books, Games People Play and I'm O.K., You're
O.K. It provides script analysis, insight, role-playing,
spontaneous responses, introspection, non-competitive-
ness, TA Rorschach. It provides participants with information about the three different ego states: Parent,
Adult and Child. Players pass superficial communications
and "win" insight into their behavior.

2233. PERSONALYSIS
Administrative   Research Associates   s/c
Players: 3-4
Participants will "understand themselves better," "isolate
their strengths and weaknesses." Changes are planned to
enable them to have "more" satisfying relationships.

2234. SENSITIVITY
Buzza Cardoza   Sensitivity Games, Inc.   1-2 hours
Players: 4-8
Real life role-playing is demonstrated. Participants draw
folders which contain mementos of events which happened
to some particular individual. Participants try to "become" the person whose folder they have and to communicate that person's characteristics to the other members
of the group.

2235. UNGAME, THE
Uniquity   Didactic Systems
Players: 2-6
This unusual game creates "an atmosphere in which
players share feelings." Questions are in units either

for students or married couples. Players answer "Tell it like it is" cards and "improve" interpersonal communication.

2236. YOUTH CULTURE GAME, THE
Contemporary Drama Service   3-5-hour session
This improvisational theatre-game helps players "develop personal values with insight." Individual acts and their consequences are "lived" within the "total environment of youth's 'real' world." "All at once and wholly both students and teachers see, feel, learn how today's world and its structures affect them personally."

PART IV

SOURCES

353

PRODUCERS, DISTRIBUTORS, SPONSORS

ABC Media Concepts see Xerox Films

Abt Games Associates, Inc.,
    55 Wheeler Street, Cambridge, MA 02138

Academic Games Associates,
    430 East 33rd Street, Baltimore, MD 21218

Academic Media,
    1736 Westwood Boulevard, Los Angeles, CA 90024

ACI Films, Inc.,
    35 West 45th Street, New York, NY 10036

Administrative Research Associates,
    Box #5, Deerfield, IL 60015

Adult Leisure Products Corporation,
    Locust Valley, NY 11560

Advanced Ideas Company,
    68A Broadway, Arlington, MA 02174

Advanced Research Projects Agency,
    1400 Wilson Boulevard, Arlington, VA 22209

AFL-CIO see American Federation of Labor and Congress of In-
    dustrial Organizations

Airlie Productions,
    Airlie, VA 22186

Allied Artists Corporation,
    230 West 41st Street, New York, NY 10036

Allied Motion Picture Center, Inc.,
    302 G Street, S.W., Washington, DC 20024

American Academy of Motion Picture Arts and Sciences,
    9036 Melrose Avenue, Hollywood, CA 90069

American Advertising Federation,
    1225 Connecticut Avenue, N.W., Washington, DC 20036

American Association for Higher Education see National Education
    Association

American Association for the Advancement of Science,
    1515 Massachusetts Avenue, N.W., Washington, DC 20005

American Association of University Women,
    2401 Virginia Avenue, N.W., Washington, DC 20037

American Bankers Association,
    1120 Connecticut Avenue, N.W., Washington, DC 20036

American Broadcasting Company,
    1330 Avenue of the Americas, New York, NY 10019

American Civil Liberties Union,
    22 East 40th Street, New York, NY 10016

American Council for Better Broadcasts,
    15 West Main Street, Madison, WI 53703

American Council of Public Relations Associates,
    1 Dupont Circle, Washington, DC 20036

American Council on Education,
    1785 Massachusetts Avenue, N.W., Washington, DC 20036

American Dental Association,
    211 East Chicago Avenue, Chicago IL 60611

American Documentary Films,
    336 West 84th Street, New York, NY 10024
    379 Bay Street, San Francisco, CA 94133

American Educational Films,
    1726 Westwood Boulevard, Los Angeles, CA 90024

American Educational Publishers (AEP),
    Columbus, OH 43216

American Educational Theatre Association, Inc.,
    762 Jackson Place, N.W., Washington, DC 20466

American Federation of Film Societies,
    144 Bleeker Street, New York, NY 10010

American Federation of Labor and Congress of Industrial Organizations,
    815 Sixteenth Street, N.W., Washington, DC 20036

American Film Institute,
    1707 H Street, N.W., Washington, DC 20036

American Foundation on Automation and Employment; Public Affairs,
    Albany, NY 12201

American Heritage Films,
    Marion, OH 43302

American Historical Association,
    400 A Street, S.E., Washington, DC 20003

American Institute for Research,
    Box 112, Palo Alto, CA 94302

American Institute of Banking,
    1120 Connecticut Avenue, N.W., Washington, DC 20036

American Library Association,
    50 East Huron Street, Chicago, IL 60611

American Medical Association,
    535 North Dearborn Street, Chicago, IL 60610

American Oil Corporation,
    910 South Michigan Avenue, Chicago, IL 60605

American Personnel and Guidance Association,
    1607 New Hampshire Avenue, N.W., Washington, DC 20009

American Society for Information Sciences,
    1140 Connecticut Avenue, N.W., Washington, DC 20036

American Theatre Association,
    Suite 500, 1317 F Street, N.W., Washington, DC 20004

American Video Network,
    P.O. Box One, Eau Claire, WI 54701

American World Films   see   American Documentary Films

Amherst Games Company,
    Box #5, Amherst, MA 01002

Amidon and Associates,
    5408 Chicago Avenue South, Minneapolis, MN 55417

Ampex Tape Exchange,
    2201 Estes Avenue, Elk Grove Village, IL 60007

Appleton-Century   see   Appleton-Century-Crofts

Appleton-Century-Crofts, Education Division,
    440 Park Avenue South, New York, NY 10016

Applied Simulations, International, Inc.,
        1100 Seventeenth Avenue, N.W., Washington, DC 22036

Arizona State Department of Public Instruction,
        1333 West Camelback Road, Phoenix, AZ 85103

Arthur Barr Productions, Inc.,
        1029 North Allen Avenue, Pasadena, CA 91104

Associated Educational Materials, Inc.,
        14 Glenwood Avenue, Raleigh, NC 27601

Associated Instructional Materials (AIM) see Association Films

Associated Press,
        50 Rockefeller Plaza, New York, NY 10020

Association Films,
        600 Madison Avenue, New York, NY 10022

Association for Childhood Education, International,
        3615 Wisconsin Avenue, N.W., Washington, DC 20016

Association for Educational Communications and Technology see
        National Education Association

Association for Education in Journalism,
        425 Henry Mall, University of Wisconsin, Madison, WI 53706

Association for Higher Education,
        1 Dupont Circle, Washington, DC 20036

Association for Study of Negro Life and History,
        1407 Fourteenth St., N.W., Washington, DC 20036

Association for Supervision and Curriculum Development see Na-
        tional Education Association

Association of American Indian Affairs,
        432 Park Avenue South, New York, NY 10016

Association of American Publishers,
        1 Park Avenue, New York, NY 10016

Association of Departments of English,
        62 Fifth Avenue, New York, NY 10011

Association-Sterling Films,
        866 Third Avenue, New York, NY 10022

Audio/Brandon (International Cinema)
        34 MacQuesten Parkway, Mt. Vernon, NY 10550

Au-Vid,
P. O. Box 964, Garden Grove, CA 92642

Avco-Embassy Corporation,
1301 Avenue of the Americas, New York, NY 10019

AV-ED Educational Films,
7934 Santa Monica Boulevard, Hollywood, CA 90046

AV Productions, Inc.,
125 West Goethe Street, Chicago, IL 60610

Bailey Film Associates (BFA),
Box 1795, 221 Michigan Avenue, Santa Monica, CA 90404

Battelle Memorial Fund,
505 King Avenue, Columbus, OH 43201

BBC-TV (British Broadcasting Corporation),
630 Fifth Avenue, New York, NY 10020

Beacon Press,
25 Boston Street, Boston, MA 02108

Behavioral Research Laboratories,
866 Second Avenue, New York, NY 10002

Bell and Howell,
Old Mansfield Road, Wooster, OH 44691

Bell Telephone Company,
600 Mountain Avenue, Murray Hill, NJ 07974

Benchmark Films,
145 Scarborough Road, Briarcliff Manor, NY 10510

Berne   see   McGraw-Hill

BFA   see   Bailey Film Associates

Billy Budd   see   University of California

Blackhawk Films,
Davenport, IA 52808

Boston South End Community Center,
Boston 02108

Boston University, Educational Media Center,
Boston, MA 02215

Brandon Films,
221 West 57th Street, New York, NY 10019

Brigham Young University, Educational Media Center,
    Provo, UT 84601

British Film Institute, Information Service,
    42 Lower Marsh, London, S. E. 1, England

Broadcast Information Bureau,
    535 Fifth Avenue, New York, NY 10017

Bro-Dart Audiovisual,
    1600 Memorial Avenue, Williamsport, PA 17701

Bureau of National Affairs (BNA),
    9401 DeCoverly Hall Road, Rockville, MD 20852

Business Education Films,
    5113 16th Avenue, Brooklyn, NY 11204

Buzza-Cardoza,
    1500 South Anaheim Boulevard, Anaheim, CA 92803

Cahill   see   Charles Cahill and Associates, Inc.

Canadian Broadcasting Corporation, (CBC), Learning Systems,
    Box 500, Terminal A, Toronto, 116, Ontario, Canada

Canyon Cinema Cooperative,
    Room 220, Industrial Center Building, Sausalito, CA 94965

Carousel Films,
    1501 Broadway, Suite 1503, New York, NY 10036

Cartrivision   see   Video Center

Cathedral Films, Inc.,
    2921 West Alameda, Burbank, CA 91505

Catholic Audiovisual Association,
    Our Lady of Angels College, Glen Middle, PA 19037

C-B Educational Films   see   University of California

CBS Electronic Video Recording,
    51 West 52nd Street, New York, NY 10019

CBS News   see   Columbia Broadcasting System

CCM Films   see   Crowell, Collier, Macmillan

Cedar Rapids Community School District,
    346 2nd Avenue, S. W., Cedar Rapids, IA 52404

Center for Applied Linguistics,
     1717 Massachusetts Avenue, N.W., Washington, DC 20036

Center for Democratic Institutions,
     Box 4068, Santa Barbara, CA 93108

Center for Mass Communication (CMC), Columbia University,
     562 West 113th Street, New York, NY 10025

Center for Urban Education,
     105 Madison Avenue, New York, NY 10016

Central Virginia Educational Television see WCVE-TV

Centre for Educational Television (London) see Great Plains In-
     structional Television

Centron Educational Films,
     1621 West Ninth Street, Lawrence, KA 66044

Chamber of Commerce of the United States
     1615 H Street, N.W., Washington, DC 20006

Champion Papers and Fiber Company
     36 South Wabash Avenue, Chicago, IL 60603

Changing Times, Educational Services,
     1729 H Street, N.W., Washington, DC 20006

Charles Cahill and Associates, Inc.,
     5746 Sunset Boulevard, Los Angeles, CA 90028

Charles E. Merrill Publishing Company,
     1300 Alum Creek Drive, Columbus, OH 43216

Charney see American Documentary Films

Chicago Area Television College,
     Chicago, IL 60607

Christian Film Service, Inc.,
     2308 Seventh Street, Charlotte, NC 28202

Churchill Films, Inc.,
     662 North Robertson Boulevard, Los Angeles, CA 90069

Cinema V,
     585 Madison Avenue, New York, NY 10022

Cinema Service,
     517 Dexter Street, Seattle, WA 98101

Cinema 16/Grove Press,
    80 University Place, New York, NY 10003

Cinema Workshop,
    P.O. Box 4085, Greenwich, CT 06830

Cinerama, Inc.,
    1345 Avenue of the Americas, New York, NY 10022

Civic Education Service,
    1735 K Street, N.W., Washington, DC 20006

Classroom Film Productions,
    22 Glenwood Avenue, Raleigh, NC   27602

Colonial Films,
    752 Spring Street, NW, Atlanta, GA 30301

Columbia Broadcasting System (CBS),
    51 West 52nd Street, New York, NY 10019

Columbia Cinematique,
    711 Fifth Avenue, New York, NY 10022

Columbia Pictures see Columbia Cinematique

Columbia University Press,
    136 South Broadway, Irvington-on-the Hudson, NY 10533

Common Cause,
    2030 M Street, N.W., Washington, DC 20036

Communicad: The Communication Academy,
    Box 541, Wilton, CT 06897

Communication Workers of America,
    1925 K Street, N.W., Washington, DC 20006

Communications Group West,
    6430 Sunset Boulevard, Suite 204, Hollywood, CA 90028

Communicative Arts Press,
    159 Forest Avenue NE, Atlanta, GA 30303

Connaught Films, Inc., Ltd.,
    245 East 63rd Street, New York, NY 10021

Connecticut Department of Mental Health see International Film
    Bureau

Contemporary Drama Service,
    Box 457, Downers Grove, IL 60515

Contemporary Films see McGraw-Hill

Cornell University, Department of Communication Arts,
    Ithaca, NY 14850

Coronet Films,
    65 East South Water Street, Chicago, IL 60611

Corporate Communications,
    18 West 45th Street, New York, NY 10036

Corporation for Public Broadcasting,
    888 Sixteenth Street, N.W., Washington, DC 20006

Council on International Non-Theatrical Events (CINE) see National
    Education Association

Counterpoint Films,
    5823 Santa Monica Boulevard, Hollywood, CA 90038

Creative Arts Studio,
    814 H Street, N.W., Washington, DC 20001

Creative Communications and Research,
    460 35th Street, San Francisco, CA 94030

Creative Educational Materials,
    P.O. Box 244, Dekalb, IL 60115

Creative Film Society,
    7237 Canby Avenue, Reseda, CA 91335

Creative Studies, Inc.,
    167 Corey Road, Boston, MA 02146

CRM Productions (Psychology Today Films),
    9263 West Third Street, Beverly Hills, CA 90210

Corwell, Collier, Macmillan (CCM),
    34 MacQuesten Parkway South, Mt. Vernon, NY 10550

Current Affairs Films,
    24 Danbury Road, Wilton, CT 06897

Curtis Audiovisual Company,
    Philadelphia, PA 19114

Dana Productions,
    6249 Babcock Avenue, North Hollywood, CA 91606

Dearborn Public Library, Audiovisual Department,
    4500 Maple Street, Dearborn, MI 48126

Denoyer-Geppert Audiovisuals,
    355 Lexington Avenue, New York, NY 10017

Didactic   see   Didactic Systems, Inc.

Didactic Systems, Inc.,
    6 North Union Avenue, Crawford, NJ 07016

Dimension,
    Box 811, Denville, NJ 07834

Document Associates,
    880 Third Avenue, New York, NY 10022

Doubleday and Company,
    1371 Reynolds Avenue, Santa Monica, CA 92705

Dupont Company,
    Wilmington, DE 19899

Dynasty, International
    815 Park Avenue, New York, NY 10021

Eames   see   Classroom Film Productions

Earlham College, Department of Psychology (c/o R. Johnson),
    Richmond, IN 47374

Eastern Educational Network,
    381 Elliott Street, Newton, MA 02164

Eastern Michigan University, Audiovisual Department,
    Ypsilanti, MI 48197

Eastern Pennsylvania Psychiatric Institute   see   Psychological Cine-
    ma Register

Eastman Kodak Company
    343 State Street, Rochester, NY 14650

Educational Audiovisual, Inc.,
    Pleasantville, NY 10570

Educational Commission of the States,
    300 Lincoln Tower, 1960 Lincoln, Denver, CO 80203

Educational Communication Association,
    National Press Building, Suite 960, Washington, DC 20004

Educational Communication Industries,
    100 Green Street, Doylestown, PA 18901

Educational Communication Systems, Inc.,
145 Witherspoon Street, Princeton, NJ 08540

Educational Development Center,
15 Mifflin Place, Cambridge, MA 02128

Educational Film Association,
250 West 65th Street, New York, NY 10023

Educational Games Company,
P. O. Box 363, Peekskill, NY   10566

Educational Institute of Broadcasting,
647 Sepulveda Boulevard, Los Angeles, CA 90049

Educational Media,
809 Industrial Way, Box #39, Ellensburg, WA 98926

Educational Media and Technical Institute for Communication Research,
Stanford University, Palo Alto, CA 94305

Educational Media Council,
1346 Connecticut Avenue, N.W., Washington, DC 20036

Educational Methods,
20 East Huron, Chicago, IL 60611

Educational Press Association of America, School of Journalism,
Syracuse University, Syracuse, NY 13120

Educational Research,
P. O. Box 34, Somerset, NJ 08873

Educational Research Association,
1019 S.W. 10th Street, Portland, OR 97208

Educational Research Systems,
P. O. Box 157, Shrewsbury, MA 05145

Educational Resource Information Center (ERIC),
Stanford University, Palo Alto, CA 94305

Educational Services, Inc.,
44A Brattle Street, Cambridge, MA 02138

Educational Television,
140 Main Street, Ridgefield, CT 06877

Educational Testing Service,
25 Nassau Street, Princeton, NJ 08542

Educator's Progress Service,
Randolph, WI 53956

Edward Small Productions,
     1041 North Formosa Avenue, Los Angeles, CA 90046

Electronic Video Recording (EVR)   see   Video Center

EMC Corporation,
     1855 East 6th Street, St. Paul, MN 55101

Encyclopaedia Britannica Films, Educational Corporation,
     425 North Michigan Avenue, Chicago, IL 60611

Entelek, Inc.,
     42 Pleasant Street, Newburyport, MA 01950

ETC   see   University of Hawaii

Evergreen   see   Grove Press

Eyegate House, Inc.,
     146-01 Archer Avenue, Jamaica, NY 11435

Fairbanks Productions,
     North Vine Street, Hollywood, CA 90028

Family Films, Inc.,
     5823 Santa Monica Boulevard, Hollywood, CA 90028

Film Associates,
     11014 Santa Monica Boulevard, Los Angeles, CA 90046

Film Center, The,
     515 12th Street, N.W., Washington, DC 20005

Film Classic Exchange,
     1926 South Vermont Avenue, Los Angeles, CA 90007

Film Distributors, International,
     2223 South Olive Street, Los Angeles, CA 90007

Film Library Information Council,
     101 West Putnam Avenue, Greenwich, CT 06830

Film-maker's Cooperative,
     175 Lexington Avenue, New York, NY 10016

Film News Company,
     250 West 57th Street, Suite 2201, New York, NY 10019

Film Quarterly, University of California Press,
     Berkeley, CA 94704

Films, Inc.,
     1144 Wilmette Avenue, Wilmette, IL 60091

Films in Review,
    32 Union Street, New York, NY 10003

Finley and Sons, Inc.,
    605 Third Avenue, New York, NY 10016

Fisk University,
    17th Avenue North and Jackson Streets, Nashville, TN 37203

Fleetwood Films, Inc.,
    34 MacQuesten Parkway South, Mt. Vernon, NY 10550

Florida State University, Educational Media Center,
    Gainesville, FL 32603

Ford Foundation,
    477 Madison Avenue, New York, NY 10022

Fordham University,
    East Fordham Road, Bronx, NY 10458

Foreign Policy Association,
    345 East 40th Street, New York, NY 10017

Foreign Policy Association Services,
    127 Peachtree Street, Atlanta, GA 30303

Fortune   see   Time-Life Films

Foundation for Research on Human Behavior,
    508 East William Street, Ann Arbor, MI 48108

Four Star International Company,
    10202 Washington Boulevard, Culver City, CA 90230

Franciscan Communications Center,
    1229 South Santee Street, Los Angeles, CA 90015

Free Circle   see   Perennial Education, Inc.

Free Press,
    866 Third Avenue, New York, NY 10022

Games Research, Inc.,
    500 Harrison Avenue, Boston, MA 02118

Gaming Resources Center, Environmental Simulation,
    University of Michigan, Ann Arbor, MI 48106

Garrand Publishing Company,
    Champaign, IL 61826

General Electric Company,
    570 Lexington Avenue, New York, NY 10022

General Motors Film Library,
    3044 West Grand Boulevard, Detroit, MI 48202

General Services Studios,
    1040 North Las Palmas Avenue, Los Angeles, CA 90038

George Peabody College for Teachers, Division of Surveys,
    Nashville, TN 37203

George Washington University,
    2121 Eye Street, N.W., Washington, DC 20013

Ginn and Company,
    191 Spring Street, Lexington, MA 92173

Glatfelder Company, Film Library, Dept. of Creativision, Inc.,
    295 West 4th Street, New York, NY 10014

Great Plains Instructional Television, Library,
    University of Nebraska, P.O. Box 80669, Lincoln, NE 68508

Grossman Publishers,
    44 West 56th Street, New York, NY 10019

Grove Press, Inc., Film Division,
    53 East 11th Street, New York, NY 10003

Guidance Associates,
    757 Third Avenue, New York, NY 10017

Gulf Publishing Company,
    P.O. Box 2608, Houston, TX 77002

Handel Film Corporation,
    8730 Sunset Boulevard, West Hollywood, CA 90069

Hanna-Barbera,
    3400 Cahuenga Boulevard, Los Angeles, CA 90025

Harcourt Brace Jovanovich,
    757 Third Avenue, New York, NY 10017

Harper see Harper and Row

Harper and Row,
    10 East 53rd Street, New York, NY 10022

Harris Tuchman Productions,
    750 North Highland Avenue, Hollywood, CA 90038

Harvard University, Educational Media Center,
    Appian Way, Cambridge, MA 02138

Harwell Association,
    Box 95, Convent Station, NJ 07961

Haverford College, Political and Social Simulations Newsletter,
    Haverford, PA 19041

Head Box, The, Educational Products Division,
    P. O. Box 4762, Clinton, IA 52732

Henny see Mass Media Associates

Henry Strauss Associates,
    733 Third Avenue, New York, NY 10017

Historical Records, Inc.,
    Box 4204, Bergen Station, Jersey City, NJ 07304

Hobi, Inc.,
    Department 15-109, 7 Delaware Drive, Lake Success, NY
    11040

Hoi Polloi, Inc.,
    230 Fifth Avenue, New York, NY 10001

Holistic Press,
    160 South Robertson Boulevard, Beverly Hills, CA 90211

Hollywood Film Enterprises,
    6060 Sunset Boulevard, Los Angeles, CA 90028

Holt see Holt, Rinehart and Winston

Holt, Rinehart and Winston,
    383 Madison Avenue, New York, NY 10017

Houghton-Mifflin Corporation,
    110 Tremont Street, Boston, MA 02109

Human Relations,
    755 Prospect Street, P. O. Box 2054, Yale Station, New Haven,
    CT 06540

H. W. Wilson,
    535 West Taft Drive, South Holland, IL 60473

IBM World Trade Corporation,
    821 United Nations Plaza, New York, NY 10017

Ideal Pictures see Audio/Brandon

Ideas see   University of Iowa

Impact Films,
       144 Bleeker Street, New York, NY 10012

Imperial International Learning,
       Box 548, Kankakee, IL 60901

Indiana University, Audiovisual Center, Media Library,
       Bloomington, IN 47401

Industrial Audiovisual Association,
       P. O. Box 656, Downtown Station, Chicago, IL 60690

Information Film Producers of America, Inc.,
       Box 1470, Hollywood, CA 90028

Information Resources, Inc.,
       1675 Massachusetts Avenue, Cambridge, MA 02138

Institute of Cinema Service,
       29 East 10th Street, New York, NY 10003

Institute of Communication Research,
       Stanford University, Palo Alto, CA 94305

Institute of Visual Training,
       40 East 49th Street, New York, NY 10017

Instructional Development Corporation,
       P. O. Box 805, Salem, OR 97304

Instructional Simulations, Inc.,
       2147 University Avenue, St. Paul, MN 55114

Interact,
       P. O. Box 262, Lakeside, CA 92040

International Business Machines see IBM World Trade Corporation

International Communication Association,
       Box 1020, Athens, OH 45701

International Communication Films,
       1371 Reynolds Avenue, Santa Monica, CA 92702

International Film Bureau,
       332 South Michigan Avenue, Chicago, IL 60604

International Film Foundation,
       475 Fifth Avenue, New York, NY 10017

International Learning Corporation,
    245 Southwest 32nd Street, Ft. Lauderdale, FL 33315

International Pictures <u>see</u> Audio/Brandon

International Society for General Semantics,
    540 Powell Street, San Francisco, CA 94108

International Tape Association,
    315 West 70th Street, New York, NY 10023

International Teaching Tapes,
    P.O. Box 865, Lakeland, FL 33803

Intext,
    Scranton, PA 18511

Iowa State University, Film Production Unit,
    Alice Norton House, Ames, IA 50010

Irving Lesser Enterprises,
    Room 1527, 250 West 57th Street, New York, NY 10019

Jam Handy Organization, Inc., c/o Scott Graphics,
    104 Lower Westfield Road, Holyoke, MA 01040

John Wiley and Sons, Inc.,
    605 Third Avenue, New York, NY 10016

Johns Hopkins University, Department of Social Relations,
    (c/o Professor James Coleman, Mrs. Sarane Boocock),
    Baltimore, MD 21218

Journal Films,
    900 West Diversey Parkway, Chicago, IL 60614

Journal of Broadcasting, Temple University,
    Philadelphia, PA 19122

Journalism Education Association, Journalism Department,
    Wisconsin State University, Eau Claire, WI 54701

Kansas State University, Educational Media Center,
    Manhattan, KA 66504

KCET-TV,
    1313 North Vine Street, Los Angeles, CA 90028

Kent State University, Educational Media Center,
    Kent, OH 44240

KGW-TV,
    Portland, OR 97207

KLUS (Las Vegas) see Great Plains Instructional Television

KNME-TV,
    1801 Roma Avenue, N. E. , Albuquerque, NM 87106

KOGO-TV see KQED-TV

KQED-TV, Bay Area Educational Television,
    525 Fourth Street, San Francisco, CA 94107

KRMA-TV, Denver Public Schools,
    1261 Glendarm Place, Denver, CO 80204

KUON-TV, University Educational Television Association,
    1600 R Street, Lincoln, NE 68508

KVI-TV, Central California Educational Television Association,
    P. O. Box #6, Sacramento, CA 95801

Landers Film Associates,
    P. O. Box 69760, Los Angeles, CA 90069

Lansford Publishing Company,
    2516 Lansford Avenue, San Jose, CA 95125

Learning Corporation of America,
    711 Fifth Avenue, New York, NY 10022

Learning Games Associates,
    2253 Medford Road, Ann Arbor, MI 48104

Learning, Inc. ,
    131 East Sixth, Scottsdale, AZ 85251

Learning Research Association,
    1501 Broadway, New York, NY 10023

Liberty-United Artists, Inc.,
    6920 Sunset Boulevard, Los Angeles, CA 90028

Linguistic Society of America,
    Box 8120 University Station, Austin, TX 78712

Little Brown Publishing Company
    34 Beacon Street, Boston, MA 02107

Los Angeles Times,
    Los Angeles, CA 90053

Lutheran Film Association, c/o Lutheran Foundation for Religious
    Drama, St. Peters Center, 16 East 56th Street, New York,
    NY 10022

Lyceum, Inc.,
    Box 1225, Laguna Beach, CA 92651

McGraw-Hill,
    1221 Avenue of the Americas, New York, NY 10020

Macmillan Company, Educational Services,
    866 Third Avenue, New York, NY 10022

Mahnke Productions,
    215 East Third Street, Des Moines, IA 50318

Mandel Film Corporation,
    8730 Sunset Boulevard, West Hollywood, CA 90069

March of Time   see   Time-Life Films

Maryland Center for Public Broadcasting
    Bonita Avenue, Owings Mill, MD 21117

Maryland State Department of Education,
    State Office Building, Baltimore, MD 21201

MASCO,
    P. O. Box 382, Locust Valley, NY 11560

Mass Media Associates,
    2116 North Charles Street, Baltimore, MD 21218

MCA, Inc.,
    100 Universal City Plaza, North Hollywood, CA 91608

Media and Methods, North American Publishing Company,
    134 North Thirteenth Street, Philadelphia, PA 19107

Media, Inc.,
    1015 Florida Street, Ft. Worth, TX 76102

Media Mix,
    4701 South Grand Boulevard, St. Louis, MO 63111

Media Plus, Inc.,
    601 Riverside Drive, Suite 11D, New York, NY 10024

Mental Health Research Institute,
    University of Michigan, Ann Arbor, MI 48104

Metro-Goldwyn-Mayer, Inc.
    10202 West Washington Boulevard, Culver City, CA 90230

Metromedia, Inc.,
    277 Park Avenue, New York, NY 10017

Michigan State University, Educational Media Center,
    East Lansing, MI 48823

Midwest Educational Television, Inc.,
    1640 Como Avenue, St. Paul, MN 55108

Miller-Brody Productions, Inc.,
    342 Madison Avenue, New York, NY 10017

Milner-Fenwick,
    3800 Liberty Heights, Baltimore, MD 21218

Milton Bradley Company,
    Springfield, MA 01101

Minneapolis Star Tribune,
    1425 Portland Avenue, Minneapolis, MN 55415

Minnesota-Mining <u>see</u> Three-M Company

M. I. T. Center for International Studies,
    Cambridge, MA 02138

Modern Film Rentals,
    2323 New Hyde Park Road, New York, NY 11040

Modern Language Association of America,
    62 Fifth Avenue, New York, NY 10011

Modern Learning Aids,
    P. O. Box 302, Rochester, NY 14603

Modern Media Teacher,
    38 West Fifth Street, Dayton, OH 45402

Modern Talking Picture Service,
    1212 Avenue of the Americas, New York, NY 10036

Modern Video Center, Division of Modern Talking Picture Service,
    4 Nevada Drive, Lake Success, NY 11040

Modern Videotape Library,
    1212 Avenue of the Americas, New York, NY 10036

Moody Institute of Science
    12000 East Washington Boulevard, Whittier, CA 90606

Motion Picture Association of America,
    522 Fifth Avenue, New York, NY 10036

Motivational Media,
    1001 North Pointsettia Place, Los Angeles, CA 90046

Motorola, Inc.,
  9401 West Grand Avenue, Franklin Park, IL 60131

Motorola Systems Teleprograms,
  4545 West August Boulevard, Chicago, IL 60651

Mt. Pleasant High School, c/o David Del Porto,
  San Jose, CA 95113

Mountain Plains Educational Media Council, Stadium Building,
  Room 320, University of Colorado, Boulder, CO 80302

Museum of Modern Art, Department of Film,
  11 East 53rd Street, New York, NY 10019

National Assessment of Educational Progress,
  1860 Lincoln Street, Denver, CO 80203

National Association of Broadcasting,
  1771 N Street, N.W., Washington, DC 20036

National Association of Educational Broadcasters,
  1101 Dupont Circle Building, 1346 Connecticut Avenue, N.W.,
  Washington, DC 20036

National Association of Manufacturers,
  1776 F Street, Washington, DC 20006

National Audiovisual Association,
  3150 Spring Street, Fairfax, VA 22030

National Audiovisual Center,
  General Services Administration, Suitland, MD 20023

National Broadcasting Company, Educational Enterprises,
  30 Rockefeller Plaza, New York, NY 10020

National Business Education Association,
  1906 Association Drive, Reston, VA 22030

National Cable Television Association,
  918 Sixteenth Street, N.W., Washington, DC 20006

National Center for Educational Media,
  1180 Avenue of the Americas, New York, NY 10026

National Center for School and College Television,
  Box A, Bloomington, IN 47402

National Council for Social Studies see National Education Association

National Council of Churches,
    475 Riverside Drive, New York, NY 10027

National Council of Teachers of English,
    1111 Kenyon Road, Urbana, IL 61801

National Curriculum Committee of Journalism,
    Journalism Education Association, Wisconsin State University,
    Eau Claire, WI 54701

National Dental Association,
    P. O. Box 197, Charlottesville, VA 22902

National Education Association,
    1201 Sixteenth Street, N. W. , Washington, DC 20036

National Educational Media, Inc. ,
    5250 Ventura Boulevard, Sherman Oaks, CA 91403

National Educational Television,
    10 Columbus Circle, New York, NY 10017

National Educational Television Film Service, Audiovisual Center,
    Indiana University, Bloomington, IN 47401

National Film Board of Canada,
    1251 Avenue of the Americas, New York, NY 10020

National Information Center for Educational Media (NICEM),
    University of Southern California, Los Angeles, CA 90015

National Institute of Canada,
    680 Fifth Avenue, Suite 819, New York, NY 10009

National Institute of Real Estate Brokers,
    155 East Superior Street, Chicago, IL 60611

National Instructional Television Center,
    Box D, Audiovisual Center, Bloomington, IN 47401

National Medical Audiovisual Center,
    Atlanta, GA 30333

National Science Foundation,
    1800 G Street, N. W. , Washington, DC 20550

National Service Board for Religious Objectors,
    Washington, DC 20006

National Society for the Study of Communication,
    P. O. Box 336, Tampico, IL 61283

National Telefilm Association, Inc.,
    8530 Wilshire Boulevard, Beverly Hills, CA 90211

National Thespian Society,
    1610 Marlowe Street, Cincinnati, OH 45224

National Training Laboratory for Applied Behavioral Society   see
    National Education Association

National Visual Communication Association,
    230 Park Avenue, New York, NY 10017

NBC News   see   National Broadcasting Company

Nebraska Educational Television Council for Higher Education,
    Lincoln, NE 68508

New Century,
    440 Park Avenue, New York, NY 10016

New Day Films,
    779 Susquehanna, Franklin Lakes, NJ 07417

New Town, c/o Barry R. Lawson,
    57 Cherry Hill Road, Norwich, CT 06360

New York Newsreel,
    28 West 31st Street, New York, NY 10001

New York Public Library,
    Fifth Avenue and 42nd Streets, New York, NY 10018

New York State Education Department, Division of Communications,
    Albany, NY 12203

New York Times,
    229 West 43rd Street, New York, NY 10006

New York University, Film Library,
    26 Washington Place, New York, NY 10005

Newsfilm   see   University of California

North American Films,
    P.O. Box 919, Tarzana, CA 91356

North American Rockwell   see   Business Education Films

North Carolina State University, Educational Media Center,
    Raleigh, NC 27607

North Carolina State, Public Instruction Department,
    Raleigh, NC 27602

Northeastern University, Educational Media Center,
      Boston, MA 02115

Northern Development Concepts,
      P. O. Box 1381, Broomfield, CT 06804

Northern Idaho Jr. College,
      1000 West Garden, Coeur d'Alene, ID 83814

Northern Illinois University, Educational Media Center,
      DeKalb, IL 60115

Northern Virginia Educational Television Association,
      8333 Little River Turnpike, Annandale, VA 22003

Northwestern University, Film Library,
      Evanston, IL 60201

Norwood Films,
      926 New Jersey Avenue, N. W. , Washington, DC 20013

Official Films, Inc. ,
      445 Park Avenue, New York, NY 10022

OFM Productions,
      1229 Santee Street, Los Angeles, CA 90028

Ohio State University, Department of Cinema,
      156 West 19th Avenue, Columbus, OH 43210

Oklahoma State University, Educational Media Center,
      Stillwater, OK 74075

Oregon State University, Audiovisual Instruction and Cooperative
      Extension, Corvallis, OR 97331

Oregon State Bar Association   see   KGW-TV

Oxford Films,
      1136 North Las Palmas, Los Angeles, CA 90038

Pacific Telephone
      140 New Montgomery Street, San Francisco, CA 94105

Paradigm Films,
      2248 Broadway, New York, NY 10024

Paramount Pictures,
      Gulf and Western Plaza, New York, NY 10073

Parker Brothers,
      190 Bridge Street, Salem, ME 01970

Paul S. Amidon and Associates, Inc.,
   5408 Chicago Avenue South, Minneapolis, MN 55417

Pennsylvania Department of Education, Bureau of Instructional Service, Box 211, Harrisburg, PA 17126

Pennsylvania Newspaper Publishers Association,
   2717 West Front, Harrisburg, PA 17105

Pennsylvania State University, Educational Media Center,
   University Park, PA 16802

Pepperdine College,
   South Vermont Avenue and 79th Street, Los Angeles, CA 90044

Perennial Education, Inc.,
   1825 Willow Road, Northfield, IL 60093

Pflaum/Standard,
   2285 Arbor Boulevard, Dayton, OH 45439

Philadelphia Film Corporation,
   885 Lancaster Avenue, Berwyn, Pa 19212

Pintoff   see   Brandon Films

Pioneer Screw and Nut Company,
   401 Broom Street, New York, NY

Planning Games Associates,
   316 West Seneca Street, Ithaca, NY 14850

Polymorph Films,
   331 Newbury Street, Boston, MA 02115

Population Dynamics,
   3829 Aurora Avenue, North Seattle, WA 98101

Portofilms   see   Perennial Education, Inc.

Pound   see   Mountain Plains Educational Media Council

Prentice-Hall, Inc.,
   Englewood Cliffs, NJ 07632

Princeton University,
   55 Mountain Avenue, Princeton, NJ 08540

Prism Enterprises,
   531 Dawson Drive, Camarillo, CA 93120

Probe Associates   see   Video Communications, Inc.

Project Simile II see Simile II

Protocol Films, c/o Dr. Celeste Woodly, Protocol Material Develop-
    ment Center, University of Colorado, Boulder, CO 80302

Psychological Cinema Register, Audiovisual Services,
    The Pennsylvania State University, University Park, PA 16802

Psychological Films, Inc.,
    1215 East Chapman Avenue, Orange, CA 92666

Psychology Films,
    205 West 20th Street, Santa Ana, CA 92706

Psychology Today Films/Games,
    P.O. Box 60278, Terminal Annex, Los Angeles, CA 90060

Public Broadcasting Service,
    955 L'Enfant Plaza North, S.W., Washington, DC 20024

Public Opinion Quarterly see Columbia University Press

Pyramid Films,
    P.O. Box 1048, Santa Monica, CA 90406

Quill and Scroll,
    School of Journalism, University of Iowa, Iowa City, IA 52240

Radio Corporation of America (RCA),
    1133 Avenue of the Americas, New York, NY 10019

Radio WTTW,
    5400 North St. Louis, Chicago, IL 60625

Raindance Corporation (Video Underground)
    8 East 12th Street, New York, NY 10013

Ramic Productions,
    58 West 58th Street, New York, NY 10019

Rand Corporation,
    1700 Main Street, Santa Monica, CA 90406

Rand McNally and Company,
    P.O. Box 7600, Chicago, IL 60007

Random House/Singer,
    201 East 50th Street, New York, NY 10022

Rank see Roundtable Films

Reader's Digest Association,
    Pleasantville, NY 10510

Real World Leaning, Inc.,
    134 Sunnyvale, San Carlos, CA 94070

Recording Industry of America, Inc.,
    1 East 57th Street, New York, NY 10023

Reiss Associates,
    230 Fifth Avenue, New York, NY 10001

Rensselaer Polytechnic Institute,
    Troy, NY 12181

Republic Corporation,
    2900 Avenue of the Stars, Los Angeles, CA 90067

Republic Steel Corporation,
    P.O. Box 6778, 1025 Republic Boulevard, Cleveland, OH 44115

Research Analysis,
    McLean, VA 22101

Research Games,
    48 Wareham Street, Boston, MA 02118

Response Environments,
    200 Sylvan Avenue, Englewood Cliffs, NJ 07632

Reynolds, Stuart see Stuart Reynolds Products

Riverwood Productions,
    115 Tompkins, Pleasantville, NY 10570

RMI Film Products,
    701 Westport Road, Kansas City, MO 64111

Robert Kennedy Memorial Fund,
    1035 30th Street, N.W., Washington, DC 20007

Robert Sharpe see Wolper Productions

Roche Films, Department of Professional Services,
    Nutley, NJ 07110

Roemer-Young Associates,
    245 West 55th Street, New York, NY 10019

Roundtable Films,
    113 North San Vicente Boulevard, Beverly Hills 90211

Samuel Goldwyn Productions,
    1041 North Formosa Avenue, Los Angeles, CA 90046

San Diego Area Instructional Television Authority,
5164 College Avenue, San Diego, CA 92115

San Francisco Newsreel see Canyon Cinema Cooperative

San Francisco State College, Library Services Center,
San Francisco, CA 94101

Sandak, Inc.,
180 Harvard Avenue, Stanford, CT 06901

SANE (Citizens Organized for a Sane World),
318 Massachusetts Avenue, N.W., Washington, DC 20002

Scholastic Audiovisual,
906 Sylvan Avenue, Englewood Cliffs, NJ 07632

School Marketing Service, Inc.,
1414 Avenue of the Americas, NY 10023

Science Research Associates, Inc.,
1900 East Lake Avenue, Chicago, IL 60611

Science Research Institute,
259 East Erie Street, Chicago, IL 60611

Scott Educational Division, Educational Media Laboratory,
104 Lower Westfield Road, Holyoke, MA 01040

Scott Foresman and Company,
1900 East Lake Avenue, Glenview, IL 60025

Screen Gems Company, c/o Columbia Pictures,
711 Fifth Avenue, New York, NY 10022

Selchow and Richter,
2215 Union Boulevard, Bayshore, NY 11706

Sensitivity Games, Inc.,
9 Newbury Street, Boston, MA 02116

Silvermine Films, Inc.,
49 West 45th Street, New York, NY 10018

Simco Enterprises,
3012 Samoa Place, Costa Mesa, CA 92626

Simile II,
Box 2023, La Jolla, CA 92037

Simulation Councils, Inc.,
P.O. Box 8248, San Diego, CA 92112

Simulation, Inc.,
    P.O. Box 140, Carmel, IN 46032

Simulations and Games, Sage Publications,
    P.O. Box 776, Beverly Hills, CA 90210

Simulations Publishers, Inc.,
    Dept. 329, 44 East 23rd Street, New York, NY 10010

Simulmatics Corporation,
    16 East 41st Street, New York, NY 10017

Social Studies School Service,
    10,000 Culver Boulevard, Culver City, CA 90230

Society for Visual Education,
    1345 Diversey Parkway, Chicago, IL 60007

Southern Speech Association, Department of Speech,
    University of Florida, Tampa, FL 33618

Southwestern Bell Telephone Company,
    1010 Pine Street, St. Louis, MO 63120

Special Libraries Association,
    235 Park Avenue South, New York, NY 10003

Spin-a-Test Company,
    P.O. Box 823, Pleasanton, CA 94566

Stanford University, Educational Media Center,
    Palo Alto, CA 94305

Stanley Bowmar Company,
    622 Rodier Drive, Glendale, CA 91209

State of New York, Education Department,
    Albany, NY 12201

State University of New York,
    1400 Washington Avenue, Albany, NY 12203

Stephen Bosustow Productions,
    1649 Eleventh Street, Santa Monica, CA 90404

Sterling Educational Films, Inc.,
    241 East 34th Street, New York, NY 10016

Storyboard, Inc.,
    165 East 72nd Street, New York, NY 10021

Strauss see Henry Strauss Associates

Stuart Finley, Inc.,
    3428 Mansfield Road, Falls Church, VA 22041

Stuart Reynolds Products,
    9465 Wilshire Boulevard, Beverly Hills, CA 90212

Sutherland Educational Films,
    8425 West Third Street, Los Angeles, CA 90048

Syracuse University, International Relations Program,
    Syracuse, NY 13210

Swank Motion Pictures,
    201 South Jefferson Avenue, St. Louis, MO 63166

Tapes Unlimited,
    13301 Puritan, Detroit, 48233

Teaching Film Custodians,
    25 West 43rd Street, New York, NY 10036

Teaching Films, Inc.,
    2518 North Boulevard, Houston, TX 77006

Teaching Technical Corporation,
    P.O. Box 3278, 7471 Greenbush, North Hollywood, CA 91606

Teamsters Union,
    25 Louisiana Avenue, N.W., Washington, DC 20001

Technicolor, Inc.,
    6311 Romaine Street, Costa Mesa, CA 92627

Technology Application Project (TAPS),
    P.O. Box 1028, Corvallis, OR 97330

Teleketics (E. R. Moore Co.),
    1229 South Santee Street, Los Angeles, CA 90015

Teletape Productions, Inc.,
    1355 LaSalle South, Chicago, IL 60603

Television Information Office,
    745 Fifth Avenue, New York, NY 10022

Telstar Productions,
    366 North Prior Street, St. Paul, MN 55104

Texture Films, Inc.,
    1600 Broadway, New York, NY 10019

Therapeutic,
    3111 West Beverly Boulevard, Los Angeles, CA

Third Eye, The,
    151 West 26th Street, New York, NY 10001

Thorne Films,
    1220 University Boulevard, Boulder, CO 80302

Three-M Company, Minicom Division, 1002 3 M Center,
    St. Paul, MN 55101

Time-Life Films,
    Time-Life Building, Rockefeller Center, New York, NY 10020

Time-Life Video see Time-Life Films

TRAFCO,
    1525 McGavock Street, Nashville, TN 37203

Transworld Films,
    332 South Michigan Avenue, Chicago, IL 60604

Tribune Films, Inc.,
    38 West 32nd Street, New York, NY 10001

Twentieth Century Fox,
    444 West 56th Street, New York, NY 10019

UNESCO Publishing Division, United Nations Center,
    317 East 34th Street, New York, NY 10017

Ungame, The,
    P.O. Box 964 Garden Grove, CA 92642

Uniquity,
    2035 Glyndon Avenue, P.O. Box 990, Venice, CA 90291

Unitarian Universalist Association, Office of Research,
    25 Beacon Street, Boston, MA 02108

United Artists Corporation,
    629 Seventh Avenue, New York, NY 10019

United Auto Workers,
    8000 East Jefferson Street, Detroit, MI 48214

United Films, Inc.,
    1122 South Cheyenne, Tulsa, OK 74101

United Nations Films and Television Distribution see UNESCO

United States Department of:

    Agriculture, Motion Picture Service,
    1850 South Building, Washington, DC 20250

United States Department of: (cont.)
    Commerce,
    Washington, DC 20250

      Defense: Air Force,
             Pentagon, Washington, DC 20330

             Air Force Library Film Center,
             8900 Broadway, St. Louis, MO 36125

             Army,
             Pentagon, Washington, DC 20310

             Navy,
             Pentagon, Washington, DC 20310

    Health, Education and Welfare,
    9000 Rockville Pike, Bethesda, MD 20014
    5600 Fishers Lane, Rockville, MD20852

    Health, Education and Welfare, Educational Materials Laboratory, Educational Media Branch, U.S. Office of Education, Washington, DC 20402

    Health, Education and Welfare, Public Health Service, National Institute of Mental Health Library, Atlanta, GA 30333

    Labor,
    Third and Constitution Avenue, N.W., Washington, DC 20210

    State,
    Washington, DC 20547

United States Government:

    Federal Communications Commission, Research and Education Division, Washington, DC 20013

    General Printing Office,
    Washington, DC 20250

    Information Agency,
    1776 Pennsylvania Avenue, Washington, DC 20520

    National Archives,
    Washington, DC 20409

    National Audiovisual Center, c/o General Services Administration, Washington, DC 20409

    Office of Emergency Management <u>see</u> National Audiovisual Center

United States Government: (cont.)
    Office of Information, Motion Picture Service,
    Washington, DC 20250

    Office of War Information see National Audiovisual Center

    Veterans Administration,
    Vermont at H Streets, N.W., Washington, DC 20560

United World Films, Division of Universal City Studios, Inc.,
    2001 South Vermont, Los Angeles, CA 90007

Universal Education and Visual Arts,
    100 Universal City Plaza, Universal City, CA 91608

Universal Pictures see Universal Education and Visual Arts

University Associates Press, Inc.,
    Box 615, Iowa City, IA 52240

University-at-Large,
    70 West 40th Street, New York, NY 10018

University Media Division of Technology Planning Center, Inc.,
    2378 East Stadium Boulevard, P.O. Box 1433, Ann Arbor, MI
    48106

University of California, Educational Media Center,
    2222 Fulton Street, Berkeley, CA 90024

University of California, Film Library,
    Los Angeles, CA 90032

University of Colorado, Educational Media Center,
    Boulder, CO 80304

University of Hawaii, Educational Media Center,
    Honolulu, HI 96813

University of Illinois, Film Production Center,
    501 South Wright Street, Champaign, IL 61820

University of Indiana see Indiana University

University of Iowa, Educational Media Center,
    Ames, IA 52240

University of Kansas, Audiovisual Center,
    Lawrence, KS 66044

University of Kansas, University Film Association,
    Lawrence, KA 66044

University of Kentucky, Educational Media Center,
    Lexington, KY 40506

University of Maine, Educational Media Center,
    Orono, ME 04473

University of Maryland, Educational Media Center,
    College Park, MD 20792

University of Michigan, Television Center,
    400 South Fourth Street, Ann Arbor, MI 48103

University of Minnesota, Audiovisual Library Service,
    2037 University Avenue, S.E., Minneapolis, MN 55455

University of Missouri, Educational Media Center,
    Columbia, MO 65202

University of Nebraska, Instructional Media Center,
    1600 R Street, Lincoln, NE 68508

University of Nevada, Educational Media Center,
    Reno, NV 89507

University of Ohio, Educational Media Center,
    Athens, OH 45701

University of Oklahoma, Educational Media Center,
    Norman, OK 73069

University of Southern California, Department of Cinema,
    University Park, Los Angeles, CA 90007

University of Southern California, Political Science Department,
    c/o Dr. Robert Goodman, University Park, Los Angeles, CA
    90007

University of Texas, Educational Media Center,
    Austin, TX 78712

University of Utah, Educational Media Center,
    Salt Lake City, UT 84112

University of Wisconsin, Bureau of Audiovisual Services,
    Madison, WI 57306

Urban Media Materials, Inc.,
    6806 Freshmeadow Lane, Flushing, NY 11365

Urban Systems, Inc.,
    1033 Massachusetts Avenue, Cambridge, MA 02138

Valley Instructional Television Association see VITA

VC Newsletter,
    P.O. Box 526, Beverly Hills, CA 90210

VCI see Video Communications, Inc.

Video Center,
    12221 Nebel Street, Rockville, MD 20852

Video Communications, Inc. (VCI)
    Suite 208, Chevy Chase Center, 35 Wisconsin Circle,
    Chevy Chase, MD 20015

Video Concepts Corporation,
    Box 138, Brookfield, CT 06804

Video Educators, Inc.,
    Box 11, Hershey, PA 17033

Video Nursing, Inc.,
    2645 Girard Avenue, Evanston, IL 60201

Videocassette Industry Guides,
    4731 Laurel Boulevard, North Hollywood, CA 91607

Videorecord see Video Communications, Inc. (VCI)

Virginia Department of Educational Film Production,
    Richmond, VA 28216

VITA (Valley Instructional Television Association),
    P.O. Box 61, Sacramento, CA 95801

Walden Film Corporation,
    153 Waverly Place, New York, NY 10014

Wall Street Journal,
    30 Broad Street, New York, NY 10004

Walt Disney Films,
    500 South Buena Vista Street, Burbank, CA 91503

Walter Lantz Productions,
    861 Seward Street, Los Angeles, CA 90038

Warner Brothers,
    200 Park Avenue, New York, NY 10017

Warren Schloat Productions,
    150 White Plains Road, Tarrytown, NY 10591

Washington, D. C. Public Library,
    Washington, DC 20036

WAST (Albany, NY) see Cornell University

Wayne State University, Educational Media Center,
    Detroit, MI 48202

WCU-TV see Carousel

WCVE-TV, Central Virginia Educational Television Corporation,
    1904 Old Farm Road, P. O. Box 3237, Richmond, VA 23235

Western Behavioral Science Institute,
    1121 Tonney Pines, La Jolla, CA 92037

Western Electric,
    195 Broadway, New York, NY 10007

Western Speech Association, Department of Speech,
    Oregon State University, Corvallis, OR 97331

Western Video,
    1541 North Vine Street, Hollywood, CA 90028

Westinghouse Group W see Westinghouse Learning Corporation

Westinghouse Learning Corporation,
    100 Park Avenue, New York, NY 10017

WETA-TV, Greater Washington Educational Television Association,
    Inc., 3620-27th Street, Arlington, VA 22203

Wff 'n Proof Learning Game Association,
    1490 South Boulevard, Ann Arbor, MI 48104

WGBH-TV,
    125 Western Avenue, Boston, MA 02134

Whitworth College, c/o Ronald R. Short,
    Spokane, WA 99128

William Brown and Company,
    135 South Locust, Dubuque, IA 52001

Willoughby-Peerless,
    110 West 32nd Street, New York, NY 10001

Wilson, H. W. see H. W. Wilson

Wisconsin State University, Educational Media Center,
    Oshkosh, WI, 54902

Wittich _see_ Intext

WNET Educational Broadcasting Corporation,
    304 West 58th Street, New York, NY 10019

Wolper Productions, Inc.,
    8489 West 3rd Street, Los Angeles, CA 90048

Wombat Productions,
    72 Tarrytown Road, White Plains, NY 10607

Women's Film Cooperative,
    200 Main Street, Northampton, MA 01060

Women's History Research Center, Inc.,
    2325 Oak Street, Berkeley, CA 94708

World Tape Center,
    123 Tucson, International Airport, Tucson, AZ 85706

Worldwide Affairs Council of Philadelphia,
    John Wanamaker Store, 13th and Market Streets, Philadelphia,
    PA 19107

Worldwide Games, Inc.,
    Box 450, Delaware, OH 43015

Woroner Films for Motorola _see_ Motorola

WQED, Metropolitan Pittsburgh Educational Television,
    4337 Fifth Avenue, Pittsburgh, PA 15213

Wrather Corporation,
    270 North Canon Drive, Beverly Hills, CA 90210

WTTW-TV,
    5400 North St. Louis, Chicago, IL 60625

Wyeth Laboratories,
    P.O. Box 8299, Philadelphia, PA 19101

Xerox Educational Services,
    600 Madison Avenue, New York, NY 10022

Xerox Films,
    245 Long Hill Road, Middletown, CT 06457

Yale University, Educational Media Services,
    New Haven, CT 06520

Zipporah Films,
    54 Lewis Wharf, Boston, MA 02110

PART V

CROSS-CATEGORY INDEX

Titles in this index are arranged under subject
categories which appear throughout the main section
of this bibliography.   The numbers following each
title refer to other subject categories in which the
individual film, tape, etc. may be found useful.

FILMS

1. ANIMAL

2. ARGUMENT

3. BUSINESS/ORGANIZATIONAL

Management

Negotiation

Personnel Development

4. CROSS CULTURAL

Ethnic

International

402   Communications

Prejudice

Urban

7. EDUCATIONAL TECHNOLOGY

8. FAMILY

9. FREEDOMS

10. GROUP DISCUSSION

11. INFORMATION SYSTEMS

12. THE INTERVIEW

13. INTRAPERSONAL

14. LANGUAGE

15. LEARNING THEORY

16. LISTENING

17. MASS MEDIA

Advertising

Broadcasting

Film

18. MOVEMENTS

Civil Rights

Peace

Women

19. NONVERBAL

20. PARLIAMENTARY PROCEDURE

21. PERCEPTION

22. PERSUASION

23. POLITICAL

Campaigns

The System

24. PROCESS/THEORY

25. PUBLIC SPEAKING

26. RHETORICAL TOPICS

History/Criticism

Aristotle and the Scientific Method: 2, 11, 21
Aristotle's Ethics: The Theory of Happiness: 9, 13, 21
Assassination of Julius Caesar: 23
Communication which Evaluates and Criticizes: 2, 3, 25
Death of Socrates, The: 2, 9
Galileo: The Challenge of Reason: 2, 9
Good Night Socrates: 4, 21
Great American Speeches: 2, 5, 16, 25
Greeks: In Search of Meaning, The: 2, 9, 13
Historian Series: Inductive Teaching of the Historian's Method
    of Inquiry: 2, 9, 14, 21
Historical Method of Inquiry: Answering Questions: 2, 9
Historical Method of Inquiry: Classifying Information: 2, 21
Historical Method of Inquiry: Dealing with the Mind: 14,
    21
Historical Method of Inquiry: Deciding What Is Fact: 2, 21
Historical Method of Inquiry: Proving Hypothesis, 2, 21
Need for Greek Philosophy: Plato and Aristotle, The: 2, 9
Plato's Apology: The Life and Teaching of Socrates: 2, 9
Plato's Drinking Party: 9, 21
Resolve of Patrick Henry, The: 9, 23
Socratic View of Philosophy: 2, 22
Trial of Socrates, The: 2, 9, 22
You Are There--A Series: 2, 5, 22, 25

Philosophic

Albert Schweitzer: 2, 4
Animal Farm: 9, 13
Answering Soviet Propaganda: 15, 22
Arnold Toynbee: 4, 15, 21
Bertrand Russell: 4, 9, 13, 21
Bertrand Russell Discusses Happiness: 4, 9, 13, 21
Challenge of Ideas, The: 4, 22
Chess Game, The: 2, 4, 18
China: A Hole in the Bamboo Curtain: 4, 9
China: One Quarter of Humanity: 4, 9
China: Rise of Communist Power, 1941-1967: 4, 22
China Under Communism: 4, 9
Communism: 4, 9
Communism: Defense Department Films: 4, 9, 22
Communism: The Soviet Model: 4, 9, 22
Communist Accent on Youth: 4, 9, 22
Communist China: 4, 9, 22
Confrontation: 4, 9, 18
Conversations with Eric Hoffer Series: 4, 8, 9, 13
Dag Hammarskjold: 4, 9
Dialectical Materialism Interpreted: 4, 9
Electronic Labyrinth: 7, 11

Religious

27. THERAPY

Individual

Group

VIDEOTAPES/VIDEOCASSETTES

4. CROSS CULTURAL

6. DYADIC

7. EDUCATIONAL TECHNOLOGY

9. FREEDOMS

10. GROUP DISCUSSION

11. INFORMATION SYSTEMS

Computer Revolution: 7, 15, 24
Information Systems: 3, 7, 15, 24
Systems Analysis and Design: 3, 7, 15, 21, 24
Understanding Computers: 3, 7, 15, 24

13. INTRAPERSONAL

Growth: 21, 25, 27
Joshua in a Box: 15, 22, 27
Motivation: 15, 22, 27
Personality and Social Behavior: 15, 21, 27
Self, The: 15, 21, 27
Sensation and Perception: 15, 19, 21, 27
Stress: 15, 21, 27

14. LANGUAGE

Dialects of Various Languages: 4, 15
English Fact and Fancy Series: 4, 15, 21, 24
Language and Thought: 4, 15, 19, 21, 24
Language as a Behavioral Phenomenon: 15, 21
Meaning: 13, 21
More Linguistic Approaches: 21, 31
Philosophy of Logic and Language, The: 15, 21
Speed Reading Systems: 15, 21, 24
Success Through Word Power--A Series: 4, 21, 24
Summary of Unit I: Language Propositions and Syllogisms: 15,
    21

15. LEARNING THEORY

Aspects of Behavior: 4, 13, 27
Conversation with B. F. Skinner: 27
Development: 27
Educational Psychology--A Series: 13, 21, 27
General Psychology--A Series: 3, 13, 21, 22, 27
Intelligence and Human Abilities: 13, 21, 27
Interaction Analysis: 13, 21, 27
Learning: 13, 21, 22, 27
Learning: 1, 13, 21, 27
Learning and Reinforcement: 13, 21, 27
Personality: 12, 13, 21, 27
Perspectives on Learning: 13, 21, 27
Psychology: 13, 21, 27
Psychology I: The Principles of Behavior: 21, 27
Psychology II: Man and His Motives: 13, 21, 27
Psychology Today--A Series: 13, 21, 27
Simulation: 7, 11, 21

Skinner at M.I.T.: 7, 11, 21
Tools of Psychology: 2, 7, 11, 21, 24

16. LISTENING

Analyze Every Audience: 21, 24, 25
Communication: Talking and Listening: 5, 21, 25
Listen Accurately: 21, 24, 25
Listen Critically: 21, 24
Listen to Some of Your Fellow Classmates: 10, 21

17. MASS MEDIA

Broadcasting: Television Right of Access: 9, 26
Broadcasting: Thirty Years Retrospect: 3, 9, 26
Citizen Kane: 9, 23, 26
Communication and Society: A Conversation: 4, 7, 26
Communications and Education--A Series: 7, 9, 22
Communications Revolution, The: 7, 9, 22
Early Art of the Cinema: 7
Environment and Development of Public Relations: 3, 22
Exits and Entrances: 3, 26
Film and Society, The: 3, 9, 22, 26
Future of Public Relations, The: 3, 22
Giving the Public What It Wants: 3, 15, 22
March of Time Series: 7, 15, 26
Marshall McLuhan: Picnic in Space: 7, 15, 26
Mass Communications: Effects: 21, 24
Movies March on: 7, 26
National Association of Educational Broadcasters Convention: 3,
    7, 15, 22
Networks and the Rating Game, The: 3, 9, 26
Professional Public Relations--A Series: 3, 22
Promotion, The: Its Role in the Total Marketing Program: 3,
    22
Promotional Campaign, The: 3, 22
PR Process, The: Communicating: 21, 22, 24
PR Process, The: Evaluating: 21, 22, 24
PR Process, The: Fact-Finding: 3, 21, 22, 24
PR Process, The: Planning: 3, 22, 24
Public Relations, What Is It, Who Is It?: 3, 22, 24
Publics of Public Relations: 3, 4, 21, 22
Television Today: A Series: 3, 7, 15, 22
That You May Know: 3, 7, 22, 26

22. PERSUASION

Persuasion: Appeal to Emotions: 2, 17, 23, 25
Propaganda: International and Domestic: 4, 23, 26
Propaganda: Its Power: 4, 15, 23, 26

26. RHETORICAL TOPICS

America in the Sixties: 4, 23
American Time Capsule: 4, 23
Challenge of Modern Psychiatry to Religion, The: 9, 15, 27
Communists, The--A Series: 4, 9, 15, 23
Communists, The--A Series: 4, 9, 15, 23
Contemporary Issues--Series 70s: 3, 4, 9, 23
Evolution of Communism: 4, 9, 23
Freedom and Obedience to Law: Plato: 2, 9, 23
Humanities: 4, 13, 15, 23
Humanities, No. I--A Series: 5, 13, 15, 27
Humanities, No. II--A Series: 5, 13, 15, 27
Mahatma Gandhi Leads India to Nonviolent Protest: 4, 9, 18, 23
Other Vietnam, The: 4, 9, 23
Philosophy of Communications and the Arts: 4, 15, 24
Philosophy of Education--A Series: 9, 15, 23
Philosophy of Human Rights, The: 4, 9, 15, 23
Philosophy of Religion--A Series: 2, 4, 9, 15
Philosophy of Social Science: 4, 9, 15
Protest and Communication: 4, 13, 21, 22
Religious Experience: 4, 13, 21
Rise of Adolph Hitler: 4, 9, 22, 25
Selling of the Pentagon, The: 9, 17, 18, 22, 23
Sixties, The: 4, 9, 23
Struggle in Ireland: Bernadette Devlin: 4, 9, 23
Student Dissent in Perspective: 4, 9, 18, 23
Time Machine Series, The: 4, 9, 23
Two Old Men: Noah and Socrates: 4, 9, 13, 23
Under the Clouds of War: 4, 9, 23
Way Back When: 4, 9, 23
What Is the Good Life: Aristotle: 4, 13, 15
What Is Virtue?: Aristotle: 4, 13, 15

27. THERAPY

Addiction: 4, 8, 13, 15
Communication: Concept and Skill: 6, 13, 15
Communication in the Nurse-Patient Relationship: 6, 13, 15, 22
Counseling the Adolescent: 6, 13, 15
Interpreting Body Language in Everyday Practice: 13, 15, 19
Need for Dialogue, The: 10, 13, 15, 22
Transactional Analysis for the Practicing Physician: 13, 15, 22

SIMULATIONS/GAMES

2. ARGUMENT

3. BUSINESS/ORGANIZATIONAL

Management

Negotiation

Collective Bargaining: 4, 16, 21, 22
Exercise Negotiations: 4, 10, 16, 21, 22
Grievance Handling: 10, 16, 21, 22
Grievance Handling (Non-Industrial): 10, 16, 21, 22
Handling Conflict in Management: Conflict Among Peers: 6, 10, 16, 21, 22
Handling Conflict in Management: Superior/Subordinate-Group Conflict (Game I): 6, 10, 16, 21, 27
Handling Conflict in Management: Superior/Subordinate-Group Conflict (Game II): 6, 10, 16, 21, 27
Handling Conflict in Management: Superior/Subordinate-Group Conflict (Game III): 6, 10, 16, 21, 27
Market Negotiation Management Game: 6, 16, 17, 21
Settle or Strike: 4, 6, 16, 21
Strike: A Simulation of Late Nineteenth Century Labor-Management Relations: 4, 6, 16, 21
Union Organizing Game: 4, 6, 16, 21, 22

Personnel Development

Academic Department Game, The: 10, 15, 21
Achievement Game, The: 10, 15, 21
Appraisal By Objectives: 6, 12, 15, 21
Appraisal Game, The: 6, 15, 21
Assumptions Game, The: 2, 13, 15, 21
Buy: 17, 21
Communicating for Results: 6, 14, 21, 24
Communication: 6, 14, 21, 24
Communication Game, The: 6, 14, 21, 24
Communication Game, The: 6, 14, 21, 24
Communications: Problems and Opportunities: 14, 21, 24
Confidence Building Game, The: 6, 10, 13, 21, 27
Creativity Exercise: 13, 15, 21, 27
Edplan: 15, 21
Employment Market: 6, 10, 12, 15
Enterprise: 4, 6, 10, 15, 21
Exercise Attitudes: 6, 22
Exercise Communication: 6, 14, 16, 19, 21, 24
Exercise Evaluation: 6, 15, 21
Exercise Objectives: 6, 15, 21
Exercise Organization: 6, 15, 21, 24
Exercise Success: 6, 13, 15, 21, 27
Life Career: 4, 6, 13, 15, 26
Peter Principle Game, The: 13, 15, 21, 27
Selecting Effective People: 6, 12, 13, 15, 21
Simulated Community Training Game: 6, 15, 21
To Develop and Sharpen Communication Skills: 6, 21, 24
Work Assignment: 6, 13, 15, 21
Work Game, The: 6, 10, 13, 15, 21
Writing Game, The: 10, 13, 15, 21, 24, 27

Sales

Market Strategy: 4, 17, 22, 27
Principles of Effective Salesmanship: 4, 17, 22
Sales Game: 17, 22, 27
Sales Promotion: 17, 22
Sales Strategy: 17, 22
Salesmanship in Action: 22, 27

4. CROSS CULTURAL

Bafa Bafa: 10, 15, 21
Balance: A Simulation of Short-Range Economic-Hedonistic
     Goals Versus Long-Range Environmental Goals: 10, 15, 26
Black Experience, The: 9, 18, 26
Cities Game, The: 9, 23
Coffee Game, The: 3, 23, 26
Community Decision Games: 3, 23, 26
Crisis: 3, 23, 26
Culture Contact: 15, 23, 26
Dig: 15, 26
Dignity: 3, 9, 18, 26
Diplomacy: 9, 23, 26
Game of Brinkmanship, The: 3, 23, 26
Ghetto: 8, 9, 18, 26
Grand Strategy: 9, 26
Impact: 17, 26
Inter-Community Simulation, The: 3, 23, 26
International Simulation: 9, 23, 26
Life in Israel: 9, 23, 26
Mythia: A World Affairs Simulation: 9, 21, 23, 26
New Town: 9, 23
Potlatch Package: 9, 18, 23, 26
Sanga: 8, 9, 18, 23, 26
Security: 9, 23, 26
Simulation: The Decision-Making Model: 3, 23, 26
Sitte: 9, 23, 26
Sunshine: 9, 18, 23
Telecity: 10, 18, 23
They Shoot Marbles, Don't They?: 3, 9, 23, 26
Tracts: 9, 18, 23
Transit: 3, 9, 23
Urban America: 9, 18, 23
Urban Games: 3, 18, 23
World Game: 3, 18, 23, 26

6. DYADIC

Abelson-Baker Interview, The: 3, 12, 21
Compatibility: 6, 13, 15, 21
Couples: 6, 8, 13, 14, 21

26. RHETORICAL TOPICS

Philosophic

Campus Crisis Game: 9, 18, 23
Conducting Planning Exercises: 3, 4, 9, 23
Cope: A Simulation of Adapting to Change and Anticipating the
    Future: 7, 23
Dynasty: 4, 9, 23
Ethics: 13, 15, 21, 23
General Agricultural Farm Simulation: 3, 4, 9, 23, 26
Humanus: 7, 9, 11, 23
Micro Society: 3, 4, 9, 23
Puzzle: A Simulation Enabling Students to Perform the Tasks
    of a Biographer-Historian: 4, 23
Society Today: 4, 9, 23
Starpower: 3, 4, 9, 23
Values: 13, 15, 22, 23

War

Brinkmanship: Holocaust or Compromise: 4, 9, 23
Conflict: 4, 9, 23
Confrontation: The Cuban Missile Crisis: 4, 9, 23
Guns or Butter: 3, 4, 9, 23
Mission: A Simulation of Our Involvement in Vietnam: 4, 9,
    23
Nuremberg: A Simulation of War Crime Trials of 1945-1946:
    2, 9, 23
Peace: A Simulation of War-Peace Issues During the Wilsonian
    Era: 4, 9, 23

27. THERAPY

Blindfold Game, The: 13, 15, 21, 22
Cycle: An Interaction Unit Introducing the Stages of the Human
    Life: 13, 15, 21
Feel Wheel, The: 13, 15, 19, 21
Games People Play: 13, 15, 21, 22
Group Therapy: 10, 15, 21
Insight: 13, 15, 21
Interaction: 6, 15, 21, 22
Juvenile Delinquency Game: 8, 13, 15, 21
"Now" Communication Game, The: 8, 13, 15, 21
"O. K. Game," The: 8, 13, 15, 21
Personalysis: 13, 15, 21, 22
Sensitivity: 13, 15, 21
Ungame, The: 13, 15, 21
Youth Culture Game, The: 8, 13, 15, 21